"Tarn's books have inspired a wild, almost religious devotion among readers. His work is a tremendous force field in which world and perception collaborate in the construction of innovative formal 'architextures' for a sensual language that has no like. Tarn is one of the most elegant and formidably intelligent minds in contemporary poetry. His books open up a means for us to be delighted again to belong to this world."
—FORREST GANDER

"While poetry is narrowing its concerns, Tarn risks a scale epic enough to contain mountains and oceans. He keeps his lines of communication open to more than one life form, with a prophetic sureness of direction."
—GEOFFREY O'BRIEN

"Tarn, a poet in Goethe's image, has spent over fifty years writing a poetry invested in the lessons of modernism, yet informed by the disciplines of anthropology. His poems are transformations of a classifying, structuring imagination into visionary utterances."
—PETER O'LEARY

"One of the most outstanding poets of his generation."
—KENNETH REXROTH

"Anthropologist, editor, critic, and translator, Nathaniel Tarn is above all a poet. Poetry is at the center of his personality and his activity. His work, in full growth, reveals a rich temperament, a remarkable linguistic inventiveness, and a vision both original and universal."
—OCTAVIO PAZ

"Tarn's poetry redefines nature and art for human culture, bringing a genuine psychological and linguistic curiosity about the human mind, about what it means to be human."
—BRENDA HILLMAN, *Jacket*

"Catastrophe, exile, a deliberate going against: these concepts all contribute to our understanding of Tarn's late style, tense, dissociative, darkly brooding, abruptly furious, suddenly elevated to a point of dizzying sublimity."
—NORMAN FINKELSTEIN, *Poetry in Review*

ATLANTIS, AN AUTOANTHROPOLOGY

DUKE UNIVERSITY PRESS Durham and London 2022

ATLANTIS, AN AUTOANTHROPOLOGY

NATHANIEL TARN

FOREWORD BY JOSEPH DONAHUE

FRONTISPIECE: Author. New York, 1985. Photo: Nina Subin.
ENDPIECE: Author. Fort Tarn, Tesuque, New Mexico, 2000s. Photo: Janet Rodney.

© 2022 DUKE UNIVERSITY PRESS
All rights reserved
Project editor: Annie Lubinsky
Designed by Aimee C. Harrison
Typeset in Garamond Premier Pro by Westchester Publishing Services

Library of Congress Cataloging-in-Publication Data
Names: Tarn, Nathaniel, author. | Donahue, Joseph, [date] writer of foreword.
Title: Atlantis, an autoanthropology / Nathaniel Tarn ; foreword by Joseph Donahue.
Description: Durham : Duke University Press, 2022.
Identifiers: LCCN 2021020921 (print) | LCCN 2021020922 (ebook)
ISBN 9781478015284 (hardcover)
ISBN 9781478017905 (paperback)
ISBN 9781478022527 (ebook)
Subjects: LCSH: Tarn, Nathaniel. | Mendelson, E. Michael, 1928– |
Poets, French—Biography. | Anthropologists—France—Biography. | BISAC: SOCIAL
SCIENCE / Anthropology / Cultural & Social | BIOGRAPHY & AUTOBIOGRAPHY /
Literary Figures | LCGFT: Autobiographies.
Classification: LCC PS3570.A635 Z46 2022 (print) | LCC PS3570.A635 (ebook) |
DDC 841/.914 [B]—dc23
LC record available at https://lccn.loc.gov/2021020921
LC ebook record available at https://lccn.loc.gov/2021020922

Cover art: Janet Rodney, photograph of Nathaniel Tarn, Elder Principal in Cofradia
Santa Cruz, Santiago Atitlán, Guatemala, 1979.

TO ALL MY (M)OTHERS

I is a throng of voices.
—JANET RODNEY, *The Book of Craving*

Dites-moi à quelle heure je dois être transporté a bord . . .
—ARTHUR RIMBAUD, 1891

No, one wasn't just one. One was ten people, twenty, a hundred. The more opportunities life gave us, the more beings it revealed in us. A man might die because he hadn't experienced anything, and had been just one person all his life.
—JOSEPH ROTH, *Right and Left*

CONTENTS

Galleries appear after Throws 10, 20, and 30.

Nathaniel Tarn: Through the Gates of Atlantis

JOSEPH DONAHUE

On those vast shady hills between America & Albion's shore;
Now barr'd out by the Atlantic sea: call'd Atlantean hills . . .
—WILLIAM BLAKE

I

Nathaniel Tarn's *Atlantis, an Autoanthropology* is a far-ranging testimonial
to the life and times of a fictional character. Our protagonist, who's been
everywhere, met everybody, done more in one lifetime than might most
in multiple reincarnations, is also the most prescient poet of our time. Fic-
tional, but not. This Atlantis is not fiction but is the history of a fiction, an
imagined identity made actual of a pseudonymous poet, Nathaniel Tarn,
taken up, lived to the extreme, by one who wished to locate his being out
of an exhausting profession into a life in poetry. The tale told is nothing less
than a meditation on modern identity, an adventure in self-understanding
that lays bare the social, familial, historical, and personal forces making us who
we are, making us not want to be who we are, then making us want to be-
come another. Nathaniel Tarn has lived words famed in his natal tongue: *Je
est un autre.* Our author and our self-created protagonist, "Nathaniel Tarn,"
named thus legally on becoming an American citizen, has had such a rich life

that his very pen name would seem to have its own ontology encoded within it, never to be quite revealed, despite the disarming candor of the following pages.

II

A well-credentialed, widely published Franco-British anthropologist, Dr. E. Michael Mendelson created Tarn, all those years ago, to save his creative life from the censure of his profession. Now Tarn returns the favor. (Borges, in eternity, will decide who the ultimate author of this book is.) Let's simply note that the signatory, Tarn, has devised an exceptional way to write his double life: the Throw. These Throws create an ever-absorbing mix of time, tone, place, and narrative, all the while acknowledging the author's pervasive philosophical concern and the source of his deepest terror, arbitrariness. Tarn draws the idea of the Throw from the practice of making pottery, so alerting us, as if we need a still more erudite prompting, to see what is so pervasive through the work: his affection for craft culture of all ages and all places. While utilizing to vivifying effect this formal innovation, *Atlantis, an Autoanthropology* is also haunted by the throw, by another sort of throw, the throw of the dice of our lives: the fate set in play for us, each and every day. Tarn is tantalized by the possibility of stable, permutable forms, within which contingency can be recognized and can even provoke delight. Each Throw of Tarn's prose takes us places, returns us to places, takes up ideas, celebrates friends, documents events, spins a tale, laments a loss, sings whatever is well made. Both in form and content this book is a continuous meditation on the interrelation of freedom and fate. We begin at the beginning: our individual's story, as told by Tarn. The opening Throws move through acutely rendered accounts of early years, gracefully weaving a dense social and cultural web. It's a world full of feeling, lightened of any lugubrious dwelling on what was. Tarn, writing with his twinned capacities, those of the poet and those of the anthropological observer, can, with a single well-turned detail, catch the intersections of multiple worlds: the natural world, the world of personal feeling, and the full social fact of being alive in a time and a place.

III

Imagine a child during the Battle of Britain, holed up in a hotel, Nazi bombs falling all round. Or a Jewish refugee life in England as the war rages. Or the indignities of the classroom. Or the pain of learning to be English but never being quite English enough. Throws divide the telling of a double life into serial renditions of fate, within which myths, mountains, fabrics, temples, money, gossip, sex, family, and portraiture take on the impromptu gravitas of tarot cards. The Tarn-to-be finds his way, through the war, through school and college, through the cafés of Paris. He finds he's not alone: Claude Lévi-Strauss, André Breton, Marcel Duchamp, and George Steiner are there. Many others whom history remembers pass through the Throws. So too, we meet and feel a fond regard for those the world has yet to hear of, but who are known to the poet, for insights, gifts, abilities, kindnesses, and in some cases, yes, slights. They all return here. Throws can tell you what a wonderful lunch on a certain day was like or can unfold brief, marvelous essays, philosophical asides worthy of Emil Cioran, Elias Canetti, or Roberto Calasso. The flow of the prose keeps us close. Museums, poetry, poetics, religious systems, love affairs, travel arrangements, the sublime, all are recurrent stations in a life lived in devotion to detecting the shapes that culture makes. At any moment in this textual Atlantis, this fieldwork from nowhere, Tarn might be finding his way to an abandoned temple, or sketching out cultural networks, or casting a cold eye on academic life, or delving into ecstasies, or sounding out despair. He might be evaluating a hallucinogen taken while driving or giving us the skinny about having been proclaimed a god.

IV

Before his birth, Tarn had two fields of expertise (the double, doubled!). He had lived two scholarly lifetimes of hands-on experience regarding two immensely complex subjects, Mayan culture and Burmese Buddhism. But then, the intrigue of identity begins at birth if not before, in 1928, in France, to a French-Romanian mother and a British-Lithuanian father. His family fled the continent of Europe for England as the war began. He-who-would-be-Tarn learned quickly how moving between cultures sharpens one's wits. Our narrator lived the discipline of anthropology long before he met Lévi-Strauss. He clearly sensed the double life ahead; he was already writing poetry in his native French, publishing poetry under yet another pseudonym. It becomes increasingly less clear who created whom in the legend of poetic vocation that this book spins out, where a French-born English poet finds in mid-century anthropology the truest singing school. In these pages, an apparently effortless lyricism arises from what in other hands would be simply the routines of fieldwork. (Fellow travelers such as Octavio Paz and Kamau Brathwaite offer equivalent examples of how a visionary poetry can draw so robustly on the intellectual disciplines of our age.) From the perspective of his immense and distinguished body of poetic work, his anthropological writings shine in a poetic light. Such works as *Scandals in the House of*

Birds or even, as Mendelson, *Sangha and State in Burma: A Study of Monastic Sectarianism and Leadership,* arise from a conviction that the totality of human life across time can be to a meaningful degree fathomed. They work out the logic of some of Tarn's most moving and luminous poems. (Consider his masterpiece, "Palenque.") Anthropology informs as well his landmark contribution to poetics, "The Heraldic Vision," gathered in *The Embattled Lyric,* where Blake and Victor Turner assist the poet in a critical rethinking of projective verse, ethnopoetics, and much else. His vast poetry embodies Robert Redfield's dream of fathoming different worldviews. Tarn makes cosmological empathy integral to the act of writing. Each Throw of his prose attests to a lifetime practice of notating, reflecting upon, collating, categorizing, and more, feeling the pain and delights of others. He models a deep and never-ending initiation into the human sciences, which shine with a restored heroism in his works.

V

The belief that origins and ends can be known, or at least imagined so fiercely and particularly that they can be understood to be "known," the proposal that culture at its most exalted is within reach of anyone willing to look hard for it, is embedded in the first word in the title. Atlantis gives the book its title but appears nowhere within it, which is in keeping with its nature. The science of man, and the individual life of practitioner of that science, lie on the far side of a grammatical equal sign, as if they derive from a place that never existed or certainly no longer exists. A watery abyss opens on the left-hand side of the comma. Is this the autoanthropology of a life lived in Atlantis, that most lavishly orchestrated absence in Western tradition, that place of first promise and last catastrophe? Are the rituals and daily practices of a life lived in oblivion about to be revealed? The title hints at an anthropological lineage that predates anthropology while claiming a literary historical one, where Atlantis has long been linked to America, the land where Nathaniel Tarn, who had longed for America as a wartime schoolboy, saluting a nearby stars-and-stripes flag, devouring a life of Lincoln, made a new life and career as a poet. The lost continent compels a further curiosity: Is Tarn's Atlantis not that of Plato or Bacon or Moore, or Donnelly or Guénon, but rather the last mountaintops of the sunken land located by William Blake between England and America? Did Tarn, on his way between continents, harbor in Atlantis? Lack of mention confirms the suspicion. Recall that in *America: A Prophecy* Blake can see, from the still-visible peaks of that lost land, Orc, an initially terrifying figure of boundless creative and revolutionary fury, who, transmuted and set free to the winds, will blow from Blake's work all through the Tarn universe. *Atlantis, an Autoanthropology* shows a Tarn who shares with Blake outrage at inequity, delight in heretical religious thought, reverence for sexual love, and an acute grasp of the origins of social conflict. And more: like Blake, our narrator has a keen eye for artisanship. He can see eternity in the weave of a fabric, in the excellence of an everyday utensil, in the demeanor of a ritual mask, in any curio or icon or altarpiece. This is in keeping with the progressive political vision inherited from anthropology, from MacDiarmid, from Neruda, from his own conscience, and confirmed for him in his visit to Atlantis.

A commitment to a vision of a cosmos arising from the possibility of a just social order had already begun to delineate itself with *The Beautiful Contradictions*, written in the mountains of Wales, no doubt looking toward those bright summits from which, Blake says, we might pass into the Golden world. Atlantis is, for Tarn, the vantage from which the glories and tragedies and the still living hope of human cultures can be seen. It is also, within any culture, the point, possibly obscure, where access to the Golden world might present itself to the metaphysically driven sojourner. All of Tarn's writing, taken together, is a single initiation into what Blake would call the visionary forms dramatic, where mind, heart, eternal truths and historical contingencies contrive a life in transfigured time.

VI

The book at hand is the bright summit of a life of writing, a life that has passed though world after world, and continually finding itself reborn within a next. Passing, that is, again and again, into and out of, the gates of Atlantis, that land of forests and palaces, sometimes remembering them, sometimes not, sometimes imagining a glory beyond them where the soul reunites with the One, sometimes, and never so eloquently as in his recent poetry, despairing to ever taste transcendence, ever to feel ecstatically torn open to the cosmos. (Readers familiar with his immense poem *Lyrics for the Bride of God* will recall Tarn's long-standing interest in gnostic agonies.) Tarn's *Atlantis, an Autoanthropology* is an ode in prose, an intellectual hymn, a spiritual confession, a tall tale, a night of great talk, a warm welcome, a feast of thought, a lesson in how to look, how to think, how to endure, how to grasp the moments we ourselves enter and exit. Page after page brings worlds, some we know, some we dream about. It's a book bearing witness to a life lived, and suffered, and transformed into art.

I have usually known how to finish a poem, rarely how to finish a work in prose. The temptation to see, know, and do everything—while kept at bay in poetry—is rarely overcome in prose. This book could have been written by consulting fairly voluminous diaries, kept more or less uninterruptedly since 1939, but I would never have finished. So, except for a date or two here and there, I have chosen to write it out of what sits in my memory. Should you wish to learn more, an archive exists at Stanford University.

For a variety of reasons largely connected to pressure of work, the book has been composed over a period of pretty well exactly thirty years: 1973–2003, with a few additions here and there up to 2013 and then a few more in 2019. Over such a period of time, views, opinions, and understandings may well shift their ground and even radically change. I have allowed this to happen in the writing without necessarily striving for consistency, limiting myself to indicating at times the rough date of composition of some chapters, here named "Throws" for reasons which will appear in the text.

The title has three references. The first is to the fact that I have never (yet) been able to experience the sensation of being only one person. (I do though expect that this is a possibility to be reached before departing the planet.) The second is that each one of us has rarely been able to limit himself or herself to interest in a single subject. The third is that we are profoundly "contextual"—meaning that we never seem able to think of ourselves alone but only of ourselves in the context of the communities and societies in which we have lived at any given time.

I have left out of this book most of our domestic life. Although this runs the danger of leaving some folks feeling excluded, I wish, for the time being, to try to avoid any possible pain to others as well as to myself.

One last point. Readers will discover that I have met many people. I list as many as I possibly can. Those not mentioned are extremely likely not to have been forgotten. The heart is the place. I beg their forgiveness. I do wish, however, to record, among acknowledgments, the poets Joseph Donahue and Peter O'Leary, who have helped greatly in bringing this book about. Peter, especially, has shared the task of preparing the book for the printer. An old man's warmest gratitude to both. Bounden thanks to the two heroic outside readers who recommended so strongly that this book be published by Duke. It is very painful not to be able to thank them in person.

Fort Tarn, June 30, 2020

Throw One

1.1 05.13.1973. The spring slow, held in by rain to the south, the cold front apparently not developing fast enough, the migrations spotty. Out at 5 a.m. to confirm the miracle, to witness the birth of color again: that for which his blood streamed in the firmament, etc. If it be not here, in this ultimate land, then where? And, in fact, the ultimate land riots with color. No fauna so rich, no flora—no ornithology certainly.

The first creeps. As if he remembered the snake. You call this a warbler? Guatemala/summer/1969: at the terrace's elbow, a tree suddenly full one morning of this, closely observable, bird (others out of failing sight's range: binoculars stolen at Customs). Spats made bird. *Mniotilta varia*: black-and-white warbler. Here: song: high, a whistle, this single precursor. I can find no other: it is as if he had come alone to claim my Pennsylvania for his tribe. "Be grave: they love not to be smiled on" (William Penn, 09.30.1681. Bucks County Deed Book 1, 273). Very soon before the black-and-white came *Regulus calendula*, the royal claim. American first. Spirals discretely up a tree, a motion initiatic, resulting in a coronation of fire at the top of the conifer he is working, the head opening, the gates of the skull sliding sideways away from center to reveal the fiery eye (which would have been Toulouse, 1983). A succession of baptists to the spring: the boss not yet in sight.

A cardinal, high in the bare trees, mimics the tanager. Who could be king. Others here and there, claiming holdings, establishing homes. Building their various principalities at several different levels above the Earth: some low, some middling, some high. A hierarchy, class, or caste, but of pure form: the food and habitat both discrete, interrelated certainly, but not inter-devouring. Small eyes beading down from all points of the compass at this untimely intruder.

The loveliness of an interaction of levels. Cape May, New Jersey: migration time. Huge flocks of geese approaching the viewer from different segments of the sky, one momentary tribe over another, a great escalation into the empyrean. Wondrousness of pacified space. Any well-orchestrated choreography: ballet, say, as in Balanchine, or a great air-show team: the Blue Devils, the Red Arrows, the Patrouille de France, the Italian Frecce Tricolori.

Completion is of the effort (is of the process), thus at any time,

Initial rituals:

1.2 The intruder lies low, in a cot perhaps, looking up. In Paris, France, 1928. Pressed down by the weight of the sky: a distant sky or a mediating ceiling—impossible to know. The intruder is very small, filial, eyes tilted up at any father that might present himself. However distant he will always remain, it is always the father who seems to prime. The air is . . . yellow, appears to be yellow. White-coated men, white-bearded it may be, forming a semicircle around his feet, looking down on him. Almost as if their heads were fruit among branches. They are very clean. They might be priests, doctors, or both. It is impossible to know whether the intruder is in exile already or is going to have his exile confirmed by some drastic, irreversible action. Or whether the action about to be implemented is a sending into exile. There is nothing ominous about the situation: it is benign. Not at all like the events of ages three to six: dying every one of those years with great regularity at Easter, all doctors out of Paris for the holiday, being painfully resurrected from pus an inch away from the heart and such-like horrors, the small body full of needles in every limb. On the wall opposite the bed, the shadows of huge trees in the hospital yard hallucinating throughout a distant wind.

The beginning of the "I" who can say "I" is a selection in space and time: it may as well be here. It would be good to know in which cardinal direction the intruder's feet were pointed. At this stage, however, that datum cannot be retrieved.

The beginning is relatively simple. The end is nothing short of the world. Then the return.

1.3 Procedurally, the word in question would seem to require invention. If that be too ambitious, let us (note, for future definition, the "us") build on those seniors of ours, those predecessors, and, with their help, take off into the future. Let there be a word "informaction." The growth of this word into its meaning has interest at this juncture. Observe:

"In" for input. I am willing to adopt, of past formulations, the notion that this universe comes in at our senses—provided that the notion of senses be wide enough for this usage—and that we focus upon the incoming world an attention ever more refined. The process of attention opens the hearing to a voice that has as little beginning or end as the *Tao* or Way itself, a voice that, provisionally, we might accept as sourcing from deep within any one of us, but that deep requires further exploration. The voice, in other words, exists within us from our own beginnings: we hear it or not as we are able to or as we please to decide. The pleasure must be worked at, hard, for the noises of the world about us will do their darnedest to drown it out. The relation between an "us" and an "I" will have to do with the depth at which the voice operates in the body—or the refinement of its hearing. For the time being, let there be the mystery that the deeper the body is an "I," the more collective, the more *us-lich* or even *uns-lich*, to coin a term, will be that voice. Let there be no interference with the mysteries.

Re the Way—should anyone consider this a "mystery," let it be defined as that gigantic wall, probably made of iron, standing at the back of one who awoke from a dream knowing for certain that there was no cessation of the wall's presence in any dimension whatsoever—that it reached upward and downward beyond any conceivable measurement and sideways on both sides with an equal lack of end. The dream is of that rare same nature as the opening of the skull: events occurring once or twice in a lifetime, *nada mas*, not more. Forgive the occasional irruption of foreign tongues. I believe in more than one language.

Attention to the "in" gives that which we work on form. To inform a text means to make it—make it: the claim, the success and the holding/the plot/ all in one. Upon that: Homestead. Praxis.

If it be a text or texture we work on, that text is an action brought about by the work, in-formed by it, given breath. The action of weaving in space and time brings about the poem of our day. We are familiar from our fathers in this art with the concept of a poem that includes all of history, one in which all actions are contemporaneous. And we might add that prose should be at least as well written as poetry.

In a lifetime, it is unlikely that one action will suffice. An action, a forma-
tion, inserted into the continuum as an information will serve as springboard
to yet other actions, yet other textures. Information bears in it a crux: the
crux of this matter becomes *informaction*. Even the alphabet aids us in this
regard. Skip a middle letter *b*, and you are home.

Say now that this lurch forward bears the weight of the procession of
memory. Uncertain steps, from an arbitrary point in time, move forward into
their own remembrance of themselves. Remembrance is an imperfect tool at
best—but, here too, refinement operates. *Summa Memoria*: a recuperation,
a diving into the wreck of precision, bringing up, from time to time, as the
matter arises, a leavening, ever more profound, of the selfsame existence.

A scrap left out for dogs or cats becomes a meal. Becomes a commu-
nion. A communion may or may not reveal the presence of a living deity
within it and, hence, within ourselves: it is too early to say. The priesthood
works on as if the divinity were present or as if, by its informactions, a divin-
ity could be induced to breach into our lives.

Us, Durkheimianly, the possibility of that breaching.

All the ordinary, "common or garden," black whales, surrounding the
white.

1.4 Nothing else I can think of at this juncture lays a greater claim to being
the first American poem—for that touching all our peoples is understood—
than the 435 plates of John James Audubon's *Birds of America*, the forms
of which, derived from water, are now on view for the first time, but only
for a while, at the New York Historical Society. In Japan, an older hand at
these things, they would probably be housed in a temple and permanently
on show as a "national treasure."

New York, 05.12.73. The mass of Audubon's work bears down on me for
the first time, and that it all started from France! 06.30.28: beginnings of this
intruder, 50 rue François Premier, Paris, France. Audubon had the advantage
of a sunny disposition in the isles: my isles came much later, when I had al-
ready created them in my own head.

Let it be a detail here merely. Of the work which went into those plates, I
learn now, three watercolors were absent in the purchase of 1861. One plate,
the California condor, was subsequently found. Two others are still at large
if not destroyed.

These two plates are of blue birds. Comment on one only. On that first,
never-to-be-forgotten American day among warblers (Princeton, New Jersey:
05.10.70), two blue critters had been missing in the riot of discovery: the

cerulean and the black-throated blue. Gazed at lovingly in the pages of Roger Tory Peterson, these birds had become a haunting.

Saint John, US Virgin Islands, 06.12.70. In the dark grove high on the island above our plantation hotel, among palms and lianas, a stop for hummers. The glasses focus on a branch at random, searching the gloom for the small vibrations. Suddenly, from the multiple wings about him, a male black-throated blue enters up stage. Wintering here as the black-and-whites had wintered in Guatemala. Small, infinitesimal web in the pattern of islands—part of a spiraling return to an early voyage on the American spine.

It might have been thought that a son eventually addicted to books would receive from his progenitors more than a single volume. Of those remembered far back as emanating from a father, one alone stands out: perhaps the only one. It had not, I believe, been purchased but, rather, had been recuperated from an old hoard or found in a bin thrown out to the elements.

The book, still with me in one of the libraries deposited here and there among these wanderings, was a copy of Maurice Maeterlinck's *L'oiseau bleu* in a small paperback edition with a rather battered blue cover. Its receipt touched me for years, perhaps because it had been specially acquired. The book as object and gift: I doubt I read it.

Back of that: Michelet's *L'oiseau* with a gaudy tropical long-tailed pair on the dust jacket. Blue in their feathers certainly but also the orange of a fiery sun. Read with French-speaking mothers at an early time.

Some ten to fifteen early-childhood books somehow survived World War II and returned. One is a Fabre on insects, and there are two or three red-and-gold Jules Vernes. Not one piece of a large army, running from Roman to Napoleonic times, not one toy of any kind—not even the German Shuco toy car or the battered police helmet my brother and I used to fight over. After the war, not one of several dozen toy mini-soldiers of a second army bought during the London Blitz survived: no sandbag rows, not one airplane, nor the tanks and antiaircraft guns, nor the rising-falling barrage balloon that I recently saw in a Madison Avenue store for more than eight hundred dollars. Where did they go?

In the nineteen-nineties: there was still no closure. So, in search of such, there is now in the study one whole shelf full of collector-quality French, Scots, English, Italian, Russian, and American lead soldiers and many shelves bearing die-cast cars, planes, and ships.

1.5 Antwerp, Belgium, circa 1937. Age more or less nine. The weather is fine. The apartment sunlit. Perhaps it is raining, but the rain is illuminated.

There is a carpet. Our beds, my brother's and mine, with their wooden book-cases surrounding two sides of the room, our desk, two-sided, in the same wood—a fine piece of art deco that survives in a London house until the seventies. We are playing some game. My mother might be knitting. The interminable conflict between my brother and me (he teasing, I reacting with some violence and getting punished for same) momentarily stilled. A great peace within as if everything had suddenly been stopped and the whole far lengthier future was humming about us on all sides. For whatever reason, the distant park, a park called Park of the Nightingales, is not being visited today: but its treasures, its long lawns and odoriferous bushes, its waffles and cream-cheese-on-rye with giant radish slices and spring onions, perhaps its deer and birdsongs, stand securely a few miles away ready to be visited on the next day. As few other things stand secure in a world perpetually vanishing—a world in which nothing appears but to disappear and never be seen again.

A world in which, every morning, while the other kids rush around the playground, three eleven-year-old Jewish schoolboys perennially discuss the oncoming war. One, gawky and bug-eyed with thyroid problems, is called Steinfeld. Disappears. The other, Wiener, small and bulky, is said to have become a doctor in the United States.

In an explosion of love, remembered for all time, whether the memory be of the thing itself or the memory of the memory, I leap demonstratively toward my mother and say, over and over again, until she wonders what has bitten me, "I am so happy; I am so happy."

A woman toward whom inexplicably, despite her overwhelming beauty and unbounded kindness and sweetness, I have not been able, for a great many years now, to feel any emotion whatsoever. No doubt because, while promising her help with Father after an endless number of disagreements, she again and again always ended by taking Father's part.

Throw Two

2.1 05.15.2003: some twenty years after Throw One. "Completion" is not a word that should ever come near this book. Should it do so, you would never be quit of it short of, say, thirty volumes. An original idea had been to spend old age reviewing a diary that had begun in 1939 with records of air raids during the London Blitz and only very rarely been interrupted, also innumerable letters to and from innumerable people, also records of travel, work, and publishing activities—in short, a long and complex life. This is not feasible. Best to leave all those records to be dealt with by others, should there be any others, should they so desire, well before the Sun decides to slam into the Earth. Concentrate on whatever saliences are left in memory and leave things at that. This is what is left of a life at age seventy-seven—come June 30, 2005.

The original project for this autoanthropology in the seventies of the last century was defined as "a thematic study of a structure provisionally baptized Nathaniel Tarn." Concentration would be not on the facts of a life, day after month after year, but on some of the concerns that had worried at that life and which might have made it interesting as an aspect of its time rather than as a one-shot, and thus ultimately arbitrary, narration. A major theme in the original text was concerned above all with the sempiternally unsolved but ever-interesting problem of the relation between a whole and its parts. Also a kindred problem: the relation of order to disorder. As a totalizer in those days—totalizer in the structuralist sense—the matter of a complete record was an aim of inestimable value. Exhaustive explanations now being regarded by most literary theorists as impossible, perhaps valueless after all, much in the original text could now be excised. Yet if some seventy-seven years are to be accounted for and some care taken over projections into however many years are left to this structure, the guiding themes of an individual's prime cannot altogether be ignored.

Perhaps a word about why the text was abandoned in the first place. As well as a poet since age five, Tarn had been an anthropologist for some thirty years, beginning with studies at the Musée de l'Homme, the Ecole des Hautes Etudes and the College de France, Paris, in 1949–50, continuing with work at the University of Chicago (including field experience in Guatemala), 1951–53; the London School of Economics and the School of Oriental & African Studies (S.O.A.S.), 1953–58; fieldwork in Burma, 1958–59; and teaching at the S.O.A.S. in 1960–67. Resigning from "the best Southeast Asia job in the world" in 1967, Tarn worked at Jonathan Cape, publishers, London, for two years (Cape Editions and Cape Goliard Press) before reentering academia in the United States and, after a spell at Princeton, teaching comparative literature at Rutgers from 1970 to 1984. "Comparative literature," it should be added, was a discipline whose existence, however legitimate it was deemed to be by its practitioners, Tarn failed to recognize.

In 1977 or 1978, Norman Hammond, a young and noticeably ambitious Mayanist, joined the Archaeology Department at Rutgers. Within a year or so, Tarn was co-teaching with him, responsible for the modern and contemporary Maya. Eventually grants from a leading anthropological research organization (the Wenner-Gren Foundation), the Social Science Foundation, and others were obtained for an impossible project defined by Tarn: "to find a language for certain kinds of cultural anthropology which would not be untrue to the scientific record while not abdicating a single aspect of its literary potential." Why impossible? Because there would be no limit to this: not even in a James Joyce, a Gertrude Stein, a Louis Zukofsky. The market would be challenged. The market would say no. The whole point of the experiment—to destroy technological jargon and make anthropology available to all—would be lost.

This project's preparation took from 1975 (the original attempt at writing the autoanthropology stopped in December 1974) to 1978, ending in participation in an archaeological dig at Cuello, Belize, in the latter year and a year's residence in Santiago Atitlán, Guatemala (the place Tarn had studied some thirty years before) during 1979. This preparation led, after too many decades, to *Scandals in the House of Birds: Shamans and Priests on Lake Atitlán*, a book brought out in 1997 that had no success whatsoever and whose career was rapidly aborted by the publisher's demise two months after publication.

The point of all this? The style and texture of *Scandals* is not all that dissimilar to the style of the original seventies text of the present work. In particular, Tarn notes the dating of paragraphs, sections, and chapters; the interweaving of time periods (in *Scandals* the 1952–53 research and the 1979 research with reference, also, to another stay in 1969); and the general allegiance to thematics in both works.

Tarn's book on the Burmese Buddhist Order of Monks and its role in Burmese politics, originally designed as one of three volumes, also took many years to be completed and published. It had in fact also been abandoned during Tarn's stay at Princeton and was rescued by another anthropologist and very substantially edited and *rewritten*. All these abdications, all these deposits of "babies" at the door of post offices, libraries, convents, and orphanages were not only the result of academia's scourge but also of the impossibility of doing more than one thing at a time. Writings on *weikza*—followers of a future Buddha—and on Spirit cults remain in notes. The Burma work was seen above all as proof of the impossibility of running at least two lives at one time: something Tarn had been trying to explain to his parental generation forever without any success. It was not until much later that the ability to spend more than one life at a time was finally achieved.

2.2 One name is Nathaniel Tarn. Another is Edward Michael Mendelson. Mendelson is a Customs name given to the paternal grandfather arriving in Britain from East Europe. For Tarn this was never a real name. Edward was owed to some member of British royalty admired by father, possibly Michael as well. Edward became Teddy. After too many encounters with female voices calling "Teddy" at small dogs in the street, I became Michael at Cambridge but kept E. Michael in anthropology.

2.3 In Lithuania the name, Father had said, had been something like Taurogi, or Tauroga, or Tavrogi, or Tavroga. Now it happens that a famous historical event in Napoleonic times was an armistice at Tauroggen (aka Taurogé) signed on June 21, 1807, by Napoleon and Tsar Alexander First. An encyclopedia gives Tauragé Municipality in the Samogitia region as a Lithuanian place close to the border with Kaliningrad Oblast (that is, Königsberg: Immanuel

Kant's city). The name originates from *Tauras* (auroch) and *Ragas* (horn), hence the coat of arms. The place was known as Tauroggen in German and Tauroggi in Polish. Tauragé is very close geographically to Kudirkos Naumiestis Municipality (now named after the composer of the Lithuanian national anthem), alias Wladilawó (Polish), Neustadt-Schirwindt (German), and Nayshot Shaki (Yiddish) in Suvalki County, from which our family apparently originated. There is a bridge in the village that leads to Kaliningrad. The multiplicity of identities in that perpetually war-torn region may be germane to this autoanthropology. Some four thousand Jews were killed by the Wehrmacht near Tauroggen in 1941.

There is only small difference between the name Tavroggi (still found in a variety of forms in the Kudirkos Naumiestis annals) and the Polish city name Tauroggi. Is it possible that the family name might have been derived from neighboring Tauroggi? In any event, Tarn derived a second pen name (Michel Tavriger) from his father's sparse information while a student in Paris in 1949–50. A school pen name is lost.

2.4 As there are people in London to this day who cannot deal with anyone else but Michael, so there are also many people in Paris to this day who cannot deal with anyone else but Michel. The origin of Nathaniel is a secret of mine that I have never revealed, whereas Tarn was taken from the French river near which I spent the summer of 1963 after a disastrous love affair. N.T. was used as the definitive pen name for years before first publications and became a legal name with American citizenship. Do all that many people know that the first question you answer in the "Land of the Free" is "Under what name would you like to be known?" You go into the ceremony under an old name and come out under a new one. Thus, the republic flatters a poet's intuition that his or her first right should be to choose his or her own name.

On my return from Guatemala to London in 1953, British "social anthropologists," in the throes of the formation of an extremely fruitful but also very chauvinistic theoretical movement, were somewhat scornful of the American training I had received and absolutely candid regarding the fact that "poetry"—which had caused no trouble at the U. of C. in the Windy City—"should be deeply buried and come up as anthropology" if I were ever to amount to anything in the profession. There were also some episodes of insult and deprecation. This prompted the living of at least two lives for a good ten years, one as E.M.M., one as N.T. These two names were sometimes as inconsiderate as to force me to move alternately between two different corners of a room on social occasions. However, holding the two lives apart became a lifelong habit. Another factor was my noticing that people very often become tediously suspicious and unwholesomely curious on hearing the faintest rumor that someone is in fact someone else. The British are especially susceptible to expressing shock and dismay at any hint of such a thing. It is, of course, an old European tradition that writers should have noms de plume or noms de guerre. In my youth there was scarcely a contemporary poet who was not, in cold fact, someone else. For reasons of this kind, great care was taken to hide all traces of the origin of certain other works written and/or published under other names that are therefore completely untraceable.

The parental generation. Mother: Yvonne Cecile Leah Suchar (originally Sucher perhaps), whose family, originally from Odessa in Russia and eventually Rumania, had been French for a time: she came to Paris as a small child and remembered seeing German zeppelins above Paris in World War I. Her mother, Jeanne, known to Tarn as Mémé, the dearest person in all of Paris. Her father, Morou, a fine singer and sculptor (said to have made one of the statues surrounding the Bucharest Opera), became very ill from a combat wound during that war. Childe Tarn saw him in bed, 17 rue de l'Arc de Triomphe, a very kind man with a sweet smile inside a white beard. Claude, Yvonne's younger brother, who left a long manuscript on the family, writes that Morou suffered agonies before dying. Morou's brother was a great ballistic expert the French Army should have used, but he was unwell and so irresponsibly killed off by being ordered to perform menial services. The family had many connections with Russia. One of the men had been director of the Black Sea merchant fleet. A cousin, Pauline, claimed to be from Odessa during Tarn's student days and spoke fluent Russian—mainly with Paris's large cadre of Russian taxi drivers. This branch of the family continues on down to this day. A story I like: Morou sitting in a café enjoying his drink. A lady with a little dog sits next to him and begins to cherish the dog in French repeatedly and very loudly. Morou mutters in Rumanian something like "Oh, go and rub your nose in it yourself!" The lady responds fairly violently in Rumanian. Morou is also said to have shaken hands with Verlaine once in a Paris cafe or restaurant—possibly the Procope.

Father: Mendel Myer, nicknamed Marcel—probably by wife, Yvonne. A family legend makes them bookbinders in a village of Lithuanian horse thieves. His father, Solomon, left for England, in the 1880s I suppose, and became, it is said, a peddler in Wales. Moving to Manchester, he transformed himself into a man of parts and, eventually, head of a synagogue in which Tarn experienced an unspeakably lonely bar mitzvah during World War II.

He was also a Mason of high degree, and so was his brother-in-law, Uncle Jack, an amiable rake. There were connections with France and Belgium in the industrial-tool business and eventually in the precious-stone business so that Father worked in Paris at one time and met Mother there, later settling in Belgium. Relatives remained in Manchester, perhaps still do: Solomon's home, on Cheetham Hill Road, ended up as a "Royal Society for the Protection of Animals" home for cats.

A cousin became professor of medicine at Liverpool University and masterminded the creation of the British National Health Service—for which deed he was made a peer of the realm. He is alleged to have bent over Tarn's cradle and to have promised the babe a great career in medicine (Tarn only met him nearly thirty years later at his own wedding lunch). There was always much speculation as to whether Tarn or his father would eventually be made a peer, at the end of which it was discovered that a *life* peerage seemed to be in question, with no available succession.

Half the family from Neustadt continued across the Atlantic to America and became the Shuberts of Broadway. Schubart had been the name of Grandfather Solomon's father's wife. The Shuberts had always pretended, somewhat fraudulently, that they were born in Syracuse, New York, where they had eventually landed up. Tarn met two of them once. No recollections. They were said to be somewhat unpleasant, quarrelsome, materialistic, and hardheaded people in reaction perhaps against their own father: a man who is said to have combined extreme religiosity with a great taste for the demon drink. Family gossip has it that Father and his younger brother Harry were entertained by the Shubert brothers in New York, with introductions to Al Jolson, with whom they shared many a good time, as well as to Barbara Stanwick (Father's date) and Sylvia Sydney (Harry's date). Tarn was unfortunate, given later circumstances, not to have been born into that branch: a sorely missed American childhood and adolescence would have been provided. In the seventies a book about the Shuberts was found to have been written by an academic person, mistaking their Neustadt completely and picking a town close to Gdansk/Danzig that must have been far larger. However, other books, notably those by Foster Hirsch and Jerry Stagg, got the origin place right. In the 1980s, Tarn tried and failed to get a modest little grant from the Shubert Foundation to help finance his trip to Lithuania and his family research.

2.5 Which was the first language: French or English? Perhaps both? No one remembers. An initial nurse was French. Dominated by jealousy, she would stick pins into the babe and get him to howl on the phone in order to bring the parents back from evening outings. She, or a close successor, made him walk too early—so that his feet pointed inward for years afterward. Father caught her at work one evening and threw her out. Eventually, a North of England woman, Eileen Gregory, stayed with the family for ten years or so. She was strict, albeit well-loved. If "naughty," the child would be placed under a cold-water tap, after which he is alleged to have become very "amorous." Later Eileen became a famous Hollywood figure, working with the children of Charles Chaplin, Fred Astaire, Charles Boyer, Fred MacMurray, and the like. She lived in West Hollywood, holding down three charity jobs until her ninety-third year. Tarn took her to lunch a number of times when in Los Angeles, the last occasion being two weeks before her death in November 2002.

A great deal of life was taken up by being promenaded daily on the Champs Elysées, which the child was named the "king" of by a concordance of governesses because of a certain haughtiness, reserved especially for little girls. The "haughtiness" probably a product of shyness: both persisting for life. One of these girls remained "in love" for many years, sending many presents and *billets doux*. A great day came when Tarn and his younger brother, Neville, were very spontaneously collected by a maternal uncle, Edmond, and whisked off to a cinema on the avenue for an introduction to Mickey Mouse. The children were fitted for school clothes once a year by a tailor coming from London. There are various attestations concerning a craze for flowers and for the opportunity of delivering "expert" critical pronouncements insisted on at any garden the family chanced to visit.

One "social" memory regarding shyness. Being taken to a children's party and standing alone with a nurse or companion in the middle of the floor of a large sitting room. Peeing in one's pants uncontrollably out of sheer terror. Bedwetting continued well into the early teens, causing much consternation in an English boarding school.

2.6 There was a move from rue Francois Premier to no. 1 avenue du Président Wilson, a very short street at the bottom of the avenue Marceau near the river Seine. In 1936 came a relocation to Antwerp, where Father wished to join his parents and brothers. A cozy town that had changed very little by the eighties—as Tarn witnessed fifty years later, recognizing many old haunts with ease: a very strange experience, walking from the past in one's head into the present and seeing what coincided and what did not. School was the Lycée d'Anvers, a bilingual (French-Flemish) school on Nervierstraat, where three friends spent playground time discussing oncoming World War

II. There were trips to dune forests looking for mushrooms and one ride, in a fine Packard that once lost a wheel along the way, to the Dutch tulip fields. Preceded by many goldfish pets, a canary called Tino Rossi, which never sang and was probably female, as well as a red-bellied salamander: both died in an earthquake while the family was visiting friends in Brussels. This visit was memorable for my being fed an oyster for the very first time.

On tramway no. 2 from home at 33 Avenue Van Ryswick to Nervierstraat, a black tie was worn on three occasions: the deaths of King George V of England, Queen Astrid of Belgium—a passion—and Franklin D. Roosevelt. This was on Tarn's initiative. Even today, there is a portrait of the great beauty Astrid on a shelf in the study, and her black-framed memorial postage stamps are set in the Belgium albums.

Occasionally, both in summer and winter, the brothers were sent to a children's camp: the Home des Esserts in Leysin, Switzerland, run by an old couple with Nazi sympathies. Parents were ignorant of this allegiance. Skiing was discovered as a great joy—and very sadly lost during World War II as a result of rising to six foot two. Wonderful hikes in the mountains added to a passion for flowers and landscape: one day spent mostly climbing a rocky mountain stream was especially heavenly. A run across a huge field during a thunderstorm was also part of such a day. Swimming on the lake near Chillon occurred a number of times: on one occasion, Tarn felt immensely brave when clinging to a rock flooded by waves made by a passing lake steamer. There was the lick of a cow's tongue on a hand as he stood by a fence with his back to the animal. There was the swing of the great house sleigh that fetched the children at the station at the start of a winter stay. There were times playing with a toy yacht on a large pool in the garden. There was a party at the house where everyone was heaping their plates with food, while one boy—a little *nebbish* already—took only one piece of meat. For Tarn, tears almost, and an indescribable tenderness over that inexplicable poverty. The pain repeated ever since at similar witnessings of a state akin to orphancy. On another occasion, eating noodles, Tarn feared he would die laughing at the inner vision of a cross-eyed cat coming up in conversation. Unable to stop laughing, he was punished by being seated out of doors. In the great cold, while he still laughed, his noodles turned to concrete. There was also the older Japanese boy who twisted the arms of younger children behind their backs very painfully if they refused to say "Heil Hitler." One of the favorite pastimes was woodwork, and Tarn still owns a paper cutter surmounted by an edelweiss he made at Leysin. Likewise, one could make lead soldiers from molds and paint them there.

Many summer vacations were taken on the Belgian Coast at Le Zoute in a rented villa called, after Kipling's *Jungle Book*, Shere Khan. Next door was Rikki Tikki Tavi, and people would drive the boy nuts as they passed repeating that sonorous name. A favorite memory concerns a time when an evening paper (was it *Le Soir*?) offered prizes for sand castles built by the sea's edge. Tarn's was destroyed early, but it was said that there was a kink in his shoreline position, and to his astonishment, a tennis racket with blue bands was the reward. Very popular was the game of "selling and buying" paper flowers (made, often very ornately, by mothers and grandmothers) against seashells, a pastime that, astonishingly, still survived in the 1960s. The brothers, devoted cyclists, made maps of the hundreds of little cycling alleys serving as streets among the villas and trees of the dune areas. Tarn has always been nostalgic for that coast and took his own children there, at Den Haan, when they were small. An excellent location from which to visit the great Romanesque barn of the no longer extant Lissewege Abbey together with the town of Damme, and to revisit Bruges and Ghent. Mother had taken Childe Tarn to Bruges very shortly before the war to see a great Memling retrospective. A painting of the flaying alive of some saint never left his memory.

Throw Three

3.1 A sudden awakening at 03.15 hours. Gazing at the skirting of the wall on the right of the bed, wondering whether to turn on the light and read or not, and, if so, what. A strange object, out of place, near the books: large garden spider. Decisively trap it under a drinking glass, sliding a postcard under the glass—the usual gambit—and get it back into the garden. Strangely, some weeks ago, a similar sudden awakening with similar result. That spider, more or less in the same place, smaller but more repulsive: fat and hairy. A carpet under the glass is not conducive to sliding: on that first occasion, a messy business. Sleep finally achieved through avenues of frail legs bent into every angle those legs seem likely to assume.

3.2 I know now that this book was to start with a small spider which, until about three days ago, lived on the bathroom ceiling upstairs. A small, compact, elegant, almost military spider. Robert the Bruce would have loved it. In the last hours of its occupation, this spider had seemed determined to discover a small crimp in the ceiling from which, perhaps, it could fasten or cause to depend a threadway to the ground. As it began its up/down work, it was caught and deported. An intention to mark the theme of a passage from an "Above" to a "Below" with this spider—leading from section 1.1 of this work to section 1.2 had been forgotten. So frail is the web of this quest.

3.3 As a baby, subsequent to 1.2 no doubt, the following? Lying in a bed or more likely a crib, at dawn, or perhaps at dusk, I, the intruder into this world, gaze at a pair of curtains. These are obliterated by a giant spider. Was it even there? Spider has taken on and retained the form of death for a whole existence. While rereading this Throw—08.24.2020—I suffer a large, very painful reddening on the left big toe, which could only have been a spider's bite in the night.

3.4 Atitlán fieldwork, Guatemala: 1952–53. A small apartment in the school director's house consisting of two rooms. A front room giving on to the "street," furnished with a desk and two chairs. Back of this, another smaller room with a camping cot. At the height of the spider season, waking every hour to find the walls covered with very large black spiders. Walls not at all smooth: cheap stucco finish, yellowish, giving the spiders every conceivable foothold. Too many for removal. Leads to a matter of killing them either by swatting or, exasperated by fear, loathing, and sorrow, pursuing the unfortunate beasts with Flytox. The larger animals are covered with the juice until they wallow in a pool of noxious liquid whose fumes are the odor of nightmare for several months.

Burma, especially in Rangoon and the south: 1958–59. Large garden spiders, on the one hand, Buddhism on the other. Determined not to kill, the object is to try to induce the spiders to leave the room. Tenaciously, they always manage to cling to unworkable surfaces from which it is impossible to remove them. In the chase they can lose a leg or two. These cripples end up killed in the end. A terrible disgust at killing: the loathing compounded a hundredfold. Small triumphs of will and ingenuity: the use of various objects to form a corridor leading out of the room. Very successful with mice later in Mandalay.

In Penne du Tarn, after the love disaster, the same problem on the stone walls of a local house.

Japan: 1961. I had written to a young French Sinologist, who had been kind enough to oversee my accommodations, that I would like to try living in a temple. Mention of arachnophobia. He meets me at the Kyoto station. Everything is arranged, but first we will go to his apartment. As we climb the stairs, a spider larger than any I have ever seen greets us at the threshold.

During dinner another appears on the floor. I am led to the temple as to an abattoir.

Left alone in a delightful room, view the *tatami* matting with terror. No elevation of the mattress off the floor, nothing between body and crawling legs. I insult the *tatami* by drawing a protective oval of DDT powder around the sleeping place. Sweating copiously in the heat, lie for some time in the dark, mistakenly convinced there will be no sleep at all.

Morning opens small, ground-level windows onto miniature gardens from which plant leaves bow into the room. A small stone Buddha meditates under one plant. Survival! A girl brings breakfast. Squat to enjoy it, gazing at one of the two windows. Large leg suddenly thrusts into sight with the grace of a ballerina's testing itself in the wings prior to entry. Within a moment, with a sidling movement, the whole giant comes into view. With a groan of horror, move cushions and breakfast into the farthest corner of the room glaring at the animal, helpless as a mouse before a snake. The girl returns at my summons and is about to kill when, with copious gestures of piety and reluctance, I indicate unwillingness to let this happen within a temple precinct. She shoos the intruder out the window, and I prepare for many sleepless nights. However, an impending typhoon eventually takes me to another location.

3.5 Circa 1937 or 1938, on the dunes of the Belgian coast, I had concocted a poisonous mixture rammed into the bottom of a jam jar and separated from the gas chamber by a large wedge of cork. Somehow, powders or liquids seeped into the chamber reducing butterflies to a mass of unclassifiable juice. Butterfly collecting was abandoned at the time when other gas chambers were being tested, prepared, and used.

Sometime later, circa 1941–42, bird egg hunting was abandoned in the Derbyshire wilds when disgust intervened. The clean collection, consisting in the selection of one egg from a clutch, all too often ended in debacle when one unsuccessful blowing led to the sacrifice of another egg.

Nothing like hunting ever marred this existence. Once, in Derbyshire, lured out by a friend with an air pistol, led to shooting a duck in the backside. Never again. Much later, lured by an embassy friend into a wild-pig hunt near Mandalay, Burma, refusing to carry a gun and reduced to thrashing around in low thorn trees for protection against murderous-looking tusks.

3.6 We have an entry into collecting. The accumulated possession of things that seem like bliss to some vanity of vanities (in that wisdom consists of discarding possessions rather than adding to them). The defense: that possessions, if intelligently chosen, lead to much pleasure and to some semblance of scholarship. Collecting: the classification and study of documented items a different matter from accumulation—for example, letting postage stamps pile up in boxes without any work ever being done on them until the boxes become, yes, a pain and an obstacle to any form of rational existence.

Possession of a closed, ordered world that ("anal" or not) will please, will not betray or talk back too loudly, and which may increase in value as time goes by (when one is unsuccessful at saving for one's children in any other way). Walter Benjamin's claim that each book bought is saved from savagery. Above everything, the books and smaller things like stamps, badges, toys—whatever—have a major role in *sustaining* existence. This means that divestment, when age demands it, is most difficult. Even if certain books have not been used for years and may never be used again, they signify *coherence and home* when you pass by. They eventually feel like your flesh and blood. And yet wisdom is felt to educate children into not accumulating!

Grounding this, the matter of order made in spite of ever-threatening disorder, the constant reiteration of order, the rage against the irruption of disorder (loss, misplacement, memory blocks, etc.) into an ordered cosmos—all of this requires a guiding concept.

3.7 Let there be heraldry—elsewhere elaborated in my writing into the "heraldic consciousness." Its fascination being connected with theoretically unlimited variations or transformations of content within a standard, relatively simple form. A love of which brands one who, long ago, fell from a great height into loss and pain and cannot any more bear the thought of an open, infinitely expanding universe. Does the relatively simple form provide no more than a guarantee of stability, a guarantee of order within which the ludic function may be exercised? Delight in closed rather than open gardens, an early passion for the *hortus conclusus*—the enclosed garden sensed as illuminated by no outside light but by a subtle inner light, a light, though apparently sourceless, born of itself from within. The whole issue of pastorality/wilderness also brought, at a later date, into question.

Delight in transformation, then, within some kind of format. Do not underestimate the joys of this; nurse no contempt for the swaddling bands which some are trapped in by birthright! There but for grace go you . . . are we not prisoners, all of us consumers?

Early childhood delight consisted remarkably often in the imagination of a slight variation within a standard mode. Most times, this imagination played around color. Looking hard at a favorite pencil whose fate in life was, say, to be a yellow pencil (the rind, not the lead), ecstasy would be approached by thinking of what this pencil would look like if fate were to change it into blue. Likewise a privileged toy car, bouncing and roaring along on its rubber wheels, would change from orange to red, or blue to green.

Is it not so that the charm of many "collectibles" (hateful word but now at large in the language) resides in their being a system of transformations? But- terflies, birds' eggs, postage stamps, toy models, coins: most of these have one form and a great—though not infinite—variety of content. Nor does the so- phistication of collecting stop here: it spreads into the visual field, where the world in its infinite variety becomes prey. A passion for American warblers, genus Parula especially, heralds in one observer that cast of mind. Or for the liveries on men and machines: trains, cars, airplanes. We are in the realm of *la pensée classificatrice*—although I cannot remember at this writing whether Lévi-Strauss dealt with collecting or not. Heraldry itself, of course, betrays the classificatory instinct in a culture where social relations, within an accep- tance pale, are part of a steady world order where everybody can, eventually, even when once unmasked, be recognized and recognizable.

You do not have to move far from this to get to a fondness for uniforms, badges, insignias, decorations—everything which helps a person "dress to kill"—in trappings once characteristic of the military life, now lost for the most part except in the case of certain ceremonial regiments in certain armies. This aspect of design is determined by order and hierarchy, every- thing, again, that reads and promotes order in a disordered world. It is trag- ically unfortunate that this particular order treats other orders of the same kind as phenomena disordered and fit for destruction. "To kill": Oh, no! It does not have to follow that a fondness for such decoration means a love of war. It may, in the end, merely indicate a passionate desire to belong.

"It is not to be known that we ask," I once wrote, "but to be recognized."

3.8 That collecting and heraldic systems go hand in glove then, whether the collector be one of our senses, like that of sight, or a possessional enterprise, must arise out of this need for order, this all-encompassing thirst and require- ment for security. Progress of more than one kind, in the work and in the spirit, which would seem to require of us today that we adopt an open view of the universe and of that labor which we choose to perform here, may well go against a most intimate grain in the human spirit—that grain which organizes the known geography into emblems, pivots, cardinal directions, ordered systems of signatures among stones or stars—the very grain which, from another angle, those very workers in open-field systems often like to think of as their favorite lore. If then one part of the mind weighs anchor and sails across never to be charted seas, insisting on unbounded and interminable *periploi*, another part of that same mind may legitimately choose to tie itself down within very old topographies? And so: the poem? No discussion of the poem today would seem complete without the notion that freedom in one aspect might have to call for a lack of it elsewhere and that the spirit will trigger in one direction what it will have to inhibit in another. We touch on the question of structure and process within the making of the poem. S. and P.—no other obsession is so potent, nor is any theme so close to the problem of the all and the many.

Throw Four

4.1 Le Zoute, Belgian coast, summer 1939. Very suddenly Tarn's bunch is on the ferry to England with car and all. They end up at Colwyn Bay, Wales: he does not know why, perhaps because paternal grandfather had been a peddler there in youth and felt it safe. The family sitting in a large circle in a hotel lounge, as war is declared, listening to Chamberlain's speech. World War II beginning. Grandfather is weeping: a mystery. Mother does not elucidate. Brother Neville and Tarn expect the bombers to show up immediately and see spies everywhere. Anyone walking on the beach, especially, is bound to be a spy. There is some stay in this place, even a house taken, then a series of moves, mostly in coastal regions. There were weeks in Torquay, Devon. Here the bunch was joined by paternal uncle Harry—the handsome bon vivant who later, in the R.A.F., landed the outlandish job of air attaché to the Nizam of Hyderabad—and Merton, the son of Father's sister Annie, later with the British Army in the Middle East. They had stayed behind to pack things up and had caught the last ship out: both of them now down with jaundice.

Later a stay in one of the hotels on the beach at Brighton, Sussex. Interminable bouts of ping-pong, cordial friendships with waiters, and a bandleader playing every night at the hotel. Somewhere in all of this, a seaside meeting of important personages, including Daladier of France. Father, in the corridor, shouting *"Vive la France!"*

4.2 After a while, Tarn and brother become boarders at the preparatory school for Clifton College "public" (i.e., in Britain, private) school in a small town neighboring Bristol. Clifton is chosen presumably because it is one of the few British "public schools" with a Jewish "house": a boarding unit inhabited uniquely by Jewish children. The house stands across the street from the famed Clifton zoo: the lions roar all night every night. Tarn experiences massive timidity: still feeling French? Unsure of his English—if it existed at all? Fear at entering a foreign classroom for the first time.

It was believed that this place would not be bombed—or not early. It was. Life was full of savage small-boy cruelty. There were epic battles between catapult-wielding sharpshooters using tight paper pellets, deleterious hazings in the collective basement bathrooms, beatings with canes: Tarn being beaten on more than one occasion, often grabbed by a master at the scene of some crime though actually not the perpetrator at that juncture. A major disappointment: not being allowed to join the Boy Scout Cubs. Some question of a quota. Little gangs would play at "tracking" on the huge wild downs near the school, close to the Clifton Gorge with its world-famous suspension bridge, and pay daily visits to the barrage balloon stationed nearby. Monthly candy rations were eaten immediately on purchase, making him feel sick so that he would not hanker for candy until the start of the next month. The last week of any given month was torture.

At a certain point, boys began to disappear from the dormitories. America the whispered destination. Tarn longed to be told that he would go, but it turned out that Father, although seemingly past military age, was not allowed to leave. Mother would not go without him, and neither of them would let the boys go alone. After the whispered scene, work in class would ensue, and on return to the house, one boy had disappeared. This too was a mystery.

4.3 Weeks in the Cumberland Hotel at Marble Arch in London while the great Blitz went on outside. The antiaircraft guns set in Hyde Park very close by. Sometimes you slept in the blind corridors, away from flying glass. One night, parents walking up and down arm in arm in the corridor. A bomb falls nearby: Mother jumps so high her head almost hits the ceiling. On most nights, as the sirens sound, guests move downstairs: everyone wandering around in pajamas or asleep on the floor, kids trailing teddy bears or dolls. At the all-clear, Father carries the boys up to their rooms and puts them to bed. Tarn is eleven at the time.

Still angry all these years later that nothing of the Blitz was seen, only heard. That one might have witnessed the burning of St. Paul's Cathedral and other such sights continues to rankle. Not going near broken, flying glass was the reason. As for loud noise—from then on for a lifetime, anything like it causes Tarn to jump. Spouse, Janet Rodney, believes this is PTSD.

Because school was in abeyance, much play occurred in the hotel rooms: mainly with the miniature army, the fighter plane made by Frog Models, and others such. There were visits to Selfridges a few blocks down the road on Oxford street to add to these collections. On one occasion, a broken awning over one of the big windows and a bleeding body lying on the ground surrounded by passersby: someone had decided to leave the planet. A visit to Kew Gardens was a highlight of this time: Tarn spent so long in the greenhouses smelling the plants that a strange fever occurred holding him down in bed for a few days.

It was difficult to read, and the impression left with the boy was that the Blitz had made him forget Latin, maths, and the violin he had begun at Clifton Prep: these subjects were never successfully returned to. (On the other hand, it is true that maths had always been hideously difficult, even at the Lycée d'Anvers.) The only book remembered as inspiring at this time: a life of Abraham Lincoln. The dream of America begins—unless it was already fed by reading Fenimore Cooper or Mayne Reid in Belgium.

4.4 Family leaves a few days before there is a palpable hit on the subway station next door and large numbers of wounded people are brought into the Cumberland. Direction north: Grandfather is assumed to have wanted to get back to Manchester—where there is family—or to have thought it safer. Tarn's group ends up in Buxton, a small town in Derbyshire. First stay in the Sunderland Hotel, a boardinghouse along an avenue opposite a great park in which such communal buildings are set. Parents, much impoverished, had now begun the mean and skimpy boardinghouse life that lasted most of the war, interspersed with the occasional rented house. One-inch markers on the baths above which hot water is not to reach. Showers unknown. Rush for the dining room at the bell to get the best helpings. Communal evenings with other "guests" in Victorian sitting rooms.

The brothers are boarded out to a ghastly secondary school from which they escape regularly for little meals cooked by Mother on a small stove in the parental Sunderland bedroom. Fortunate removal to a good day prep school, Holm Leigh, from which it is possible to get back to Clifton. Eventually, there is a Buxton house with a garden at the back in which first paintings are created: irises, marigolds. There is a piano that Brother Neville fails to master. His brother then tries in order to "show him" and does not manage to do so. Also a garage in which Tarn's plane-building epics are enacted. Ends by designing his own flyers. One of them, the *Triumph*, a pale-blue thing edged with navy blue, furnished with too much rubber, ascends like a rocket to a great height, somersaults, dives nose down into the ground, the propeller rammed right back into the tail. But it flew! A visit from Uncle Harry allows Tarn to put on his R.A.F. overcoat and cap. There are nature walks and egg collecting for a time on the nearby moors: immense, fearsome, wuthering—from which a grouse, exploding between your feet, can scare you almost to death.

At thirteen, a terrifying bar mitzvah in Manchester. Hebrew lessons have not been very successful, and excuses have to be made because the full ritual cannot be memorized. A massive thunderstorm during a totally sleepless night at the end of which Tarn squeezes into the parental bed. These events are mostly communal, but Tarn, as grandson to his grandfather the temple president, has to stand alone. At a huge lunch afterward, unknown relative after unknown relative proffers presents and exhortations. There is a touching one: a beautiful watch with a very large and long rectangular face covering the whole wrist, handmade by a generous, unknown distant cousin and kept until now, although it did not work for very long.

An early "love" for a young girl who rides by the Buxton house on her bicycle. Lying hour after hour on a couch near the window every day, waiting for her to come by.

4.5 At this age thirteen, a move to Clifton College proper becomes possible. The school evacuated to Bude, a seaside resort on the north coast of Cornwall. Life is raw. There are nightmarish rugby games on the freezing cliffs in which you are so inept that remaining in a very low-ranking team, running up and down a field with far smaller boys clustered around your knees or calves and trying to bring you down, is regular fare. A boy-scoutish, pre-cadet formation known as the Terriers forces escalades up sheer concrete walls, scramblings along tree trunks over a back-country canal many feet off the ground, rope swings, cliff falls, and other terrors. To balance this, many excursions into beautiful parts of Cornwall and Devon—Tintagel, Clovelly—some of them as an R.A.F. officer cadet in uniform with a less athletic routine: marches, inspections, rifle training, and the like. The brothers are set to learn fencing with a ferocious ex-sergeant-major to improve stamina. Underneath he is a generous man.

There are some kind and interesting masters: Guy Lagarde (French or Swiss?), for whom there is considerable affection; Michael Mounsey (art); Donald Davie (biology), who gives Tarn the run of his library and introduces him to Thurber, Runyon, and other Americans. There is one ominous class master, a Scotsman, who manages once to lift Tarn from last to first in the class in Latin and hold him there for two or three weeks through sheer terror. One of his reports reads "This boy would amount to something if he could forget Virginia Woolf for a while and concentrate on Shakespeare." There had been some kind of "mystical" experience: a sense of superhuman freedom and virtual levitation for two or three weeks—after a reading of Woolf's *Jacob's Room*.

Much painting. Once a very large oil of Stravinsky's *Rite of Spring* is so unbearably exciting that Lagarde is hauled out of his bedroom next to the dormitory at a late hour to look at the work. Eventually, first prize is won for a painting of a barn, and art as an alternative to writing is long considered. A prize is also won for designing a new terrace where the houses rented by the school then stood. Anxious to purchase books with the prize money, art master Mounsey is pursued during a few days without the prize being forthcoming. Finally, a measly half-crown is turned over: no doubt a lesson is buried in there somewhere. Tarn goes in for prize after prize (the winners are announced at mealtimes in the huge hall) in order to buy books. The first, for history, entails reading of Trevelyan's *Garibaldi and the Thousand*, which is learned virtually by heart. The school store, with its volumes of Tennyson or Matthew Arnold imprinted with the school crest, is spurned in favor of contemporary fare: a Faber paperback of Siegfried Sassoon, some Auden, some Isherwood, and others of that stable found in a bookstore in Bude. At a later date, when the school is back at Clifton, a first Lund Humphries volume of Henry Moore's sculptures is purchased in London. On the way home, at a gallery selling ethnographic objects, Moore is discovered to be downstairs. Entreaties to the gallery owner lead to a not very graciously given signature (Moore remains downstairs), which elicits exclamations of surprised approval from the headmaster when the prizes are later given out. For an unknown reason this book has disappeared.

Frequent profound depression, manic in remembrance ("I think I have been depressed since the day I was born"), is a constant problem. The only cure, following on from Lincoln, was a reading about the first American pioneer settlements in Nevins and Commager's *America: The Story of a Free People*—the volume still owned and reread recently together with Howard Zinn's less optimistic classic. A *Daily Telegraph* map of the United States is tacked to the wall above the bunk, and the capitals of the forty-eight states are learned by heart. An army base is situated near the school, and on many evenings the lowering of the Stars and Stripes gets to be saluted by this schoolboy all by himself. The magazine devoted exclusively to the US issued by Penguin Books is regularly devoured. The dream of America continues. Some attention must have been paid to the war. One day, during Latin prose, the fear-inspiring teacher allows his flock out onto the downs: immense D-Day fleet rounding Cornwall before moving into the Channel. We are among the first to see it. After five minutes of exhilaration, noses are once more plunged into Latin composition. Another of this man's pranks is uneffaceable. Very suddenly one morning: a student screams at the top of his voice. Thunderclap. Out of his mind? The terrorist—who later becomes headmaster of the Scots "public school" Loretto—is laughing. It appears that there has not been enough feedback from his boys of late, and he is waking them up.

4.6 Not long afterward, the school goes back to Clifton. The Jewish house provides a hideously boring, conventional Jewish education as well as sleep-inducing Sabbath services in a small synagogue within the building. Clifton classwork patterns change. Conventional Judaism has been aesthetically un-entrancing since the beginning, when Father took one very occasionally to synagogue in Antwerp. The architecture unattractive, *idem* the animated and markedly irreligious conversations that frequently went on during services (the matter of the temple being a community meeting house was not yet in the mind's understanding). As for having to raise a cap to dozens of strangers, it was tedious in the extreme.

Tarn attains the rank of house prefect (only advantage: a study cubicle of one's own); his first swoop on noisy critters happens to net Neville, who cops a "hundred lines," which have to be secretly "forgiven" the next morning. After this, there are exceedingly few swoops.

Hearty detestation of school life. Expulsion courted many times. On one occasion, a final three-hour examination yields a totally blank paper to the apoplectic supervisor. The headmaster, a blond giant who later becomes vice-chancellor of Nottingham University, withholds permission to go on vacation, then lifts the final exam: "I'm sure enough work has been done." There are visits to movies and theaters downtown (even the Old Vic's

Shakespeare performances are out of bounds!) crouching on a taxi floor and hiding a very distinctive school cap in a back pocket. The boldest move is a nighttime escape with some fellows to walk all the way into Bristol while the town is celebrating V-Day.

A one-armed World War I music master and organ virtuoso, Douglas Fox, scares his charges to death while teaching them Handel's *Messiah* and Mendelssohn's *Elijah*. Brings his bony fist hard down on their skulls. (An already developed obsessive-compulsive streak whirls the music around in Tarn's skull for weeks afterward.) Fox also brings good things to the school: one visit is by Benjamin Britten and Peter Pears for the *Michelangelo Sonnets*. Tarn acquires the vinyl records and is entranced by them (although his very first purchase is Delibes's *Samson and Delilah*). Boys are also taken to Bristol Philharmonic concerts: one discovery is Sibelius's Second Symphony. Fox's devotion is discerned: he receives a present from Tarn and, greatly touched, corresponds for some time afterward.

Poems are published in the school magazine under a pen name: one poem somehow gets a prize and is published in the teachers' magazine *English*, constituting a lifetime first publication.

I had had one literary meeting. Edwin Honig, an American GI, had somehow arrived at Clifton. As a poet, he had translated Lorca, whom I worshipped at the time. We walked on the downs. A century later, we had some correspondence.

4.7 Vacations are spent in Gerrard's Cross, Buckinghamshire, where parents had settled after Buxton. Again: a boardinghouse followed by a rental. Coffee every Saturday downtown in the same coffeehouse where girls are admired and appraised. Intense and hopelessly timid first loves, perpetual enstorming by powerful emotions. It is the custom—eventually discovered—for everyone to be with everyone else at one time or another, and all the brides are friends of one another. Bluestocking and poet Rosemary, with whom long ardent conversations on D. H. Lawrence are the order of the day, is the first to be courted. Then Miriam appears. Melancholy passion. A decision on one of the only pieces of pure action Tarn has ever dared to carry through. One day, Miriam, leaving the café on her cycle, is followed for miles also on a cycle and accosted with a blurted confession of terminal loneliness. This results in an invitation to the local tennis club, which is accepted, although the subtle artistry of tennis is completely unattained. Later, Lynette, who bestows a first kiss under the cherry trees in her garden one night, and then Anne, with whom matters might have become more serious had there not been a move to London. There are dances at the Bull Hotel, a well-known establishment where the movie *Colonel Blimp* is eventually made. Tarn, totally unable to ask anyone to dance, chews the inside of his cheek out with anxiety, attempts by various means to make himself look "interesting." One time it is Lynette, the first ever to move in his direction, who rescues him by asking him to dance: the beginning of that brief friendship.

4.8 The war homes even here. On two occasions, a ceiling falls down on the brothers' heads. On the first occasion, Tarn is knotting a necktie in the bedroom mirror and sees a sudden ominous crack appearing in the ceiling. Grabbing Neville, he rushes him out. On the second, the ceiling falls in on Neville while he is asleep. The Bull Hotel bar is a resort of R.A.F. pilots whose glamour is for Tarn a matter of fantasy. On one occasion, Mother is invited to a party and takes her son: the party is entirely for Scots Guards and Wren (Women's Royal Navy) officers. More excruciation at sensing that one probably looks older than his age and fearing that people will wonder why he is not in uniform. Eventually, a Wren asks the boy to dance—after which Wrens become a leading object of affection. At another dance, the evening is spent with a buxom woman soldier. For a brief period there is work with the Women's Land Army on a nearby farm, positioned at the chaff hole of a large machine and having to take several showers afterward. The first money earned purchases Carlos Romulo's *I Saw the Fall of the Philippines*. An amusing disgrace is suffered on being sent out with a large horse to work on a field. Rain sets in. Worries about the horse catching cold: the animal saddled with Tarn's raincoat is led back to the farm, meeting with some hilarity from other workers. Many war movies are seen alone at the theater near the coffeehouse, after which ardent walks home meditating on the better life that the world is bound to experience after the war.

A few visits to London are managed despite parental opposition to such during the V1 and V2 flying-bomb period. Invariably have to do with bookstores. On one occasion, somewhere in the suburbs, a ticket is bought to a revelation: the boy's first ballet performance . . . by the Rambert company.

4.9 Back at school, life is felt to be more and more intolerable. At seventeen, one year before the accepted time, urgent demands to be allowed to take the Cambridge scholarship examinations. On a birthday, visiting parents are dragged around to see a dozen teachers, each one of whom declares that this is far too early and nothing but disappointment will result. Tarn determined. Eventually, from London to which the family has moved, a train, sardine-packed with competitors, all "swotting" until the last moment. Ego won't swot. On arrival, assigned by the porter of King's College (the first choice) to a small room over a fish-and-chips shop, dank and crawling with spiders. Totally unable to sleep because of excitement and arachnophobia, Tarn finally collapses an hour or so before wake-up time. Fearful of being late, enters the first exam without breakfast.

Several ordeals. A tactical invention causing some self-pride at the oral examination by King's faculty: discoursing on a set subject, then finding a link to another subject in order to demonstrate the colossal breadth of your expertise. On one evening, entertained in the lodge by the old classicist Provost Sheppard, who glowingly discourses on the founding myth of King's. Much about how some will be chosen and some not, and how fortunate the chosen will be. An awestruck vision of how, at any given moment, any destiny whatsoever is not in your own hands.

Many weeks later, returning to the apartment at 16 Wendover Court on the edges of Hampstead, London, from a shopping expedition with Mother, an official-looking envelope on the doormat behind the door. A history scholarship to King's. The money is piddling, perhaps $150, the honor substantial. Clifton is totally dismayed: two very young boys, Jews to boot, have succeeded where the cream of the crop, including the head of school, has not. The latter is said to have ruined his chances by answering the question "And what is your opinion of the Bard?" with a bemused "What Bard?" Ego's class master muddies the waters by stating, in his letter of congratulations, that because of some "profound intellectual flaw," he will not be impressed until his boy wins a double first during his stay at King's. Little does this man seem to know the adage that those who parrot their teachers get double firsts while the best minds get double two-ones.

Throw Five

5.1 09.30.74. Begun a year and three months after Throw Four. Throw One had been a source of contentment in the interval, knowing that the seed was there and available. It stood on its own. It had even appeared with drawings by the author's hand in the first magazine "supplement" ever devoted to N.T.: in S.U.N.Y. Binghamton's *Boundary 2*. The university semester had ended; the year had ended: a summer stretched out delusively long. Unknowingly, this *Atlantis, an Autoanthropology* had been launched. When that was realized—and, jointly, the fact that the poetry volume titled *Lyrics for the Bride of God* was unfinished—the *AAA* was abandoned for the time being, and the *Lyrics* were taken up again.

Another idea had been to return to Santiago Atitlán, where everything had begun: *remshush ulewu, remshush akal*: world center, navel of earth and sky. I had lived there for a year in 1952–53 for anthropological research toward a Ph.D. at the University of Chicago. I had returned in troubled personal circumstances during 1969 and stayed some six or seven months. It seemed to me that it would be possible to build a book around my experiences of this place. The text would weave in and out of time periods, reaching into travels made before and after 1952. I had in mind a kind of *millefeuille* in which, by association, one travel memory would be laid upon another until a complete layer cake had been constructed. The book would be concerned with my understanding of the world through the act of moving around: part travel book, part autobiography. This eventually became, a long time later, *Scandals in the House of Birds: Shamans and Priests on Lake Atitlán, Guatemala.*

5.2 Poetry had begun at age five. Mother still had the proof of this on paper. It had continued around age nine when, to the astonishment of Antwerp teachers—even provoking a ceremonial visit to our home from them—an essay exam had been answered with a poem *"L'Hirondelle"*: "The Swallow." It continued during the war with pathetic little lyrics inspired by battle reports bound in a notebook with the drawing of a Free French flag on the cover. A return to French in Paris after the war had failed miserably. Only twenty-fifth-rate Apollinaire was produced. Nothing then happened until a walk in the old colonial Botanical Gardens of Maymyo, Burma, in 1958–59 during anthropological research there.

5.3 A move from anthropology to publishing in 1967 and a further move into teaching literature in 1969 can perhaps serve to document a problem in the apprehension of reality. A major problem for me. Living in Princeton in 1970, I had recently interviewed Gary Snyder in a piece titled "From Anthropologist to Informant." My own experiences and memories had crept into the interstices of this text, cryptically reduced to initialed notes in order not to detract from Gary's remarks. Gary had found the right note on which to end the piece, asking, "And now, what about you?"

In the depths of this project lay uncertainty about the medium of prose. In childhood I had told Mother that I would never write a novel. In novels it was the fiction that worried me: the act of adding a story to the immense sum of already existing stories disturbed me profoundly as an unwarranted intrusion into the order of the universe. It would raise the question "Why this story rather than any other?" The demon of the arbitrary. I had always read fiction with unease, and even then it had to be long fiction: an exhaustive story, which would allow the suspension of disbelief for as long as possible, allow the sense that the world no longer existed, that the story had replaced it. A book of short stories has always felt to me like a collection of amputated limbs, bleeding with the loss of the bodies that had once been attached to them. No amount of theory about the perfection of the genre (its musicality, its closeness to the act of the poem) could defeat this unreasonable attitude. I had made mine the surrealists' distrust of fiction: André Breton's works, more documentaries than novels seemingly, and Aragon's marvelous

Le Paysan de Paris had appeared to me, when I read them in 1949, to confirm all my distrust.

5.4 Then, before I understood the role that *la prose du monde* could one day play in my own poetics, prose had become akin to an instrument of torture. Any poet who has been through the mill of academia and suffered his or her thought to be ground down into papers, articles, and theses for academic consumption will shudder when reminded of how tyrannical editorial bureaucracy can be. (Pause to note that, from now on, I will use my conceit of "burrokrassy" and "burrokrasstic" in lieu of the orthodox rendering.) Manuals of style for the composition of such works tell the story. Begin with the mania for standardized punctuation, syntax, and academic jargon, continue to the strangulation of thought and expression in its most intimate details, and you have a prison from which very few academics have been able to escape. My sharpest memory of this: a passage in an article of mine on Burma in which I had written that a monk, on completing a ritual, had drunk a "soda pop," resulting—among dozens of other maniacal requests—in the order to substitute the words "mineral water." True, this was in academia and in Britain . . .

Behind this, of course, the fervent attention to correct detail in an academic book, which has to be the scholar's trademark. But life, in fieldwork, gallops at you with the speed of light. Sleep is a luxury. Day after day passes in often, perhaps usually, inconclusive interviews; accumulations of detail that, for months, refuse to fit into any pattern; rituals half understood and rarely completely witnessed (never perhaps to return in the course of a year's cycle!); beliefs incorrectly expounded or incorrectly grasped to be checked, counterchecked, and checked again, with different "informants," before the stubborn morass can be distilled into the philosopher's stone of theory— that theory, then, to be checked against other theories, themselves in the process of contradiction and evolution. The resulting book never an end but a beginning toward another text, a revised edition, a completely new work, perhaps in another field, another time, another country. And besides, the wench has lain dead for many an age.

For a thousand librarians, lying prone under the great weight of their books, like defeated monsters under the feet of Hindu Kali, how many times may there appear a Jorge Luis Borges?

5.5 Initial few days of a sabbatical year—a first. So many changes in this life: there has never been the possibility of enjoying such underfinanced freedom.

The idea for "a prose work" sits uneasily in the gloom, unformulated, untested, fetal. The powers that be would, at this stage, be perfectly satisfied with a new book of poems: I have the elements of what might become one. No move beyond these elements. To all the kind souls who ask where I am going now, what I am going to do with this freedom, which far-flung locales I am going to add to my existing roster, I have answered: going to stay still, in my own place, in my own house, in order to be able, to attempt, to begin, to write. The demon inside, the slave driver, casts aside fantasies of Provence or Bali or the Himalayas. The Lake at the world's center insistently summons the muse of prose, the goddess of sustained explorations.

There have been some obscure and painful growths (distracted by the warblers, the "confusing fall warblers" passing through this garden, dividing the year one more time). Say you wrote down a memory, then looked into diaries for the original record of the fact behind that memory? Text-ure would be enriched? The role of the "heraldic consciousness" as a theoretical base from which to explore this scriptor's psyche, the groundwork of his most intimate preoccupations? One is assured that there is interesting reading in the theory of autobiography, of travel literature, of narrative. A simple instance of the feasible: beginning with a first-person narrative for the present, a third-person narrative for the past? And those temptations of "honesty," supreme fiction of absolute truth to fact and event? Reminders of Robert Redfield's comment on the "long text" of my doctoral thesis: "This is the most painfully honest thesis that I have ever read: no scholar to date has ever recorded as minutely, as painfully one might say, his own doubts alongside his own certainties, echoing the doubts and certainties of informants, the questions still at large in the whole field." Of course, one had been employed in 1952–53, not altogether enthusiastically, as a guinea pig in an investigation of how Redfield's concept of "worldview" would play out in a field study of ritual and belief . . .

No reason not to go to the library—the Princeton one preferably—and immediately take out these works on autobiography, travel literature, narrative. To find oneself at the end of the year with a huge sheaf of notes ready to begin. The next sabbatical seven years away.

5.6 Paris, circa 1950. A room at my maternal grandmother's apartment. I had bought a plant, one of those delicate, thousand-leaved ferns: a maidenhair. By staring into this plant, all the ideas in one's head at the time would dance their way into a coherent pattern. Who knows, some new ideas might emerge, born of the existing ones, to complement and complete. Looked into the plant. Wrote *Mémoires d'un jeune savant qui se voulait poète (Memoirs of a Young Scholar Who Wanted to Be a Poet)* in one go, in my own handwriting (with fine black ink), and drawings at the end of each chapter. It remains unpublished.

5.7 Deathly fear of incompletion at the heart of this project. Where are the crutches? Do I not still search this way in regard to poems—should the first lyrical impulse meander off into more than lyric, looking like Demeter for Persephone? Do I not still rush then into the accumulated mythologies of all races to locate some echo of the impulse, some branch on which the melody can be hung? The spider's web be hung?

I am to be the spider now, determined at last to spin out of his/her own body alone, with no help from air or gravity, that perfect web.

(The other day, finding a web at the door, unthinkingly destroy the spider's house. The next morning, same web again in the same place. So moving: no destruction possible!)

Inhibit study of webs and insect architecture. No. Find out how webs are built. Eventually. But not now, not now.

5.8 We may be obliged, as so often before, and with Peer Gynt, the great circumambulator, the great *pradakshina* expert in our own culture, to "go round about." It is easier to meditate in movement than while sitting still. (A monk at Daitokuji Monastery, Kyōto, Japan, 1961, at my very first "sitting": "Among beginners, there are those whose bodies sit perfectly still but whose minds are wild, and there are those whose minds are still while their bodies thrash around like demons possessed.") Let the prose itself be travel, move where the spirit wills without destination. Forget that my own travel plans have always included destinations. If an inn be pleasant, the food tasty, the host or hostess accommodating (the hostess especially, shall we say, accommodating), stay there another day and perhaps another. Why not throw away the guidebook altogether, casting aside the fear of missing a good thing into the maw of its *dueño* devil?

No later than two days ago, a poet to me, on being asked if he liked his place of residence and work or had ever had thoughts of change: "Nathaniel, I never consciously think of the future, or attempt to influence the way in which it might fall out for I think this would detract from the value of whatever moment I might happen to be living in or through. Therefore, if I should move one day it would be in response to a call from the outside suggesting that a move should be made." The perfect Buddhist, *nichtwahr*? Said with great authority. I find it hard to believe.

A woman friend, commenting on this: "Yes, perfect. But why should he have made such a point of it? There are times when only consideration of the future can make the present operative."

"There are vibrations in the air at present," the poet continued, "that lead me to think such changes as you suggest may come about. But I shall wait for them." Ah! Vibrations! Ah! Vibes!

Many vibrations of late concerning the golden virtue of passivity. An interlocutor recently: "Why not consider non-action as a form of action also? Why not non-interference with the given until it is truly given, firmly and squarely before you, so that all the elements for decision are present?" I am a control freak. I have relentlessly tried to plan every moment, every achievement to date. I always envisage a destination. Let there be an end to that now. Let this book go where it will; I will not care one jot. As for the reader?

5.9 Great weariness this morning. Strong desire to sleep. Get down onto the floor and sleep. Almost overcoming the other urge: to write ten pages or so. Invocations to coffee and tobacco, guardian goddesses of prose—see Balzac. This day the dice are to be cast, the Rubicon crossed. The book to be pursued relentlessly at the rate of ten pages per diem. Is that not what prose writers do according to all accounts? Blessed circumscribed labor: gone the arrows, thunders, and lightnings of the poet, the sudden inspirations on a bus, or while eating chocolate ice cream, or in the middle of making love! No more of those interminable interruptions, at any moment of day or night, turning from visions to notebook. And if it should be eleven pages, or thirteen, or even twenty? Perish the thought: the book will be that much longer. We have an art! Let us fill it with matter!

The weariness?

A fear.

That the throw will not be perfect.

5.10 The throw? A potter throws, making a pot. Following printer and poet Janet Rodney Tarn, I have been learning to make pots. First act, first movement. As the Maya would say, on the Lake, *el primer viaje. Viaje*: not a trip here but the transit from one act to another, a going that always supposes repetition, a succession of goings and returns. The *viaje* of a saint's icon to church: it will return to its *cofradía,* its chapel of origin, after the church service is done. The trajectory of a dance that will bring the dancer back to his starting point. An act of love, one in a series of acts of love to be repeated, at intervals, as long as the lovers are alive.

Why should the throw be perfect the first time? Is there no possibility of correction, or of starting again if the throw has gone wrong? Chinese story of the painter who is commissioned by his emperor to paint a duck. He keeps the boss waiting for months, even for years. The emperor comes to the studio, remonstrates. The painter sets up paper and ink, throws his duck in one moment, hands it to the boss, turns away.

There are many arts and crafts in which the original throw must be *the* throw, in which no corrections are permitted. Sometimes it is the medium: no room for mistakes. Sometimes it is the spirit in which the artist moves: making it new, making it right, the very first time. It may be self-defense: you can only, by mistake, die once.

It may also be, less nobly, because the artist hates correcting. (Was it D. H. Lawrence—the great British novelist, the great American poet—who rewrote each draft of a novel afresh: corrections approached, each time, as new throws?) Or s/he believes that corrections are somehow debilitating? Did the Maya gods get tired, at the center of the world, creating men of water, then of wood, then of mud, scrapping the unsuccessful trials each time or allowing them to crumble—before one final throw managed to stand upright, looking back into their own eyes? In archaic thought, first trials are *mistakes*, rarely "sins."

At the heart of every throw of poetry, I have always silently prayed that it should be perfect or need the strict minimum of interference toward perfection. I am as capable as anyone of sitting down to a long session of corrections and of taking a poem through several drafts to satisfaction. Once the thing is in progress, there may indeed be much satisfaction in drafts. Then why the initial fear? An act is fearsome only when being contemplated: in the action itself there is nothing but action. In the act itself the problems in the act evaporate in the acting.

Yet the process of corrections is also subject to fear of the throw. The poem is left to sleep in a file for days or weeks until some form of compulsion evolves toward correction. Sleep is best because it makes the poem a total stranger. *Transmutemini! Transmutemini!* as I once wrote in a copy of my first book for Igor Stravinsky. Then the correction takes place, in one throw, and usually the version holds. Usually: not always. The wisdom of "sleeping on a problem." Even in passivity, the right moment has to be awaited.

There is yet another fear. Years ago I noted "It is always difficult for me to write a poem before I have done all the other work that I can conceivably do on that day, until I am weary and exhausted. Otherwise, the poem would sear the page like acid." I might have added "and burn away, invisible." The theme recurs in the poem of *Lyrics for the Bride of God* titled "Sparagmos: Pen/Ink/Paper/Penna."

There is the fear of what comes before the throw. Is everything in its right place in the mind? Has the unconscious, awake or asleep, worked well enough for the throw to be perfect? There should be no fear. No vacant space fast gathering in the mind like threatening mist. Not that fearsome excitement, akin to some kinds of impatient sexual excitement, invariably arising when the throw-which-is-about-to-be reveals itself, in its first stages, as being insufficiently prepared for, unresolved.

I find myself using "corrasable" paper and correcting each typing mistake as I make it (05.27.2013: gentle present reader: these are precomputer times!), unwilling for this throw to be imperfect. I even begrudge the time it takes to make a correction.

The fear of one's own energy in an uncontrolled state. The fear of one's own conquest of the world—which is only asking to be conquered!

Rastignac! De Rubempré! What shackles!

The diamond body is not a body you clothe yourself with. It is a body that is put upon you by the world as a prerequisite for your necessary actions. You wake one day to find yourself clothed with it, as in the only armor that is not a prison.

5.11 The weariness. An attempt to fly from the throw. Deciding that the throw must be put off once again is revolting—that it is not time yet, that alchemy has not taken place in the crucible, that the philosopher's stone is not yet prepared.

Throw the stone in the dung heap! We have gone round about.

Outside it is extraordinarily quiet. It has been quiet all morning except for the warblers. Before beginning to write this, I remember catching myself with the thought that I might have wished for noise or some other interruption. Coleridge's person from Porlock. There was, in a sense, such a person: seeing a certain woman, in a store, just before homing to the typewriter. For reasons now lost, the sight of her had saddened me. The fact that I had just spent a happy night with a lover mitigated that pain. For whole minutes, the thought of the happiness and the thought of the woman in the store had fought with each other, attempting to determine a mood, to seek out whether an action might be possible or not. Peer Gynt had to step in, resolutely, and continue his journey round about. Silence continued, affording no excuses.

Throw Six

6.1 Cambridge was liberation: smoking, drinking, the opposite sex, attending lectures or not—more or less as you pleased. Only tutorials were mandatory. An induction ceremony in which the provost applied hands and, at your request, did *not* admit you in the name of Jesus Christ. "Digs" during the first year: a room in a boardinghouse beyond Magdalen College on an avenue bordering a canal with a fish-and-chips shop round the corner. Many a dinner wrapped in newspaper. A bicycle to get around. In the first week, total self-cloistering to read all of Romain Rolland's *Jean-Christophe* in one go. Call it a celebration.

The surprising discovery that because of the discipline in which a scholarship had been gained, history, not English, was to be studied. No rebellions in those days against this sort of fiat. Interesting lectures from Herbert Butterfield and Michael Postan, two masters. First tutorials in a huge volume of J. R. Tanner's *Tudor Constitutional Documents*: not by any means exciting.

6.2 For the rest of the time—i.e., the second and third year—scholar's privilege brought a room in college down by the river with a view of the world-renowned chapel, the eighteenth-century Gibbs building, and Clare College. Two rooms in fact: the front one with the view, a bedroom at the back overlooking the provost's garden. Down in the basement a number of baths and the coal containers from which very heavy sacks had to be carted up to the front room's fireplace. Meals in the great hall with ancestral portraits looking down. Disgusting food (a rabbit dish full of maggots once) but, perversely, a famous cellar with excellent wines and liqueurs. No opposition was ever successful: tradition is tradition. Other colleges had other traditions and, who knows, might have enjoyed excellent food with indifferent wines. At least no obligatories as for Wordsworth, Coleridge, etc.

Almost everyone older: this was the time when troops were returning from the war; we were still in the days when they were mostly officers. Peter Phillips was a friend on the same staircase, very solitary, somewhat neurotic. He disappeared after the end of the last term and could never be found. A "gang" came together little by little: David Rowse, Christopher Moorsom, Richard "Dickie" Muir, Peter Dixon. Ardent intellectual passions; fascination at one time with René Guénon, Ouspensky, and Gurdjieff; interminable talk about getting away from the Bomb; growing dissatisfaction with an England weary of war and unable to rest and recover. Very little play. The routine comprised rising around midday; eating bacon, eggs, and sardines year in year out to save money for books; reading—often without even bothering to dress—on a couch in the front room for a great many hours at a stretch. Sometimes, nauseated by this, rushing out into the street and begging the first acquaintance met with to convey one to a cinema. Dinner in hall and bed. There was much companionship among these boys; many parties were given, many—as in the case of Dickie's—so overwhelmingly gay that Rowse and Tarn were often the only straight men in the room. King's had a reputation! A few epics. One night, returning from a pub, Rowse and Tarn decided to paint a frieze from the Egyptian Book of the Dead all around the walls of Rowse's main room. It took hours. Some time later, the boys were congratulated by the college head porter for their enterprise and presented with a bill for restoration.

6.3 In the third year, English was finally a possibility. Tarn "read" English as a devoted, nine-in-the-morning-by-any-weather fan of Prof. F. R. Leavis: his responsibility being to rouse from bed the other devotees. However, tutorials were with Prof. F. L. Lucas: a greater contrast between two men it is not possible to imagine. Lucas was very patient, but on one occasion when he was presented with a three-line essay on Herrick, that patience was sorely tried. With only a year to play with, Tarn decided to concentrate entirely on the Elizabethans: only Wordsworth, Coleridge, and Keats (abiding loves) to be exempted from this ascesis. A small typescript of poems poses as part of a final "thesis" offering. Very soon after seeing Laurence Olivier's *Hamlet* movie newly arrived in town (sitting through two consecutive séances on the first day), the Tripos exam was written entirely on this film, earning our hero his first Two One. In effect, Tarn and a friend had posed as university journalists before this, visiting the awe-inspiring sets of this *Hamlet* as well as the ballet film *Red Shoes* and some others. Fortunately, the university rag accepted an article based on the imposture.

There were fancy-dress opportunities. On one occasion, a whole Hamlet costume was designed: black tights; black silk blouse with billowing sleeves and collar ringed with white silk cord; a mask in black cloth, red ribbon, and a white cord design of a hangman's noose descending onto the bridge of the nose. Hair powdered white. Very successful.

Women friends were few and far between in those days. Only two women's colleges, replete with ladies often called "bluestockings" who were not, it appeared, very interested in romance. This led to the most intense frustration. A first great love, Ruth, a Londoner Czech refugee of great beauty, remained chaste and eventually preferred to marry an Israeli musician. Devoted and bounteous Wendy, an "English rose," picked Tarn up off a sofa at a college party but did not keep him. (Many months later, met again, Wendy is about to move to Germany to marry an R.A.F. officer but teaches her ungrateful friend a few things about sex that he had never known before. For sheer gentility she is remembered with unearthly affection ever since.) The frustration led to many a piece written in wrath and submitted to various Cambridge literary venues, all praising the benefits of coeducation and railing against the gender imbalances at the mighty university. The inevitable waste, the bulldozed kitchen/midden of this adolescence! Where sexual maturity had occurred between a fourteenth and a twenty-fourth year and been unused. Blasted by the mores and beliefs of anglo-saxondom!

A great many years later, considerable shock is experienced when visiting a King's College that has blissfully become coeducational.

The May Balls after exams were the one and only time in the year when occasions for being a daredevil presented themselves. The balmy weather, magnificent architectural settings, glamorous dresses, and surfeit of youth conspired to create rare magic. On one occasion, without even buying a ticket, Tarn pushed a drink-besotted Moorsom into the river behind the college and made off with his date, a bona fide heroine of the French Resistance sporting a Croix de Guerre! On another, two boys made a pact to exchange two sisters every two hours or so, but our hero eventually kept the preferred sister without honoring the pledge. Outside of the May frolics, there was one occasion on which Tarn and Rowse managed, unseen and unintercepted, to bring wooden planks from a construction site to the river, creating a bridge over which two young ladies arrived to spend the night with them in Rowse's rooms. This could easily be a cause for expulsion if not, at the very least, "rustication" (temporary suspension of attendance). There was also Tarn's creation and presidency of a Cambridge Ballet Society, with many a party in his rooms for the likes of Nadia Nerina of Sadler's Wells, Zizi Jeanmaire of the Roland Petit Ballet, and Ram Gopal, the Indian master. Nerina subsequently married a first-year friend of Tarn. When elsewhere, Tarn followed his balletomane habits as much as possible: his record being assisting at a performance for twenty-four uninterrupted nights on end—many at Covent Garden. Margot Fonteyn was the great passion (flowers sent to her, a signed photo received back). He has always felt that, had he been some years older, he would have gone for her.

6.4 Moments of great joy at intellectual discoveries—kissing a book after reading it still a sign of lasting allegiance and respect. There were also moments that could be described at the time under no other sign than that of the gnostic: moments in which mental activity—the forever tumbling, jumping, and circling squirrel in a cage—was still, and another, meditational frame of mind took over, another kind, infinitely sharper this time, of attention. One such evening moment came while sitting on a bench along the wall separating King's and Clare and looking at a huge tree on the river not far from Tarn's rooms. The tree seemed to grow in size until the orb, become huge, had the appearance of what might be imagined as Yggdrassil—the central world tree of the ancient sagas.

Somewhere in this book, the dream of a great iron wall may appear, one which has no dimensions this side of infinity. In the vision it literally stretches out forever in every possible direction. Now imagine a sea which does the same. Imagine that the Earth is all sea—that no land whatsoever exists, only weather and wind. Every imaginable thing else is water: there is nothing else in existence except water. Anything that can be made has its basis in water. Suppose then that we are waves continually being formed on the water by the action of wind and gravity. The waves come and go eternally, but they do not change the composition of water.

You will soon perceive that, in this image, we have always been born and have always been dead or, alternately, we have never been born and will never die.

At a later date in, say, the nineties: it is also true that time is the greatest of all illusions. Each one of us is, at one and the same moment, in our mother's womb, in our daily life, and in our grave. And this is true of everyone, in all periods, all epochs, all histories—which reduce themselves, in one kind of imagery, to a single world breath. Only thus can anyone move to come to terms with unending injustice, with the relentless and rigorous apartness and self-containment of each individual fate. Only this way is human fate brought back into a true semblance of equality.

Again very much later, in the new millennium. Morning coffee. Gazing at a vase of flowers. "The point is" and "The point is not" fuse, merge, become one. Then a great silence, a great peace. Then a great many moons of depression rise, are felt to have been lifted. Or not. We know that plants have many voices, that a great deal of music issues from them, yet we are usually blessed, above all, with and by their magnanimous silence.

6.5 Some winter vacations were spent in Switzerland with parents: the most pleasant was at St. Moritz, where nightly visits to a restaurant/bar being taken care of by a very sweet waitress followed a day of skiing. A charming young girl in Tarn's party and a British skating champion provided some romantic interest.

Three summer holidays were more substantial. The first, with Charles Gordon, took in a Spain still very much under Franco, a Spain where you could leave a bag in the middle of a plaza and return many hours later to find it untouched. The trip began in Barcelona, staying in third-class hotels often impossible to distinguish from brothels. A lovely lady gave Tarn a copy of Adolfo Bécquer's Romantic-era poems, although there had been no commerce between them. These little hotels came with a full complement of bedbugs or lice, whose ferocious attacks would leave your whole body scarlet and itching beyond belief. Sleepless nights were spent staring out the window and chain smoking. Going to the beach in a streetcar one day, a scandal was occasioned by the wearing of shorts. You fell in love with Gaudí and the Louvre-sized Museum of Catalan Romanesque art in Barcelona and with the Moorish splendors of the South—excepting the Great Mosque of Cordova, whose qualities never managed to impress.

Madrid was reached in a third-class *correo* train so slow that it was possible to get out, walk along with the train, and get on again a few minutes later. A trip of twenty-four hours with people sleeping on top of each other three deep in the corridors reaching all the way into the toilets. The boys got out at one small village, sleeping in a bright-blue room after a dinner of tomatoes and garlic shared with a priest. First-class tickets the next day but neverthe-less landing up in third class again. A sandwich bought at one station half eaten before a tickle in the throat revealed a half-consumed nest of ants.

There were visits from Madrid to Toledo, Segovia, Avila, Seville, Granada, and other classic towns: landscape, architecture (the Segovia skyline espe-cially), art consumed in great eye and throatfuls. In Malaga the ships were seen at night about to depart for Africa, arousing fiery further travel long-ings. In a small restaurant there a dog came up to one customer at table. The man bent down kindly toward the dog and, in a very low voice, asked "*Y que pasa en Cadiz?*" There was a sojourn at a very small beach called Punta Um-bria de Huelva in Andalusia, where everyone walked around all day in paja-mas. It was reached by night in a small fishing boat from Huelva—a long trip under the stars. A delightful flirtation with a dark-haired, dark-eyed young girl took place here, hands held under the sand to escape the vigilance of a grandmother who constantly lamented that such a sweet young man would never reach heaven for failing to be a Catholic. Letters followed for a couple of years together with photographs: one displaying the huge mantilla worn during Andalusian fiestas—a favorite.

After a reading of *Death in the Afternoon* and much else, bullfighting was a serious part of this journey. The great matador "Manolete" was seen at To-ledo: unfortunately, it was not one of his good days. In Cordoba a friend took it into his head that an extremely unwilling Tarn should pretend to be the young American matador Barnaby Conrad, whom he had met recently in Madrid. Taken around town, bought a superb pearl-gray Andalusian hat, an eventual rendezvous in a small bar to hear a very old man singing flamenco ("no voice left but plenty of *sentimiento*") resulted in our hero being carried back to his hotel in a state of massive inebriation: only wine and minute fried fish had been provided. Waking several hours later with the realization that Conrad was fighting in town that very afternoon. A hasty departure in taxi and train followed pronto. On returning from the South, the railway station buildings were covered in black crepe to announce "Manolete's" death.

The second-year vacation was spent alone in Italy. Limited to Florence and Venice, although a day's trip with American Express to Siena, including a stop overlooking the towers of San Gimignano, was invested in so as to wit-ness the Palio horse race. Excellent seats came with this, but the expectation of seeing Sienese art at the museum and cathedral was completely frustrated. You may reckon that, wherever you landed, some one thousand paintings were studied per day in all the churches, palazzi, and museums available to visits. Solitary from start to finish, there was never a conversation, never an acquaintance to interrupt the concentrated campaign on Italian art. Tarn lived from espresso to espresso.

Then again Spain. This time company occurred at Grenada. On the Alhambra hill stood a bizarre old hostel. It happened to be reached at night. You were sent by the old German owners to a "swimming pool" at the bottom of a large garden infested by large rats. Rooms were bedbug ridden: you began in a fairly decent one and were gradually, if staying on, reduced to a variety of hovels. An anthology of guests. A pleasant young Grenadan stayed here in the summer with the aim of meeting foreign girls: commerce with Spanish young women was out of the question. For Tarn, a stormy affair with a young Parisian of Russian origin. There was a visit to Linares (where "Manolete" had been killed) for the memorial bullfights. The town seemed to adopt the young couple: the only tourists in sight. Magical evening *paseos* ranked in memory among the most enchanting evenings of a lifetime. Somehow there were always choice seats at the *corridas* reserved for the pair by citizens concerned for their enjoyment.

(Many years later, the sad discovery that "Manolete" was very much pro-Franco.)

Linares was followed by a stay on Ibiza a long time before tourists took it over in the sixties. The farmers still wore velvet black pants; it was possible to buy antique ribbons, flutes, and castanets. The Carthaginians were much in mind during *periploi* of the island in small fishing boats. Every morning a few soldiers stood their mules in a circle, brushing and grooming them. The trip back to Barcelona took place in a storm. The whole ship's company, animals included, was sicker than it ever seemed possible to be.

Throw Seven

7.1 The earliest fantasies belong to Perseus. Lady to be found in a dark wood, usually strapped to a tree. Dark wood beside the sea. The lady naked, of course. Never quite sure of whether I arrive on a white horse or on more modern equipment. The unstrapping is perfunctory, and I am not aware that there ever was any snake or dragon to be dispatched. Linchpin of the seduction is usually an extensive discourse. Going, in as much detail as can be mustered, into a rehearsal of everything that will one day be laid at her feet. This is a quest.

There is some ambiguity as to whether her presence during that quest is wished for or not. On the one hand, I want to perform the deeds in her company, hand in hand with her and, doubtless, body to body at appropriate moments. On the other, there is considerable charm in the thought of long journeys, or one long journey subsuming all possible journeys, at the end of which I would return carrying the world in my hands. The world represented as a series of collections encompassing all known objects. Also as knowledge: by the time of the return all would be known that could be known about anything and everything. Whether the possession of knowledge is sweeter than the ownership of treasures it is difficult to tell. I am sure that wisdom wins out in the end.

The degree of nudity of the lady is always to some degree problematical. Because no information is forthcoming from parents or guardians, the imagination of the female body is left to chance. When the discourse ends, the lady, persuaded by this speech and little else, falls into the hero's arms and grants him her initial favors. These forest meetings are exhausting, especially when they are subject to repetition.

7.2 Paternal grandmother's apartment, Antwerpen, Belgium, circa 1936. To keep the nine-year-old Tarn quiet and prevent him from squabbling with his brother, he is seated in an armchair in the corner of a large dining room. After a number of such sessions, at the end of which a penny is the reward, the child discovers, at the foot of the armchair, a battered old copy of *Life* magazine. In the middle of this there is an illustrated article on a strip-tease performance. The woman, clothed to the last in G-string and nipple guards, closes the act by undoing the G-string, turning round at the same time, and vanishing through curtains at the back of the stage. The last sight caught is of a bare backside left behind between the curtains. It is ascertained that (1) a female rear is not all that different from a male rear (hair has not yet grown on the child) and (2) the sight of such an isolated pair of bare half-moons is not unexciting.

7.3 Leysin, Switzerland, circa 1937–38. The home for children run by an old German couple with distinctly Nazi leanings. Sleepwalking at night. The matron obliges you to lodge your face in her neck every evening and say the Lord's Prayer. I vaguely believe that I should not be doing this. I have not been made aware of the reason why my penis looks different from everyone else's and, when bothered, invent the story of a terrible accident that must have deprived me of my foreskin in early childhood. Such is the price of a dearth of information. I continue to wet my bed, as I shall do for many years. On one occasion, I am sitting at lunchtime opposite a young caretaker in her teens with whom I have fallen in love. The matron, from the head of the table, jokingly reprimands me for wetting my bed again on the previous night, and the girl smiles in complicity—with the matron or with me it is agonizingly impossible to tell. I am profoundly mortified.

The terrace: a large esplanade in front of the house, where the children are put down to nap after the midday meal. I lie next to a little girl who has shown me, or will shortly show me, her nakedness by lifting her dress over her head as I happen to pass by the door of her dormitory. We enter, under the blankets, into an exploration of each other's parts, in the course of which

I discover a place between a small girl's thighs that I had not known before. Cleft and minute hole. Buttocks already known.

7.4 Bude, Cornwall, 1941. Clifton College has been evacuated. On the day after arrival, I am waylaid by a boy who acts as a kind of professional informer and who takes me out on the dunes in front of our house and asks me if I know where babies come from. Uneasy thirteen-year-old ignorance. Boldly, with no euphemisms, he clarifies the picture. I am horrified, unable to comprehend how what was seen in Leysin could grow so large. Days to assimilate the message. The same young gentleman informer announces that he will give a set of lectures in his dormitory after lights out. The price of admission being the value of a candy bar. The proposed subject is "sex." Muster courage and enter his dormitory. On the bunks, six or seven pairs of eyes, all agog. Our teacher, mouth twisted in a permanent leer, begins with a description of female breasts and the manipulations necessary to give them pleasure. Barely a few words from him before some officious prefect, inspecting the dorms, discovers me skulking in a room not my own. I claim the confusion of a new boy looking for something he had mislaid. Loss of a candy bar. Still no information.

7.5 London, 1946. Cambridge student for some months and still a virgin. Closest friend at the time claims huge experience and is begged repeatedly for help. He eventually finds an attractive young actress who is willing to initiate. Nowhere to go except the parental apartment. Parents away one night, we steal back to my room like two thieves. I am so concerned for my parents and so ignorant of my duties that my teacher becomes impatient. The night is a fiasco. A second lady is a rather more mature person assigned to look after me while I visit the set of Olivier's *Hamlet* movie. At the end of the day she takes me home and to bed. Quickly bored, she falls asleep.

7.6 How did my fantasies fare at this time, and did I still wish to lay the world at some girl's feet? I believe they did so continue. At Cambridge, the Czech girl, Ruth, was someone who deserved the world. But Wendy, the first true mistress, must have introduced a degree of reality into such matters, and as a result, perhaps, she was very ungratefully treated.

Paris, 1948. What, in my notebooks there, had brought on as savage a satirical streak as I have ever mustered? Against woman and, in particular, against woman's sex? Doubtless the sheer wretchedness and frustration of gender relations before the "sexual revolution" of the sixties: one's own failings projected onto the women one met and with whom one tried to come to terms.

7.7 Jump to attitudes toward the female body and an understanding of how these are determined by a vision I have called "heraldic."

Diary entry, undated, probably circa December 1974:

"It has taken longer to figure out—but now with some suddenness in fact—that woman's body also partakes of, or is seen through, the prism of one particular heraldic vision. [2003: a more "liberated" text would have specified any body of any gender.] There is a model in the mind, or in the sensibility, unconscious by and large, though it may become conscious with age, to which the various female bodies encountered approximate. Size, shape, texture, complexion . . . all these come into play. A certain element of tidiness, of primness almost; a median size between the bloated and the skimpy; a well-ordered structure with no spill overs has the initial preference.

"Once again, it appears, the love of order and the fear of disorder. The paradisal body is co-terminous with Eden as the most finely-honed of world models, the most . . . classical architecture? There is also the behavioral aspect of the heraldic vision: manners, etiquette, elegance. Perhaps the whole manner in which woman behaves toward the male in close proximity is involved here—the subtle interplay of giving and withholding; aggression and defense; come-on and put-off—whose balance is vital to successful union. I recall Konrad Lorenz's writing on mating—on how subtly the patterns of aggression have to give way to the patterns of love, the signals inhibited in the one case and the others triggered off—the slightest mistake in the ritual order, the slightest variation in the prayer ending by excluding the god. . . .

"Another variant in canon-formation: the proportion of part to part. In one body, all proportions may, taken individually, be somewhat exaggerated—but all work harmoniously when taken together. Totalization, in the work I am doing at the moment, being both the whole model and the relation of individual parts of the model to the whole."

Was all of this written before or after becoming aware of the sense of *blazons* in the French tradition, meaning small poems describing in great detail the physical features of a woman's body with praise or criticism attached? I no longer remember.

Need it be said that, by and large, with whatever modifications a woman writer will care to make, the same kind of considerations will probably, at times in any event, characterize a woman's attitude to the male? And indeed the purview of any individual body toward any other loved body of whatever sex?

"Now: if one could be less 'heraldically' minded oneself! I have met men who admire, love and make love to with pleasure almost any female body they encounter. The code is not pre-structured in the mind as the woman comes toward them: the password is acceptance of whatever shape the bounty of heaven reveals. The question abuts on the whole topic of order and disorder; structuration versus non-structuration or, perhaps, process; closed versus open systems. In keeping with the direction in which I believe myself to have been evolving, a weakening of the heraldic obsession in one's aesthetics would seem to be nothing but a benefit?"

7.8 "And yet, within the vast abundance of shields, is there to be no preference, no selectivity? If a certain body-type triggers a response in the form of a thrill the poem is heir to, is this not to be considered a very ground of a poetics at all? I am still not sure. . . .

"What is the fate of a body of fantasies as it wears itself out against the mores of the tribe insofar as these permit or inhibit access to the object of desire? Some will always be seducers; others will always drown in their own timidity. The timid will, all their lives, envy the brash from afar. This said, however, some kind of revolution in mores has taken place in our time, and our own age, in relation to it, will have placed us—rather like, for Christians, those born before Christ and those born after—in a more or less privileged position. How many parents in recent times must have witnessed the behavior of their offspring and bitterly felt how near they had been to a great deal more pleasure than their *floreat* brackets had ever allowed them?

"What of the great ship Freedom that had been missed? Freedom? Fling off all clothes! Freedom? Marriage to the winds; swap wives or seduce the girl next door in full view of our wives and with their blessing! Freedom? Swing in a perpetual orgy with a Kama Sutra at the back of our minds! The guide books are ready on publishers' shelves: a *vita nuova* opens out, bright with massage parlors, gang-bangs and other forms of easy pickings. Some fledgling Molière, mute and inglorious as yet, waits in the wings to cast this comedy.

"However, a complicating factor in the recent situation has been that currents of liberation, running this way and that, do not necessarily reinforce each other but may, on occasions, find themselves in flagrant contradiction. From the point of view of a man who has lived his life before the 'sexual revolution,' this current may seem to be contradicted by the current we know as 'Women's Liberation.' Our prospective partners discover they have souls; careers; agendas; scenarios which send us into corners like bad boys or throw us out of the house altogether. Uneasily, we prepare to wash the dishes one day out of two; to adjust our hiring practices; to draft laws of non-discrimination. The partners still not satisfied. Up from their backs, freedom in the bed! Above all, an immense upheaval in the male mind: the realization that this may be the revolution of the century: not a single other you can think of even begins to match it in importance."

7.9 So much for the notebook extract. In the two or three years of "liberty" following the breakdown of a first marriage, I have found myself wondering whether the male situation at this juncture is not truly insoluble. What are the conditions today of a successful relationship? What is left when the alleged "penis envy" of woman has shrunk to such minimal proportions and her enjoyment of being treated as a "sexual object"—if it ever existed—has disappeared altogether? (I do not believe that I have ever objected to being treated as one!) When perfumes and so many other allurements begin to be banned? When the most elementary forms of male sassiness necessary in the male mind to the initiation of the mating dance are relegated to the category of aggression?

As a lyrical poet, it has in the past been almost a precondition of writing that I should feel in some sense to be pursuing a female whose role becomes that of Muse. The female complains: "Muse? Whazzat?" Ego: "How about: inspirer of strong emotion vis-à-vis the perception of an exemplar of beauty, leading to poem, leading to gratitude and the request that permission should be granted to allow the world and its goods to be laid at Muse's feet?" Female: "No, don't want that. Depends on *you* making the money—now *I* want to make the money. Don't like pedestals (Ego never conscious of having offered pedestals!). Want to be a poet, me, myself: no more Muse. 'Muse kaput.'"

Artemis turning Actaeon into a devourable stag will not do, unless we are more masochistic than even we were led to think. So biological aggression of any kind is inhibited, the path to the love signal eradicated *ab initio*. This is where we came in. The woman poet refuses the very concept of "Muse," claims the right to rip off a male body if she pleases as one would hack into little pieces any sleeping Endymion.

However, could we not agree to live and let live? Are desire and consequent pursuit not to be allowed to survive? Might "Muse" not be of either or any sex and still be a "Muse"? I see no other way to the survival of lyric. Let Wordsworth turn in his grave: we need a new preface to a language unheard of as yet, a dialogue, a two-way language, preserving the ancient sources, allowing any god his femininity, any goddess her masculinity as well as the traditional prerogative of both cases.

Stronger by far than she has ever been in her capacity for allowing or refusing pursuit, American woman has found herself using every trick in the book: show/no show, give/retract, promise/renege ... perhaps she is right after all these eons. She used to be a very vulnerable and, frequently, battered person. The puritanical tradition achieved two objects. On the one hand, it gave a great many women born before the middle forties a great distaste for, and a mistrust of, their own bodies. "I hate my own body, cannot value it. Yet it is the only part of me a man values and, if I do not give it, I shall not achieve my goal (and what other goal is there?): to be a healthy mother in the suburbs. I must therefore give—but I will make man pay by withholding the mind and spirit he is unable to value." Result: lifelong frigidity.

On the other hand, male trained to "score" with very little consideration for the woman he scores. New York, circa 1952: my astonishment at meeting a very presentable and highly educated young woman so battered by her previous boyfriend that any kind of intercourse has been almost impossible to her for many months. In this light, necking and petting as the outcome of fear (pre-pill times: pregnancy also very much in play!) is understandable but may cause such frustration in the male that battering may result? In this light, my manifestos in defense of tenderness to women (often misguidedly identified as "Latin") could be considered a contribution to the embryonic stage of the "revolution."

As for laying the world at someone's feet, can I be sure that this ambition has survived? I led my youth as if there was nothing else to do with it but use it as preparation. I am not sure whether I *lived* that youth or not—but this ties in with the problem of whether one can ever live an art as well as live a life. Ambitions were almost always betrayed, sooner or later, by a lexical torrent. Initially timid, I would, when finally tempted to try, give my story such ample play that the lady of the moment was either swept off her feet on the instant or, far more likely, bored forever. Not women only: the whole world was a stage for my role in its own conquest. And when "scoring" was unsuccessful, as happened most times, I daresay that the tale itself became its own reward. The loss was glossed over with a semblance of beauty "for its own sake," and I retired not so much to nurse wounds, as to accumulate more goods and more knowledge against the day when the finest creature of creatures would finally accept to step into my house.

7.10 Something must be said about the relationship of beauty to loss: the theme of elegy. I have been saying good-bye to beauty since I can remember:

the sense of loss and, specifically, the sense of beauty lost have been with me from the beginning. It is my form of weeping the *lacrimae rerum*, my form, no doubt, of expressing whatever primal loss I may have suffered, far back in childhood jungles, when Mother stepped aside from me for a moment in some manner never recorded, when my brother was born, or when some toy went spinning forever irretrievably out of reach (and I knowing that!). Do these universal banalities need recording?

All the same, I stop at the fact that it is *beauty* that is lost, not love, not companionship, not some sense of participation in the world (although there is that primordial exile we'll come to eventually). Next, I stop more dramatically at the recognition that the loss itself contains its own consolation. It is almost as if it were necessary to lose, to feel the sense of loss, in order to appreciate the lost beauty as beauty. I tell myself with fear that it is perhaps the very sense of loss that is the beauty, for starting from that sensation and then going around, heavy-looking, pregnant with loss, gives one a *sérieux*, a look of wisdom, of fulfillment, that links one in kinship with prophets, seers, mystics, saints, ascetics, the mighty fathers in the college of the sky. The world is beautiful because there is a cancer at its heart; there is an immemorial loss and fall at its center: it is that loss, that fall (*a felix culpa?*), which imparts to the world both wisdom and beauty. My motto from the start in the heraldic design I drew for a shield in childhood: "*Videre et Scire.*" To see: what else than beauty? To know: what else than beauty? Mr. Keats and truth. Mr. Henry James saying of Italy, somewhere in *Portrait of a Lady*, that it is a country where the pain of beauty can be comforted by endless knowledge. Is this correctly quoted? I do not remember many quotations. The sense of this one has been with me since adolescence.

In any event, is it not then but a short step to realize that you may actually court an experience of loss by making sure that you never lay hands on beauty at all? By letting it go from the start, by never claiming it in the first place? Since writing began, I have thought of committing a book called *The Failure*: it has never been committed. How many times has a lack of daring in the temperament not served to cancel any attempt at winning anything? Irrespective of whether anything is ever to be won or not, whether any dance can be initiated between two people, say, unless the energy in each of them decides in confrontation with the other to move toward that other—so that two passivities are mysteriously transmuted into two activities, then fused into a single movement that goes by the name of love. How difficult it was in youth to remember "Arletty's" *C'est si simple l'amour* in Marcel Carné's movie *Les enfants du paradis.* Youth was a terrible burden. And yet this great concern for beauty: is that not, above all else, the mark of the poet?

05.25.13: How sad and masochistic all this sounds in retrospect!

7.11 Honolulu, 1961. I teach at the London School of Oriental & African Studies. At the Tenth Pacific Sciences Congress, where I have convened a seminar on the sociology of Theravāda Buddhist institutions in order to be able to continue on to Japan, I finally get to meet a scholar whose work on Burma, though still unpublished, I have found very valuable. The man and academia have never jelled. He exists now on the fringe of university life, living off some small business. He has a Chinese wife or mistress. There is not much nightlife on Oahu—despite the ads—and academic parties bore us stiff.

My friend disappears every day to a certain bar. He invites me to join him "whenever you have the time and have exhausted everything else." I finally accept one evening to find that my friend's routine is nightly contemplation of a Chinese cigarette vendor of great shapeliness and sweet disposition. He buys cigarettes every evening and exchanges some small talk. Astonished at the evidence that the matter could be taken further—the lady appears willing—I lecture my friend on the "Latin" worship of the flesh and the idiocy of American Puritanism (I am still French at that point and breakfast every morning with the French contingent, led by the famed geographer Pierre Gourou). My friend answers sadly that experience has taught him to value these underdeveloped situations. Nothing but disappointment could follow from actually consorting with the girl, whereas nothing but nightly pleasure arises from his minimal contact. After some two weeks of this ethereal romance, my friend went back happily to his domesticity. Perhaps he was anticipating what age brings with it in this respect.

7.12 The whole wretched syndrome of the one-and-only, sick pivot of "romantic love" is blatantly at work in a relationship that has never come to fruition at a time when I am writing such poems as "Addio Romantica" and "The Last Illusion" in *The Traviata* (*La Traviata* means "The Lost One") section of *Lyrics for the Bride of God.* The *Lyrics* had begun, in part, as a paean of praise for a manic love at a time when that love was drifting ever closer to Scylla and Charybdis. When the ship crashed on both rocks at once, a change of heart had to occur, and the *Lyrics* became elegiac.

What am I saying? Was the first section, *The Kitchen*, not already full of foreboding? Had there not been the interim folly of *The Artemision*? Even more to the point, had I not always known that I was an elegist? Had the *Lyrics* ever changed direction, or was I merely imagining that they had? Was I already in mourning at the time of celebration?

Circa January 1972. I am writing some poems that I believe to belong to *The Kitchen* section although I later discover them to belong to *The Invisible Bride*. I am dealing with terrible conflicts of allegiance. I have just written the third poem, whose refrain is a monotonous "I die." As the last act of the morning, I instinctively change "I die" to "she dies."

I go out in order to shop but stop to glance at my mailbox. There is so much in the box that I drive back up to the house and sit in the car looking at the mail. At the very bottom of the pile—an envelope so small I might have missed it. She is never coming back. There is no shopping that day. After a long gap, *The Invisible Bride* section continues in full sail toward its elegiac conclusions.

7.13 *Tout lasse, tout passe, tout casse.* In some such order, Guillaume Apollinaire, the most nostalgic and elegiac of poets. At this age, I have already gone over the mountain, already laid treasures at someone's feet, already brought in the collected loot and displayed it in one haven. The passion for order has not disappeared. Rather, it has shrunk into a particular receptacle, like a braided river electing at long last to flow in one bed only. I remember being worried for many years by an apparent inability to focus on one pursuit, one subject, one discipline. How would I ever become a writer if painting, music, history, philosophy, anthropology, science, and the like engaged so much of my attention and strength? I used to say that "the larger the house you wish to build, the more the bricks," but this was small consolation.

Unbeknown to myself, however, the process has taken place. Much too much, perhaps, has been sloughed off, and poetry is left. "I came to poetry late" says one poem. If you were to ask me how it is that I am now a man of nine books or so, I would honestly have to tell you that I see it as no less than miraculous. Ambition has, at least in part, been replaced by achievement; the not-done has, in ways that I, but mainly others, must judge, has been done. I have written these books and not others. I can go into a bookstore now and not weep, literally weep, as I used to do in my student days, at the thought that I did not know why I should buy these books and not others.

I can perhaps live with a woman without wondering what it must be like to make love to Aphrodite (there is a piece in *Lyrics* about this—though inverted in that the speaker cannot imagine loving a woman after chancing to be favored by Aphrodite). It is in this manner that we prepare, from a long way back, to die—by having lived thusly and not otherwise. Everything perhaps depends upon the acceptance of that "thus." If it can be achieved, it brings great peace. The revolutions of the wheel of why and why-not reveal themselves as the only revolutions that could have taken place, as blessings, however terrible the wounds they may have inflicted, on oneself, still more on others. Alas, still more on others! Life is a blessing in the teeth of its manifold curses.

Now it only remains to read the dreams aright so that the future may round off the past, whatever that future brings.

August 2019: it is now recognized that we are in an era which is bringing about the liberation of a very great set of "minorities" into every kind of equality with straight white men of every conceivable form of ethny and gender. It is infinitely more than high time. The only thought that survives: what happens to the glamour of flirting and lovemaking? Is there still any room for that?

Throw Eight

8.1 At the end of Cambridge, dissatisfaction with England will not rest. Tarn had been to Paris very shortly after the war for an idyllic reunion with the city. His father's brother David had introduced him to a plump and buxom young girl, Françoise, with whom he chastely enjoyed the city sights and corresponded for some time afterward. This was the same David who had given him a great treat when a child in Belgium. Arriving on a rare visit, he had taken the boy to a bookstore and told him to select what he wanted—without limit. On a second day, the same happened in a shop selling cacti. There was a third day, unremembered now. Every child should have such an experience of *unlimited* bliss. However, it may have been David who, still earlier, had brought a white teddy bear three times the size of the child, who howled without stop until the creature was hidden away. The thought remained that an extreme fear of dogs may have resulted from this plush creature.

More than visits to Paris were required, however. Tarn told his parents that he would move to Paris for a time and obtained a modest survival kit from them.

Bilingualism was a major obstacle. To write in English or in French? Obviously, it would have to be French. It would have to be French completely—everything had to be done "completely"—and English would have to be forgotten. How *could* I have thought that? But more than one language is a boon for everyone except the poet. For the poet it is torture.

Tarn moved into a furnished room in the apartment of a Mme. Amado not far from his grandmother Mémé's place at no. 17 on the rue de l'Arc de Triomphe, close enough to provide most evening meals. Mme. Amado loved conversation and Tarn had a transient fervent interest in Catholicism arising from the reading of biographies of certain women saints. At the time, Victor and Russian-speaking Pauline Natanson, passionate bridge players and cousins to each other, lived with Grandmother. When they moved to a place of their own, Tarn moved into their room. Conditions were somewhat primitive. There was a bath, but it did not function. Bathing took place at the weekend at a washstand in the bathroom, dividing the body into three parts and using up several basins of water heated in the kitchen. Uncle Claude had his room and office opposite Tarn's, and Mémé had a small sewing workroom right at the back of the apartment, out of which she had in her later days run her small clothing business.

Disoriented and uncertain how to proceed, the student remained a student and kept college discipline, reading weighty matter such as the *Divine Comedy* and Étienne Gilson's great history of medieval philosophy. Paternal uncle Harry, living again in Belgium but coming frequently to Paris, tried Tarn out for several jobs through the good offices of his current lady friend. She had important contacts in French society. For a moment, something was mooted at the United Nations: it was never clear what. There was also a possibility as tea-and-coffee busboy rejoicing in a title like "third assistant director" to a movie person: I could have been an actor! A lack of results in these pursuits was unfairly ascribed by the lady friend to the boy's "moods" and duly reported back to London. However, as a *bon viveur* Harry would take his nephew out on each visit to one of the best restaurants in the city. An astounded novice learned that enjoyment of *food* was a possibility in this life. On an Antwerpen visit, before the move to Paris, he had been taken by this same Harry to a nightclub and set up with an attractive young woman who took care of him for the whole night. During the Paris years, there were also meetings in other countries, Spain and Italy among them. Youth might have been rather different if Harry had not always lived at some distance away.

Eventually, something materialized at the French radio on the Champs Elysées, and Tarn read the news in English there a few nights a week. There was also a job as a part-time reviewer and translator on the English-language version of a weekly tourist guide, the *Parisian Weekly Information*, also on the Champs Elysées. The director was a pleasant gentleman and allowed the boy to write just about anything, even some quasi-philosophical manifestos. Nightclubs: sitting alone with a free bottle of champagne, too timid as usual to acquire any kind of company. On one memorable evening, Carmen Amaya, a flamenco dancer very well-known at the time, and a bunch of her people suddenly irrupted into the empty club and began dancing furiously all over the minute floor, almost knocking the spectator off his feet as he leaned back away from the volcano. Later came theater, ballet, and art. There were magical evenings at the Marigny with the Jean-Louis Barrault company and the lovely decors of Christian Bérard; more sober evenings of Sartre and Camus with the legendary Louis Jouvet; Jean Cocteau with Jean Marais; August Strindberg, Eugène Ionesco, or Sam Beckett with Roger Blin in smaller theaters in Saint Germain des Prés and Montmartre. Also at the Marigny there were great evenings of ballet: the premiere of Zizi Jeanmaire's *Carmen* with Roland Petit was especially fiery. Some fashion reviewing was included—with visits to the great couturiers, although this, sadly, came to an end when a translation misfired: the French *hanche* became haunches instead of hips!

8.2 *Combat*, a marvelous newspaper in which Albert Camus had had a leading role, was devoured every day. It featured wonderful cultural pages, and two or three of them per week were of major importance. A great deal was written in these days about French anthropology: the African work of the Marcel Griaule group or the Oceanian efforts of Maurice Leenhardt. Much popular attention went to ethnographical travelogues: slide and film shows often given at the Salle Pleyel: later it appeared that some professional anthropologists had mixed feelings about these, and Claude Lévi-Strauss himself refused a prize generated by that business. One day, Tarn saw a movie about his generation in St. Germain des Prés: Jacques Becker's *Rendez-vous de juillet*. The story concerned a young man (Daniel Gélin) interested in that kind of "ethnography" and trying to set up his departure for exotic lands. In the course of the film he visited the *Musée de l'Homme*, an anthropology museum situated in one of the two art deco buildings at the Palais du Trocadero, opposite the Eiffel Tower esplanade. This building also held the Maritime Museum while its twin housed the *Musée des arts et traditions populaires* (French ethnography), a collection of casts of French monuments, and the *Théâtre national populaire* (T.N.P.), also a favorite haunt. Large quotations in gold by Paul Valéry shone just below the roofs.

Our student, who prided himself on trying to know every museum in any town he visited, realized he had been in Paris a whole year without knowing the Trocadero ensemble and went off one morning to the Anthropology Museum. It was huge . . . and overwhelming. In a corner, near the elevators, some posters advertising lectures and courses. Details were taken, and, back home, trembling set in for three whole days. An impression that the future was entering into one's body. On the third day, Tarn went back and enrolled, determined that this project would remain secret until the first examinations had been taken. If Mémé wondered where her grandson disappeared to several days a week, she appeared to keep her counsel. The secret would have been maintained had it not been for a parental visit to Paris two weeks before the B.A. equivalent finals. Had Grandmother said anything, and did they come to check on their son? Logistics compelled the admission that a "respectable" profession had been found. There were considerable doubts about fieldwork among "savages," but the prospect of academic rank and eventual professorships helped to keep these at bay. The parents were dubiously pleased.

8.3 First teachers were Marcel Griaule at the Sorbonne and eventually his colleague Germaine Dieterlen—as well as others such as Jean Rouch the musicologist and filmmaker. Griaule's *Dieu d'eau*, which, much later in English, became *Conversations with Ogotemmêli*, had been appreciated for its astonishingly comprehensive and almost Egyptian initiatic system. Tarn soon knew everything that had been published on the Dogon and the Bambara of the then French Sudan and followed the work for years. Griaule had a transcendental sense of humor but was very solidly grounded: the lectures were most amusing and often ribald. He was mainly concerned with inculcating fieldwork procedures and often compared them to police work, telling his class that they could do worse than get some instruction from Paris's finest!

There were other lectures at the museum in prehistory, physical anthropology, museography, and so forth. On one occasion the already redoubtable Lévi-Strauss was tremulously approached after a lecture and asked—on behalf of the parents—what he thought of a future in anthropological research. The approach was inspired by the maestro's second wife, who worked at a bookstore on the outskirts of town, but the question was inane and was met with marked severity and some degree of contempt. This teacher especially belonged to the generation of "I teach and speak, you listen and learn"—very different from the American counterpart. It was the first of three problems with Lévi-Strauss.

The second year was also centered on the museum under the auspices of the *Centre de formation aux recherches ethnologiques* (C.F.R.E.), directed by the prehistorian André Leroi-Gourhan and conceived of as a kind of apprenticeship. There was even a week-long field trip to the barge dwellers on the canals near Paris, the excitement being provided by the rumor that incest prevailed on these barges. Life was led rather muddily in tents under fierce rain: the trip hardly pleasant. Of greater interest were the free courses on Southeast Asia by Paul Lévy at the Fifth Section of the *Ecole des Hautes Etudes* as well as those by Lévi-Strauss on North American Indian mythology at the same E.H.E. and later at the *Collège de France* nearby. Tarn's Americanophilia was fed by these accounts of the US Southwest and the Pacific Northwest even though, by then, he was adopting the anti-American rhetoric of the average French student. After early written efforts on the barge people and the gypsies of Andalusia, Tarn catalogued the Assam Naga collection at the museum and wrote a paper on "Naga Tiger Mythology"— both for Paul Lévy. Admiration has been maintained through the years for the E.H.E. and the *Collège* and their system of free education in which a subject was taught—when there happened to arise a teacher worthy of it—to students of varying backgrounds, often of advanced age—some, it seemed, almost off the street. Regret has subsisted that work could not be done with the likes of Georges Dumézil in Indo-European studies or Paul Demiéville in Buddhist studies.

Close friendships were developed with Isaac Chiva, a Rumanian Jewish refugee who later became an authority on French ethnography and Lévi-Strauss's number two at the new Laboratory of Anthropology attached to the *Collège de France*; Claude Tardits, later an Africanist; Alexander McDonald, a lifelong Scots-Frenchman, later a Tibetologist; Bernard Laffont, later in Laos; Georges Condominas, later among the tribes of Vietnam. Many were married, and their wives, Isabelle Chiva, Ariane McDonald, and Claudie Tardits, were students also or otherwise part of the group.

Tarn was taken to meet Lucien Biton, a bank clerk and one of the world's major Buddhologists, whose passions were Orientalism, philosophy, anthropology, Surrealism, and erotica. His major interest involved the relations between early Greek and early Buddhist philosophy: his favorite philosopher, Sextus Empiricus. A small, intensely lively man, he had, for reasons that remained unclear, decided never to publish. His small apartment, rue du Théâtre, contained a huge library on all his topics as well as a substantial collection of ethnographic objects that he bought with his first wife. Visits were on Sundays, sitting bunched up around a table in the main study, and included a vast amount of talk and a collation of wine and small *friandises*, salt and sweet, that he shopped for himself and presented with many comments on provenance and very obvious pride. During these meetings, Lucien held forth at enormous length: the Great Monologue (French this time) of a type only encountered much later as the Great American Monologue among poets such as Robert Duncan and Kenneth Rexroth. Tarn's spiritual foster parents, the painters Henri and Nō Seigle, were always there, and Rolf Stein, an eminent Sinologist and Tibetologist, was a frequent visitor. It was often said that the greatest masters came to Lucien to have their theses read and approved. Biton was a ferocious collector, visiting even *les papiers*: places where old books could sometimes be found trashed as waste paper. He claimed to have launched his collection by subtracting the volumes of a famous Orientalist collection one by one from under the backside of a librarian at the *Bibliothèque Sainte-Geneviève*. The man had kept warm this way in the middle of winter. Lucien very generously helped Tarn to build a library at reasonable prices, and for many years after leaving Paris, Tarn and he continued to find books for each other, Lucien keeping elaborate accounts in a nineteenth-century hand. Of course, no Paris visit ever omitted at least one afternoon at the rue du Théâtre.

Sometime in the early nineties (by then Henri Seigle, not an easy man, had become fed up with Lucien, and the Seigle no longer came), a last visit was paid to Lucien, who had remarried an astringent philosophy professor after the death of his very dear first wife. His body was devoured by cancer, a leg had been amputated, yet he held forth for four hours to Tarn and Rodney with his customary ferocious and opinionated panache as a grand adieu to an old friend. The performance, without a single shred of self-pity, was enormously touching and impressive. Tarn has never known what happened to the library.

8.4 The early times in Paris were heady days and nights. One of the first celebrities met with, at a party, was Jean Lurçat, the artist responsible for the renaissance of French tapestry in the fifties. His talk was almost entirely about the Spanish Civil War and demonstrated to our student that men often belong to one war only: Lurçat appeared completely uninterested in World War II, for instance, which, of course, gradually revealed itself as Tarn's own war. There was a visit, ill-remembered, to Jacques Villon's studio in a country house on the outskirts of Paris and a long talk, equally ill-remembered, in a magnificent garden, with Salvador Dali, which may have been brought about by Caresse Crosby. Dali, a Franco person it was later found, struck Tarn as markedly literate and well informed sociologically on the European scene.

Tarn wrote an unsolicited essay on "Spiritual Paternity in the Poetry of Jules Supervielle," which, ignoring the fact that he was not actually reviewing, he sent to the admirable magazine *Critique*—devoted entirely to learned and extensive book reviews. He was in short order amazed to receive a summons from Georges Bataille, a major French writer, in his office near the Opera. Bataille handed him Supervielle's new *Oublieuse mémoire,* intimating that he should write a short note for the back of the next issue. Amazed again, he found that his piece appeared instead at the head of the issue, and this began a relationship with *Critique* that lasted many years. The next day, Supervielle, evidently delighted, called Mémé's apartment and invited the student over for a talk and a gift of a very early book. On the way in, a beautiful young girl was also recognized—whom Tarn had once fallen for in the street—as the poet's daughter but was found, alas, to be already married! Was this to Pierre Bertaux, the proponent of a very unorthodox theory about Hölderlin and a hero of the French Resistance?

A first book was dreamed up, an essay that came out eventually as "La légende de Saint Germain des Prés." Serge Jacques, a young photographer, contributed pictures of sites, cafés, nightclubs, authors, and artists of the famous quarter now a tourist favorite, while Marcel Jacno, a friend of a friend of Tarn's mother and a well-known typographer (he was responsible for the packaging of Gauloises cigarettes, the masterful *Théatre National Populaire* posters, and the looks of many famous brands of perfume), designed the book. Unfortunately, our student's text was entirely rewritten by the fly-by-night publisher (allegedly for tourist consumption!), who also absconded with any profits. The author used the pen name Michel Tavriger on this book and a couple of other items in an attempt to get close to what the family regarded as the ancestral name. The friendship with Jacno was a lasting one, continuing into the years when he lived in a wonderful studio on the Île Saint-Louis. On his arrival in Paris, Tarn had gone from door to door on the island looking for a room: it did not take long for him to realize that this would remain a dream. It is a dream he still nurtures from time to time. Jacno, a very quiet, patient, and kind man, was a member of the French Communist Party and was amused by Tarn's "spiritual" interests. He would never preach but say with a wide smile, "You will see. It is only a matter of time."

Some interesting contacts arose out of an article on the paintings of Victor Brauner in Tarn's little tourist rag. Georges Mathieu, an abstract painter, royalist, and publicist, took the writer under his wing for a time and introduced him to Brauner and other painters. Serge Charchoune (enough was not known of his Russian background for this to be appreciated at the time) and other artists were met on various occasions through the Seigle. Now for these very Seigle.

8.5 In a bookstore off the boulevard St. Germain, a painter couple—Henri and Nō Seigle—were encountered with immediate mutual sympathy and, all being friends of the store owner, a conversation somehow began about Surrealism. The works of Dadaists and Surrealists had been devoured at school in Cornwall with the same kind of passion as was roused by Virginia Woolf, early Auden, Isherwood, and others such, but—their wartime migrations to the States and other safe havens being unknown—they were believed to have died long ago in the homeland lost to World War II and had become mythical beings. The Seigle were happy to assert that they were not at all dead and that some of them could be visited and sat with at the Place Blanche café in Montmartre on almost every Sunday of the year! The Seigle were themselves members of the group.

These sessions were attended for about a year, mainly because of a desire for company in that Tarn was not at all sure how he felt about Surrealism, all the more so because it was surviving in its very late stage as a formal group. He therefore stressed an English identity and did not commit himself to any actions but enjoyed Breton's humor and superbia, especially when the master expatiated on the "atrocious habits" (drinking Coca-Cola, for instance) that his daughter Aube, sitting next to him, had picked up during their time in America. (In 2019, in Paris, Tarn purchases the *Letters of Breton to Aube*, published by Gallimard.) Benjamin Péret, Toyen, and a handful of others were the last survivors of the sempiternal purges. There is a memory, which may be faulty, of a onetime visit from Max Ernst. Octavio Paz came regularly; he, a Sino-French young woman, Monique Fong (who later became a United Nations interpreter and friend of Marcel Duchamp), and Tarn often walked back to Paz's place, although his still being married to his first wife, the distressed Helena, caused some difficulty. Tarn owns an inscribed copy of *El Laberinto de la Soledad*, which came out around this time: many further books arrived at a much later date.

The Seigle became lifelong friends and began by taking Tarn under their wings at classes that they offered on evenings once a week in the home of a couple, members of the group. The man in this couple was Jean-Louis Bédouin, who eventually wrote the Breton volume in Pierre Seghers's collection *Poètes d'aujourd'hui*. The classes were in the esoterica of all cultures and came with beautifully illustrated notes prepared by the two painters. Nō Seigle was a relative—niece perhaps—of an immensely erudite esotericist master, and she remained a lifelong spiritual searcher (eventually Buddhism, then Krishnamurti), the only being who might be called "enlightened" known in this lifetime to this writer.

The rationale for the classes was related to Breton's call at that time for an "occultation of Surrealism," and Breton was kept informed of the experiment. But hoary political contentions still haunted the group, and there came a point when allegiances were challenged in the "Pastoureau affair," which, once again, was related to problems with the relation of the group to the Communist Party. The copious annals of Surrealist excommunications contain some reference to this. The Seigles' wartime experiences of internal conflict in the Resistance had left them, Henri especially, with a hatred of the extreme Left. They defended the "occultation" position. Somewhere in all this and for reasons that never became clear, Bédouin turned coat and accused Tarn at the café of writing a book about the existentialists (his *Légende de Saint Germain des Prés* picture book): a scandal that was thought to require an immediate public purge! Tarn had to walk out, and at this point, in solidarity, the Seigle walked out as well. Considerable amusement was occasioned by Tarn having called Breton "*Monsieur*" on departing. The regret remained that the famous apartment on the rue Fontaine had never been visited and that the only autographed item one had been left with was a questionnaire about magic. The excommunication had lasting effects. Many years later, Tarn proposed to translate some Breton poems and *L'amour fou* for his London book series Cape Editions. A grant from the National Translation Center at Austin, Texas, was obtained but had to be refused: word came from Paris that this effort would be verboten.

Most evenings were spent, in one way or another, in St. Germain des Prés, where Juliette Gréco, *Ma Grecque*, and the Frères Jacques sang at La Rose Rouge; Léo Ferré at the St. Thomas d'Aquin; a couple of American actors, Lee Payant and Gordon Heath, at the Abbaye, where you applauded the songs not with clapping but with finger snapping, and the Club Saint-Yves, a 1900s club famous for its *cerises à l'eau de vie*. Tarn would often walk back all the way to the Arc de Triomphe at a very fast pace, the prostitutes hailing him as *l'ouragan*, the whirlwind. During those walks, the thought that any separation from this city would result in death or disaster was a frequent one.

Academic life continued with very few breaks. One remarkable experience is worth recording. One night, Alexander MacDonald, Pierre Laffont, and Tarn took a train south to see the prehistoric caves at Lascaux. They were able to buy a ticket, go in, admire the astounding paintings, go out, buy another ticket, and go back in. A couple of other sites were visited, now lost to memory. In much later times, Lascaux was closed to all but professionals, and a replica of the famous monument was built for tourists.

8.6 Love affairs, however, continued, mainly unhappily, "even in Paris." Conditions were poor and unconducive to romance: most times, hotels specializing in three-hour rentals had to be resorted to. Uncle Claude used to like to go to *thés dansants*, where you had to dance with totally unknown partners—a sort of European variant on the singles bar concept—but never once did our student pluck up the courage to ask someone, and besides he was not a dancer. However, Claude was glad to have the company. There were, successively—but the order is doubtless incorrect—a young woman who modeled and sold gloves in a city boutique, another who sold men's shirts in a shop that Uncle Harry frequented, a very hysterical young German. Close platonic friendships, always problematic in one way or another, arose with Monique Fong, of the surrealist group, and Varvara Pitoëff, an unbelievably intense young actress and member of the famous Russian Pitoëff theatrical family.

More important was young Marie Helène, who lived with her father in an apartment near the Passy metro station and spent summers with her mother in the South of France. She claimed, and it was doubtless true, to be completely lesbian, having experienced a long affair with an older woman. Tarn, massively smitten, persisted. Finally, a night together in a hotel was agreed on: "to see [in Marie Helène's words] whether the homosexual link could be broken." Both parties were extremely nervous, and drugs were produced that, it was believed, would help matters along. The Beatrician body lay all night as still and cold as marble. However, marble freezes everything in its vicinity. Even after this debacle, our hero continued smitten and went down to see M.H. in the South of France. He was treated kindly but told very clearly that there was no future to be hoped for: he was "a very fine person but not the kind of male she had required." Had she desired rape? On a desolate night train ride back to Paris from Antibes, the initials M.H. were carved into the back of Tarn's left hand. Later, M.H. was heard of at Cambridge, where she had somehow met up with Tarn's old friends. It was reported that she made many advances to young girls. One of the friends became smitten in his turn but was no more successful than anyone else. Not long afterward, this friend, having entered the Foreign Office, discovered that he was gay.

The scene for one drama was Lévi-Strauss's aula at the *Collège de France*. These classes were exciting because of the maestro's teaching, because many members of the *Tout Paris* made a habit of coming—a venerable custom in an intellectual city—and because of the presence of a very beautiful young woman with whom Tarn lost no time in falling passionately in love. A fine Swiss edition of de Nerval's *Aurélia* had been inscribed in pencil with all our scholar/poet's favorite quotations. One day, the lady in question left in the middle of the class. She was followed and persuaded to have a coffee while explanations were proffered. The *Aurélia* was politely refused and her lack of availability referred to. Was it then made clear that she was the maestro's friend and future wife, or did this become clear later? Absolutely disconsolate, our hero walked back down the avenue Saint-Germain and thought, in his desperation, of calling on Germaine Dieterlen. She was most understanding and comforting in a motherly way.

Another kind of bizarre romance occurred with P. de B., a young Cuban socialite of rich and seemingly aristocratic but politically and economically dubious parentage. Another Cantabridgian, Christopher Moorsom, who was always trying his friend out with strange introductions, told Tarn to call on her at the Ritz in Paris, where she was staying with her mother and older sister. P. was an exquisite, dark-haired, huge-eyed, perky-nosed flower of Latin youth. A great deal of mystery surrounded her at the Ritz, and visits, walks by the Seine, even an afternoon chastely spent on the home couch, rue de l'Arc de Triomphe, were always interfered with or endangered by demanding scheduling problems and undefined requirements of mother and sister. A great deal of Catholic rhetoric was also deployed by the young princess—about sharing her love between Jesus and her beau—most of it fairly clearly directed toward the preservation of chastity. Had one been less victimized by timidity and a strongly held belief that advantage should never be taken without clear consent, matters might have proceeded further. They never did. It was once rumored that P. was only fifteen at this Parisian time. Much later, after several appearances and disappearances, P. married Christopher Moorsom, gave him some daughters, and is said, by many concerned, to have become a harridan.

8.7 Poetry was not working. Everything was written in French—a factual diary, the *Journal Quantitatif,* and one for cogitations and meditations, the *Journal Qualitatif,* as well as the "Mémoires d'un jeune savant . . ." previously mentioned. However, the poetry was felt never to rise above twenty-fifth-rate Apollinaire: it was as if, whatever one tried, the influence of this beloved poet would never diminish. Whether the idea of abandoning French ever arose at this time is uncertain, indeed doubtful. Certainly, French continued to be used well into the next period in Chicago. It was also the case that, in cosmopolitan and multilingual Paris, the idea of escaping from the English language remained completely illusory.

One responsibility to France had been delayed. In the middle of his studies, our student, much to his surprise, had suddenly been summoned to a *Mairie* and found himself lined up, in the raw, before a French military commission. The news that he had been classed as unusable by the British Army when at Cambridge ("no officers needed at this time"—it was believed this might have occurred because the examining doctor was a writer and relative of the Philip Gosse who had inspired Tarn's adolescent orchid-hunting ambitions) was of no interest whatsoever to the French doctors. The matter of ongoing studies had not been cleared up, and military service loomed. A very kind gentleman friend of Uncle Harry's, the Colonel de C., set about obtaining a delay so that studies could be completed. A substantial variety of ministries and military quarters were visited in various parts of the landscape, many papers obtained, many hands shaken, and the delay was eventually obtained. The very kind and gallant colonel was dutifully thanked on holidays every year.

A more practical issue was that of a professional future. Any possibility of ethnographic fieldwork from a French base appeared to be most uncertain. Lévi-Strauss did not seem to be founding a lineage. Most anthropology had been, and continued to be, written in English. Smith-Mundt and Fulbright grants were obtained and led, after all the documentation and fingerprinting, to departure for the New World on the old French Line ship *De Grasse* in 1951. Imagine the feelings involved in standing at the bow of the ship, looking back at France and distant Paris—the city that was never to be abandoned.

The Atlantic crossing was agreeable, including a dinner at the captain's table with a blonde American dancer as partner, although most attention was paid to another student, a tall, leggy, literary person who, unfortunately, was going to a very distant university. The approach to Manhattan was as impressive as it had been for the hungry and tired, although the city's flanks where the ship eventually docked seemed curiously old-fashioned and dilapidated. The first night in New York, staying with Dutch friends and onetime coworkers of Tarn's father in a high-rise neighboring Lincoln Center, was unforgettable: looking out and witnessing the private lives of multitudes framed by hundreds of windows. This was followed by visits to the Institute of International Education, where the young woman responsible for the American venture became a "family friend." An encounter with a young lady working in a bookstore, using the French accent gambit, was also enjoyable until, some hours having gone by on an impromptu date, our student admitted that although he was indeed French, the accent was faked . . . and exhausting. He was forgiven.

Throw Nine

9.1 Major mystery of this life to this life. How can the work so often reflect such joy, even such ecstasy, when the life, most of the time, is experienced as pure hell? In no way whatsoever is this an exaggeration. It is not a manner of speaking. Don't even try to think of any kind of comfort. At the same time, do not feel concern for those who coinhabit. There were a great many years, yes, when moods were uncontrollable and relationships perished as a result. But softening techniques have been developed over time, principally humor. Never eradicated altogether. But you would rarely know now how close at all times the knife is to the vein.

Why pure hell? Mainly because of unrelenting depression and anxiety. This has been analyzed and found to be clinical/chemical depression: I suspect there may have been a bipolar element in youth, but the top part of this eventually dissipated and the bottom half was left. Difficult to tell depression and anxiety apart. Seems they are friends in a very tight circle, one leading inevitably and virtually every time to the other. Since as far back as one can remember. I would often ask the Seigle, in the splendor of late adolescence in Paris, "'Why is it that, not for one moment, not ever, can I experience *joy*?' Why do I say, 'I do not love life, but my poetry does?'"

From as far back as I can remember, I have called the ground of this anxiety "the demon of the arbitrary." I am obsessed by the simple question, applied to almost every aspect of life from the least to the most important: "If the all is unavailable, why this rather than that? Why that rather than this?" Accompaniment to the hoary old problem of free choice. If I have nothing specific to do—although actually every time I do have—why should I turn left rather than right, or right rather than left, when I leave the house? Only occasionally the feeling that everything has been determined from the start—but this does not eliminate the fundamental anxiety. One of the most frequent manifestations of such feelings: standing in a bookstore looking at a good dozen or more desirable books. Problem one: I cannot afford all the ones I need or want. Problem two: which then shall I take? Complicated by the knowledge that, all my life long, I have been able to buy books instinctively some ten years or so before needing them. Ever stop to think that some people who need books just as badly have no money at all and cannot buy even one? Rarely: I have always been too self-centered to react well to such injunctions—like the wartime parental "Eat your beans; the children in Greece do not have any." In any event, because my feelings have always been contextual, very frequent meditations on such poverty only add to the anxiety.

Anxiety worsens as the years go by. Nothing is free from it: statements, discussions, phone calls, letters, meetings, talks, lectures, readings, interviews, photography sessions, complaints to firms or authorities—involving interlocutors or not—*any* kind of dialogue or correspondence whatsoever, anything to do with the telephone. Writing (especially articles, even more so, reviews). Any task to be performed. Medical visits and procedures. Travel plans.

A few years ago, I was diagnosed with a touch of obsessive-compulsive disorder. Not a physical form: rather one reflecting mental processes. It has grown. Anxiety is a magnet for OCD: as soon as anxiety is manifested in any shape, form, or degree, OCD fastens onto it and will not let go. The effect is devastating. Let us say that a worry occurs. The average person will think about it, try to resolve the associated problem or deal with it if possible, and then put it aside. Only rarely will this worry take over the mind to the extent of shutting out everything else. In the case of OCD, this takeover is exactly what happens: the subject of worry repeats itself continually, forms a kind of interminable loop that never rests. This can go on for days and nights until the worry has passed, is replaced by another worry, or somehow gets resolved. Imagine how this interferes with sleep. If there is a worry on going to sleep, you will awaken sometime between say 1.00 and 3.00. Then OCD immediately presents the mind with its worry-of-the-moment, one squirrel immediately follows the first, and continuing insomnia results. Add that modern conditions are torture to OCD sufferers insofar as the general "busyness" of the population has reached such levels that *responses* to requests, enquiries, needs . . . of any kind whatsoever make themselves rarer and rarer (the modern form of an answer is no answer). "Manners" have gone to hell.

Like many syndromes associated with anxiety and depression, OCD appears to be mainly chemical in origin and can be subjected to certain antidepressants. I have experienced the fact that there are some anti-ds. that will, literally, "transform your life." The effect does not last. The main hitch is that side effects can be so devastating that the medication cannot be used. Worry persists in seeing oneself as a "chemical man": does this, for instance, interfere with necessary emotions, bring about anhedonia, or menace creativity such as it is? After years, I am still waiting for a successful drug that will not produce these various side effects, although there is no doubt that treatment is improving.

But I have heard it said that no one who has not experienced clinical depression can ever know and understand what it implies. Some autobiographical writings are available.

9.2 Back to the one person with whom one appears to have been most emotionally involved: Father. Everlasting regret that there was never the courage to sit down once, once and for all, and to say, "OK. Let's take the time now. I really mean let's once and for all take the time, *make* the time. Tell me what it is you would like to tell me. Tell me what makes *you* so anxious that you can never explain it to me in full, that you can only deal with it by issuing orders and always impatiently and in the worst of tempers. You obviously feel you never have enough time to explain it because I never have, or seem to you to have, enough time to listen. Let us agree that the business interests you wish to explain are usually Greek to me, that they bore me to exasperation, that I normally do not want to hear the stuff in any shape or form although, this time, I firmly intend to make the effort."

Knowing, as one might think this, that the courage would never be found to say it and that the ground of such a conversation, in the form of a *relationship*, did not really exist.

Father often saying to visitors, "Yes, I have two sons: one a poet, one a painter: how on earth did that happen or [as a feeble joke] why did this have to happen to me?" Father often reported to have praised his sons behind their backs as he would praise his wife without her ever knowing.

And so, year after year, every time one came into their house, being captured at the door, before anything could be said, before Mother could be greeted, before the difficulty of managing moods in a transitional situation could even begin to be handled (one aspect of anxiety: passing from one place to another, from one situation to another, especially when it involves other people) . . . and being taken into Father's room and sat down and told that "this" would only take a minute. Which would take a good deal more.

In essence, Father, who had suffered very serious losses by leaving Europe, was managing funds that were, perfectly legitimately, put into my name and my brother's name in order to protect us if anything should happen to the parents but also, no doubt, because there were advantages to such devolutions. In early days, I believe, there were attempts to explain why and how this was being done, to demonstrate the advantages, to argue the pros and cons, to delineate the risks if there were any. This was undoubtedly mixed with a desire on Father's part for us to take an interest in, and show approval of, his good deeds. In the end, however, his defeat was acknowledged in that papers were simply handed over with the instruction "Sign here" or "Sign there." There was something infinitely sad about all this. When it was over, one felt one was being finally allowed out of the room—but only to join in some futile conversation or, usually, some nerve-racking meal. Over the years, the matter became even more painful and depressing because of the fact that it seemed as if nothing would actually ever be parted with at the right time for our benefit before the final exit. It was not greed: it was discouragement at sempiternally being told that "there would be enough" when in fact it was becoming more and more clear that war and market forces would eventually reduce this "enough" to a pittance.

Most times, there was one action that the unfortunate man could not forgo: some discourse about the fact that things were not going well, that business was unsatisfactory, that friends had failed, that the national or international situation was unfavorable, *und so weiter*. So and so had behaved badly; so and so was an "unprincipled bastard"; all those people were "swine." A recital of facts and figures could mean nothing because the context was unknown and no information had been absorbed that would allow comparison of one situation with another. Sympathy was obviously being asked for but in such a manner that it could not be proffered, given, or received.

A disaster. Attempts to understand his anxiety? And then to relate this to a behavioral feature of one's own anxiety: the Tarn habit of asking a vital question before it could be forgotten. Or ignored under the pressure of some other question or ongoing event.

9.3 How many years has it taken to ration those questions, statements, or explanations: to work out carefully when the best time would occur for these matters to be raised or sprung so that the most favorable results would be obtained in return? When with individuals born with diplomatic talents, such methods seem to arise so naturally it is never a problem to come up with them because instinct does all the necessary work! Or is this an illusion too?

The rage, sometimes, that some should find so easy what one found so appallingly difficult!

Unto the *n*th generation! So that Father also suffered from anxiety—and/or depression I do not have the precise means to tell—and the question is: how far back did this go? All the way to extreme youth, when he was sent, at something like sixteen, to learn a trade in the Low Countries? Completely alone, except for whatever family he was put to board with and for the yeshiva he was set to study in? Or later, when the German invasion of Western Europe and especially Belgium had taken place and the family had apparently lost a factory and turned from the manufacture of industrial precision tools (using precious stones) to trading in those stones alone? Although he was a pupil and footballer of the reputed Manchester Grammar School (for how long before going abroad?), the mind seemed furnished with virtually nothing. Nothing was ever read except the newspapers: in later years, with television, the "news" was ferociously followed and then hours of purely innocuous "entertainment" involving little beyond the British sitcoms. Despite some kind of religious education (a kosher household had apparently been abandoned on marrying), very little grasp of anything in Judaism beyond rituals and superstition. One pathetic memory. Father: "Those stories in the Bible—Moses and all that: bobbymices, no?" "Bobbymices" was the term for stories, for myths and legends, for nonsense. Some form of anxiety about death? I am not certain. It took many years for me to find out that bobbymices was actually the Yiddish *bubbe meise*: old wives' tales!

How many questions unasked of parents, of grandparents, because the only thing desired was to get out and away from family as soon as ever possible! When, at the very ultimate last, a tape-recording interview was set up, it was too late.

Everything, for Father, ended up by becoming a matter of money. We never went out for a meal without having to study very carefully what dish would please us in some measure without being one of the most expensive on the menu. There was never any possibility whatsoever of spontaneity in the choice of a place to eat or to stay in the face of Father's icebound opinions that this restaurant, this hotel, that shop were those at which the best prices could be found. It is not that he was ungenerous. He would sometimes give remarkable gifts, although always of his own choosing (something Mother always complained about), but, in essence, he did not know what or how to give or how to begin to find out what might be desired, what might give pleasure. There had been that gift of Maeterlinck's *Bluebird*, mentioned before. There was the choice offered, at my age of fourteen, between a typewriter or a microscope—the typewriter eventually to arrive from those Dutch friends in New York. Most other gifts were enmeshed in the financial procedures described, in pocket money or in allowances, and could not be appreciated as gifts. A mere sigh of relief took the place of an expression of true gratitude.

It is also true that any expression of emotion was warded off by Father in one way or another. It was as if, far back, all emotion had been found to be wanting, as if humanity was incapable of producing genuine emotion. Occasions for conflict—usually at the dinner table and usually bringing about digestive troubles (I suffered from stomach aches of one kind or another through the whole of childhood and youth)—arose from the fact that having "sacrificed everything" to give his sons, and especially his elder son, a fine education, this education had turned the son into an arrogant prig. The standard comment being "Yes, you may know about $x, y,$ or $z,$ but you know nothing about life." It took many years for any kind of expertise on my part to be overtly considered worthy of any attention whatsoever. Passionately addicted to collecting (saving this book or that object from barbarism, as Walter Benjamin once pointed out), I tried for a long time to get my parents to finance art acquisitions that my pocket money would not cover. I did say once "It could have been women; it could have been horses: it was books." I find it hard, however, even today, to bear the thought of all the fine objects of art I could eventually have loved—let alone sold eventually to help the family—if they had trusted my judgment. As it was, their apartment was one of the most sterile places I have ever known.

An expression that came into Father's mouth more often than any other was "It is a pity that. . . ." This ontological dissatisfaction could not fail to have a paralyzing effect. I do not know exactly what role this played in Brother Neville's difficulty in taking responsibility for himself as a painter. I do not know how to calculate the amount of extra effort it took to enable me to function at all. Obviously, a great deal of effort was expended on trying to "impress" this parent because I always remember saying that "if I met a man, I had to tell Father that I had met a prince; if I met a prince, I had to tell him about meeting an angel; if I met an angel, I had to confess to having encountered God."

9.4 There were also the frequent fits of paternal temper and of rage—the main cause, when all is said and done, of one's inability to speak to an unchallenged father "face to face." "God forbid" that you should spill some wine or food on the dinner tablecloth: a look of thunder would come over his face followed by a variety of unsettling expletives. As if Father were the one this had been aimed at, as if he were the one to be directly and personally insulted. This meant, in the long run, that Mother would have to be the person who would intercede.

This situation led to another very painful one: I do not know whether to ascribe my emotional deadness toward Mother to it or whether sources are to be found much further back. In brief, it almost invariably happened that Mother began by seeming to understand your own complaint or problem and to take your own side—after which she would state that she agreed with Father—thus leading to a sense of absolute abandonment.

I cannot say that I know very much about the relations between my parents. Father left a document that I discovered among his papers when he died, asking for it to be read out aloud to Mother, in the presence of my then wife Patricia and Brother Neville. It was a devastating indictment of Mother, written at a time some thirty years before when he had probably been very perturbed by her having become very close to a doctor friend, accusing her of never having paid the slightest attention to his interests, his business, his concerns. I did not read this document aloud or show it to anyone except Patricia, being certain it would have killed his spouse. Mother always used to say that she had fallen in love with Father on meeting him in Paris—in spite of his having gone off to India on business for two and a half months immediately after the engagement and in spite of his extreme undemonstrativeness. He had behaved like a nineteenth-century macho in ascertaining her virginity on their first night. He had somehow allowed his cousin Jack Pearl to come with them on their honeymoon. I found out only relatively recently that Mother had had an affair with Father's brother David early in the marriage and had decided that he was the one she should have married. In Father's last few years, Mother had very frequently raged against him on the slightest pretext (his invariable insistence on turning off lights to save electricity would be one of them) to the point where Neville, who had had the most to suffer from him but lived in London and so saw more than I did, began to feel very sorry for the man.

I do not believe that I became aware of Mother's problems with anxiety until very late. In old age, she talked about it a lot. Perhaps it had become worse after Father's death: she continued to live in their apartment, which was rather large for one person. There had been much talk about getting a smaller one, but Father was undecisive. She told us repeatedly that she would lie awake at night and worry—mostly about us and our children or grandchildren. Whenever we pointed out to her how sterile all this was, she invariably replied that she had nothing else to do. True. We heard repeatedly how first her parents, next her husband, had prevented her from making something out of her life: she would have liked to be active in some branch of medicine. I had pointed out to her when she was middle-aged that she should find some occupation, hobby, or serious pastime; made many suggestions; brought her many documents, programs, and brochures on a great variety of possible activities. Nothing. Especially in old age, she would rarely forgo an opportunity to ask me whether I believed in an afterlife or not, invariably adding that she hoped there was no such thing.

Back to Father. A very salient part of what I considered to be his superstitions—but probably like much else (his distrust of banks inter alia) related to losses and dangers incurred during the war or to the everlasting anti-Semitism that he had witnessed as much as anyone in Continental Europe. Related to the latter was his attitude toward marriage "out of the faith." As boys, we would frequently be lectured on the fact that no commitment should ever be made to non-Jewish girls, his attitude to them being love-them-if necessary-but-leave-them, there being at all times "plenty more fish in the sea." He would often remark that one would be sailing along very happily in a marriage or relationship until the day when a spouse would suddenly make some disparaging remark: is it likely that he himself at some point may have been the victim of such? He was especially hard on American women. I believe that he lived in great fear at all times that one of us would incur his wrath on that subject.

When I declared in 1955 that I wished to marry Sasha, the sister of my Cambridge friend Christopher Moorsom, Father would only agree on condition that she would convert. Foolishly, being still unquestioningly dependent on the parents, I went along with this. Sasha made the attempt for a time but, being doubtless on other grounds unsure of her commitment to me, eventually made this process into one reason for our breakup. Neville went further and married a non-Jewish woman. Unbelievably, Father actually managed to extract a promise, or what he took to be a promise, that there would be no children of the marriage because he did not wish to have non-Jewish grandchildren. When a son was born nonetheless, Father behaved outrageously for years whenever that family would come to the house, and it has always been a matter of wonder to me that Neville stood for it. For some reason I am still unsure of, Neville also had Mother problems and has always taken Father's side, having somehow become persuaded that Mother worked against our interests. For my part, I have spent years trying to redress the balance in Father's arrangements so that Neville and his family would eventually know some measure of justice. Neville died of cancer early in 2020.

With the onset and progress of age, I have felt more and more sorrow and, I guess, pity for my father, a greater closeness to him, and overwhelming regret that I never found out who he was. I wish this were true for Mother also. Unaccountably—although some curiosity remains about the identity of this very splendid (a famous beauty in her youth), kind, and often overwhelmingly loving person—it is not.

9.5 Anxiety and language. Unlike Mother, who never mastered English completely, Father spoke English well, with a tendency to try to raise its class level a little when he felt that to be appropriate. He wrote clear, albeit a little stilted, letters but did not explain himself very clearly in our verbal confrontations. Was he stumbling over himself from anxiety?

I have had a lifelong habit of rehearsing letter writing and conversation, especially conversation, before these take place. Driving a car, lying in bed with insomnia, taking a walk are all occasions for this. I believe that this habit is related to an anxiety that the best, the most effective, the more carefully tailored way of making a statement requires preparation, very careful thought and rehearsal so that, when the moment of delivery arrives, the message is sent out like a *saeta*, the arrow straight and true of one mode of Spanish flamenco. This is also related to the notion of "throw," requiring that delivery should be once only, utterly clear and irrecuperable. If you have won, fine. If you have lost, hack it and go on to the next thing without regret. Of course, this is the method of a "control freak" always trying to make sure that anything is ready as well as it can possibly be in advance, without room for slips, mistakes, drift, loss, disaster. Admirer, in theory, since my youth of Surrealist ideals in the matter of *écriture automatique*, I have to ask, *contra*: is there ever art without control?

Anxiety, yes—but also something else? A poet, a writer, is known, or should surely be known, first and foremost, for his or her ability to say as clearly and precisely what s/he means. If you are not running wild in hundreds of different ways today, any lack of clarity or imprecision has to be carefully examined before acceptance. If this is the case, then rehearsal and practicing are basic functions of the craft. Perhaps there can be no art without some degree of anxiety.

This whole argument should reveal why I have had and continue to have trouble as a reader with the modernist and postmodernist phenomenon of disjunctiveness. The stance is grounded in communication theory: the rules for effectiveness in most media are strict. There is a line this side of which communication takes place, but on the further side of the line it does not. It need hardly be said that tolerance of disjunctiveness varies: there will always be a reader or listener to claim that s/he has understood or gained something from a text that others, even most others, will have found totally opaque. Personally, I have most times regarded such claims with extreme suspicion because, on pushing that person, on insisting s/he tell me exactly what it is s/he claims to have understood or gained, s/he has been found wanting and ends by sidestepping the whole issue. To me, therefore, there are limits to any communicative system's expansion beyond which the system cannot stretch on pain of failure. As long as humans remain human and do not radically evolve (or possibly return to) other modes of perception, linguistic usage must remain limited in the same way as politics must remain limited: the ideal of "perpetual revolution" is a fine one as an ideal but remains for the foreseeable future an impossibility. Various essays have shown that belief in the push and in limitlessness is necessary to the illusion of an ongoing process of creation but that it is also necessary to know that all process eventually has to fall back into structure—i.e., to bear and tolerate limits—from which, when the impulse is present, process can set out another time.

9.6 Limitation has other interesting aspects. Are the aging more tolerant of limitation? Two mechanisms seem to have been at work in the later poetry, the place where most confession still occurs—not in the sense of blabbing out one's "innermost" feelings but in that of revealing what thematics of concern best identify a certain poetic code. One mechanism is synecdochic. Unable to face the anxiety involved in capturing the "all," aware of how much redundancy and tedious repetition can be generated by such attempts, the poetry settles for trying to represent part of the all as if it were the all—mastery, of course, depending on which part is selected and how cannily the part in question is located and chosen. The other mechanism involves dealing with a desire to witness, understand, control, or own a given thing, where the desire has been frustrated, as if the satisfaction of the desire were less important than the recording of it in such a manner that the failure stands successfully within the poem in full lieu of the unavailable fulfillment. The

"Narrative of the Men and Women Who Became Stars" in the book *Seeing America First* is a good example of this—where not getting to see a comet despite all efforts turns into a satisfactory record of a more tragic failure: that of the astronauts whose *Apollo XI* vehicle exploded at the time when the poet was trying and failing to get a glimpse of the hurtling star.

Throw Ten

10.1 A curious ritual known as "orientation" took place at Yale. Insofar as it looked like an ersatz Cambridge—our dormitory standing very close to a feeble imitation of King's College chapel—the place very quickly became depressing. After a unisex place like Cambridge, hope had dwelt on a coeducational establishment like, say, Berkeley, Kansas, Oklahoma ("Amerika")! Yale was frustrating even though an effort was made on one occasion by the authorities to bring in some student nurses for a tepid evening's dancing.

   Some thirty students from all parts of the world, many far older than Tarn, were placed under the inexpert care of a young journalist assistant professor. Unsure of himself in his position at the university, this young man continually harassed his charges into having "problems." It was the first time for Tarn that the word "problem" had become so problematic. However, this was the era of Freud's greatest influence in the States: single-handed, he stood for all of psychology and philosophy to boot. Even the young girls one eventually met insisted on the impossibility of not having problems. There was also the journalist's mind-boggling sense that "coming for the first time to a 'democracy'" would naturally engender a host of problems! It was impossible for us to claim that democracy existed anywhere else. Our student continued to insist that he had never felt as much at home as he had upon this very first landing in the United States. And, oh yes!, "democracy" was a word and concept known in Europe.

Desperate to avoid writing papers on Jefferson, democracy, the frontier, and such (all of these had been amply "done" at Cambridge), Tarn called on prominent local anthropologists and begged for their help, insisting that, with so little time, every moment should be spent in the discipline. Much kindness on all parts. George Murdock discoursed on kinship theory and gifted a number of publications of the human relations area files. More excitingly, Ralph Linton told at great length—and doubtless not for the first time—the story of how he had been bewitched by Ruth Benedict. None of this helped overmuch, although our student was eventually allowed to present a term paper (previously written in Paris) on Native American mythology.

Two amusing moments. On his very first morning, Tarn ventured out to a small diner for breakfast and ordered eggs. "How do you want them?" Totally nonplussed, it had to be admitted that one knew of avian offspring only as boiled, poached, or fried. The look of bewildered disgust on the cook's face was treasured for many years. On another occasion, Tarn managed to induce half his colleagues to purchase Yale sweatshirts and show up wearing them on a single day at breakfast. The journalist exclaimed that Tarn had at last "caught the spirit" of the venture.

Excursions were organized to New Canaan (the Phillip Johnson glass house and, in another residence, a first sight of a Jackson Pollock), to the United Nations, to a baseball match (incomprehensible!) in New York, and to the Roosevelt family home at Hyde Park on Hudson. On every occasion, group photographs were taken—though, as much as possible, one's own suspicion-prone presence made itself scarce.

10.2 There were a few days back in New York and on the coast before leaving for Chicago. On Tarn's own volition and without introductions, very brash visits were undertaken in New York to Abraham Kardiner (psychological anthropology) and in Washington to Mathew Stirling (Mesoamerica) and James Fenton (Iroquois) of the Smithsonian, who provided a very welcome Chinese lunch, and to D'Arcy McNickle (Native American activist) at the Bureau of Indian Affairs, who gifted a still-confidential World War II antiwar document of the Hopi people. The University of Pennsylvania Museum of Anthropology at Philadelphia provided another visit in the company of Monique Fong, whom Tarn had met at the surrealist cafe. At a Columbia University lunch with Julian Stewart (South America), Harry Shapiro (physical anthropology), and Alfred Kroeber (Amerindians and general theory), the great Kroeber broke silence only to say, "Take a good scarf to Chicago, young man; the cold is terrible there!" *Mein Gott* was he right! Then came the train ride to Chicago in a night sleeper.

10.3 A first semester was spent at International House, but its sentimentalism and paternalistic rules about the separation of the sexes were absurdly old-fashioned even then, and eventually a series of apartments was shared with Claude Tardits, another budding French anthropologist. Because just about all the graduate students were married, the two Ts were invited everywhere as a couple. Socializing was not particularly brilliant: arrival at the door, beer can shoved into your hand, football or baseball match on the TV. The two Ts did become famous for their extremely elementary "French" salad dressings, so dinner at their place was considered a privilege.

Fred Eggan, author of a well-known book on Hopi kinship and social organization, was especially friendly at registration time and anxious to talk with people who had studied with Lévi-Strauss. This soon revealed a problem: the two Ts were thought to be far more knowledgeable than they were in fact, and no amount of throwing themselves on their knees in front of the faculty and confessing to massive ignorance seemed to make any difference. The boys soon realized that all of theoretical anthropology (structuralism aside) had to be studied in American textbooks and monographs. The result was infernally hard, round-the-clock work, extremely little play, and virtually no getting to know the city until the end of the year. Tarn gave papers on Lévi-Strauss's *Structures élémentaires de la parenté* in Eggan's class and on myth in the work of Leenhardt and Griaule in Robert Redfield's, and sent back to Paris reports of Sol Washburn's exciting advances with genetics in physical anthropology (Sol's classes took place in the early morning, when Chicago winds could cut like razors). One visiting professor, the Winnebago specialist Paul Radin—who may conceivably have been a paternal relative and told Tarn he thought his family had been bookbinders in a village of horse thieves—had made himself unpopular in some quarters of the profession through somewhat eccentric outspokenness. He made no bones about "keeping company with the Europeans in preference to the Americans." He would show up, invited or not, whether for breakfast or for dinner, with a package of meat under his arm, demand to be fed and entertained, and spin interminable yarns and portions of his complex life story—completely eliminating any possibility of doing any homework.

Eventually, Tarn became a member of Redfield's "Comparison of Total Cultures" seminar, which that strange mixture of an eighteenth-century English gentleman and American pioneer ran with two other faculty members: Gustave E. von Grunebaum, an Islamic specialist, and Milton Singer, later a specialist on India. Tarn was struck by the fact that standard French education in the history and methods of philosophy, known by French youth as *philo*, was not a part of American general education and that Redfield, as a result, was doing much in his anthropology to introduce philosophical concerns into the discipline. When Redfield visited Paris and gave lectures there, the first was fully attended and the next two extremely poorly. Letters were received at Chicago from old colleagues wondering how on Earth one could be working with such strange teachers. Some of the letters waxed fairly ferocious.

10.4 To enjoy "a real American campus with good-looking girls and ice cream," the two Frenchmen went to Melville Herskovits's seminars on African anthropology at Northwestern. It was good to get away from Chicago's "gray Gothic." Herskovits was most welcoming and even invited the boys to a Tanglewood concert. In Evanston, Tarn met the Yoruba specialist William Bascom and his Cuban wife, a meeting that led to a Cuban trip during one vacation. The urge to get out of the United States for a while had grown strong. A student friend had a car and drove single-handed all the way to within a few miles of Miami—where the pair fell asleep in the car—with virtually no stops. The radio blared "Blue Tango" incessantly: Peter Bogdanovich's movie *The Last Picture Show* has the soundtrack of that year exactly. There had been an Easyriderish episode when stopping for gas in a small southern town, the boys being told for no other reason than showmanship "not to go up *that* street," but the gentle hills of Kentucky and their horses in the early-morning sun had also delighted. A very warm day in Miami was spent walking up and down hazardous sidewalks outside the huge beach hotels. In the evening, the radio at a small b. and b. announced that a coup had taken place in Cuba and that General Fulgencio Batista had returned to power. Tarn, without the hundred dollars extra needed to try Jamaica or some other island, paced his room all night, phoned Pan Am at four a.m., was advised not to go, and went. The plane was full of Batista supporters going home. Tarn sat next to the new chief of police.

A fine hotel room cost very little because the tourist season was ruined. Within hours, Argeliers León, a musicologist, had been hauled out of Havana University and took his visitor to a Santería priest, where the three were soon flinging chicken blood around the walls of the room and discussing the Afro-Cuban pantheon of Catholic-Yoruba deities. Tarn became friendly with this *santero* and used to visit him backstage at the famed Tropicana nightclub, where he played drums for the paradisiacally beautiful dancing girls. Various visits were made during the stay to ritual sessions. At one of them, a dance with the initiates dressed completely in white, our ethnographer learned for the first time that drums could make you physically sick. In the main plaza of Havana, you could walk round the arcades and pick up a good collection of the colored bead necklaces, each of which denoted a deity. A collection of these includes a heavy initiation necklace for the deep-sea goddess Yemaya, whose "son" the young Frenchman was declared to be. (The collection with manuscript field notes was donated in 2018 to the International Folk Art Museum in Santa Fe, New Mexico.)

The great and justly famed painter Wilfredo Lam was contacted through surrealist acquaintances and fried up a delicious tomato dish one day in his studio a few yards away from Batista's main army camp. He was also generous with a drawing and some books, and a correspondence went on for a while after that visit. There were calls on the senior masters of Cuban anthropology, Fernando Ortiz and Lydia Cabrera. Slightly scary brushes with the Army occurred at night, one of them on the way to the Tropicana, included having to get down from the bus and being frisked with a revolver in one's back.

A very tall young Afro-Cuban lady was encountered in a city café in the wee hours after coming back from the Tropicana. Devoted to literature, she kept a notebook by her chamber pot into which she had copied her favorite poems. She quickly became obsessed with the idea that she should be taken to Paris to become the second Josephine Baker. Prompt skedaddles from a number of hotels became necessary.

10.5   These were exciting days for a young pro. Rides to New York whenever possible (four or five to a car with one stop in a cheap motel on the way) gave a taste of city life, which there was no time for in Chicago. The great June 1952 Wenner-Gren Foundation "Anthropology Today" meetings, for instance, came with an introduction by Lévi-Strauss to Roman Jakobson and an impassioned conversation about structural linguistics in a downtown bar. This was one of the very few, perhaps the only occasion for this writer, in which the Paris maestro behaved in a relaxed way with his erstwhile student. A connection with Marcel Duchamp was established through Monique Fong, and Tarn drank coffee with him on 14th Street on a few occasions, with subsequent visits up to his bare studio furnished with a chess set. Duchamp did not talk much. Still timid, Tarn would expatiate overlong on his studies. Duchamp would tell him that he was "far too clever for the likes of him and that he understood very little of what his young friend was saying!"

Graduate friends were on their way to becoming leaders in their fields in later life. Among them were Manning and June (a Tarn crush) Nash (Guatemala, Burma), Charles and Zelda Leslie (Mexico, India), Victor Gourevitch (theory, philosophy), Ed Bruner (Indonesia, North America), and Robert Fox (Philippines).

Entertainment came rarely. There were parties at times, and Tarn became known for a song that was known as "Tarn's song" and usually requested: it was a French medieval song "*Sur les marches du palais*" ("On the palace steps"). One English Department friend, a guitar player, was involved in these sessions, but departmental borders were fairly strictly observed. The two Ts, whose second apartment, near the El, stood so close to that of a black couple that their bed could be touched by extending a hand out the window, spent evenings in a number of jazz clubs in which they were the only whites and, on one occasion, a church where services were musical and entranced. These were the only occasions on which jazz ever "made sense" for Tarn in the fullest possible way. Such visits were often followed by rides back on the El from downtown at 2 a.m. with newspapers blowing around in desolate, vacant-looking lots. In New York, "Birdland"—John Coltrane and Charlie Parker were heard there—was one haunt; another was Dave Brubeck's place in the Village.

There were girlfriends, but it was difficult to get beyond the "necking" stage without ritual declarations of passion (declarations in such straightforward terms as "I love you" even though neither you nor the girl necessarily believed in the statement), and these were spurned by sophisticated young Europeans. It was required of a young man that he should put undue strain on his body by an unconscionably long period of courtship, the physical expression of which could only manifest in the areas of head, shoulder, arm, or knee of the lady friend. Freud continued to loom large: one young lady after every episode in bed would sit bolt upright and insist on running through every aspect of the action in relation to her last meeting with her analyst. This grew rather tedious. Another belle, Margaret, pride of her graduate department and an efficient young librarian in her spare time, was the daughter of a theology professor and greatly enjoyed sex on condition that several gin and tonics were provided first. Her great desire that love should be made in her home was regarded with considerable wariness: Tarn was most unwilling to face the potential wrath of irate Protestantism one cold Chicago morning or to consider a theology professor as a potential father-in-law. There was a young red-haired lady from Finland, member of a group numbering five Finns or so whose leader was a young theology student—but you would never have known this was his calling. The friendship was very tender but had no time to develop before departure for fieldwork. Beverly, a very sophisticated young woman working in publishing, had a minuscule apartment in the Village in New York, a very pleasant place in which to endure a city summer. This relationship also fell victim to departure from the States. Family names are lost.

Tarn learned very much later that, had he known about it, he could probably—Fulbright rules about returning to countries of origin notwithstanding—have gone on to a small place in the Carolinas known as Black Mountain College under the tutelage of a poet by the name of Charles Olson. Conjectures abound on what might have happened there, successfully or disastrously, and how life might have been entirely transformed. In the event, he was now one of the Redfield group, and the boss wanted him to work on one of his concepts, that of worldview, originally known by its German name, *Weltanschauung*. One of the novice's first duties was to compile a critical bibliography on the concept—in the course of which he may just possibly have invented the word "ethnopoetics," later claimed by Jerome Rothenberg. Or come close. He had very much wanted to do his work in South Asia or the Far East, but Redfield persuaded him that he was young enough to take a detour. "With your aesthetic sense, I am going to send you to a place in which you will bless me every morning on opening your window." The mandate was to reach Lake Atitlán, in the Guatemalan highlands' Department of Solola, choose a village, and settle down in it. As an initial introduction, Tarn was sent, with a generous supply of pocket money, to Harvard for a three-day visit to Ben Paul, an anthropologist who had already worked at the village in which he would spend almost his whole professional life: San Pedro la Laguna, on the lake. The visitor was greatly impressed by the handsome brick buildings with the red heraldic crests over their entrances.

10.6 After a few interesting days going into Chicago to buy basic equipment came a train ride to St. Louis with a stop there and a short walk outside the station, then on to Houston. There was time before the plane to walk through the center of town on a Sunday morning: colossal, white-on-white buildings all the way and totally deserted, an almost surrealist experience.

A few days in Mexico City. Visits to Miguel Covarrubias at his dance school—his illustrated books on Mexico and Bali already owned and much admired; to Alfonso Caso, head of the Instituto Nacional de Antropología e Historia, who was inordinately generous with his publications (he later visited in Atitlán accompanied by a very handsome daughter); to the Colégio de México for a lecture by Diego Rivera; to all the available museums and sites of murals; to ballets and concerts; to the waterways of Xochimilco; in short, to a miraculously attractive and lively city before it had fallen prey to pollution and immense overcrowding. And having the huge mass of the Pyramid of the Sun at Teotihuacan entirely to oneself, climbing it alone, was an experience virtually initiatic, an opening of the doors into all the mysteries of Mesoamerica. How solitary travel could still be in those days (in India and Nepal also, after Burma), how unconscious one could be of the privilege of seeing things without being crushed to death by other people—and how miserably different thirty or so years later!

10.7 Guatemala City was a much smaller and less significant place. After a few days there, getting the lie of the land and making professional visits, the bus to Panajachel, a longish trip before the highways, which came in the seventies. Nothing had ever been seen more beautiful than the first appearance of Lake Atitlán and the gradual revelation of its volcano-sheltered landscape as the bus curved round and round from its rim down into the little town of "Pana"—again the sense of an initiation, an opening into the heart of this New World. Tarn had been recommended to a German pension run by Milly Hanstein, the mother-in-law of a fellow anthropologist, Richard Adams, a heavenly, engardened little home from home in which to acclimatize. Then the choice of the big place across the lake, the head place of the area: Santiago Atitlán. Doubtless, the fact that—unlike all other villages—it was linked by a daily boat with Pana played a part in the selection, but previous writings on Santiago had also whetted the appetite, especially those of Samuel and Eleanor Lothrop on some of the rituals. The dramatic costume, the women's huge halo-like headband (*cinta*) especially, was another draw to one who would soon succumb to the wealth of textile beauty all over this country.

10.8 Through the good offices of Ellida Cabrera, a young lady who was connected to the Instituto Indigenísta in the city, a couple of rooms were obtained in the house of the school headmaster a block or two from the church and the main plaza. A bedroom giving onto a garden at the back in which a Chicago-purchased camp cot was put down. A front room, giving on to the street, came with a table serving as desk, a simple desk chair, and a camping armchair. A wooden window beside the desk and curious pairs of eyes, both young and old, perpetually hoisted up to the windowsill and staring in at all hours. Desperately needed privacy at times only obtained by shutting that wooden window, especially at night, when reading would take place in the armchair between two candles precariously balanced on its arms. Joyce's

Ulysses borrowed in Panajachel for starters. Food provided by the young wife of the headmaster: black beans, rice, a few greens, incredibly tough chunks of meat—a whole year of vicious heartburn. At night, large spiders all over the walls. But, true enough: every morning, on opening the little window onto the little village huts with the Fuji-pure shape of San Pedro volcano beyond, the recognition that Redfield had been right and that, the stench of trash and excrement in the streets notwithstanding, few places in the whole wide world could be as beautiful as this.

Much fear and anxiety had been suffered before arrival—mainly with the vision of going out and speaking but never being spoken to. For a week to ten days, Tarn pounded the streets, greeting passersby, met by curious stares or complete indifference. He may simply have been taken for a tourist: there were many such coming in on the daily launch. Eventually, however, he was taken up by a group of young men, one Juan Sisay in the lead, with awkward first conversations in one's room; stabs at linguistic education; the first tentative questions, often incredibly inane. One question stands out in memory as blush provoking, to Salvador Sisay, a cousin of Juan's: "What about stories?" "Stories? What kind of stories?" After much waffling, Little Red Riding Hood is offered as an example. Salvador looks very thoughtful. "Well, you see, Don Miguel, there are no wolves in this country—but if there were, I very much doubt that they would talk. . . ."

Eventually, the work, while trying to keep Redfield happy in regard to his concept of worldview, centered on the traditionalists practicing the often extremely secret Maya-Catholic religion and their rivalries with the young Catholic revivalists (headed by Juan Sisay) and the budding Protestant movement then led by another friend, Pedro Ramírez Mendoza. The story was eventually told in a huge, unwieldy "long text" of some seven hundred pages deposited at the University of Chicago and a ninety-nine-page shorter version, the Ph.D. thesis proper. Redfield had intended to publish the latter but died of leukemia before he could; it eventually saw the light many years later in Guatemala City as *Los Escándalos de Maximón* and became a kind of classic quoted by every tourist guide in the country. It was amusing at times to be sitting in a bar or restaurant and hear this going on. Eventually the book was pirated. There was also a very detailed field diary and typed field notes that remain at Stanford in manuscript.

10.9 Fieldwork can be a hard and lonely business. A day goes pleasantly and may have produced some valuable information, some piece of the huge jigsaw puzzle you are, day in/day out, trying to understand. As likely as not, it is followed by a day on which everything fails: an agreeable "informant" sud-denly goes sour; a rendezvous is missed; an action or event announced for one day occurs on another; you have been badly, perhaps deliberately, misled; the new piece of the puzzle (treated to the interminable checking and rechecking with different "informants" any information whatsoever has to be constantly subjected to) is revealed to be useless. Whole days, even weeks can go by with-out any progress made. Sometimes the very notion of "progress" becomes questionable. There are anthropologists who are relentless questioners, who seem to enjoy drilling into people's minds and souls a long time after the "in-formant" has shown signs of weariness, upset, or even anger. Not this one.

Tarn could not do this and often used to say that he should have been an archaeologist: "While stones speak, they do not, on the whole, answer back." Arriving in Burma in 1958—after years of working on the Maya puzzle and having, perhaps, reached one level of the solution (shown to be shal-low in later work in 1979)—he felt something like despair at facing a very sizable new puzzle, packs of blank note cards, and a bare filing box. When he eventually left anthropology, the sense of relief at no longer having to ask questions was overwhelming. Gary Snyder, suggesting in the 1970s the title "From Anthropologist to Informant" for a Tarn interview with him, put his finger on this sense, and Snyder had not even been a full professional anthropologist!

One particular aspect of religious study in Atitlán was especially wearing. The rituals carried out in the warm, comforting, odoriferous, candle-illuminated little *santos* chapels known as *cofradías* had one major drawback. It is part of "service" to the saints that an officer, a male *cofrade* or female *tixel*, should accept at any time of day or night—and even be woken from sleep in order to accept—a drink of the ferocious cane sugar alcohol *aguardiente*, commercial or home-brewed, or a smoke: cigarette or cigar. This acceptance was highly ritualized: the receiver having to thank, in flowery terms, each individual colleague, the saints, and eventually God himself, then usually pulling a long face in real or feigned disgust as the inevitable moment came to take a sip, a gulp, or a drag. Having had enough was never an excuse. General drunken-ness prevailed virtually the whole time, and this time could stretch to three days and nights, or even a whole week, without stop. You would dance to the melodious and heartbreakingly plaintive marimba music; wear your butt out hour after hour on the hard *cofrades* bench; your knees on the hard-packed floor in endless prayers, always in danger of having a colleague weeping on your shoulder, whispering incoherently in your ear, lying asleep across your knees or, at worst, being heavily sick over your ceremonial clothes. I had been instructed to wear the ceremonial woolen black coat and the red scarf of a *principal*: a village ceremonial elder.

10.10 It was necessary to take breaks. You might take walks. One long one involved leaving Santiago at dawn, with thin circular clouds like puffs of smoke surrounding volcano nipples and, after crossing the hill range surrounding the lake, ambling down for several hours through ever-thickening forest toward the Pacific Coast—dreaming of fortunes to be made from the fabulous orchids on the sides of the path if only you could have gotten them back to the States. Spending some time on the archaeological sites of the coast, then two or three days later, the hard trek back up, some seven hours or so. Another walk was the one, in the far North, from Huehuetenango, all the way across hills, valleys, and plains to Todos Santos: again a matter of a whole day. The long walk down from a tall hill into Todos Santos, villagers coming up and kissing your hand under the impression you were a priest. You slept on a table in the church sacristy that night, and it was suggested that you hire a horse to take you back. Anxiety about horses kept you awake all night; you sent a man back with his nag at the crack of dawn and walked all the way back. There was also a trip with the photographer George Holton and his wife to Nebaj—a Quiché village reputed in every guidebook to refuse people who wished to stay overnight. You *did* stay without trouble, sleeping on straw in the municipal hall, waking to find a black widow spider under your waist.

Many of these walks, or bus trips, would involve the acquisition of textiles. You would arrive at a village in the morning, put the word out that you were interested, view items brought to you in the afternoon, and leave by evening. Redfield was generous in providing small sums to feed this passion (the collection is now in the Museum of International Folk Art, Santa Fe, New Mexico). Occasionally, it was possible to go further afield. A rail trip to the Atlantic jungle classic Maya site of Quiriguá with a young woman from the American Embassy (until she was warned off the "foreigner"). A plane trip to another great classic site: Copán, led by the legendary Alfred Kidder, arriving, as it happened, on the day that a Rotary Club was having its picnic but finding Copán so "human" and comfortable that nothing could detract from it. A further plane trip to the Peten jungle site of Tikal. Uncleared in those days. After a night in a hut, hacking your way to Temple Five, sitting at the top, seeing the plane coming back early, scuttling across the jungle so as not to miss it.

Stays in Panajachel provided some relief. A painter, Pat Crocker, who had worked for years on illustrations of Maya costumes and had a beautiful house in town with a fine library, was one host, a difficult one at times with his drinking habits and his sexual orientation, but most kind. The city was another possibility with friends at the French Embassy and boisterous visits to the ladies of the night, after which a five a.m. departure in the bus for Pana and the sun-soaked ride in the boat back to the village were astringent recalls to duty. Anthropologists would come through: Paul Rivet and Henri Lehmann from the Musée de l'Homme among them. In Santiago, Maurice Herzog, "conqueror" of the Annapurna and later French minister of sports, was a very pleasant visitor, as was Alfonso Caso of Mexico City. There were women, encountered on the boat from Panajachel or in the Santiago church, mystified at the sight of a young gringo performing strange ritual tasks with the Natives. One attractive young lady, no longer a girl, was traveling with her mother and turned out to be the daughter of an American general. When she left, too early, for the colonial capital city of Antigua, our anthropologist followed by another boat, chanced to get a small plane ride from the lakeshore to Antigua, and arrived at the ladies' hotel as a very surprising apparition. The general's daughter behaved ungenerously: at her age she should have known better. Undoubtedly, there were other trips, adventures, and encounters, now lying forgotten in the diaries.

10.11 After a year of all this came the time for departure, and a huge drinking bout materialized, starting at nine a.m. in the cemetery over the grave of some friend recently dead and continuing throughout the day in various locations. In the evening, Tarn's friends wrapped an extra belt around his waist—locals tended to drop clothes when under the influence—and marched around the town with several others, ritually shouting "*Solo Dios!*" with index finger pointing upward and setting up much howling: an unholy racket. The headmaster said the next morning that Don Miguel had been taken for an Atiteco. Some thirty glasses of highest-proof alcohol, much of it mixed with 100 percent chili juice, acted as an absolute purge, thus avoiding the mother of all hangovers. Never ones to waste anything, Juan Sisay and friends arrived to take away sheets and other household things left behind, carried Tarn's huge wooden box of textiles and goodies down to the boat, and saw him off for the last time. At the city, the box was handed over to Pan American Airlines.

Further travels were in order. Stops in Mexico. The first flight was from Guatemala City to San Cristóbal de las Casas. Tarn had never expected to see the lake again, and suddenly there he was—in a prop plane with some degree of leisure—flying over the lake from the Pana side northwest toward Chiapas. Came as shock, almost as heartbreak, yet with a curious sensation that this was a promise that you would return. In fact, for years afterward, a frequent dream: setting out for the lake, the whole long journey to reach it, then being prevented by something from actually crossing to Santiago.

At San Cristóbal, visit to the Danish anthropologist Franz Blom and Gertrude, his photographer wife. A very large colonial house surrounding an equally large patio. The huge sitting room full of masks and other splendid things, many suspended from the ceiling. Visiting the chapel under restoration, marveling at the patio as large as a village square. Blom's European gentility.

On toward Oaxaca. The idea was to travel by bus at night so as to be able to tour, visit, and work during the day. First sight of the mighty Zapotec ruins of Monte Albán. Purchase of a rough woolen Oaxacan blanket, black with white borders and a huge red sun in the middle. A ceramic candelabrum also—which arrived in a hundred pieces in London, was stuck together by Mother, and survived for many years. Somewhere on the journey north, sensing that the weather was too warm and giving a fine heavy sweater to a pauper. The next dawn, freezing: out of the bus and into some hovel of a hotel, burrowing deep into the bottom of a bed, taking an hour or more to get warm.

Mérida, the Yucatán. Chichen Itza and Uxmal, the latter especially impressive for its architectural styles and its great solitudes. Again, the luxury of seeing great sites by oneself. There was news here of Alberto Ruz l'Huillier opening the great tomb at Palenque that very moment. Thoughts of taking a train there and realization that there simply was not enough money in hand. Somehow, Pan Am had been persuaded to send the big box of "ethnographic samples" for free to Mérida, last stop in Mexico before New Orleans. Hours spent in the Mérida office getting the box to go on for free to the States. Moneyless. Broke. Decision to try to sell one pair of boots and one photographic tripod. Stand in a street. Boots useless in this place and every photographer already in possession of a tripod. No alternative to begging for a meal. By chance, fall upon the French owner of a restaurant, who very kindly obliges with a dinner.

In New Orleans, finally, something has to be paid for the box. Arrive in Chicago with little more than a nickel in hand.

Holland America Line ship *Rotterdam* back to England. Catch a filthy cold from all the going in and out of air conditioning in Chicago and New York, also on the ship.

G1.01 Author, Mother, Neville. Paris, 1930s.

G1.02 (*top left*) Father. 1930s.   G1.03 (*top right*) Favorite Uncle Harry. Hyderabad, India, World War II.   G1.04 (*bottom*) Author. King's College, Cambridge, 1945.

GI.05 Patricia. London, 1960s. PHOTO: NATHANIEL TARN.

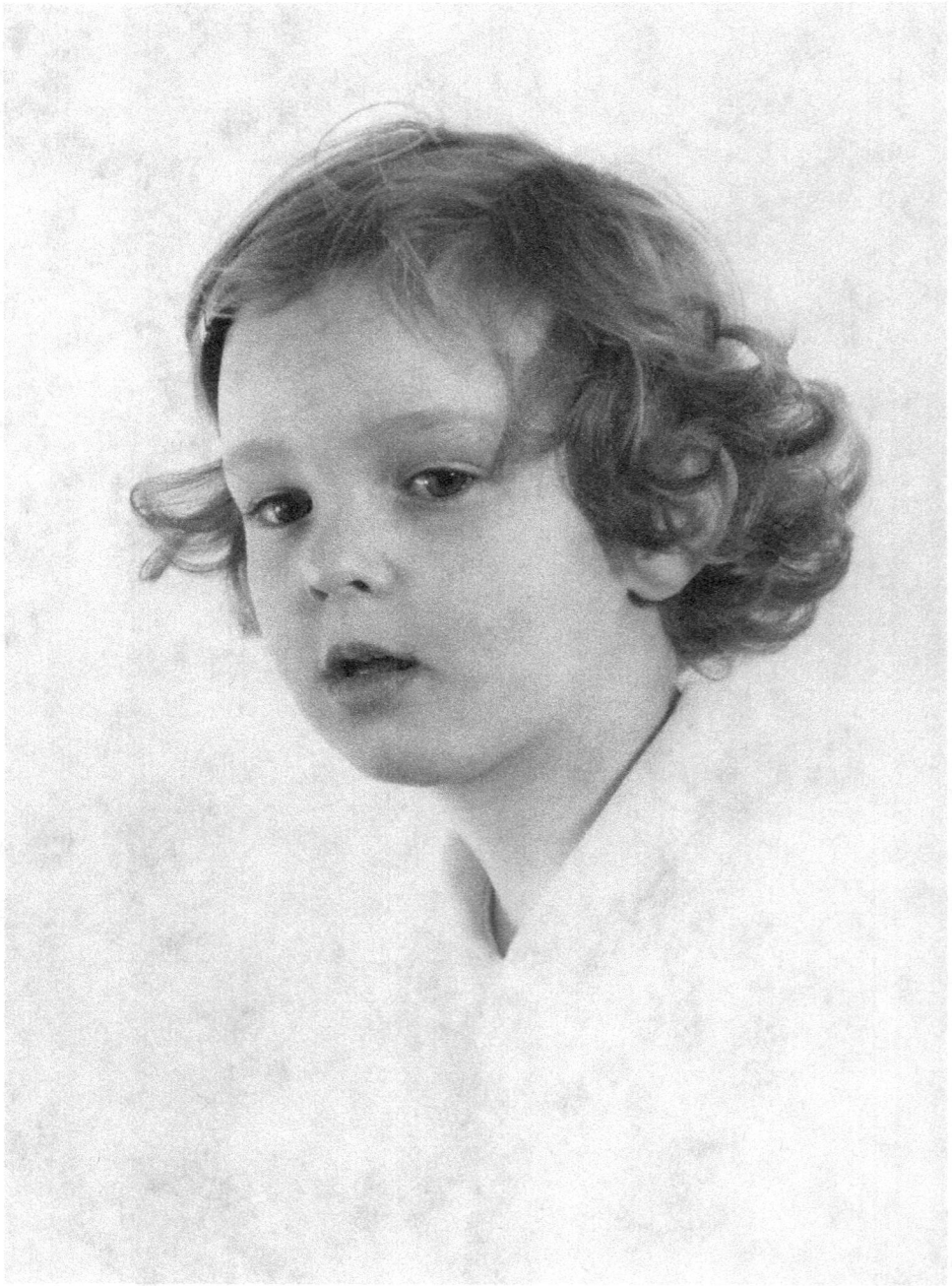

GI.06 Andrea. London, 1964. PHOTO: RICHARD CHOWEN.

G1.07 Henri and Nō Seigle, painters. Paris, 1964.   G1.08 (*bottom left*) Nicolas Chiviliu, principal, shaman. Santiago Atitlán, 1952–79. PHOTO: JANET RODNEY   G1.09 (*bottom right*) Author. Amarapura, Burma, 1950s. PHOTO: PATRICIA.

G1.10 Patricia with spirit wives. Taungbyon, Burma, 1950s. PHOTO: NATHANIEL
TARN.

Throw Eleven

II.I Santiago Atitlán, circa 1952. A calm evening is wrenched apart by a sudden storm of words shouted in a high-pitched female voice just outside my window. Has she gone mad? Open the window and see a young person standing awkwardly with a basket on her head, her extended arm caught at the wrist by a young man wearing a panama hat. The female—no more than a girl in her late teens as I now realize—continues to shout: even had my Tz'utujil been better than it was, I doubt I could have understood much of that fiery torrent. By looking closer, I now make out that the youth is also giving voice, albeit very low and, it seems, very sheepishly. It does not look as if he is holding the girl's wrist with enough strength to forbid movement: it is clear that she prefers shouting her imprecations to any escape. The boy, for his part, looks thoroughly miserable: he has obviously been ordered, by relatives, custom, or love, to hold his ground. The pair thus stands locked in a conspiracy, reminiscent of the way in which street dogs are locked together after coitus, turned away from each other, back to back, looking shamefacedly at passersby and panting—although dogs have the good grace to keep silent.

I have just witnessed my first Atiteco declaration of love. This awesome scene, which usually takes place on the Lakeshore as the girls fetch water in the evenings—the boys lying in wait along the steep paths—is apparently de rigueur even in those cases (and there have to be some) in which the girl is not impervious to the boy's charms. The torrent of language attests to her outraged maidenhood (notwithstanding the fact that premarital sex is frequent); it is evoked a number of times if the boy persists, after which, upon some sign from the girl, the boy's elders begin visiting the girl's, and a new set of rituals impels the young couple into matrimony. At these meetings, the girl continues to make herself scarce and to serve the guests if need be only with a show of the utmost distaste and reluctance.

Whatever else it may suggest—and this, to me traumatic, scene led to a series of hypotheses on the role of sex in the Christo-pagan worldview of the Maya that became important to my work—I here use the event to introduce the general topic of plain versus ornery speaking in public and private affairs. The life of "indigenous" or "preliterate" folk, note, is not necessarily characterized by an overabundance of plain speech. On the contrary, recalling the interminable powwows that usually precede, among such peoples, the act of coming to the point in any important matter whatsoever, we may surmise that devious speech (the art of a Ulysses), ample rhetoric, and even downright hypocrisy undoubtedly play their part in achieving any semblance of consensus or unanimity. It is a matter of whether you want your democracy to preserve the appearance of healthy dissent natural to any large concourse of beings or whether you require the living universe to be satisfied only by the semblance of absolute unity on every issue. There are times for a yes and times for a no. The whole question is how you say these two words with the minimum, or maximum, of hurt to an interlocutor and the ears in the surrounding bushes, trees, rivers, and mountains.

11.2 Are we approaching the realm of courtesy and manners? It may be so. My parents, bless them, tried for a lifetime to coat my rebellious and dyspeptic demeanor with a veneer of good manners. They still mutter today, staring hard at the small boy skulking in a forty-six-year-old frame, that I have spent most of my existence dragging down the finest possible "bringing up." Best schools, best teachers, best models to emulate. Lodged first in a culture renowned for courtesy (until modernity's frenzies gripped *le gentilhomme français*), then propelled by war's hazards into the culture of the gentleman par excellence, dear old ruler of the waves, Britannia's. The British have always addressed the waves with the greatest respect, thus ensuring, until the much-needed breakdown of empire, a long and prosperous imperial history as well as occupations for the best families' scions. Over the years, I grew to understand that the word "sorry" was the imperial keystone of British manners. England is a country in which you apologize to someone who has just trodden on your toe or knocked you sideways on the platform of a public bus. Also one in which you thank your tormentor schoolmaster when he has just thrashed the living daylights out of you by a well-administered beating with a cane. I had finally come to wonder whether the appalling grayness that had settled on the British in the wake of World War II had not come about as the result of a new imbalance between the ex-ruler and the ex-ruled. Suddenly, there was, in short, no longer an empire to be polite to while enjoying the fruits of its sweating backs. As a result, the natural aggressiveness hidden in the politeness backfired upon the unfortunate upper castes so that they spent most of the postwar years gnawing at their own vitals and louring at their compatriots in streets, theaters, restaurants, offices, or shops. It was only the relative cheapness of life in Europe that might prevent Americans from seeing America first, but in the Olde Countrie, leisurely, courtly, and accommodating travel abroad was no longer on offer.

11.3   As a student in the United States in 1951–53, I had no special occasion to give thought to American manners: they did not appear to be dissimilar to those I was used to in Europe. One even got habituated to the honorable petting and necking ethos: I realized on seeing Bogdanovich's movie *The Last Picture Show* that, for some strange reason, the ethos experienced in its culture had formed the basis of a sense of America as *home* and the eventual call to a return from exile. Of this more later. By 1970, youth had discovered itself in America to the extent of waging a noticeable war on its parents in the form of the "counterculture." Women had discovered their rights and were leaders in this—alas not a revolution, but still a rebellion. So had a host of "minorities." The streets were no longer safe, nor were classrooms nor teachers' offices nor beds. Trains no longer ran on time—if slums on wheels could still merit being called trains; the intelligence of burrokrassies had suffered permanent deconstruction, and everyone had at one and the same time found a voice so that nothing could be heard distinctly anywhere. It even became mandatory to discuss the life of academia with students, to allow them into the councils of the professoriate in all matters ranging from promotions to course structure and to beg for their evaluations of teaching at the end of each semester. This led later to the mania of asking for "surveys." Where in the universe could a righteous man (query: "universe"; query: "righteous"; query: "man") lay his weary head?

It was impossible to follow a person through a door—especially a swing or revolving door—with any hope of its being held open long enough to avoid disfigurement. Holding a door open long enough for a woman to precede you would occasion either an unpleasant snigger or, if the woman were old enough, an astonished gasp of thanks and a distant look of memorization, as if the lady in question were an Australian Aborigine suddenly coming face to face with the dreamtime.

On more than one occasion, the public highway suddenly became a living hell. One day, in Princeton, I parked my car, slowly and carefully enough it seemed to me, in a public parking lot. A black face intruded upon the driver's open window, preceded by a large fist, and voiced the intent to bash my teeth in because I had, unwittingly of course, grazed the owner of the head's spouse on the street just before entering the lot. I was called a "faggot" in the same ritual of aggression and, not knowing how widespread this usage had become, was left to wonder what on Earth had had the time to be noted in my demeanor to occasion this comment. Until it dawned on me that this was "racial conflict." Around this very time I had attended "Black Power" meetings on campus and been frisked by the uniformed guards. Many years later: astonished at finding the whole archive of the Panthers on the shelves of Stanford Library.

11.4 New York City, circa 1952. Walking along Broadway, or was it Fifth, I spy in the window of a men's clothing store some attractive neckties at an affordable price. The ties are black with yellow letters on them, and the letters are Greek. Enter the store and begin choosing among the ties, while salesmen hover nearby. "Tell me," I ask a salesman, "can these ties be purchased by anyone?" A look of utter astonishment steals over the man's face. I explain hastily that I am assuming these ties refer to campus fraternities. In England, I continue, there are such things as regimental: college and old-school ties. The whole point of such ties is to serve as instruments of recognition between members or ex-members of such groups. The system would, of course, collapse into nonsense if any Tom, Dick, or Harry were to flaunt these ties. (To this day this custom obtains, and one can even be publicly accused of usurpation if such has occurred.)

The salesman ignores these explanations. With the patient look of a missionary explaining the mysteries of the Trinity to a naked savage, he proceeds to expound the basic tenets of democracy as it pertains to the free market. The discourse swells—the man is obviously a graduate—and expands into a general condemnation of every nation in the world that is not the good old U.S. of A. and ends, after some asides to the effect that no harm is intended, no slur upon Britain especially, in a round of expletives denoting that he, the salesman, would rather be roasted in Hell than see any legal clause enacted in the Congress, the Senate, or the Supreme Court whereby any individual in the whole expanse of this Great Land should see himself forbidden to purchase any necktie that caught his goddam fancy. Conciliatory by now as any missionary, I hastily buy a tie and retreat into the streets.

11.5 Two different readings of the word "democracy." In the 1950s it is clear that a caste-ridden society across the Atlantic (namely Britain) faces a caste-less society (you are still supposed to believe) on this American side of the "pond." When does the world lose its innocence? My parents speak of the end of time as taking place in 1914: Europe loses its charm forever as well as its manners. To us, from this vantage point in the 1970s, the world loses its innocence between 1939 and Vietnam.

Britain, I have long felt, bears the brunt of World War II and is unable ever to catch up. There is no rest, no respite. Deprivations continue: rationing and the end of empire. The minorities and the workers awake, home from the wars in which the blood of Cockney batmen has flowed in the same channels as the blood of their county officers. A poet or two arises in the provincial wilds, challenging with excoriating accents the supremacy of London. Britain begins to listen to itself on stage in the words of proletarians like the "Angry Young Men." The social structure falls apart, or pretends very efficiently to fall apart; sheer weariness does the rest. This weariness also contributes to the decline of English gentility. I speak of gentility on the streets—the matter of courtesy and politeness—for, in poetry, Britain had died so to speak in the arms of William Blake or, if one wishes to be charitable, in those of Gerard Manley Hopkins or perhaps (why not?) in those of T. S. Eliot.

In "vital" fields such as trade, commerce, political, and burrokrasstic alliances, it is necessary to do one of two things. Either you can shore up the ruins with a pretense at good manners that will keep the oil flowing and the consumer running or you can pretend that the society is not disintegrating at all, that the old virtues of individualism are merely exasperated by ever more troublesome times—and continue to pretend that all is well with courtesy. In the end it is all one. The more you are assaulted in the streets and in public places, the more mellifluous the voices become on radio and television. And because these are the stuff that our dreams are made on, public parlance also waxes, day by day, more nonsensical.

11.6 In all countries, at all times, there are purists sitting in the editorial offices of dictionaries, academic presses, and libraries whose life task it is to deplore the downfall of the current language and to propose countermeasures. The US is no exception, and there have been many critics to point out that the media (is!) ruining us. Nor is this the only country: a book could be filled with jokes about B.B.C. English. Here the anthropologist must keep a sense of balance. A changing language is not necessarily a language in decadence. In the ever-accelerating mobility of US fashion, the language and its slangs evolve with bewildering, albeit invigorating rapidity. The media, of course, is always caught in the act of catching up. This manifestation, known as "co-optation" by the radically minded, consists of the sudden appearance of items of slang and subgroup lingos among the ads that are the staple of commercial broadcasting. Of course, the ads themselves are sometimes the source of creativity. By and large: is the media behind or in advance of the language? Hard to know.

11.7 In keeping with the thesis that the media conspires to maintain alive a vision of a unified society where none exists, we can locate the major enemy. Its name is euphemism: the substitution of a mild, indirect, or vague expression for one seen as offensively harsh or blunt. Mildness, indirectness, and vagueness are the very characteristics that most blunt a language, and the degree to which the English language is finally being blunted in the United States is nothing short of disastrous. In fact, there is a need for a concept in language akin to the concept that has grown up around the need to preserve our physical environment. We need to talk not only of physical, but also of mental or cultural, pollution.

There was at one time, and there remains in many parts of the huge country, a tradition of blunt American speech: folk speech as opposed to consumerized speech. The latter is found mostly in burrokrasstic, technocrasstic, academic, and political circles and their oceans of jargon. Jargon here: a new terminology evolved not so much because no language exists at a given time to account for new developments and discoveries (where jargon would be legitimate) but because some wish the right to work in a certain field to be limited to a certain elite. Lectures, speeches, seminars, briefings, orientations, conferences, and their publications have become not only hard to follow sometimes but mainly satanically boring. The omnipresent lack of precision and incisiveness often makes one wonder whether anyone is any longer capable of sheer thought.

11.8 In the fifties, at Chicago, I was impressed by the extent to which the American student or teacher always seemed willing to keep open, or to reopen, any given question. Sometimes ad infinitum. The culturally continuing tendency to "rap" and the belief that any problem can be talked to a conclusion if verbally manipulated for a sufficient length of time does make you wonder, though, whether this is not part of the decadence. In the end, will any amount of talking take the place of real thought? I am not, in these seventies, unknown to be hard on students when blather seems to me to be substituting itself for a hard workout of the gray matter.

Just how much is euphemism responsible for all this? How much is linguistic vagueness a result of a desire not to offend? I have wondered whether the absence of *philo* (with its search for truth as overriding any desire to please) in American education played a role here. There is nothing evil in the desire not to offend, and in many cultures this desire is not only carried to very great lengths but is very clearly linked to individual or group survival. The question of how much one can ever trust any interlocutor, of course, will have to loom large as the obverse of this.

At the end of the Nixon era, the voice of Senator Sam Ervin achieving its enormous impact by bringing the hills and the wilds back into American speech with the vengefulness of a whole people outraged by the sordid activities of its leaders. Just as in the first years of the new millennium the voice of Senator Robert Byrd. But the daily experience of talking to the average citizen? No change. The academic chairman unwilling to tell me frankly about a negative response to my application for promotion, the trader reluctant to point out how shabby some aspect of my domesticity in need of his attention has become, the young woman shy of letting me know that my advances are not likely to be reciprocated—all speak with the voice of the traditional friend, whose cosmic task it is to be responsible for telling you that your breath is not as fresh as it should be on this fine spring morning. I confess that I still fail to understand my new compatriots much of the time because I do not believe that they are telling me exactly what they think.

Of course, there is the matter of the code. How often has someone not been able to understand me because I was not using the code appropriate to a given situation or transaction? Codes, of course, are responsive to changes and evolutions in language, slang, and economic-political diction, but is not their overall effect that of narrowing the bands within which language can operate at any time and in any space? Is the linguistic aspect of American Anglophilia ("Oh, I can never get enough of listening to your voice") dependent on a perceived lexical versatility of the Brit? Do codes not work against linguistic inventiveness, set the mind in unmovable grooves, strangle the very evolution of thought itself? And is it not this, when all is said and done, that made the sixties counterculture, tragically, into a rebellion rather than a revolution: the sheer absence of clear, above all organized, thinking?

Perhaps we have to go right back to de Tocqueville for all this and his fears concerning the "tyranny of the majority." Or we can invoke Ralph Waldo Emerson on "our smooth times." How about the following in "Self-Reliance": "Well, most men have bound their eyes with one or another handkerchief, and attached themselves to some one of these communities of opinion. This conformity makes them not false in a few particulars, authors of a few lies, but false in all particulars. Their every truth is not quite true. Their two is not the real two, their four not the real four, so that every word they say chagrins us, and we know not where to begin to set them right. . . . We come to wear one cut of face and figure, and acquire by degrees the gentlest asinine expression." Emerson continues by writing of "the forced smile which we put on in company where we do not feel at ease in answer to conversation which does not interest us. The muscles not spontaneously moved, but moved by a low usurping willfulness, grow tight about the outline of the face with the most disagreeable sensation." Were we Americans lost as far back as that?

In the nineties now, and in the new millennium, I am exhausted by the number of times I have to listen to the interminable blather of consumer society. Do I have to "enjoy my beverage" or "a pleasant experience" or "a flight" almost any time I breathe? Am I "mandated" to "have a good morning, a good afternoon, a good or wonderful night" every day of the century? It can get worse: "Enjoy the end of your day," "Enjoy the rest of your telephone call." Am I forced to respond to any inquiry whatsoever that "I am feeling just fine" when in fact I feel like hell and hate the inquirer? How many zillions of times do I have to be told that my call "is very important to us" when it is clear that the "us" hardly gives a flying fuck about the call? Is there a mind behind these statements, these inquiries? *La donna de la mia mente?*

(I am amused by the recent order to the French population that it should greet anyone with a hearty *Bonjour*! as an antidote to the perceived massive impoliteness of said population [bad for tourism], especially the Parisian. God forbid that one should forget to say it! And how forcibly one is reminded to come up with it pronto if one happens to have forgotten! [Disease can also be French!])

It is the business of the poet, in my view, to be as precise, as exact, as clear as possible whenever s/he writes, indeed whenever s/he utters any word at all. This does not necessarily have to interfere with any inventiveness whether lexical, syntactic, or semantic. I have been gratified by hearing a New Mexican Hispanic young woman friend of mine say, "Whenever I have been speaking to you, I feel that my language has widened." Although I can be horrified by it, I can also be pleased when another young woman, anywhere on the continent, asks "You mean you are not only a poet but a *published* poet? Oh, may I *touch* you?" Perhaps the sense that the poet defends against cancer of the language is responsible for the strange nostalgia that drives so many young people to wish to be poets—when the rewards for such a vocation are as pathetic, indeed as obscenely insignificant, as they are in a country whose language should be, and is not, its primary and everlasting treasure?

There was once a pithy, straightforward, and colorful American speech with manifold regional variations. It now seems to be lost on politicians and burrokrassts. Seeing, or listening to, a great many politicians in Congress today is a sickening experience. The impression remains that they have a vocabulary of some 150 words, not more, and that they repeat over and over the same coded messages—so that such witnessing one day is exactly the same as witnessing sixty days later. Beyond the business item of the moment, nothing in the discourse ever changes. The interminable repetition of pieties about "this great land," "our inalienable freedoms," etc. etc. etc. at, for instance, election conventions can become nauseating. Their invocations to the "Murrikan pipple" I find especially atrocious when it is abundantly clear that most of them don't give a damn about such a giant but are only thinking of the next scuffle between themselves and the "other side of the aisle." It is becoming more and more obvious that the process is in decline and that the Murrikan people have less and less trust in their representatives. Another huge problem is that of expertise among our political classes. What do these people *know* that allows them to pretend to *think*? A beloved car sticker of mine: "One nation under . . . educated." Who puts these people in power? The decline of our political classes, as abundantly manifest in the language used, will drive this empire to its end. Someone with great authority needs to lecture them about *language*.

Later comes the thought that "civility" rules the roost because the roost is a fundamentally violent place. One ends up by being afraid of saying what one thinks because the response is likely to be frightening. America, as one knows through its intolerable support of guns, is a violent country.

By the twenty-twenties manners have disappeared here altogether. Either one is blindly thanked to death in code. Or else virtually no one truly thanks anyone in language for anything. No one answers a call, a letter, an email unless there is deep friendship or business need, and folks—knowing that everyone is perpetually "busy" and have less time than you have for any kind of contact—allow matters go by until kingdom come. Know that the same lament is also heard these days in other "civilized" countries. We are not alone.

Throw Twelve

12.1 In theory, Tarn should have returned to Paris after the Guatemalan work: had the Fulbright rules not mandated return, he might well have stayed on in the United States. However, writing poetry in French had not worked out. Diaries had been kept in French until Atitlán, but English had to come back in for anthropological purposes. It began to be very clear that the future lay with English/or/American. During the stay on the Lake, a correspondence had somehow begun with Sasha Moorsom, a brilliant young Cambridge graduate and actress, sister to friend Christopher. She had been met with once when she visited Cambridge as a teenager and enchanted the whole group: it was discovered that she had been holding hands under the tea table with both David Rowse and Tarn. The increasingly romantic nature of the correspondence was part of the decision to go back to London. A return to the parental household at 164 Montagu Mansions, just off Baker Street, afforded a room, a desk, a bookcase, and maternal care. On the very day of arrival, however, parents were surprised by "something that had to be done urgently" in town. Sasha, having hidden a little while to observe her new beau, finally sat down at a café table in Chelsea. Her fresh, foxy, ravishing beauty was as overwhelming as a sunburst. A slight touch of an American accent in the new arrival was immediately commented on with surprise and, perhaps, some slight distaste.

12.2 French nationality was reluctantly abandoned but would have meant a couple of years of military service as well as other responsibilities. A necessary visit to a doctor arranged by the French Embassy in London resulted in the following sliver of dialogue: "Where do you wish to make your home?" "In this country." "In which case, there does not seem to be much point in the French Army for you?" "Doctor, that is not for me to say." "Off you go— you are dismissed."

A period of uncertainty followed, during which continued studies while writing the Ph.D. thesis and the establishment of contacts with British anthropologists seemed to be the path to follow. Visits to Cambridge and to the London School of Economics ensued. The question of poetry, which had never bothered anyone in Redfield's circle, could not help coming up. At Cambridge, Professor Meyer Fortes, a distinguished theoretician and Africanist, declared in the strongest possible terms that poetry should never enter into an anthropological discussion and, indeed, that "the sooner it was completely buried and its energies allowed to metamorphose underground and to come up again as anthropological enquiry, the better." British social anthropology was still in its formative stages and extremely ascetic, as well as nationalistic. It was at this point that the definitive split in public identity occurred and the habit of assuming pen names, acquired in France as part of a well-established European tradition, was once and for all adopted.

The London School of Economics (L.S.E.) down in the Strand became a home from home. Seminars were followed with Raymond Firth (Polynesia), Isaac Schapera (Africa), and visiting professor S. F. Nadel (music, Africa)—all of them important theoreticians. Other teachers included Maurice Freedman (Chinese in Southeast Asia).

The affair with Sasha lasted about a year. She eventually shared an apartment in Eaton Square with a young friend, Venetia. Tarn lived with her part of the time, and there were visits to Sasha's separated parents in the country. The father, Raisley Moorsom, was a very kind, eccentric, old-fashioned gentleman, an alumnus of King's, Cambridge, descended from William Wordsworth and owning some letters of the poet's. One vacation was taken in the South of France, staying with the Seigle in Penne du Tarn and moving on to stay with friends of Sasha's in Grasse and St. Paul de Vence. At the time, Sasha had a job as a producer at the B.B.C. and a couple of programs of "primitive" poetry were created with her help. She tried to interest the B.B.C. poet Roy Fuller in Tarn's work without any success whatsoever.

Problems arose when Tarn's father insisted that if marriage were to be contemplated, Sasha would have to convert to Judaism. Tarn foolishly agreed. She made a brave attempt and attended lessons with a rabbi, but her heart was not in it. Eventually came the dreadful evening in Sloane Square when Sasha broke off the relationship. Tarn fled to the Seigle in Penne, where he remained for several weeks, walking the Causse hills daily, becoming as thin as a rake, fighting spiders at night in a stone hut he had borrowed and working himself into a very strange experience that occurred on a visit to Toulouse. Sasha, not seen for many years, eventually married the sociologist Michael Young (later a famous Labor peer); wrote novels; lived for a time in Africa; visited Santa Fe once with her daughter, a Buddhist nun, in the eighties; and died of cancer in the nineties.

On returning to London, life with parents in Montagu Mansions appeared to be impossible. A room was obtained in an apartment rented by the Spillius couple in Chelsea. Somewhat influenced by the Seigle, who argued, during a Paris visit, that he should make a solid marriage as a basis for the scholarly and writing life, Tarn agreed to be introduced to a young woman by friends of his parents, a Viennese-born gynecologist Dr. Alfred Loeser and his wife. Patricia Renate Cramer—tall, strikingly beautiful, elegantly dressed, and very shy, the sole surviving child of a German refugee couple living in Northwood near London—met, at the Loesers' on January 1, 1956, a young anthropologist wearing bright-red socks but otherwise conventionally dressed. After a short and exciting courtship, they were married with much pomp and ceremony during the summer of that year and honeymooned in Positano, returning to live in an apartment rented from the art critic John Russell in St. John's Wood. From there, a move followed to 18 Manchester Street not far from Montagu Mansions.

12.3 A conference of the Historians of Religion Association in Rome, shortly after marriage, was a pleasant occasion. Rome and its sites! At the event, Christof von Furer Haimendorf of the School of Oriental & African Studies, London, a future boss, extended an invitation to join him on a visit to the great *Condotierre* Guiseppe Tucci, a Tibetologist living in a square building's palatial apartment surrounding a vast courtyard. Every one of the great many rooms in that apartment was full of glass cases containing hundreds, perhaps thousands, of valuable Buddhist statuettes while the maestro's study contained the whole front wall of a Tibetan temple! His reputation as a vacuum cleaner, going through the Himalayas sweeping up everything in sight, was obviously justified, and there was in addition the extensive collections of the Oriental Institute (I.S.M.E.O.) he directed in the city. Two salient adventures were owed to Marcel Griaule, traveling with Germaine Dieterlen and Monique, the divorced wife of the French Arctic specialist Robert Gessain. One was a special dispensation's visit to the basement of the Vatican, recently excavated, where ancient statues and architectural features were radiant with an unbelievable freshness as if made and erected on the day before. Another was a furious ride in a sports car at four a.m. to get to the painted Etruscan tombs in the countryside at dawn: here, descent from the floor of the fields into the springtime freshness of these funereal monuments was an astounding experience. Other Etruscan visits occurred, Griaule being in the best of humor and loosing his wicked sarcasm on all the old lady tourists we came across.

It is always difficult to write a thesis while fully occupied with graduate studies (or later with teaching and administration), but "Religion and World View in Santiago Atitlán, Guatemala" was finally completed in several hundred pages, and the determining oral examination, which had had to wait an inordinately long time for a visit from a member of the Chicago faculty (Fred Eggan eventually), took place in Isaac Schapera's apartment not long before the wedding. Tarn was tortured in the greatest possible detail for three hours, after which Eggan broke out the whiskey, blithely suggesting that the exam had been a mere formality and a piece of cake! A major shock occurred on the very morning of Tarn's wedding in the shape of a letter from Redfield, hoping that his missive would arrive in time for congratulations but specifying that the thesis itself would have to be reduced to one hundred pages so that it could be published with two others in a book envisaged by the maestro. With bravura, the "long text" (now a Chicago microfilm) was later abridged down to ninety-nine pages, but Redfield died before executing his plan. Tarn spent the whole reception, at the Savoy hotel, discussing the problem with his L.S.E. professors: the wedding photos show a tip of the letter protruding from a stricken Tarn's tuxedo jacket. The abridgment was eventually published as *Los Escandalos de Maximón* in Guatemala City, whereas the "long text" became praised as "foundational" by subsequent investigators at Santiago and began to be purchased by important libraries.

There had been other chores: the Chicago Ph.D. was extraordinarily tough and required two minor theses as well as a major one. Mircea Eliade was no longer on the faculty, but Tarn wrote for Joachim Wach, who had succeeded him. A curious episode: before this was settled, Tarn was sitting at the terrace of a Paris café in St. Germain des Prés. A gentleman sat down a few tables in front of him. Strangely enough, the name Wach came to mind. A waiter was sent over with a query: the gentleman was Wach. Tarn introduced himself. That is how one minor thesis was planned.

Two memories of Manchester Street, one trivial, the other not so trivial. Patricia had never learned to cook and was occupied one lunchtime with the business of making a tomato dish in the small kitchen. Tarn stood in the wooden frame of the doorway and, on Patricia announcing that she had succeeded for the first time in some cooking maneuver, decided to show his approbation by jumping. His head hit the top of the door frame with such violence that he fell to the floor almost senseless. Some celebration! The other souvenir, more substantial, involves the American anthropologist Margaret Mead, who was lecturing in London. Anxious to secure some help with his Burma plans, our student had contrived to invite her to Manchester Street. Her schedule would allow only breakfast. Once all were seated, Tarn began to pour out his problems (this was before the Chatham House grant had turned up). After listening for a while, the redoubtable lady said something like "Young man, I came here to hear about your work in Guatemala, and you have been boring me to death for the last half hour with your financial problems." There was a split second in which to decide whether to collapse to the floor in absolute defeat and humiliation or whether to realize that this was said in good part and to react accordingly. The latter was achieved, and a no-holds-barred discussion followed during which Tarn criticized the ways in which the professional hierarchy subjugated the graduate student body to its own ends. The day was saved, and Mead became willing to help, although, in fact, nothing ever came of that.

12.4 Of greatest importance became the question of what to do and where to go to continue a fieldworking career. The desire had always been for work on Buddhism in the East. A Mahāyāna area would have been preferred: either Japan or the Himalayas. Raymond Firth found various arguments for promoting Burma: among others the languages and cultures in the desired areas were so very complex. But the *main* ploy was that the London University School of Oriental and African Studies (S.O.A.S.) needed a Southeast Asia person, and Tarn would fit right in. Eventually, the back- and spirit-breaking tasks of obtaining a grant had to be initiated. The Royal Institute of International Affairs (Chatham House) was approached, and it secured a grant from the Rockefeller Foundation. The topic that Chatham House wanted covered concerned the political role of the monkhood in Burma—a subject that had been mentioned over and over in colonial times but that no one had ever documented in detail. The grant came through, but the matter stumbled on Tarn's lack of awareness of the custom for a mediating institution to take a cut for itself ("administrative purposes"), and he was scandalized and furious when the grant figures were revealed. Firth had to convene a peace meeting at the Atheneum Club, during which misunderstandings were cleared up. Even after this, interminable burrokrasstic palavers and maneuvers were needed before finding out whether entry into Burma would be allowed. Miracles of highwire ambiguity had to be performed in order to coordinate acquisitions and purchases while yet ignorant of the fate of visa applications and sailing dates. A period of studying Pāli (with Professor Jaini, later of Berkeley) and Burmese, first with an old colonial service officer, later with Drs. Hla Pe and Anna Allott, then followed for both Patricia and her husband, although only the latter worked on Pāli. The equipment needed for an eighteen-month stay had to be amassed and packed, the main item being a Land Rover car that was barely seen before being unloaded at Rangoon. There was also the small matter of getting a driving license. In mid-1958, the fatal day finally dawned, and the young couple was escorted by Tarn's parents to Liverpool and embarked on the Bibby Line ship *Derbyshire*, a very old tub that had served the Raj for a great many decades and still bore a map of the one-time empire on the front deck. A five week-long journey ensued. After a stormy and sickening start, the lights of Algiers gargling in the depths of its bay granted a first exotic sight, followed by the Suez Canal, whose main excitement was provided by a great Italian cruise ship steaming in the opposite direction. Someone had an Italian menu on board, and the contrast with the Bibby food—it was rumored that the purser sometimes purloined the goods and sold them in ports—could not have been more painful. Part of a day was spent wandering around Port Sudan, and then came Aden, with some purchases of camera equipment and other duty-free stuff, followed by the Indian Ocean. There was precious little to do on board, but the Tarns had secured copies of the first three volumes of Lawrence Durrell's new *Alexandria Quartet* and were entranced by them. A mincing British Council officer returning from leave—who was to play quite a role in later days—provided some entertainment and information. Tarn had planned a two-week stopover in Sri Lanka (then Ceylon) with the aim of

108

THROW TWELVE

visiting a number of archaeological sites, mainly those of Sigiriya and Anuradhapura. Alas, a coup (arriving for coups was something of a specialty of his) had just occurred, and all he got in the end was a couple of hours touring Colombo more or less under guard in a military truck.

In Rangoon, lodgings were at first in a British Council house dominated by a young musician: this was the mincing gentleman of the ship. He was especially trying at mealtimes, never offering a single sliver or sip of any of the delicacies he found it easy to obtain from a commissariat and then guzzling them, discoursing ceaselessly while the Tarns had to make do with the wretched concoctions provided by the host's cook. One of Patricia's first jobs was learning to deal with this individual and his bookkeeping. Contacts, plans, and projects were being elaborated and the city reconnoitered. On her first walk through a Burmese street, Patricia absolutely refused to lift her eyes from the pavement and traversed the whole length of it clutching her husband's hand. Eventually, she became completely accustomed to the routine and shared every aspect of most of Tarn's travels, actions, and visitations—becoming more and more of a partner in the work. Much more agreeable quarters were eventually found in the home of Geoffrey and Katherine Bates: the spacious home with its servants and excellent kitchen, together with a large garden and daily tea, became a source of great comfort. A Rangoon home routine was established, including a ritual *kaukswe* Sino-Burmese meal followed by heavy sleep at the weekends and visits to the Swimming Club's pool, where, sooner or later, all foreigners including social scientists gathered. Members of the American Asia Foundation were there most times, and David Steinberg and his wife became firm friends. The distinguished Sinologist Wolfram Eberhardt was a frequent visitor. Another weekend ritual took place at the home of the Bloomsbury Group member who became Burma's godlike archaeologist, Gordon Luce. He shared the home with his Burmese wife, Daw Tee Tee Luce (this is the Wikipedia spelling!), a very distinguished social worker who ran a place for juvenile criminals (including the occasional murderer) in her house, and with the great political scientist J. S. Furnivall. On Saturday evenings, Luce would bring out his old gramophone and play classical music from Bach to Shubert (never beyond) in chronological order from one January 1 to the next. It was here that Tarn first learned to listen to music intensively, with no other matter in mind. On Sunday evenings, there were readings with all visitors taking part, these ranging from Shakespeare's plays to the stories of Thomas Love Peacock.

12.5 Any fieldwork difficulties experienced in Guatemala were dwarfed to the point of ridicule by those encountered in Burma. Had Tarn, like many anthropologists, been able to settle in a pleasant village—the illusion runs—the stay might have been of a very different nature and a good deal more agreeable. However, a study at the national level required a good deal of moving around. Hence you were at the mercy of one burrokrasstic office or another for the whole eighteen months. The feeling at the time was that Franz Kafka, having failed to visit Southeast Asia, "had never really seen any of it." Would it surprise you to learn that the permit for importing the Land Rover was acquired *eighteen months* after arrival and a few days before departure while trying to sell the vehicle to one man after another, joyously kicking it and mishandling it? (Driving in the country, even on the best roads, like the Rangoon–Mandalay highway, was a nightmare, yet in eighteen months there had only been one flat.) That the papers, signed and verified, were obtained by our anthropologist by taking them into a government office with a provision of sandwiches and a cushion—behavior never seen before in such a place—conveying them personally over a whole day to different officers for a total of twenty or more signatures, after which he fell out into the street, more dead than alive, clutching the miserable prize? That you could sit in such an office, waiting for an official said to be engaged elsewhere, the same official sitting at his desk for several hours right in front of you, engaged in such vital activities as personal chats with friends or paring his toenails? That you could believe every weekend that, come Monday, you would be in prison for the infringement of any one of a zillion legal rules yet never see the inside of such a prison?

Had Tarn been American at the time, he would have benefited from the American Asia Foundation's "little errands men." The British, embassy and council, while pleased to "debrief" you at the end of your stay, defined their job as limited to helping the Burmese meet and consort profitably with British businesses. Incredible nonsense had to be suffered at the hands of at least one official. An ex-policeman with past service in Malaya who fancied himself as a writer and ended up as the British Council man in Mandalay would enjoy such pranks as hauling you into his office to inform you that the vice provost of the University of Mandalay had informed his British Honor that you had not raised your hat to him in the street a week ago come Tuesday. But our Mandalayan policeman's wrath was good and truly raised when Tarn, with no other means of transport at that time, took it upon himself to ride down in a British Council movie van from high up in Kachin State back into town. This atrocious crime was duly reported to Rangoon, and a reprimand, admittedly mild, was administered by a friendly first secretary some time afterward. This kind of daily grinding down no doubt contributed to an illness, resembling malaria in some respects but never fully diagnosed. This gobbled up the month that Tarn had reserved, toward the end of his stay, for an entry into the monkhood under the Patthan Sayadaw, a great and kind Abhidhamma specialist monk in Rangoon. Patricia was pleased that she did not have to see at the door her husband, shaven, yellow-robed, and holding a begging bowl.

In other respects, the timing of the stay was fortunate. This was the last time you could still travel all over Burma before restrictions limited tourists to a week or so and only a very few places. Eight months were spent in Rangoon, with side trips to such sites as Pegu, Prome, and Thaton, at the end of which Tarn went, together with Patricia, as a delegate to the World Fellowship of Buddhists conference in Bangkok. A truly mad few days were spent there during the conference and afterward coping with an obsessive desire to get to Angkor. The trouble was that the Thai and the Cambodians were having an intimate little war. One after the other every move connected with going through Laos or Vietnam fell through. At the end of this absurdity, Patricia fell ill and was summoned home by her father while our anthropologist, literally weeping with exhaustion, went back to Rangoon. His only consolation: a friendship made at this time with the legendary silk man Jim Thompson, who gave a small Thai painting in sympathy and enabled the purchase, for a humble fifty dollars, of a very tall one: the Buddha and two disciples over a Jātaka scene. The friendship included dinners at Jim's home: a couple of traditional Thai houses joined together and filled with a wondrous collection of Thai art. Other guests were usually scholars, especially specialists in that art. The house was eventually donated as a museum to Thailand and can thus be seen today. Also, the large Thai silk shop that had begun as a very small place in which Tarn ordered a very fine silk navy-blue suit that survived for many years. Thompson died mysteriously in Malaysia and was the subject of a book or two.

12.6 An extremely difficult time in Mandalay had to be endured alone. Obstruction from foreign residents ensured, in one way or another, that there was nowhere to live except a "chummery" for University of Mandalay junior faculty. This horror, built of concrete, unprotected by any vegetation, noisy, without any facilities, curtains, or comforts against the 120-degree heat, provided a couple of rooms and a great deal of noise from young faculty playing cards until 2 a.m. almost every night. Meals had to be taken out at three hotels. The menu was invariably the same: chicken (boiled, roasted, fried), beef (boiled, roasted, fried), fish (boiled, roasted, fried), etc. Whichever cooking method was chosen, the result was identical. Gin and tonics helped. This food was luxurious compared to the pathetic Chinese stuff you had to eat on tour. Burmese food, very much an acquired taste, was available only in homes.

Among various trips, one on the Irrawaddy river steamers, enabled research at great centers of monastic learning such as Pakkokku and Sagaing. Another, made with a very kind "informant" who was godfather to a delightful princely orphan, Ye Myint, whom the Tarns came very close to adopting, went across the Chindwin River to Monywa for the study of a famous Messianic Buddhist monastery/temple in that vicinity. Much fun was had with an elderly friend of the informant who spent a couple of hours elaborately justifying a drink (thus defying Buddhist abstention) "because of the cool of the evening" before bringing out the whiskey bottle for a few healthy rounds.

After travel alone in Kachin State, attending a great Manao festival in the far North with buffalo sacrifices, dances by hundreds of tribal men (ceaselessly shooting rifles) and women in black and red covered with rivers of musical silver ornaments, smoking opium with officers from the rump of Chiang Kai Shek's armies living it up in those hills, and throwing his shadow on the valleys of China from a mountaintop at Muse (a New Year's trip into China offered by a Burma Army officer was reluctantly refused as too problematic—it would not have been "good form" to disappear forever into the Celestial Kingdom), Tarn returned to Rangoon for an ecstatic reunion with his wife.

They then endured more time at the chummery. Relief from the heat could be obtained at Maymyo, the Raj hill station, with its old bed-and-breakfast places, little horse-drawn carriages, and other Victorian amenities. An extraordinary week was spent an hour or so north of Mandalay, during the major annual festival, at Taungbyon, headquarters of two of Burma's main spirit (*nat*) cults. About 150 *nat kadaws*, priestess brides of the spirits (women and a few gay men), congregated there, each with a booth filled with their statues and ritual paraphernalia. Extraordinary water processions of the spirit statues and hundred of worshippers on the river in a dazzle of light, frenzied dances and trances by the brides (often roping in Tarn with pink silk scarves drenched in cheap perfume), and concerts of spirit music far more melodious than the usual performance banshee were the rewards of a week's stay in the village. Data remain unpublished.

A trip was made to Mount Popa, where further *nat* studies could be made up and down the treacherously steep path lined with monasteries and cult centers, followed by a week's stay at Pagan, one of three major sites that Southeast Asia owes to India, together with Angkor in Cambodia and Barabudur (Paul Mus's spelling), Java. This miraculous place, with its hundreds of temples on the banks of the great Irrawaddy River, documented mainly by Gordon Luce, deserves whole books to itself. Lodging was at the Raj period guesthouse, shared with Sonia Orwell, George Orwell's widow, and her husband since 1958, Michael Pitt-Rivers, who happened to be staying there at the time. A nightly farce was enacted there when a little man came in selling early-medieval votive plaques with Buddhas or scenes of the Buddha's life on them. He would go to one couple one night, then the other on the next night. A great deal of anxiety was generated by this procedure, the two couples maintaining "face" all the while.

Temptations had to be resisted everywhere: despite a warning published by Tarn at the time in a Rangoon magazine, Burmese art has been draining out of the country ever since. Perhaps the Thai protect their own art by selling vast quantities of Burmese.

The major trip of this period was made by car all over the Shan States, studying Shan Buddhist history, sects, and forms of monasticism. The couple were fortunate to attend a very elaborate princely *shinbyu* (boys' monastic initiation) in the Sawbwa's palace at Taunggyi with a side visit to the Pindaya caves. There were trips on lovely Innya Lake and lengthy drives to many areas as far as Kentung over by the Thai border. Personal risk had to be taken at this time from insurgents and "dacoits" (bandits of various stripes). Cars were known to have been stopped, their doors opened, and the occupants shot without any ceremony. Perhaps good fortune was ensured through a guide/assistant who eventually revealed himself to be a member of an insurgent Shan party.

12.7 In the same way as his interests had been in conflict with Robert Redfield's, Tarn's present concerns were now in conflict with Chatham House's. He was interested in improving on theories of Burmese religion that seemed to him unsatisfactory at the time, with their radical split between Buddhism on the one hand and "animist" spirit cults on the other. Some nine months into his stay he began to discover evidence of a third component that, because of its concentration on the coming Buddha Maitreya rather than the past/present Buddha Sakyamuni, he called, for want of a better term, Messianic Buddhism. He came to consider this as his most original research area—virtually nothing systematic had been known about it—and was frustrated at not being able to give it his full attention. Study of the spirit (*nat*) cults suffered even more from a tight schedule.

Back to monks and politics. All through the Raj, scholars had talked about this or that role of the monkhood (*Sangha*), but this institution had no available face. Most rarely, if ever, did anyone come up with the name or even title of a single monk. The task of putting a face on the *Sangha* turned out to be a huge, incredibly time-consuming, and painfully detailed one. A major part of this was an interminable series of daily, weekly, and monthly visits to various newspaper, magazine, and institutional offices—such as the Ministry of Religious Affairs—to acquire complete runs (vain hopelessness of totalizing ambitions!) of their publications. Then the cutting up of hundreds of papers to isolate details of individual monks: who had had tea with whom, who had gone to such and such a ritual, who had attended a conference, who had had a hand in formulating a policy, who had paid a visit or received one from a minister . . . followed the task of acquiring *Sangha* histories in Burmese and Burmanized Pāli, especially sectarian ones, in order to push the picture as far back as possible. In the meantime, much attention was focused on the 2,500th anniversary of the Buddha's birth and the huge *Sangayāna* assembly that Burma had convoked from all Theravāda countries: an action presented by Prime Minister U Nu as a Burmese contribution to the world from which Burma would accumulate a great deal of good karma.

Several results emerged. First, a general picture demonstrated how the *Sangha*, an apparently churchless and often leaderless organization, functioned both independently (when the polity was weak) and in relation to the polity (when it was strong) all the way back to the late eighteenth century, with hints for previous periods. Second, much of this could be shown to have been governed by a monastic trait whose importance Burmans usually poo-pooed: the formation of teacher-to-disciple lineages and the relation of these to the evolution of sects. Third, this in turn played a part in the true story of the *Sangayāna* as a contemporary version of an age-old Burmese political-control mechanism: the monks who organized, ran, and eventually benefited from the big and showy event were those who cooperated with and indeed were, in some respects, part of the government. Previous to the revelation of this all-told unsurprising fact, the Burmese government's propaganda had been taken at face value. Despite the propaganda, very few foreign monks participated.

The fascinating thing about Messianic Buddhism was something of a catch-22 in that it was virtually never talked about unless the anthropologist talked of it first. Once you started, however, especially with Army officers, it was hard to stop the flow. In brief, this form of worship had existed way back into royal times and the times of wars against British occupation, at which point the cults acquired anti-European nationalist overtones in addition to those characterizing conflicts between Southeast Asian kingdoms and principalities. At the time of research, Messianic Buddhism manifested in the shape of a bunch of little men all over the country (hard to know how many) claiming to be not only the *Cakravartin* (world king) who, according to the Dīgha Nikāya scripture, would tidy up the world for the coming of the future Buddha Maitreya, but also strongly hinting at being a pre-Buddhahood incarnation of this same Maitreya (something *not* conveyed by the scripture in question). The basic aim of an adept was to acquire powers (often reaching to invulnerability—important to warriors—as well as long or even eternal life) through the arts of alchemy, cabbalistic signs, astrology, medicine, and other such disciplines in order to last long enough to hear Maitreya preaching on his arrival to Earth and thus immediately attain Nirvāna. One inroad into this material, previously never looked at, was the many popular lithographs depicting some of the more famous adepts. These were to be found on sale at religious bookstores situated on the steps of major pagodas. Another inroad was the discovery of some of the associations, occasionally monastic, run by such adepts. Much research had to be devoted to possible non-Theravāda (Sarvāstivāda or even Mahāyāna) contributions to this thinking, often by comparison with Chinese materials, but this, alas, was never finalized.

Eventually, Tarn suggested a unified model of the Burmese religious continuum running from animism at the lower end, in which you would be possessed by power (the spirits), through Messianic Buddhism, in which you accumulated the possession of more and more powers through the esoteric arts, up to "pure" Theravāda, in which you finally realized that power should be given up entirely in favor of enlightenment. The original plan was to write a work in three volumes, one on each aspect of the triad. In effect the first book, for Chatham House, took ten years to write and was then abandoned under pressure from literary interests. It was eventually, and somewhat miraculously, rescued by a Cornell University graduate, John Ferguson, who rewrote much of it in his own style and edited it down into a publishable form. It came out from Cornell University Press in 1975, and Ferguson with his family were by now close friends. All those who had to be thanked for their help were thanked in that book. In the meantime, Tarn watched while colleagues who had been in the field after him—and, in at least one case, introduced by him into "his" secrets—published their results before his. It was his fault and his problem. The other two volumes—on spirits and messianics—were never written, and only the field notes and a set of published articles remain.

12.8 Eighteen months is a long haul. Unbelievably, the time came to leave at last just before Christmas 1959. Huge boxes were packed, special care being taken (diplomatic-pouch privileges were not available as they were for some) to wrap acquired religious objects in yellow monastic robes as a token of respect and haul them off to a ship. The Tarns flew to Bangkok, where Jim Thompson's hospitality was enjoyed again in his home. The trip continued on to Siem Reap for Angkor, easy to reach this time. One unforgettable night: riding in a *cyclo* to Angkor Wat with a chanting noise swelling and swelling as you drew near so that it seemed that a thousand monks were singing in the huge building. Then finding that only half a dozen novices were practicing for their examinations there in the entrance building. Tarn has considered it a boon to have seen Angkor alone before the huge irruption of international tourism in the 2000s.

Patricia had become pregnant with Andrea on her return from London and now went back to England. Tarn dropped off the plane at Calcutta, having promised not to spend too much on acquisitions. The whole first floor of his first hotel there was taken up by one shop after another that our man was unable not to look at. Among thousands of objects, he spotted a golden Tibetan figure of a Garuda, which a boy quoted at a ridiculous price. Gritting his teeth, Tarn walked on, suddenly pivoted on his feet, and went back, only to find the boy being given an earful from his boss for nearly selling a treasure for a song. There were other stops at Delhi, Benares, Agra, Fatehpur Sikri (it was easy to get on and off planes in those days), where tourists were still few, as well as Ajanta and Ellora. At Ajanta, Tarn, desperate for rest, had to forgo that because an all-India car rally was taking place there. Crossing the Himalayas with his escort of American widows—he had coincidentally been booked on his flights with these ladies traveling on their spouses' life insurance and never ever lost them—led to Nepal with visits to Kathmandu, Bhatgaon, Patna, and hill temples (blessedly well before the days of the hippie invasion), and the birth of a great devotion to that whole area. A friendly British Council Nepali contact led him into a midnight adventure. The routine was to visit a whole string of dealers and pick out interesting items that were then transported to a central location where a selection of purchases could be made. Childishly insufficient pocket-money sums secured a few eighteenth-century miniatures (sixteenth-century ones were at ten pounds instead of five) and a wonderful *tangka* painting with multicolored squares filled with small stupas.

Then it was on to Iran: friendly stops in Tehran with British Embassy and Council acquaintances and a flight to Isfahan with its turquoise domes under snow. The effect on the mind of abstract design after India's plethora of figuration was extraordinary. An extremely friendly and scholarly man led Tarn round the great bazaar, revealing himself only at the very end as a guide in need of a fee. Some of the Scheherazadean scenes in courtyards off the market, with light slanting in on turbaned men conversing among plants and flowers, have been a mental *locus amoenus* ever since: Sufism beckons! Some bizarre expeditions into monuments with secretive purchases of tiles off the floor negotiated by the guide as well as a visit to a Jewish dealer's small shop were part of Isfahan. Gradually, the suitcase was being emptied of clothes and almost everything else.

The glories of Istanbul share a space in the mind with a shot of the widows descending to breakfast in a hotel elevator clutching little bottles of Nescafe—as if Turkish coffee were some kind of poison or, God forbid, aphrodisiac. Finally, it was three days in Athens and the ritual visit to the Parthenon, whose floor could be walked over in those days like that of any other self-respecting ruin.

More and more weary, our Ulysses found himself losing some treasured object at every stop: miraculously, Pan American Airlines brought every single thing back to him. On the last, Paris stop, it was a hat for Patricia. Sitting in a London-bound Lockheed Constellation, Tarn began vociferating about why this "cursed plane was taking so long to take off." His neighbor, much amused, told him to look out the window: he had fallen asleep and was nearing the capital. This too launched a friendship, to be resumed many years later at Princeton, with Stanley Corngold, professor of German at that institution.

Throw Thirteen

13.1 Writing in mid-1974 now. After Cambridge, Paris, Chicago, Guatemala, London, Burma, have I acquired a distaste for hard work that will remain with me for the rest of my days? In switching disciplines in 1969 on immigrating to the United States—after two years of editing at a publisher's—I condemn myself to a further spell of hard labor in that I am quite unqualified at the beginning to teach my new discipline of "comparative literature." (Additionally, I do not believe that the discipline exists.) Fortunately, the United States, if not Europe, affords a poet some degree of liberality. Not always, however: after some ten years at Rutgers, an attempt to get away from it by an application for a position in "Complit" at another university is rebuffed with a short "not qualified" written by a historian of American poetry. How flattering can academics get?

13.2 I am interested in the conditions that determine an individual's attitudes to work. Role of these attitudes in shaping his or her character. Reader, please construe "her/his" from now on when encountering "his."

Much evidence for a work/sexuality link. Somewhere among those Persean early-adolescent fantasies the dragon of hard work lurks in the dreary forest. Can one lay the whole of acquirable knowledge at a maiden's feet without hard work? Somewhere in the forest also lurk the slave drivers—for you don't make yourself crazy without having been shown the way. I have described the monster in Cornwall who lifted me from last in class to top for three weeks. There was ambivalence: I usually (masochistically?) liked such monsters. Much earlier, in Belgium, I had had a class master of the same type: Monsieur Claude. Huge, with red hair and a red mustache. My parents brought him in as a supplementary tutor at home. He drove me especially hard in mathematics.

Somehow, I loved this red monster. Many years later, after the war, in the sixties I guess, I went to see him on Nervierstraat in Antwerpen. Caught in the street outside the school stood a small, shrunken Belgian farmer. "Do you recognize me?" After some time peering, "Yes, you are the boy who wrote that poem '*L'hirondelle*' about a swallow." In the eighties, I found the stationer's shop where we bought school supplies. The owner remembered Monsieur Claude.

Behind such monsters probably stood a father—not the real one doubtless but the vision one had of him. To say the least, Father always found it hard to praise. Doubtless this arose out of an inability to enjoy. I have commented on his expression "It is a pity that." Add to this a strong preference for "useful knowledge": in his view, that which enables you to make an impression on the world. Poetry, of course, had been decreed by the gods of the father to be a "useless" kind of work: work that should always remain decently hidden in the background, a spare-time occupation, a last string to whatever small successes you owned, a *hobby* if you pleased. For years I was unable to state that I was a *poet*—and the reluctance persisted until the 2000s. Paradoxically, such a declaration was doubly dangerous. On the one hand, you would offend serious society by showing a lack of seriousness. On the other hand, you would offend against a certain code of modesty. Culture did manifestly sanction successful poets, the canon running say, in Brit terms, from Shakespeare to Tennyson to Hopkins; in American terms from say Bradstreet, Whitman, and Dickinson to say Pound, Olson, Duncan, and Dorn. Just how you ever stood a chance of entering such a canon under the double rule of offensiveness, it was hard to say. It reminded me of the rule of the Brit theatrical union, Equity. You could not act if you were not in Equity. You could not be in Equity if you were not an actor.

So: you valued "useful" knowledge and felt guilty about "useless" knowledge. As one defense, I acquired the habit of accumulating all and any kinds of knowledge. A passion for acquiring books assisted this. I have always thought of them as friends that do not answer back and still remember the delight of encountering Walter Benjamin's essay on building a library: saving books for civilization.

However: along with this came the sense that learning was a bottomless vase and that you would never surprise the parent by ending the process and never hear that ultimate praise. There would never be any kind of security. In such ways you become a slave driver to yourself: internalization, I guess. Bourgeois culture wrecks the incipient poet ninety-nine times out of a hundred. Today, "creative writing" students by the hundreds (far too many as we shall see) emerge from the woodwork declaring they would like to be poets but not knowing whether they dare embark on this commitment without some guarantee that they are "going to make it." Ninety-nine percent do not.

How can all of this not metamorphose at some point into that most wretched of all human traits: ambition? How would it be possible, in these beaten-down conditions, not to want to be the first, the best, the king or queen? Being ambitious condemns one, as all wisdom teachers have repeated ad nauseam, to a life of misery. On this dread subject, more later.

There had been the poem about a bear, written in French at age five, the swallow poem at age nine, the little notebooks with a Free French flag drawn on the cover at age thirteen. Yet as the years wore on, I must have acquiesced to hiding poetry, to backgrounding it, to allowing it only when everything else had already happened, including, I daresay, sex. Have I've mentioned the poem-searing-the-paper fantasy? I sometimes called poetry "my epilepsy." In later thinking this intruded into a theory about "rapture," but I knew from early on that poetic super-excitability did not by itself, on the whole, produce anything but hysteria, good for the trash basket. (Had I ever written the great poem "Howl," would I have recognized it?)

From time to time over the years, I would see myself as wasting my life, that all my scholarship was misguided and death-wishing, that one almighty heave might free me for the garret. The break with anthropology in 1967 (bitterly resented by at least one friend, George Steiner, who had his own reasons for not wishing me to be a poet) was of this nature—although the need for making a living did not vanish with that break.

13.3 Yet, again, was that need ever a clear one? There was ambivalence on Father's part. On the one hand, the gods clearly decreed that every man should fend for himself: "One day, you will have to get off your father's back." On the other hand, it was also true, God help us, that this father had been saddled with two hopeless sons. It was fortunate for me, the argument went, that my father had been a normal man and had accumulated enough to see us through for a time (more guilt). This "for a time" was never specified, although one was often told by Mother, before the days of recession and inflation, that there would "even be enough after the grave." Also never specified. Mother interiorized this and went on repeating such statements long after they had totally ceased to be true.

None of this ended with marriage. My delightful Patricia's delightful father was not improvident, but it was in the nature of the case that father and father-in-law could never satisfy each other. I continued to be a symbolical bringer home of symbolical bacon, living in a house not my own, on a budget not my own, a time not my own. Father-in-law, a *bon viveur*, would often send round luxuries and delicacies while being oblivious to the necessities that an enjoyable but over-luxurious dwelling and lifestyle inevitably required: on one occasion, Patricia nearly had a howling fit when I threatened to send one lot back. The absurdity of being weighted down with a career I had come to detest, unable to make a break because of these pseudo-responsibilities, made for a bad conscience at best, angst at worst. Even within the last two years, mid-sixties to mid-seventies, a biography of the Brit poet Ted Hughes has mentioned Tarn's "palatial house." It was comfortable but far from palatial. Peter Porter, an Australian scribbler, whose review of my *A Nowhere for Vallejo* said nothing about the book but repeated three times some derogatory nonsense about my leaving for the "well-paid American poetry reading circuits," once nixed a British Council grant that, he claimed, "Tarn does not deserve because he is the son of a rich Jewish merchant." As part of this work-ethic concern, I also remember convening a family meeting to persuade my folks that they should allow my brother to become a painter instead of slaving away unsuccessfully at the law (for reasons I have never understood, my brother refused). For my part, I could not forget that I would also have liked some kind of liberation!

13.4 Returning to poetry: I persisted. *Je maintiendrai*. That ambition held me together I have no doubt. I have discovered myself over the years to be slow but methodical and, above all, persistent and resilient. It has often been a great source of misery never to know when to give up. My mind returns to a project again and again over the years until I have exhausted all possibilities.

Romantic ideas of poet-hood—those very ideas that bourgeois culture promoted by opposing poetry—were central. I believe that fantasies included at all times the vision of a young poet, bedecked like Byron, enjoying a good head of hair, moving like a god (Hölderlin!) through the world's best salons, and impressing the young ladies to death. *Je maintiendrai*: did I not eventually have to write the line "I came to poetry late"?

Thus, through the years, I continued to commit poems to paper though desperate at the thought that no opus seemed to be growing. It was clear that individual poems would not do: a body of work was required. This did not begin to happen until after Burma and my introduction into the London "Group." I'll get to this later.

Gradually, ambition is elided by achievement—although never completely: the desire associated with the former unfortunately persists as a deleterious habit. The "initiation" of first publication done with, you are left with a life path without issue or residue. You may be fortunate to discover that knowledge acquisition is an accumulative process, whereas something we can provisionally call "wisdom," a good of a somewhat higher order, is a process of shedding. This dialectic is peculiar to artistic, as it is to religio-mystical, achievement. It does not prevail so much in scholarship, although there is always the final life work's distillation open to the scholar. Thus the body of work or opus grows, the process of adding and subtracting becomes ever more subtle within the body itself, as within each poem, and something—in Pound's expression—has been done as opposed to not done. *Punkt*. Period.

I have been left with certain unlikable habits that need to be eradicated, if they ever are, by going, like Peer Gynt, round about. I still have a tendency to do everything that is feasible at that moment before getting down to the major task. This goes for any "creative" writing (hateful term!): poems, diaries, essays, recording dreams, making notes. It continues to be hard to commit to the "throw." Fear of my own energy continues to prevail. I persist in overvaluing forms of intellectual activity that are not my forte while undervaluing those very forms that do enable poetry. Rational thinking from *a* to *b* to *n* has never been my strong point. After the Blitz—which seems to have brought on some kind of fall—I became "bad" at classics, maths, and the exact sciences (with the exception of biology), and it may be this that my history teacher at Clifton diagnosed as my fatal "intellectual" flaw. (Some parting gift!) With infinite pains, work in the social sciences did bring about some kind of competence in rational argument. However, I am much more at home in intuitive thinking, in making what appear to be irrational jumps.

My inheritance is that I go on distrusting that power. It has been hard for me to understand, for instance, that students wish me to teach "as a poet" in the American academy whereas I continue telling myself I should teach as a "professor."

Certain fellow poets in New York have been trying to make me understand lately how much I hinder myself by an apparent distrust of all "powers." It is true that much of what I was interested in early on—though then not exactly in fashion—has now become the rage: "spiritual," "esoteric," and "initiatic" lore of every kind abounds, especially to a ridiculous extent in Santa Fe, New Mexico. I still believe in the need for caution: there may be one "saint" for a thousand charlatans, one true teacher for a thousand "gurus," one true "initiation" for a thousand trips into the "occult." I want to come back later to the adverse effects of pseudo-orientalism. Yet my friends' arguments have value and weight. There is much that I dare not do and keep putting off: the poem "At Gloucester, Mass. after Foreign Travel," in *Lyrics for the Bride of God*, hints at some of this. Lack of daring: a form of death fear almost certainly.

13.5 What of this notion of a body of work, or opus, in relation to "accumulation"? I often felt in my "prime" that, were I to die the next day, I would wish that all my work to date would be destroyed. There is something apparently gratuitous about this. It does share perhaps in the childhood fantasy of laying the whole world—and *nothing less*—at some lover's feet. What is it that makes all this so totalizing? I believe it echoes the accumulative tendency within the process of wisdom acquisition as defined by various traditions—the Buddhist in particular, as described above. Totality is perhaps the sine qua non of wisdom acquisition as seen from a point of vantage immediately previous to the attainment of wisdom and loss of accumulation, "wisdom" here standing for "enlightenment," the resolution of all questions and all mysteries.

The body of work as held in the poet's mind cannot, because it is open in only a limited way to prediction, be much more than the vision (or "prophecy" if you like) of that total moment achieved by adepts at or before explosion. It is a fantasy like other fantasies but a powerful one. It includes the implication that one's death and the explosion are one (another fantasy), that one's powers are forever ripening, and that the last word will not be spoken until the last moment. Many poets face long years of decline. Many leave great bodies behind them without having had a chance to speak the final word (the *Four Last Songs* of Richard Strauss have always been visionary in this sense for me). Some poets—I borrow a thought of Robert Kelly's—replace the possibility of the final word by a final act. Confessional poets (ungraciously, I used to call some of them "the suicide club") often select this replacement. Anne Sexton has just chosen to disappear from the stage as this is written, and we have the interminable posthumous saga of Sylvia Plath: a blight on serious progress in the British understanding of poetry.

A little more on "totality" or "totalization." Defining the cosmological function of mythology in his essay "Mythological Themes in Creative Literature and Art," Joseph Campbell describes it as "that of formulating and rendering an image of the universe, a cosmological image in keeping with the science of the time and of such kind that, within its range, all things should be recognized as parts of a single great holy picture, an icon as it were. . . ." Going on to write of a lack of congruity between our traditional myths (closed systems) and the relativism and openness of our own lives and mind-sets, Campbell claims that the only possibility of reintegration is for traditional images "to be retained, washed clean of 'meanings,' to be re-experienced (and not reinterpreted) as art." A major poet friend, Joseph Donahue, points out that whether we subscribe to traditional religions or not, their imagery, in the end, seems to be virtually all we have left.

Anthropology with its relativistic studies of myths has given the modern artists this possibility, a process stretching from the interest in a Sir James Frazer of an Eliot or a Pound to the "ethnopoets" of our own day. The work of a Mircea Eliade on the myth of the eternal return, for instance, allows us to see each individual's opus as a ritual placing of that body of work within the original body of the cosmos. Poetic creation for each poet is a reenactment of the great events of the world's creation (*in illo tempore*—in that time) in what an Australian aborigine would call the dream time. Indeed, each opus is that creation, as spoken through one voice among many. This also is doubtless the drift of the oft-repeated claim, from Lautréamont to Robert Duncan, that we are all writing, or should be writing, the same poem. We are the chorus to the world's noise. I am well aware as I write that this is a holistic vision of poetic activity that probably disappears after the last modernists: Olson, Duncan, Dorn, Zukofsky, Everson, and their like.

Totemism and myth, in the work of Claude Lévi-Strauss, act as intellectual grids for social classification by a constantly recurring process of totalization, detotalization, and retotalization. Totalization: the establishing of a system of referential categories such that each species in a series of species abstracted from the known world of living beings will be assigned to a category until the world is exhausted and the system is saturated. Detotalization: the mental taking to pieces of such systems in ritual and liturgy for dialectical and didactic purposes, normally with retotalization in view. Thus begins all movement, all creation. A bias favoring totalization over detotalization as the ultimate creative act is open to discussion: it is also possible to see, with a different bias, the alternation, forever, of the two as characteristics of any creation—or, at worst, detotalization priming in a dust-to-dust mode.

Certain poems, or bodies of poetry, partaking of the mythic, show proof of a powerful urge, if not a compulsion, toward structuring experience in a like manner. The detotalization and retotalization of the cosmic man in William Blake's prophecies, especially *The Four Zoas* and *Jerusalem*, are of this order. It would seem that a model of social classification by means of the tribes of Albion 1, 2, 3, 4, *n*, imposed upon the tribes of Israel, the English counties, the revolutionary nations, etc. generates the matrix in which the "human composite" or "cosmic man" can be apprehended. In turn, this cosmic man serves as a prototype for all models of unity (note my expression "body of work"): the initiatic unity brought about by "individuation" in the fullest sense or by a complete spiritual "realization." Archetypal models for the same process can be discerned in such classifications as that of the Ten Sephiroth in the Kabbala.

Sociologically, some such notion as that of "ecclesia" might serve to clarify the dismemberment and rememberment of society seen as one "great man." In order for there to be an ecclesia, there must presumably have been a fall or breaking apart of the original unity: a *sparagmos*. Whether the process begins with a detotalization or a retotalization hardly matters: the process is in essence circular. All this may be useful for understanding the poem "Sparagmos: Pen/Ink/Paper/Penna," in the *America* section of *Lyrics for the Bride of God*. In this present book I have pointed out how a strong heraldic order could endow a society with a powerful sense of security: a feudal system, carrying in its heraldry the element of classificatory thought, is a world where everybody can eventually be recognized over and above his or her individuality—contrasting with a modern world where, although everyone is recorded on computers, that record is a statistical one at best, involving not individuals but classes of individuals. The resulting anomie has been amply documented from Franz Kafka on down. László Krasznahorkai is perhaps the latest exponent.

On thinking of it, the classificatory tendency within myth must also afford a sense of security. It had always seemed to me that even the most historicized of religions contain within themselves a worldview that does its best to deny history. The Christian history, for instance, contains a fall from grace at the beginning of human time that is, from one point of view, an unmitigated disaster. From another vantage point, however, the fall is a fortunate event (the *felix culpa* of the theologians), for it is the precondition of the system's divinity's greatest gift to the world: the sacrifice of his "only Son." This sacrifice accomplished, mankind is redeemed from the fall, and the way is open toward a final rehabilitation of all things. Standing outside this worldview, however, it might occur to a nonbeliever, even if he or she acknowledges an unavoidably "satanic" element within the human psyche, to ask why the whole mechanism had to be set in motion in the first place. One answer could conceivably be that the mechanism represents an understanding of what happens to every single soul on its way to wisdom. I'm sure more than one theologian has pointed this out.

Eliade has argued that the archaic mentality abhors history. His identification of myths of eternal return is a valuable one. He has simplified reality, however, for there are as many examples of "primitive" interest in history as there are examples of a lack of such interests or of an abhorrence of history. We seem to have to opt for a dialectical situation in which man sets out into the unknown on the one hand with his notions of irreversible history, his open systems, but on the other hand guaranteeing his socio-psychological order by postulating closed, nonhistorical systems—either within the framework of the historical (the circle or cycle within the line) or, more usually, encompassing the historical (the line within the circle). Such a dialectic, it seems to me, is at work in man's most immediate experience of spiritual development (as exemplified in all initiatic lore and ritual) as well as in his experience of creativity. Lévi-Strauss, in the last chapters of *La pensée sauvage*, argues with Jean-Paul Sartre on this very same topic, although the thrust of his argument, I believe, would favor history over anti-history or a-history. There is history in all cases, primitive and civilized: it is not used, not domesticated in the first case while being put to work toward unlimited "progress" in the second. I'm afraid we are stuck in the second.

Throw Fourteen

14.1 On return to London, an apartment was rented at no. 6 Kidderpore Gardens in Hampstead off the Finchley Road, followed by the acquisition of a house at no. 21 in the same street: this remained a longtime home. A "normal family life" was duly instituted. Andrea was born in 1960 and Marc in 1963. Their father had been the last to see Andrea because of an unholy rush to the hospital by the parental generation and so was determined to outfox that generation on the second birth by being present for it. A regular routine of visits to Patricia's parents in Northwood outside town allowed for quiet walks in a beautiful garden—although sumptuous meals at family gatherings where only German was spoken (it was always assumed that everyone understood) often made smoke issue from Tarn's ears. There were various holidays. One pleasant one, without the children, was to Baden Baden, where Patricia's mother was taking a cure—although Tarn was not able to engineer a visit to the Hölderlinian site at Tübingen. Another, with the children, involved taking a villa at Den Haan on the Belgian Coast. The rooms were painted white and furnished with white cane chairs and beds—an ideal setting in which to read the nineteenth-century Russians. On the morning after arrival, the curtains were drawn back and—amazement!—the same game of exchanging paper flowers for bucketfuls of seashells was still being played by toddlers as had been played in the thirties!

14.2 The nomination to what was undoubtedly the best Southeast Asia job then current arrived while Tarn was lying on his bed in the ratty Mandalay "chummery" mulling over a loss suffered through a mouse making her devastating nest in his precious box of cuttings. This appointment made our anthropologist extremely miserable, and he groaned about it for three or four days, lying in stifling heat on that horrible bed, before finding the courage to wire acceptance. The problem was the standard one: this would involve much time and energy and thus take away those commodities from the pursuit of poetry.

The School of Oriental and African Studies, however, was a reasonably pleasant place, much less of a pressure cooker than the L.S.E., and work in the department under an Austrian who had become British during the forties, Christoph von Furer Haimendorf (Assam and Nepal), was not inordinately demanding. There were pan-university meetings with other colleges, conferences of the Association of British Social Anthropologists, and lectures by local and foreign dignitaries at the Royal Anthropological Institute. Redfield's lecture there, followed by a dinner organized for his gratification at the House of Lords, afforded this old teacher great pleasure not long before his death from leukemia.

14.3 A number of interesting conferences. The Tenth Pacific Science Conference at the University of Hawaii in 1961. In order to get there, Tarn had organized a seminar on Theravāda Buddhist social institutions. His secret aim was to push on to Japan, and he brought this about by putting a claim to S.O.A.S. that some comparative knowledge would enhance the new lecturer's status and utility. Hawaii was pleasant, with institutions like the Bernice P. Bishop Museum and the remarkable Asian collection at the Honolulu Art Museum. The seminar over, anthropology was left behind on behalf of botany and ornithology: a trip to see the nene goose, another to a booby colony on a US Air Force base at which photos of the birds were solemnly handed out while cameras were impounded for the duration of the visit. Also to the point was a weekend visit to Kauai. Naively believing that food most probably grew on trees, Tarn had to confess after arrival there that the hotel stay took up all his available cash.

The Japan sojourn was intense—no other possible word for it. After a first miserable acquaintance with humid heat at the International House in

Tokyo, Kyōto was seen exhaustively, thanks to the help of the French Michel Soymié, who arranged that initial stay in the spider-haunted temple, the Belgian Hubert Durt, and the Swiss Jacques May, scholars of Buddhism all, who arranged visits to many temples, palaces, gardens, and other sites. Hauchecorne, an extremely "Nipponized" teacher of French married to a Japanese, organized an extraordinary trip to Okayama province. Train after train after train, each one smaller, eventually got the party to the village of Tachikui. The great caterpillar-like kilns climbed the hillside, and the villagers, renowned for their ceramics, were, on their own initiative, making large dishes in celebration of a Van Gogh anniversary. These were to be given to the French and Dutch embassies. Tarn and another young man kept on picking up marvelous shards, and Hauchecorne kept on telling them not to bother. Eventually a meal in a potter's house produced a large choice of rejects that could be bought for a song. The meal went on and on well past the last train's time. Hauchecorne then produced a ghost train featured on none of the printed schedules and got us back to Kyōto for dinner. On another occasion, Tarn sat through the unearthly development of a typhoon—the deadly quiet, the winds, the trees lying down on the ground, the devastation—in a small pension found after the spider-haunted temple episode. Hungry, by clambering over fallen tree trunks he reached a small bar where Hauchecorne happened to be dining. The latter admired a shirt and was promptly given it off the wearer's back, a pleasant little ceramic pot received in exchange. Departure from Kyōto involved a sad and solitary dinner at the station restaurant with a TV playing *La Traviata*, getting on the train, finding one's sleeper, and, exactly at the right moment, Hauchecorne, who had promised to be there, holding out his hand from the platform as the train slid past him.

Much work was done thanks to a thick batch of introductions obtained from the Ministry of Religious Affairs: to Buddhist and Shintō temples and to "New Religion" centers. New Religions usually involved mixtures of Shintō and Nichiren Buddhism and excelled at roping in new members when these were under stress owing to illness and other afflictions. A visit to the huge Tenri-kyō center was academic, but at the smaller Konkō-kyō place, a director decided that he had caught a missionary in the making, and a very good meal was ruined by his very pressing harangues. Eventually, some thirty men slept on the floor in one room, bothered all night by huge flying june bugs relentlessly slamming into everything, including the sleepers. One great disappointment was that the Shingon Buddhist (esoteric Buddhism) shrines at *Kōyasan* could not be visited because of damage from the typhoon. A tourist brochure picked up in the Osaka airport in 2004 seemed to show that this place has become a Disneyland!

Much else could be said about this trip. Noh theater was a major revelation: the slow majesty of both movements and music overshadowing by leagues the more dramatic Kabuki. The effect of this made its way into such early poems as "The Moon in Nō" and "René Grousset Weeping at the Doors of the Shōsōin." (Grousset was a major French orientalist.) Carmen Blacker, a leading scholar of mountain cults, was a companion. However, she was very timid and full of paralyzing dos and don'ts about Japan. On one occasion the Takashimaya department store's basement was visited in search of a formal dress: only a Sumō wrestler's stuff would do for tall Tarn. Much time was taken getting a set together. Everything is at long last assembled. Move to the cashier's desk. At this point, a Japanese man sweeps in, picks up the kit, pays for it, and disappears in a flash. Carmen, questioned and upbraided, declares that no woman in Japan can interfere with a man's actions. What was the man's intent?

The craze for *Mingei* (folk art) eventually led to a huge box being packed and sent off (it was "lost" for a full year but eventually reached London).

14.4 Other conferences over the years included one in Strasbourg, where the foundational Kabbalah scholar Gershom Scholem and the great Indo-Europeanist Georges Dumézil were in attendance. Scholem eventually thanked his young friend for a gift of his first book *Old Savage/Young City*, "which I have placed on a shelf of works inspired by my *Major Trends in Jewish Mysticism*." Crucial encounters on this trip included the statue of the "Synagogue Defeated" on the south portal of the cathedral (featured as an illustration in *The Beautiful Contradictions* and on the cover of the 2003 *Selected Poems*), a visit to the very rich Museum of Alsace Jewry and another to the magisterial Retablo by Grünewald made at Issenheim and now seen at the Unterlinden Museum in Colmar. A much later visit to this miracle led to the poem "Mathis at Issenheim" in the 2008 *Ins and Outs of the Forest Rivers*.

A conference on the history of gnosticism was attended in Messina, Sicily, with the aim of touring the island after the meetings. Edward Conze, the great scholar of the Mahāyāna Pāramitā, was staying in the hotel room opposite, and many a sandwich was shared with heavy conversation on those premises. Never intending to give a paper, Tarn was impressed by the lack of sociological attention paid to certain matters and persuaded University of Chicago gnosticist professor Robert Grant to let him give a paper. After this, the island was duly toured in a large black mafiosi Fiat: all the Greek and Christian sites round the coast as well as the magical prehistoric site of Pantalica, loud with bees, and the illustrious Segesta temple in the fields of profuse spring flowers. The diary of this tour is the only illustrated one ever kept, the traveler feeling he probably looked like a Victorian watercolorist sketching the ruins under a large umbrella. The end of the journey provided the astonishing soaring vistas of Monreale and the joys of puppetry in the city of Palermo. The road was very clear: you gather that, today, you risk life and limb going round the same circuit. *Sic transit* solitary travel like much else in modernity.

A S.O.A.S. bonus in London was the occasional tea with a far-famed translator from the Chinese and the Japanese: Arthur Waley. He shared an apartment with Beryl de Zoete, a scholar of Indonesian dance. An introduction had come about through the Portuguese poet Alberto de Lacerda, whose *77 Poems* Waley had translated, probably following an introduction to and perhaps a nudge from Edith Sitwell. Waley was apparently very pleased to have a young contact at S.O.A.S. and enjoyed hearing the school gossip while shuffling about in some very ancient slippers and making tea: as an independent scholar, he did not appear to have many academic contacts. Arthur was not the easiest man to talk to. You would make a remark or ask a question, and he would sit with his chin on his fist, apparently sunk in thought, in the attitude of Rodin's famous statue. After more than a decent interval, you would risk asking another question: whereupon he would answer the first. His extremely devoted nursing of Beryl, who had an extreme case of Parkinson's, put a break on these meetings. After her death came the great surprise of news of Arthur's marriage to a woman no one knew and that lady's biography of his totally unexpected twin lives. Many years later: another surprise—finding Arthur's papers at Rutgers' University Special Collections, bought by a librarian who had intended to work on them and, it seems, never had.

14.5 During a short "vacation" from fieldwork in Burman Maymyo on the edges of the Shan hills, Tarn had been very taken by the old colonial Botanical Gardens, still kept up rather well, and had spent some hours on successive days walking around them. Suddenly, three poems occurred very much under the spell of a *Selected* Gerard Manley Hopkins that he must have been reading at the time. Doubtless this was also occasioned by the presence at Mandalay of a young London-based Canadian poet, David Wevill, working for the British Council as an English teacher at the university. Under these auspices, Wevill was fortunate to enjoy a pleasant house on campus and was sensitive enough to ask the Tarns over from time to time, allowing them a breathing space away from the miserable chummery. The one thing it was inordinately hard to do was to get him to accept reciprocity in the Land Rover on trips to Pagan and such: the poet was constitutionally *sittlich* and refused many a good opportunity. It turned out that he was waiting for a married lady love whom he had met on a transatlantic ship and had had a violent affair with. She intended to divorce.

She eventually arrived, and her first attempt at entertaining the Tarns was memorable. First, for the sparkling white dress and huge white hat setting off her not-inconsiderable beauty and second for her utter failure in persuading Wevill's Indian cook to concoct a dish she had very much wished to offer. The couple's presence was a boon. Eventually, they fell prey to British burrokrasstic nonsense when the effeminate gentleman met with on the SS *Derbyshire* made it known to his superiors that the pair was not married. They were told to leave Mandalay and return to London!

14.6 While in Burma, the couple had spoken about a poetry group they belonged to in London where they would be glad to take their anthropologist friend. Tarn was lacking in literary company. Although a close friendship had developed for years with Alberto de Lacerda—to the point where Tarn had written a review/article on him in *Critique* that introduced the poet into the company of René Char—Alberto, with the exception of Waley, kept his literary contacts (with the Sitwells and others) so secretive that no introductions were ever forthcoming. Tarn's efforts remained solitary. Back in the UK, on the last day of moonlighting with a sociology course at an American air base, the sergeant, who had driven past Ely Cathedral several times on the way to the station, was asked to drop his charge off there. He who had never seen the miraculous edifice when a student at Cambridge filled himself with it to such good effect that a poem, "Ely Cathedral," was born of the visit. Others followed. These were duly sent out, a grid being kept showing all offers and rejections. Out of sixteen offers, one, agonizingly, took forever to be returned until, finally, the rather dry and mainly critical *A Review of English Literature* had accepted, in its vol. 1, no. 4, October 1960, a very first publication: a small poem titled "I Have No Ireland." A sharp bout of elation masked the fact that there was one typo: this was not detected until years later. Other publications followed in 1961 and 1962—inter alia in *Ambit, Outposts, Poetry & Audience, X, The Poetry Review, Stand, Peacock, Endor*—literary magazines.

For some reasons never clarified, the Wevills took their time in following up on their promise. Eventually, however, Tarn found himself a member of "the Group"—an association that, provided beforehand with a group of mimeographed poems by one author member, met every Friday evening at the home of Edward Lucie-Smith in Chelsea. Here they proceeded to tear the poems to pieces. After which, tea, cookies, and general conversation ensued. The new member did not share an aesthetic that seemed to him to descend too directly from the postcolonial "Movement" but was very grateful for the socializing. Although the eminent Ted Hughes had ceased to attend, the leading lights at the time were Philip Hobsbaum (the original founder), Peter Redgrove (probably the finest poet), and George MacBeth (following hard upon). Among those present was the young John Digby, a self-educated Cockney from Workingman's College, afflicted with a powerful stutter and the self-proclaimed pope of English Surrealism, who became Tarn's oldest literary friend. He is now one of the finest collage artists in the world, very successful in the United States, where he is married to Joan, a professor at Long Island University.

By 1963, the Group had, doubtless via Macbeth, who worked there, been offered a "signature" broadcast by the B.B.C. involving a prestigious publication of the chosen poems in *The Listener*. A group of Tarn poems inspired by Gershom Scholem's materials was chosen—their author being so naive and foolish (though perhaps also a trifle impish) as to send T. S. Eliot the cutting of the set at Faber and Faber. Need it be said: no reply. After that occasion, there were many broadcasts in Macbeth's series on the Third Program, followed by pleasant lunches. It has to be said that, of all the Groupists, Macbeth was the most friendly, unfailingly courteous, and amusing. A true gentleman, rare in the business. He was last encountered at the Rotterdam Poetry Festival in the seventies but, most sadly, died still young shortly afterward.

In the same year, the First Guinness Prize was "added to the laurels" at Cheltenham—the only major prize for poetry that this career has ever been graced with. Attending the Cheltenham Festival were John and Elizabeth Fowles, with whom a friendship swiftly developed: Fowles's first editions, from the very first *The Collector*, are all in the library. Fowles very kindly and very soon brought the poet to the attention of his publisher, Tom Maschler at Jonathan Cape. Maschler had been encountered earlier in the entourage of Sasha Moorsom but had forgotten the E.M.M. name. He was not reminded but found himself surprised when his new author appeared at his office.

In December 1963, rooms were requested (scholar's privilege) at King's "in order to complete several anthropological papers." The rooms were the ones that had been occupied as a student, but some renovations had taken place that had by now bisected them, and sleeping there on this occasion was a very curious experience. For fifteen days, work proceeded furiously on the polishing of extant poems to produce the book that, in 1964, became *Old Savage/Young City*. At one point, the poet was intercepted in the grounds, furnished with a surplice, and more or less ordered to join a service in the great chapel to perform Christmas carols and hymns for a B.B.C. broadcast. Much lip work and very little singing, but if the tape still exists, he can be seen in procession appearing to bellow lustily as the white-garbed procession exits from the building. Close to the last evening, E. M. Foster was encountered in the fellows' common room reading a paper all by himself. Feeling a burning need to go onto some sort of Elysian record as an achievement, our poet "confessed" to the elderly gentleman that he was in rooms under false pretenses. Foster was quietly generous with his time before retiring to his own quarters. There were other visits to Cambridge through the years. A sad one involved a reunion with friends from 1952–53. An ardent desire to catch up was completely scotched owing to the friends' immediately immersing themselves in liquor. One marvelous visit, however, was made in order to hear Britten conducting his *War Requiem* in the chapel. The next morning, a quick dash into Heffers Bookstore before an early return to London produced Britten standing by himself on the ground floor. A quick, effusive compliment revealed a composer eager to converse, but escape was quickly chosen up the stairs to the first floor. Such timidity costs dear. On visits to Paris, Isac Chiva had offered introductions and meetings with Paul Celan and Henri Michaux, but the novice did not feel he had anything to contribute and desisted. In the nineties the links of Chiva, college friend in Paris, and Celan were revealed in the publication of the Celan-Gisèle de Lestrange correspondence. De Lestrange was Celan's artist wife. The book also brought home to Tarn that he had, unknowingly, had a fling with Gisèle's sister during his Paris sojourn after the Sasha Moorsom breakup and had left for Chicago only six months after Chiva had met Gisèle. Gisèle had been working in the *Museé des arts et traditions populaires*, Chiva's own workplace, until he became assistant to Lévi-Strauss at the *Laboratoire d'ethnologie*.

At the time, Jonathan Cape hardly had any poetry beyond Cecil Day-Lewis and William Plomer. Design was at its nadir. Tarn refused the namby-pamby offerings of the design department, discovered to his great joy the huge folios of Edward Curtis's work in the British Museum, and selected a Northwest Coast illustration for the cover, very dramatically done in chocolate brown and black. As was the custom with first books, *Old Savage* garnered a number of reviews, many of them favorable. Later, only one reviewer, Richard Holmes for the London *Times*, consistently followed this author with attentive and intelligent criticism. Unfortunately for contemporary poetry, he later turned into an illustrious biographer of the Romantics. Maschler prided himself on being a great hunter in New York, bringing prestigious American novels (often best-sellers to boot) to British attention. He asked Tarn which American publisher he would like to have. Tarn had absolutely no idea, but Random House was a name he knew. This was aiming high though eventually foolish: Random had barely anything besides Auden. Random brought out *Old Savage* in the next year, unnecessarily changing the cover colors to olive and a sickly green. But a happy aspect of this was a friendship with the editor Nan Talese. If he had then known of New Directions (how had he not?!?), the outcome might conceivably have been different.

14.7 It may be agreed that a "literary career" began around this time with the formation of many contacts, friendships, and an international span of networks, the latter very much expanded, of course, when Tarn started formal work in 1967 with Jonathan Cape. In effect, the Cape collaboration had begun before and stretched from *Old Savage* in 1964 to that date, 1967: a fair number of suggestions made to Maschler were accepted. Among friends, Christopher Middleton, whose *Torse 3* had been found immediately impressive, was encountered at an American Embassy poetry reading and given a lift home that was interrupted when the car had to be abandoned outside Lord's cricket ground in a totally blinding pea-soup fog. For some years—until it was decided that the Brits were no longer of interest—a very fine library at the embassy was used by London poets, providing, for instance, a first hit on an LP of Kenneth Patchen reading poetry to jazz. Ted Hughes was seen from time to time, although this contact grew mainly when he took up with Assia Wevill, the wife of the Canadian poet Tarn had met in Burma. Ted's "rugged silences" were always hard to deal with and not conducive to much conversation.

On one occasion, Ted scandalized Tarn by calling him one morning and requesting that his Neruda translations be immediately taken to the British Council so that they could be read by an actor at the great Festival Hall International Poetry gathering in July 1967. One actor was going to read all the translations. Refusal was followed by a harangue, Ted gave in, and each poet had his local translator reading with him. Jon Silkin became a friendly acquaintance through his magazine *Stand*, as did the editors of other periodicals: *Ambit, Agenda, Poetry Review, Outposts*, and many others. One somewhat strangely retro relationship developed with Mary Hutchinson: a close friend of Henri Matisse, prominent in the thirties and now a patroness of the magazine *X*. This led to a collaboration and several review articles with Maurice Nadeau's *Les lettres nouvelles* in Paris. Nadeau was uninterested in English and American writing, however, preferring countries from which he could obtain subsidies—mainly Communist. One dinner at Mary's was memorable for the company of Aldous Huxley and his wife. It was a very short time since a great fire had ravaged their home in California, but Huxley was taking this very calmly. His resignation reminded Tarn of the archeologist Gordon Luce's when the Burmese threw him and his wife Daw Tee Tee unceremoniously out of Burma, leaving his famous library for a time on the Rangoon docks in the rain and depriving the couple of everything, their wedding rings included.

The playwright Arnold Wesker became a family friend: he and his wife, Dusty, often at home in Kidderpore Gardens with reciprocity at the Wesker home in Highgate. Allan and Ruth (Fainlight) Sillitoe and B. S. Johnson were also of the crowd, as were John and Elizabeth Fowles in London and at their superb home in Dorset with its long lawn leading down to the fossil-loaded cliffs. Fowles became estranged after the premature death of his Elizabeth, at one point a serious flirt of Tarn's. It was rumored that he was embarrassed to consort with writers less "successful" than himself! The publication of Fowles's *Journals* in 2004 came as a shock to Tarn with its Degree Zero anti-Semitism expressed in the need to qualify every Jew he encountered with a label, such as "the European Cocktail Jew X" and the like.

Many other contacts occurred when going out of London to various places in the British isles, either for solo or group readings. One pleasant trip led to an acquaintance with Edinburgh, then one of the world capitals of booksellers. The munificent pay was pounds five.

Principal friendship in London: Shamoon Zamir and family were very close (King's London then N.Y.U. Abu Dhabi); Shamoon wrote some of the first major papers about N.T. Anthony Rudolf and his lady, the Portuguese artist Paula Rego, were close. Italian poet Roberto Sanesi gifted Tarn with translations and readings. Tomas Segovia in Madrid idem. Dutch poet Hans ten Berge helped with travels and readings, and became a friend for life.

A difficult friendship with a literary critic who was beginning his ascent into international fame arose out of Maschler's sending him *Old Savage*. On this occasion, the critic was full of praise for the book—but it was the only time. A meeting soon afterward resulted in immediate rapport and very frequent lunches at the friend's clubs, visits to Hampstead, and visits to the friend's home in Cambridge. The friend was always worshipful when recounting meetings with celebrities: heavy breathing and significant looks would go with such remarks as "Last night, I heard a master" or "I have just had lunch with a genius," adoration of degrees and other awards and decorations bordering on the pompous. There were disarmingly frequent references to major offers of employment, either rejected or not to materialize. Disregard for America as a "derivative culture" (he had made himself vastly unpopular there) was another barrier. Conversation was extremely intimate but fraught with the friend's obsession with Jewish survival and his rule that no Jew could ever complain of anything whatsoever because s/he was a survivor of the Holocaust and should be everlastingly grateful for that. One aspect of such attitudes was that Tarn's sempiternal worries about not having time for poetry and his desire to "get out of" anthropology were thoroughly and uncompromisingly rejected. The argument ran: "You have the best anthropology job in your field; you are or, can be, a major anthropologist: nothing else is of any importance." Further, all poetry after *Old Savage* was deridingly deemed, not without barbs of barely masked irony and sarcasm, to be imitative of X, Y, or Z on the Anglo-American scene. In the end, the critic was exerting himself continually on behalf of anthropological texts he had not even read while offering no help of any kind where it was truly needed. No number of statements that good or bad/successful or unsuccessful, *this* was what Tarn wished to do, did, and would do under any circumstances whatsoever brought about any change at any time. After the discovery that the man had had a small pamphlet of poems published many years before and his acknowledgment, in one letter, that he would very dearly have wished to be a poet, Tarn began to suspect that some kind of Blakean jealousy was at work here. During the breakup of Tarn's marriage, letters came demanding to know how anyone could possibly "break up a Jewish marriage." Many of the critic's concerns were very deeply felt, undoubtedly very worthy, and most movingly expressed. However, this interference could not be accepted, and with many a sorrowful complaint coming from the other side, Tarn put an end to the relationship. That the loss of George Steiner has been in every way a serious lifelong loss is unquestionable.

14.8 For a time, Tarn enjoyed being on the "international circuit," a kind of "old boy" system in which meeting with a certain crowd in one place ensured one's invitation to the next. The first great "fix" was Berlin in 1964 at an international meeting organized by the Congress of Cultural Freedom, a powerful organ in Britain through its magazine *Encounter* before it was discovered to be subsidized by the CIA. There were a very few "political" occasions—such as being taken as a group to, and photographed informally at, the Berlin Wall—but for the most part the gathering was firmly literary. Kenneth Rexroth had been unable to attend and very kindly suggested Tarn as a replacement, which made this one-book person into one of the "key" speakers with a paper on "Poetry and the Science of Communication." Jorge Luis Borges (a lunch with whom revealed that he knew neither Hebrew nor Arabic: a surprise!), Herbert Read, Wole Soyinka, Vasko Popa (a great circuit organizer), James Merrill, Stephen Spender (always on the make), W. H. Auden, and Langston Hughes (a very delightful and kind man) were among the luminaries there. Auden was generous enough to take a *Collected Shorter Poems* to his hotel and not only inscribe it but fill it with annotated corrections. Günter Grass and Helmut Heissenbuttel were among the German visitors: regrettably, Ingeborg Bachmann was not.

Keith Botsford, a young novelist with an irritatingly "mysterious" demeanor, was in Berlin. He had joined the Congress for Cultural Freedom in 1962, but Tarn was unaware of the implications at the time. He then revealed himself as an organizer of a special gathering within the general P.E.N. meeting on the magnificent lake at Bled, Yugoslavia in 1967. The general membership of P.E.N. was not too happy about this, but the meeting was grand, with Susan Sontag, Vasko Popa, Hungarian poet Gyula Illyés, Czech poet Miroslav Holub, theater critic Jan Kott, and many others. There was an epic meal with Miguel Angel Asturias, a right-wing Jungian writer who was the Chilean ambassador to Belgrade, Pablo Neruda, and Miguel Angel Asturias (Guatemalan). The literati were supposed to be attending a local theatrical performance, but Neruda kept everyone at the table way past the starting time. Eventually, neglecting as always to pay the bill, Neruda took the group to the theater. Tarn sat at the back but saw Neruda walking down the aisle, saluting people right and left and agreeing with them as to how marvelous the first act had been.

Neruda had become a friend shortly after *Old Savage*. One day, Maschler had asked whether there was any interest in translating Neruda. Tarn felt that the master already had so many translators that it would be absurd to try to tackle him alone and, after doing *The Heights of Macchu Picchu* by himself in 1965–66, assembled three others: Alastair Reid, Anthony Kerrigan, and W. S. Merwin for a *Selected Poems* (1970 in London, 1972 in New York). Neruda was always very friendly, liked visiting Kidderpore Gardens (which he called "the cool house"), and always brought a gift all the way from Chile: on one occasion there was a black ceramic guitar-playing figure that cannot have been easy to transport—especially because his luggage may well have contained a number of them. A correspondence was maintained, including an invitation to visit Isla Negra, but this was prevented by the horrible coup against Allende and Neruda's murder. A huge amount of help for the *Macchu Picchu*, perhaps too much, had been offered (and gratefully accepted) by Robert Pring Mill, an Oxford don who was expert in Neruda's work. Meetings with him were extraordinary in their attention to the minutest detail. Pring Mill did not participate in the *Selected*.

The Bled occasion was memorable for another reason. Tarn had informed Maschler that the "three pillars" of the program he wanted to establish at Cape were Charles Olson, Robert Duncan, and Louis Zukofsky. Olson was understood to be attending Bled after reading with Ezra Pound at Spoleto immediately before and was expected daily. In his pocket, our budding editor carried a general Cape contract for Olson to sign. One day, after the conference had started, Tarn was watching a film when a huge presence crashed down beside him. Sidelong glance. "You must be Olson." "And you must be Tarn." Olson was staying in the room above Tarn's at the hotel overlooking the majestic Bled lake and agreed to come down one afternoon for a drink on the balcony. His discourse, alas, remained deeply undecipherable—as it did for a great many people at that time, it seems, except for the initiates. He signed a Jargon *Maximus*, writing "here Tarn for the future" (a standard inscription), then suggested we walk over to the party being given at Tito's villa. On approaching the entrance, but while still a ways away, Olson spied a diminutive lady just inside the door. "Excuse me," he said and slid away. Within moments, the great dancer was whirling around with the lady in his arms to the tune of some exquisite waltz.

On one occasion an exciting trip to an apparently almost deserted Prague during the Dubček window led to an immediate gift of a sum of money for the use of poems in *Plamen* magazine, visits to all the museums and famous sites, membership in the Prague Poetry Society, a dear friendship with its director Peter Pujman, many meetings with Czech writers and two young actors of the National Theater, as well as the episode at the Staranová synagogue that figures in Poem Ten of *The Beautiful Contradictions*. For some reason, this being Passover time, Tarn had determined to go to a service at this oldest temple in Europe. He arrived as people were going home. Unexpectedly overwhelmed with nostalgia, he returned the next morning and stood at the door. He was led inside and given a minor "blessing": holding the ton weight of a Torah scroll. He also participated in getting rid of some German tourists who had strayed in during the service. Then the occasion was spoiled by one of those alienating details he had always suffered from. Embarrassed at being asked for money, he proffered some dollars and was rudely told "No, not like that, slip them into the prayer book!" He had never learned the codes!

The whole site, however, with the famous graveyard and other buildings (beginning to be turned into a crowded tourist attraction on a later visit), was entrancing. A lifelong memory remains of a long walk taken one day from here all the way across the river and, climbing through the organ sounds of musicians resoundingly practicing in many baroque churches, finishing up above the lilac trees high at the crowning castle.

Throw Fifteen

15.1 Continuing from Throw 13, let there be a notion of "heraldic systems" involving a form of manageable simplicity that remains constant—the heraldic shield as a primary model—into which complexity is introduced by the manifold permutations that can be undergone by the content elements. My interest in and fascination with such diverse matters as heraldry itself—stamps, postcards, badges, medals, liveries, uniforms, birds, islands, human bodies—revel in this constant interplay of simple form and complex content.

What I look for here is the primal or archetypal form—an "idea" if you will—that stands as the model for all possible forms: it is not for nothing that Plato is often identified as the philosopher par excellence of the archaic worldview. Let us say that there is such an idea, such an "Eden" if you like, at the fountainhead of each system of topography. And add that grid-like classificatory projections onto elements perceived as possible members of a system take place in the mind as part of an attempt to impose, or reimpose as is the case here, the original Eden on the mass of formless data that the world manifests. This, it seems to me, is the initial move in any act of creation.

The first phase of this act of creation may be identified as the act of collecting, of bringing into a defined area those objects that may become relevant to any pursuit: hence, in poetry, that dawn-like shimmer of the lists

that, in primitive and archaic poetry (great shade of Homer!), have so fasci-
nated poets and critics alike through the ages. Here, much revolves around
the problem of just how the elements of any given list are gathered, on what
basis they are brought together, what the criterion is for the impression of
belonging together that prompts the collector to join things in one way and
not in another. We know, however, from Lévi-Strauss and other anthropol-
ogists, that the criteria of one culture are not necessarily apparent to another
culture: all men classify but not in the same way. There are, in nature, certain
apparently obvious selection criteria: birds, fish, animals, plants evidently be-
long together in some way that is obvious to us Westerners and can thus be
arrayed in species. Yet for any one category—plants, for example—the tribes
of the Philippines, say, or of the Amazon will perceive species differently
from a Linnaeus. Contemporary Western botanists may learn much from
such perceptions. We are dealing then with a complex network of decisions
in which it is difficult to tell the "real" from the "fantasy" basis of any given
decision. For poetics, the concept of metaphor is obviously involved.

I am as interested here in the "real" as in the "fantasy" nature of such mental
activities. To take one example, it would seem as if the behavior of islanders,
in relation to off-islanders, is a heraldic constant pretty well everywhere on
the globe, although we may have to differentiate between communities com-
posed uniquely of islands (such as those of the South Seas) and communities
composed of islands and a nearby continental "mainland." It would be inter-
esting, I imagine, to study the nomenclature of islands with this in mind:
to see how often the same terms recur, beginning with simples like "North
Cape," "South Inlet," or "East Harbor." The process of establishing social "is-
lands" on a continuous mainland—e.g., for elitistic purposes—would seem
to illustrate as well as any other the way in which a group of people might
start with an "Edenic" vision, a fantasy which they use to elect or impose
another new Eden, one that becomes sociologically real, by cutting up reality
in a certain way. That there is much to be said and studied about "historical
areas"—zoning, election districts, Native American reservations, retirement
communities, etc. in these States from this point of view—with very differ-
ent rationales and purposes, it goes without saying.

15.2 Evidently, we keep turning round and round the question as to whether
"reality" is bound or unbound, closed or open, finite or infinite—including
the mind with which we apprehend that reality. This can send us back as far
as the very creation, or not, of the universe itself: the question of whether it
was or was not created is not as insane as it appears if the notion of parallel

universes is contemplated, where our world might be some kind of fantasy in the "mind" of another. In poetics, the question stands at the back of contemporary creativity itself: whether we use traditional models and forms or not, and if so to what extent, whether we use traditional bodies of myth or not, etc. etc. etc. What is the road from a Homer to a Dante to a Pound? For Homer, we are already asking whether the poet described the society he had at hand or, more likely, whether he was recalling or re-creating (correctly or incorrectly?) a society already dead. The issue is somewhat simpler with Dante, based in his allegiance to Catholic history and tradition. It becomes open again with Pound, given his use of very varied bodies of myth and history from a variety of cultures: his selection of course. It is in fact perhaps in Pound that the closed/open universe issue makes itself most critically visible in our time. Do we then sempiternally reinvent or continue to invent—both with various degrees of allegiance to "reality"? Perhaps the mathematician or the physicist is the only one who can answer or may, one day, be in a position to give the ultimate answer. The only assurance you have, it seems, is in the ludic power or compulsion of artists to deal with models of unity for their own sakes (for their as-if sakes we might add in these confused times) as an insistent prior condition of any apprehension.

Interest in myth is strong in our era—perhaps because basic "reality" seems to be so poor in anything that could be identified as "spiritual." We are interested in returning to beginnings as the "Ethnopoetics" movement, following on Pound, makes clear. The temptation to mime ancient, well-established models of unity—even though the factual basis of these models has been extinguished—is very strong. We are constantly drawn back to the "primitive." Provided that we are not under too many illusions on this score (there is no way we can become "Native Americans," "Papuans," not even, in the case of Black nationalists, "Africans," any more than we can become, in a fully sociocultural sense, "Hindus" or even "Buddhists"), this reexamination of ancient sources gives strength. A great deal of this has migrated into the major modern movements: Cubism, Futurism, Dadaism, Surrealism, Constructivism, and the like: the beginnings of a long period in art history in which repetition through appropriation becomes standard procedure. There is, in Surrealism, a strong push toward enlarging basic "reality" through the dream, the fantastic, the occult. More, it is often forgotten that early Surrealism was not an "art movement" but conceived of itself as a total revolution with Rimbaud's "*Changer la vie!*" as its motto: "reality" was not only to be enlarged but to be utterly changed, utterly transformed. It is for this reason that the urge to add *Changer la société* to the motto made such an issue of relations between

Surrealism and the French Communist Party for so long. Enlarging the debate, it may be possible to say that even our contemporary wars act toward enlarging "reality." The average American knew next to nothing about Islam before the two Gulf wars. Now the word and a great deal about it are becoming household knowledge—as well as misunderstanding—among many.

Here again the dialectic of the open and the closed. The disunity of Lautréamont's sewing machine and umbrella conjunction—to take a famous metaphor adopted by André Breton—can be shown to be but a form of the apprehension of a more inclusive unity at the point where apparent contradictions, in Breton's formula, cease to be apprehended as contradictions. Michel Carrouge's insufficiently known classic *Les machines célibataires* (an example of structuralist myth analysis before Structuralism's time) documents this notion for a wide range of pre-Surrealist and Surrealist authors. Both Dadaism and Surrealism were powerful forces in the present move toward Ethnopoetics. Anthropologists Claude Lévi-Strauss and Michel Leiris, among others, had their early experiences of poetry and poetics in that entourage.

15.3 Any weaknesses in the fascination with models of unity? It would seem that a poet's powers are perhaps most under stress when he or she undertakes that initial act of collecting. I note that Blake's totalizations for one, while very successful at certain moments (in that of *Jerusalem*, for instance, or in that of the reunification after the *sparagmos* of cosmic man), are uncomfortably strung out at others, such as when he attempts to list the revolutionary nations from Peru to Japan or the counties, churches, and other sacred sites of the English Holy Land. There is an element of debility in the urge, constantly felt, to be all inclusive. The drive to catalog *all* elements of an important phenomenon or event, to exhaust and saturate the description, often conflicts with the urge to select in order to achieve the optimal degree of emphasis.

Suppose that we are treating a beloved body as a heraldic shield. For one much given to projections (I avoid, right now, the characterial implications of projection), it may well be that the "Eden" of the ideal physical body preexists in the mind and that this mind attempts to impose it upon anybody with which it comes into sexual contact. The temptation, then, in any lyrical throw, might be to record each and every one of the nameable parts of that body and to distinguish them from parts of all other possible bodies belonging to the same system. Thus, the hair is . . . , the eyes are . . . , the lips are . . . , and so forth. Faced with such a catalog, the poet retreats: selection and exclusion must take place, or the poem becomes unmanageable.

It would be good to know more about the interplay of these forces: obviously, the genre and structure of each poem has to be involved. There must be several different mechanisms. I may achieve my aim by selecting for praise some part of the beloved body not usually commented upon: this should lift the banal into originality. Or, bring in metaphor: such and such a part is like . . . something unimaginable before—and the trick is done. Breton achieved this in the famous "Free Union" poem.

The very force of such unusual selections is surely that they may give the illusion of totality, of everything having been said when this is not the case. The shock of surprise is such that the recognition and recall of absent components are inhibited.

This is not academic. French poets of the sixteenth century created a whole genre that we might render in English as "Heraldicizers of the Female Body." Check out the section *Blasonneurs du corps féminin* in the Pleiade volume titled *Poètes du XVIème siècle*, edited by Albert-Marie Schmidt, 1964. I need hardly add today that only cultural history to date has limited similar treatments of the male body. It may be coming very soon.

The problem in its widest aspects, however, still eludes us: selection with us is most times a matter of trusted, instinctive craft rather than reasoned analysis. And the critic, apart from the highly perceptive, truly creative individual, can only speak ex post facto. As a footnote, I would suppose that Lévi-Strauss on the activity of bricolage would be found to be pertinent here.

I come back again then to the perception that if one part of the mind weighs anchor to sail across perilous and uncharted seas in the processual aspect of creation, another part of that same mind will tie itself down to the structures of the oldest topographies. Much as this may be disliked by proponents of various forms of the "perpetual revolution," it may be that freedom in one aspect of poetic activity must be compensated for by a lack of freedom in another. Much of poetic theory in our time stresses the processual at the expense of the structural. Ultimately it is a matter, as I was already hinting in my 1964 Berlin paper, of the rigors of the theory of communication.

On the one hand, we have slavish adherence to old models in the belief that the very body of poetry is exploding or falling apart and is no longer communicating to anybody but the small cliques who produce the stuff. Incest instead of marriage. The uninhibited and totally unrestricted free play of an ego (however much it may deny the role of ego), an individual consciousness at sea in a time of great cultural diversity and ever-accelerating change, presents a real danger of communication breakdown, of irrelevance—in a word, of unreadability. On the other hand, we live in this time and no other: the stakes are high; there is everything to be gained by losing one's chains. These (1970s) are a very great time for American poetry while some other poetries, in Europe mainly, have been running ashore and beaching in sand. The challenges of living in this society are being met by great bodies of work in which the long and difficult philosophical poem is as much part of the venture as the perennial lyric. With Pound, "beloved Irish Yeats never forgotten," followed by Williams and Zukofsky, Olson and Duncan, Rexroth and Dahlen, we have a set of investigations that will rank high in the history of the American word. The point of view discussed here takes theirs as the central tradition: there are other efforts of importance sharing more or less in this experiment. But all this breaks down with the category Postmodern and the triumph of unlimited disassociation and disjunction.

15.4 Revisions and rewrites in 2004, thus in the first years of the twenty-first century. I have often wondered—pressured no doubt by those who feel let down by an insistence on a both/and model, the continued stress on structure as well as process, added to an interpretation of the new highly disjunctivist "Language" poetries as essentially incestuous, sterile, and unconvincing, bedecked in the emperor's new clothes, meaningful, if at all, as a totally inbred collective illusion—whether I have not paid enough attention to the need for enlarging, indeed for transforming "reality" as well as accepting what "reality" is under our noses compelled by iron sociological fact. What I come up against, again and again, is the question of readership, of consumption, without which our production appears meaningless. I have said a hundred times that we overproduce writers and underproduce readers, that poetry readership and appreciation (despite superficial signs ever leapt upon by the superficial media) are in free fall, that the life of the poet in American society has, for the most part, become a joke. There are always answers to such comments, but the answers always appear to me to involve incest—the production and consumption of poetry by poets for poets—and not marriage, the age-old production by poets for consumption by nonpoets: "general readers," average human beings, in order that society as a whole may be enriched. And that we are not left with specialized and very academicized cliques.

The rock against which you beat your head is that there is a need, internal to the art, to "make it new" and that this often involves pushing the edge of the envelope beyond what communication theory will tolerate. There is also the need to communicate with significant sections of the public so that poetry has a voice, has an influence, has a chance of "changing life" and "changing the world." I do not have the answer. I can only raise the question while not believing overmuch in the possibility of such changes.

Many years ago, when I began as a writer, I was fascinated with the idea of a privileged garden, a *hortus conclusus*, that would be lit only by an inner light emanating from the garden itself and no other source. I have no idea whence this vision came. Later, in some way that I cannot now recall with any precision except to know that it did not arise out of reading, I associated the idea of the creation of poetry with the hope and promise that would be contained in an absolutely unknown, never before seen or witnessed, *totally new* object that would appear one morning, preferably in a garden. Hope and promise I specify because, as a depressive, it has always been difficult for me to gather energy for the making of poetry without a surge of hope in the future not just for myself, but contextually if possible as always, for the planet and mankind. The sense of hope was intimately involved with the appearance of such a new object while depression was involved with interminable repetitions of the already existing, of "the same."

Writing in the new millennium now, I have recently discovered that certain trends in contemporary philosophy (Benjamin, Bloch, Blanchot, Levinas, Derrida) have focused attention on the notion of the absolutely new, the absolutely different, and the absolutely other—all these designed to totally avoid any repetition of anything already existing, any repetition of "the same." These trends are marked by hopes that have been associated with the idea of the messianic, of a subject matter to be called "messianic"— not a formal messianic such as exists in every traditional, established belief system—but a "structural messianic" as it were, a messianic without a Messiah, whose sole aim it is to maintain the future absolutely open by guaranteeing that nothing already said or known (hence any already conceived notion of a Messiah) can be said or known of it. This would establish a mechanism, a vision for the perpetuation of human hope and an all-encompassing idea of justice, involving justice for all of history, for the dead and the unborn as well as those presently alive.

When pushed to extremes, there is something exasperatingly fantasy-like about such views and aspirations, something that seems to relegate these ideas to the realm of language and not to the realm of any possible action. I am therefore still regularly thrown back on my notion that a both/and view of creation is required. First, there is the notion of process as an activity absolutely open upon the future so that anything that can possibly be created should have its opportunity and that the opportunity should persist *in absoluto* during the whole extent of the particular creation. Second, there is the paired notion located in the recognition that process, in art, invariably begins out of previously existing structures and falls back at the end of the act of creation into structure—though this time it is, of course, a new structure that modifies those "previously existing." Without this starting from, and falling back into, structure, no example of "reality" whatsoever could exist: an alternative world would be thinkable in fantasy but could never be brought to birth. As far as poetry is concerned, we would never have any poems, and this, in the last resort, is the only criterion we as poets can apply to the question of life, possible or not.

Throw Sixteen

16.1 The strain of keeping up the S.O.A.S. job and of launching a "literary career"—effectually leading two lives hidden from each other at times even in a single room at a single party—became heavier and heavier. Colleagues were mystified. On one occasion, not long before Tarn's departure from his job, a longer than usual stay at Maschler's "Carney," a Welsh cottage in the Black Mountains out of Hereford, resulted in a call to Professor Haimendorf that his lecturer was "stuck on a mountain" by the weather. This became a joke in the Anthro Department. Meantime, negotiations had been going on at Cape regarding the launching of the small book series Cape Editions under Tarn's editorship as well as the foundation of the little press to be known as Cape Goliard.

Tarn had suggested to Maschler that if anything worthwhile was to be done in the context of the present literary scene in England, the progressive energy of a "little press" should be married to the distributive power of a major publisher. At a party in the course of which the psychiatrist R. D. Laing had been dancing with great abandon dressed only in a pink nightgown, Barry Hall, printer and designer, and Tom Raworth, poet, of the Goliard Press had been encountered, and a copy of its Charles Olson's *West*, just published, had changed hands. One day, on bed, floor, chairs, and other furniture at home, Tarn laid out every little-press series he owned and invited Maschler over. Although Goliard had only two or three publications at the time, it was preferred, and Cape Goliard was formed with Hall in charge together with Maschler and Tarn. Raworth, distrusting the big league, preferred to depart. Separate quarters for the press were established in St. John's Wood, where Barry worked extremely hard to pull off the coup. The negotiations with Cape about status and pay were so complex that Tarn omitted asking for a share in Cape Goliard, and he was not reminded to do so.

All this had begun, as mentioned earlier, for Tarn on landing at San Francisco on his way to Hawaii in 1961 and spending some time in the basement of poet Lawrence Ferlinghetti's City Lights bookstore. The haul from there turned out to be far more important for the future than the finding of a used Galway Kinnell's *Christ on the Avenue C* for 50 cents in a Honolulu bookshop. It did not take long for Tarn to realize that everything he found to be lacking in British poetry, as well as in the works of what he called the American "suicide club" (Lowell, Berryman, Plath) offered by the likes of Al Alvarez as role models for the Brits, could be found in the writers he had picked up in California. From then on, while also finding some British authors for Cape Goliard, he joined Hall (already very much in touch) in prospecting among the "New Americans." This effort was spelled out in a piece titled "World Wide Open: The Work Laid Before Us in This Disunited Kingdom," published in Barry Miles's *International Times*. Miles, later a biographer of Ginsberg, had a bookstore not far from S.O.A.S. that was an even better source for the New Americans' publications than most places in the United States—although the late, lamented Eighth Street Bookstore in New York was a sacred resort until it closed, never to be replaced.

Many a meaningful visit to Cape occurred during Tarn's tenure. One by Ginsberg included a party at Cape's, 30 Bedford Square, in the course of which Allen went around the room sucking the suits' earlobes and whispering in their ears. Brit embarrassment can be imagined. There was also a serious dinner at Maschler's. Idem for Burroughs. Duncan came for a reading, and Tarn interviewed him for the B.B.C. All that was needed was a "Well, Robert, how are you doing in London?" or some such banality, and the interview was transmogrified into the Duncanian version of the Great American Monologue.

The July 1967 Festival Hall reading brought many things and many people together. Ginsberg and Olson participated as well as Neruda, Holub, Herbert, Bonnefoy, and a host of others. The star turned out for Tarn to be Giuseppe Ungaretti, who read, extraordinarily, by means of silence: not even *sotto voce*, but with an astonishing quiet projected only a little hoarsely out of the back of his throat. There was a huge party afterward in a large luxury apartment taken at Hanover Terrace in Regent's Park by Panna O'Grady, Olson's companion on the trip. An unpleasant moment occurred as Tarn, usually quiet and wallflowerish at parties, was sitting on a couch occupied, as it happened, by a very drunken John Berryman. Suddenly, across the room there were two of his "maestros," Olson and Dorn, crouching and snickering at Tarn "fraternizing with the enemy." Tarn had not exchanged a word with Berryman but then got him to sign a book. Dorn, first met at a reading in the Charing Cross Road with Anselm Hollo, became a good friend in later years but was not an easy person to deal with on first contact. During a visit to Essex University, where he was teaching, a call on Dorn provoked a scornful volley regarding Cape's publishing of Zukofsky's *A*. This, together with Duncan, Maschler had stolen from Cape Goliard for the Cape main list. Dorn's view was that Cape had taken the faulty American edition and simply reprinted it under its covers. The wrathful Slinger was not pacified by the news that it was a miracle that Cape had taken on Zuke at all. On most things, the main house's new ventures did not do away with counting pennies: a long correspondence with Octavio Paz was concerned largely with Octavio's wanting a new book out of Cape and having to be satisfied eventually with the reprint of a New Directions volume.

16.2 Securing everybody one might want for a publishing list was not an easy matter. Some poets like Creeley and Snyder already had United Kingdom publishers, Cape's principal rival being a young doctor, Stuart Montgomery, who produced very-fine-looking books by these two and many others at his Fulcrum Press. He was even publishing Duncan until pirate Tarn, during his initiatory trip to the United States and meeting with Duncan on Mt. Tamalpais, managed to persuade the poet that his work was far too extensive to be dealt with by only one house. On the international, pluridisciplinary Cape Editions front, the "founding editor" did not have it all his own way. Maschler occasionally discovered titles—Vaclav Havel, Bohumil Hrabal, Sklavomir Mrozek, Uwe Johnson, for example—to whose inclusion Tarn had to agree, not necessarily unwillingly. Nonetheless, the first four volumes were Olson's *Call Me Ishmael*, two titles by Roland Barthes (his first commissioned translations into English), and Claude Lévi-Strauss's *The Scope of Anthropology*, his Collège de France inaugural lecture. These were followed by science titles (von Frisch and Huxley), "political" titles (Castro, Eldridge Cleaver, and Lefèvre), and anthropological titles (Edmund Leach), as well as many literary titles (Jarry, Trakl, William Carlos Williams, Bonnefoy, Parra, Breton, Zukofsky, Hikmet), most of them being Tarn acquisitions. A substantial portion of his work went into the general list: Lévi-Strauss was an example. Occasional amusement: Eldridge Cleaver's *Soul on Ice* was abridged for Cape Editions over Tarn's counsel . . . until Maschler tumbled to the fact that he had a US best-seller on his hands and brought out the whole text in Cape hardback. An abridged Cleaver did remain in Cape Editions.

An American connection was established with Richard Grossman in New York, and visits to him were always very pleasant. There were also some harmless shell games played with titles in that context. Among Tarn's titles, *Where Babylon Ends* was done by Cape Goliard, London/Grossman, New York; *The Beautiful Contradictions* by Cape Goliard, London/Random House, New York; and *A Nowhere for Vallejo* by Random House, New York/Cape, London.

16.3 Leave from the "best Southeast Asia teaching position in the world" had been taken without unpleasantness from S.O.A.S. but with some bemusement on the faculty side just at a time when promotion to reader (associate professor) seemed a distinct possibility. The change was celebrated by a huge stock-taking and exploratory trip to the States and Canada. This began with a final anthro paper at the Asian Studies Association meeting at the University of Michigan. It went on to include visits to Maschler connections in New York: the agent Candida Donadio and the writer and publisher Angus Cameron at Knopf. In that city, Louis Zukofsky virtually sat Tarn on his knee to explain how his Catullus versions worked: the book had been handsomely published by Cape Goliard. There were visits to John Ashbery and other New Yorkers with the aim of discovering availabilities. In Aspen, Colorado, Jonathan Williams and Ronald Johnson were encountered again (they had spent time in London, turned many on to the stocks of Ezra Pound pamphlets in Peter Russel's bookstore, imparted more information on the New Americans, and inspired Tarn to start a blank book gradually filled by poets on his journeys). A memorable long mountain walk to Conundrum Hot Springs ended with Jonathan, Toby Olson, Paul Blackburn, and others all sitting in the raw in a small stone bath, later to be revived and comforted by Ronald's great cooking. A visit with Blackburn, who had just separated from his wife, revealed Paul's vitriolic feelings about her at that moment. A short poem titled "Ajax to Red; for the Tarn in August 1967" has a third stanza that reads:

I know where I am
and with whom. Name
of Sara Blackburn, one
very beautiful woman.
             Fuck her.
       I intend to.
          etc. beautifully.

16.4 Up into Canada via Big Sky Country and over to Montreal for the Great Expo Poetry Festival. Pound was firmly expected but was sick. A number of people had come up mainly to see him: Robert Lowell, Robert Creeley, and Denise Levertov among them as well as the very strange British poet George Barker, who seemed to enjoy riling and teasing Tarn, and Czeslaw Milosz, the Polish-Lithuanian poet. This was followed by a flight to Calgary, at which point Tarn realized that he could continue by train and did so on an exciting Canadian Pacific ride through Banff and Lake Louise all the way to Vancouver. A stay with Robin Blaser was occasioned by Blaser very kindly providing Tarn with his first reading on the American continent at the great aircraft-carrier–shaped Simon Frazer University—although Blaser remained permanently reluctant to offer either Jack Spicer's work or his own: Tarn never found out why at that juncture.

After a bus trip up Vancouver Island to Nanaimo, a ferry crossing, and a return to Vancouver, the expedition moved south and caught Robert Duncan, Kenneth Rexroth, and William Everson in one single reading at the top of Mount Tamalpais. A problem arose: Palo Alto had to be reached pronto for a midnight meeting with Kenneth and Miriam Patchen. Permission had been obtained from Cape for Tarn's editing of a selected Patchen. Duncan kindly commandeered a young man and ordered him to get Tarn down the mountain to the bus stop for Palo Alto. Miriam was a delightful hostess, and Patchen, very pleased to be considered in England, heaved himself out of bed in great pain as always and chatted for a couple of hours (work was eventually done on the *Selected* in Maschler's Welsh "Carney" without any reference to the New Directions selection and turned out to have only a 10 percent overlap: the Patchens claimed to like the Cape one better). After this the next couple of days brought first acquaintance with the Duncan and Rexroth versions of the Great American Monologue. Everson was not available. Back in New York, a visit to Lowell brought up his usual dismissing of Olson as "too much in the line of Pound," and a gift of used clothes "for your children" from Elizabeth Hardwick prompted the recipient to wonder whether he really looked as impoverished as she obviously took him to be.

16.5 Life was intensely busy at Kidderpore Gardens, and for the first and only time in his life, Tarn had a secretary, a very sweet girl who eventually died tragically of lymphoma. All the Cape Editions and Cape Goliard correspondence was dictated to her. Tarn's own work continued apace. A young man who also died of lymphoma, Tony White, was in charge of the series Penguin Modern Poets and placed his friend in number 7 with Jon Silkin and Richard Murphy even though Tarn had published only *Old Savage*. This was a huge gift. White was a very dear friend. His mother once said that Tony's very last, very long letter was sent to Atitlán in 1969: most regrettably it failed to arrive, and Tarn has wondered about its content ever since. The *October* sequence followed *The Beautiful Contradictions* in 1969 in a beautiful edition by poet friend Asa Benveniste's Trigram Press, another "rival" to Cape Goliard and Fulcrum. Contacts with Roberto Sanesi in Italy and the Unicorn Press people in the United States occasioned publications in both those areas: broadsides, anthology appearances, an Italian translation of *B.C.* and, at Unicorn, the first work of Victor Segalen published in English, a selected *Stelae* that, unfortunately, has never been reprinted. There were also contacts with French poets Claude Royet-Journoud and Anne Marie Albiach and their magazine *Siècle à mains* in London, out of which arose a meeting with Michel Deguy that grew into a lifelong friendship. The Seigle continued to be seen in Paris, often for the opening of their shows: at one of these Giacometti was present, and an invitation to his studio resulted. Coffee with novelist Michel Butor, an old friend of the Seigle days, would be a staple when he came through London.

Likewise with many Czechs, including dear Peter Pujman, a friend also, like many Czechs, of the Weskers. A translation conference at Bratislava was the occasion for another visit to Prague just two weeks before the Russians marched in. This was linked to a first trip to Russia as a member of the *Société européenne de culture* that an Anglo-Irish poet, George Buchanan, had persuaded Tarn to join. It was the only intellectual group at the time that claimed to be in touch with the Soviets. The official Soviets of course. This first visit to Russia was full of strange events. During the day, Tarn attended meetings. In the evening, he hung out with a young minder who had contacts with writers in the underground. One poet had lost both legs throwing himself out of a moving train for the love of a girl. He lived off translating children's books. Another took Tarn very late one night to a house partitioned into many rooms by sheets and placed an icon in his hands. It later turned out that this young man desired a record player from a dollar shop—but the gift was treasured as a gift. At one meeting of the *Société*, Tarn, on an impulse, sent a note to a gentleman opposite stating "I would rather be in the Hermitage." A note came back: "Wait five minutes, go there to entrance such and such. Present this card." It was signed with the name of the director of the Hermitage, and Tarn had the place to himself. He chose to look at the astonishingly rich Central Asian galleries.

Nineteen sixty-eight was a vintage year, first at the huge *Congreso cultural internacional* in Havana reached after an epic flight with Arnold Wesker. The pair had gone on a Cubana Airlines flight to Madrid looking forward to a brief trip to the Prado, but they were limited in the end to a drink at the Café Gijón, where Tarn had spent so much time with Spanish poets as a student. They learned post hoc that an engine had caught fire on departing London and that the aircraft had had to go back. At dawn, they were in Gander and, not content with a dinner served, demanded as a right a full eggs-and-bacon breakfast. Shopping for items not obtained in Canada the previous year included a stout pair of mukluks. All down the American coast into broiling Havana, margaritas and an immediate barrage of questions from television and radio about how one reacted to arriving in Cuba. Difficult when one had only just landed! Tarn saw Argeliers León again, now head of anthropology in Cuba, but was prevented from seeing his old friend the *Santería* priest for whom—following a promise to bring something from Africa on the next visit—Tarn had remembered to bring an Ashanti gold weight. This, while many others were taken to rituals by León, was a major, painful, and incomprehensible disappointment. It would never be cleared up. The list of people attending would fill a chapter: Sartre, Leiris, Cortázar (from whom the hilarious *Cronopios y Famas* stories could not be obtained despite a letter from Cortázar indicating he would like Cape Editions to do it), Blas de Otero, Hans Magnus Enzensberger, José Lezama Lima, and an army of Cuban poets, many of whom became friends: Pablo Armando Fernández, Roberto Fernández Retamar, and others—while seniors like Eliseo Diego and Cintio Vitier were greatly admired. Friends were also made at the Casa de las Américas and sets of their publications and their magazine added to Tarn's library. The result of all this was a Cape Goliard and Grossman *Con Cuba* volume, edited by Tarn, partly with materials previously brought out in Margaret Randall's wonderful *El corno emplumado* magazine and partly with poems from his own collections.

Everywhere one went, boxes of cigars: in the end you had to smoke one puff of each cigar and throw it away: no one wanted cigars! A three-hour speech by Fidel Castro was endured, and a visit to his house provided the collector with legendary presidential white cigar bands (one of which has gone into the History Museum at Santa Fe, New Mexico). Avoiding the arranged tours, Tarn and Wesker decided they would like to go to Santiago de Cuba. The organizers said: too far. A banner was made with *Santiago o Muerte!* in big letters, holding which the two marched around the conference site. T. and W. were eventually sent to Santiago to see the proud medical centers of that region. Later in the year came the Knokke Poetry Biennale on Tarn's beloved Belgian coast with new visits to Damme, the great medieval barn at Lissewege, Bruges, and Ghent.

16.6 It was all over in two short years. Tarn was told that his work at Cape was being curtailed because a new editor, Ed Victor, was joining the firm; because Cape Editions and Cape Goliard, despite great reviews and critical success, especially for C.E., were not making money (they needed, in Tarn's opinion, ten years to make a mark rather than two); and so on and so forth. Some personal matters were also in evidence: it was clear that Tarn was somewhat cavalier in his approach to publishing and its protocols. Indeed, the main reason was probably that Tarn wanted to remain an editor, a title hunter as he conceived of it, and not become a full publisher, laden with administrative, contractual, and other business responsibilities. There may also have been other personal matters between Tom and me.

Some curious hangovers to all this. Cape Editions continued for a time, with Maschler making the decisions before it and Cape Goliard were erased and Cape reverted to what it had always been: a very small and fine but rather conventional outfit depending mainly on American best-sellers. Much later, Maschler and his partners made a fortune by selling Cape to Random House U.K., with Tom retiring to a huge house in Provence while also keeping "Carney" in Wales. Shortly after immigrating to the States in 1970, Tarn found, to his surprise—nothing having been said—the *whole* of his Cape and Grossman stocks on a table at Barnes and Noble on Fifth Avenue for 47 cents per volume. In 1970, too, Barry Hall had left his wife and somehow persuaded Maschler to accept his running Cape Goliard from Santa Fe, New Mexico. Two volumes were brought out, both by Drummond Hadley, a wealthy cowboy and poet, friend to many friends. This also collapsed. Hall occasionally visited in New Hope—on some occasions he had ten thousand dollars in his boots; on others he needed to borrow ten dollars. After many a mysterious adventure recorded in a Tom Raworth obituary article in the British paper *The Independent* on November 2, 1995, Hall ended up in Kenya trying to run a television business and died there.

16.7 Tarn's own work, influenced more and more by the Black Mountain and other New American poets, was leaving what he saw as the narrow confines of British poetry as then practiced and had opened out considerably by the time of his third book, *The Beautiful Contradictions*. This was published in 1969 by Cape Goliard though written over the two previous years—a great deal of it at Welsh "Carney," where Allen Ginsberg had written another Cape Goliard (1968) volume: the "Wales Visitation, July 29th, 1967" poem.

Another influence, together with the Olson of "The Kingfishers," was Hugh MacDiarmid. Tarn had not been paying any attention to "the Celtic Belt" apart from considerable enthusiasm for the magical voice of Dylan Thomas in the late fifties. (He never met Thomas: on an occasion before Tarn's going up to Cambridge when a Cambridge philosopher friend, later a Dominican monk, had taken him to the Wheatsheaf pub for that purpose, Dylan was not present.) One day a London reading by MacDiarmid was suddenly announced. This, together with looking at some of the Scotsman's poetry, was a revelation (a "permission" as some would say in "new age" circles). It suddenly seemed as if the British poetry scene, topped by the Celts, was this huge mountain on the sides of which, but very low down, English sheep had been obliviously feeding. From the summit, anything could be said in poetry, as if no subjects whatsoever were barred, as if the universe and all its contents and all its disciplines were the poet's rightful province. A letter was dispatched to MacDiarmid, requesting admission into the Celtic race! No answer.

At this time, an acquaintance had been formed with Kenneth White as a young Cape inductee after finding his work in Paris, where he had been teaching. A visit to him in Edinburgh, combined with a call on Norman McCaig, occasioned a telegram to MacDiarmid, asking for permission to visit immediately: this time there was agreement. Tarn bought a huge bunch of flowers and a very large cake that he placed in the arms of Mrs. MacDiarmid as she met the two men at the gate of a small cottage. The Scotsman, sitting in an armchair in front of huge piles of newspapers, declared with many titters that Tarn had conquered the redoubtable and unconquerable Velda. A couple of hours of excellent conversation ensued, copiously humidified with libations of "wee drams." Books were signed as well as a huge pencil portrait of the hero bought in Edinburgh for ten pounds. Tarn returned to London that night unable to sleep a wink. On some later occasions, he would receive a summons from the B.B.C. to come entertain the great bard: this required visits to many pubs with a young lady producer in tow and delicate negotiations with a drunken but insistent poet to avoid the lady having to spend the night with her interim protégé. When in the States, Tarn was once thanked for a letter by MacDiarmid announcing how glad he was that Tarn was alive because he had recently read his obituary in the London *Times*! This was the second occasion for the Scotsman, apparently, on which somebody announced as dead had shown up alive.

16.8 Possibilities on the American continent had begun to open up. There was considerable interest at one time in a professorship of comparative literature at McGill, but Tarn wished to live in the United States and found himself shouting excuses down the phone from "Carney," at the time of his departure from S.O.A.S., one morning when things came to a point. In the summer of 1969 a job opened up at the State University of New York Buffalo, on the old campus. The other faculty included Anselm Hollo, James Wright, and John Knoepfle, with Leslie Fiedler as professorial overseer. Tarn taught a course on structuralism and obtained one student for another on Surrealism. Many a pleasant afternoon was spent with the other poets playing pool in downtown bars. On a holiday, the crowd enjoyed a dramatic poolside party at Fiedler's. Jerome and Diane Rothenberg were in residence at the nearby Seneca reserve and often came to the campus. Friendship with them began at that time. There was one visit to the Ginsberg and Orlovsky farm at Cherry Valley. Allen insisted on taking everyone into a field to milk a cow, a procedure laced with many delighted comments on milking generally. Barry Miles from London made bizarre comments in print on a later occasion regarding Tarn's "English gentleman's tennis clothes"—or something to that effect. The clothes were a product of his imagination. A visit to Charles Olson in Gloucester was mooted by a very Buffalonian figure, poet, and editor whose name alas I have lost. But this plan unfortunately fell through because of Olson's last illness.

16.9 Though expected back in London, Tarn decided to rest, recuperate, and think things out by returning to Lake Atitlán, via Panama. On the night of his arrival in Guatemala City, the meal at a cheap pension resulted in a devastating twelve hours of sickness spent alternately groaning on the bedroom floor and washing sheets in a very depressing concrete-lined shower room. This was followed by a move to Panajachel and the renting of a hideous house from a local Indian landlord, owner of a pension in the town. The house was well situated on the Lake beyond the river, above the photographer George Holton's delightful little waterside place. It was full of scorpions, and the platform along the front of the house was built so badly that scooping off the rainy season water at two a.m. every morning was a regular chore. It took about forty-five minutes to walk into town across the river for supplies—sometimes far longer because the river could be unfordable. The time it took for mail to reach Guatemala and foreign parts out of the country caused further severe stress to the delinquent and all others concerned.

A friend kindly sent down a suitcase (a valuable camera was stolen at Guatemalan Customs) and some books: Pound's *Essays*, Olson's *Human Universe*, a few volumes by and about the great Peruvian poet César Vallejo, and the like. Dis-intoxication from publishing habits took place: the compulsion to skim was gradually replaced by careful, longtime, and detailed reading of individual pages at an extremely slow rate. The whole of the book *A Nowhere for Vallejo* was written here.

Living at Santiago would have been too difficult psychologically, but there were one or two visits there, and Nicolas Chiviliu, the old master, was met with again. After sending a message, Tarn, who had taken a nap on a pension bed, woke to find the great man looking down at him. There were trips: to the colonial city of Antigua many times, to the dramatic fiesta at Todos Santos in the Cuchumatanes with its bareback horse races.

One day, a man arrived and started cutting down everything of value in the not very interesting "garden." Seized with rage because he loved plants and depended on the garden for bird watching, Tarn screamed the man off the property, threatening him with the wrath of the Maximón and every variety of black magic. The next day the owner arrived and threw his client out. Fortunately, George Holton was able to let Tarn have his own place because he was working for Lindblad Travel in the States and all over the world (he exerted himself so much that he died in his fifties of a heart attack in China). Holton also lent his friend a good camera that fell from his hands accidentally on return from Todos Santos. This broke Tarn's will for a while.

At the very end of the sojourn, a trip to the Atlantic Coast was arranged with the aim of seeing Livingston and the seaboard areas. The nasty house owner was a member of the all-Guatemalan group! Apart from one day-long river trip, the venture was so badly organized, the living quarters and the food so wretched, that Tarn left in the middle and subsequently claimed and obtained his money back by threatening to expose the organizers in writing.

Immigration to the United States for the whole family—Patricia and the two children, Andrea and Marc—had been organized at the American Embassy in London after traversing ravagingly interminable burrokrasstic procedures. Ironically, Tarn learned that if he had accepted the idea of joining the State Department South East Asia staff, none of this would have applied. New arrangements, also of a lengthy and trying nature, had to be made with the American Embassy in Guatemala City. Eventually, Tarn joined wife, children, and parents in Switzerland, and the group arrived at Princeton in time, with the head of the family going ahead by a couple of weeks. An event in Switzerland has remained a lifelong scar: Tarn's small son, Marc, on seeing his father, made as if to shake hands. At New York, where, unbeknown to his admirer, Olson was dying of liver cancer, Tarn stayed with his University of Chicago colleague Charles Leslie, who, despite his friend's European fears and misgivings about buying anything without long and thoughtful preparations, obtained for him a $300 Dodge Dart on the spot, the spot being the basement of the N.Y.U. apartment block in which Leslie was living. After two weeks, the new driver faced the daunting task of driving the New Jersey Turnpike and took up residence in the married quarters allotted by Princeton.

Throw Seventeen

17.1 On the sovereign importance to this writer of museums and cultural monuments. Even more than viewing landscapes perhaps, nothing in life occasions as much pleasure as a visit to a great monument.

Mystic Seaport, Connecticut: 10.12.74. Seeing Mystic Seaport about a month ago, on the way back from a first trip to Nantucket with a new friend, Janet Rodney, who had been a student of Tarn's for a year. This followed, in turn, a long summer vacation on the Atlantic, specifically Nova Scotia with his children, where his love of all things Scots had a field day, later: New Brunswick. Tarn's enthusiasm for the North Atlantic area and for maritime history is at its height. Awareness that these crazes follow each other a little too rapidly, and fear of acquiring too many documents, too many memberships in this or that society, association, museum, research group. What to do with all this stuff when enthusiasm wanes, turning to another subject? After all, I am known for never throwing anything away: the proverbial pack rat. Mind you, the economy of that is not as problematic as it sounds. Easily bored, I have learned to keep a number of subjects going at once, sometimes over long cycles of time, picking things up again as attention wanes here and waxes there. Wasteful some say, but the poet is the eternal dilettante in everything but poetry if his/her poetry is to survive.

All the way up into Connecticut the leaves have been astonishing, challenging even Vermont, where they were viewed last weekend in the course of a visit to Hancock Shaker Village, the Bennington Museum, Woodstock, and Newfane. A good selection of places for the thought in mind, viz:

Relation of museum to the heraldic vision? As a rider, what is happening to the museum today: are places not becoming museums wholesale in their own right so that you now have a village/museum, a town/museum, an area/museum, and so forth?

The traditional museum: a place where things are brought and deposited. Then, sometimes many years after, displayed with more or less tact, taste, finesse, sense of design, contextual savoir faire.

Context and the degree of abstraction from its origin that an object suffers at the museum is a major concern. Objects are deaccessioned from their own world and reaccessioned into a different world belonging to science and art. An Amerindian basket, say, can be part of a show on its originators but is more likely nowadays to be part of a basket show or to be displayed as a form among other beautiful forms. An Italian altarpiece becomes part of a show on the art-historical period it belongs to or part of another on its painter. Its "sacredness" is now moot.

Back a little: Freer Gallery, Washington, D.C.: 01.29.73. The Freer is a delicate collection of masterpieces: a gallery of Oriental art. Any object is paradigmatic, immediately calling to mind its peers in other places. The masterpiece does this for us and more, eliciting the best from everywhere, establishing its authority as it instantly organizes every time and space hierarchy in which cultural objects can be placed: *Le musée imaginaire*. (Never is food more ardently discussed than when eating a very fine meal.) The still, initiatic ravishment of these flights by oneself (their privacy, their elitism if you will): I too am part of that great column of culture that sinks into human origins and soars into human futures around which any world I care about revolves. Alone, the primary experience is one of a steadily growing, pulsing, almost ecstatic excitement, picking up increments of knowledge and discrimination: a bee or hummer among flowers. This is most difficult to manage when not alone. All the excitement passes into showing objects to the other, in forming and educating him or her if necessary or called for, at best in "sharing" favorites, views, and opinions.

Perhaps say provisionally that the traditional museum is heraldic because form is constant whereas content varies predictably. As it happens, I have sometimes grown disenchanted with traditional museums. Tiresomeness: sheer accumulation of objects/sheer accumulation of knowledge. Any difference?

THROW SEVENTEEN

Objects out of context, except for masterpieces, too easily become passive and heavy, wearing down the viewer. In the background—the old demon of the arbitrary: why see this rather than that, why this object, this museum, this town rather than that? Yet old habits die hard, and I still find myself making for a museum when arriving in a new city. Something gently absurd here: why not treat the town as a town, walking the streets, enjoying the architecture, sitting in a café watching the world go by? Of course, the unknown town is a new market. What travel agency can neglect to mention "shopping opportunities" in any tour prospectus or itinerary, however famous and extraordinary the monuments to be visited? And shopping can often be a crashing bore.

17.2 Traveling this continent brings awareness of a new concept of the museum. Call it "reconstruction." Main aim: to resurrect a bygone time and present it so that the viewer can feel that he or she is experiencing that time without discomfort. You have a time machine—but with restrooms, snack bars, and the gift shop. For gifts mainly to oneself, of course. As the years go by, the gift shop becomes larger and larger. One day the whole museum will be for sale?

Here the aesthetic is subordinated to the historical. The building or complex is situated in its original site. Whatever the object, it is brought back into context with others. An object need not be beautiful as long as it is curious: a "conversation piece." (Is this an American invention? Do Europeans need conversation pieces? Well, Balzac is very good at placing objects, items of dress, furniture, food in his contexts.) Fill a reconstructed house with furniture and furnishings, with the original objects if extant and available: if not, with the closest semblance. The historical continues to prime.

The time machine operates as a resurrector of a certain space-time vortex in a culture that has been too careless of its treasures to preserve them entire. Nantucket's survival has depended first on a sudden onslaught of poverty consequent on the obsolescence of the whaling industry. This inhibited new architectural forms. It is a matter of degree, but Nantucket for many reasons thus remains a rare "living fossil" in contrast with the somewhat artificial fossil of Mystic, say, or Louisbourg, Nova Scotia. Nantucket no longer functions primarily as a fishing center, but people still live there and it is a *nota bene* "tourist destination." The artificial no longer functions at all except in its own terms. It is part of a whole new consumer vocabulary: a something-something "of choice." A "signature" place or dish or event.

I have not had time to research how much of Mystic has been "returned." The activities portrayed at Mystic today certainly took place in the past. Are there more activities here now than before? To what extent is Mystic now a "world model" cramming as many facets of an original action into one place as possible, perhaps beyond original use?

Mystic today is divided into six working areas plus one containing conveniences: a septet. First, the ships: the *Charles Morgan*, the *Joseph Conrad*, and many smaller craft. The "Village Area" description gives an idea of what has been intended: "The craft shops and homes are representative of those found in many New England maritime communities of the 19th century. These buildings have been moved to this site, a former shipyard; one of the many old Mystic yards." This large section includes sail-making, rigging, rope-making, iron-working, barrel-making, mast hoop-making, ship's supplies, etc. etc. Also: a weaving shop, a bank, a tavern. Hunch: there is probably surplus here.

Actually, Mystic has both worlds: the museum *and* reconstruction. The museum world includes, in the "Formal Exhibits and Administrative Area," thematic collections such as "Figureheads, Scrimshaw, Paintings & Models," the "China Trade Exhibit," and "Clocks & Navigational Instruments."

Significant: rich conservation and training departments: the "Fisheries Area," the "Ships' Preservation Area," the "Mariner Training Area." This adds a dimension to the field: some interaction between past and present occurs during training for certain crafts, some of which may still be of practical use today. Something similar happens at the Bath Maritime Museum on the banks of the Kennebec River in Maine.

Compare the vast complex in northern Vermont known as the Shelburne Museum of American Folk Art. This also combines a host of whole-houses-and-buildings-with-contents (including the *Ticonderoga* steamer-and-contents) with a great many thematic shows. The difference is, to the best of my knowledge, the original unimportance of the actual Shelburne site. Contrast Shelburne with Louisbourg or the Habitation Port Royal, Nova Scotia: true archaeological revivals and not "models" of an "ideal" situation.

17.3 Consider the following for a new twist on the museum's function today. At Mystic, along with young trainees, there is a number of old men who share the docent work. This provides employment to old sea dogs and other local seniors. Now notice that some of these oldsters are in period costume and practice old-time arts and crafts. It becomes difficult to draw the line between "real" and "symbolic" activity. The old gentleman on board the *Charles W. Morgan* whaler may have been a scholar, an ex-seaman, or both; he may also have been a consummate actor. With acting, perhaps, we reach a problematic crux.

Beyond *Son et lumière,* how far are we from seeing Maya Indians dressed as priests and congregation in classic Maya costume performing ceremonies on the cleared and restored temples in the Peten and Yucatan? There is, I believe, a plan afoot to transform the whole Maya area into a major tourist destination with its own train—partly, at least, along such lines. Or pharaohs and slaves on Egyptian pyramids? On Bali, in Indonesia, an interesting situation has arisen whereby the same dancers celebrate rituals in their own temples and dance in other location shows tailor-designed for tourists unwilling to spend a whole night waiting for rituals. In North America things of this type are available. "Plymoth Plantation"—a site I have not visited—is said to feature Indians and Whites in classic costumes of the settler period. At Louisbourg, I observed the awkwardness of certain "actors" who were uncertain of whether their functions were curatorial, educational, or both. Young men in seventeenth-century French uniform were a little puzzled when having to respond at one point to a genuine, real-time fire alarm. Some elderly ladies in reconstructed houses were also divided. One would throw imaginary slops out of a kitchen window on the heads of passersby, another would dialogue gently with a colleague while spinning or weaving, while yet another would ask a little American visitor what he was studying at school and whether he was enjoying Canada. The imagination cannot help reaching forward. What if the Plymouth Indians suddenly took the plantation as some of their kin recently took Alcatraz? What if some old lady were to decide she truly was the cook in the governor's house at Louisbourg? How far are we from Pirandello? New questions arise continually.

17.4 Is there a ritual element in the creation and visiting of reconstructions? Anthropology argues that ritual must, ideally, be very precise and exact and very much based on securely remembered models in behavior and text. The most important part of ritual is repetition. One sanction or text here is that ritual is a form of re-creation of the world itself. Belief may not be a sine qua non. A psychological reassurance function may be served by behaving in an as-if manner: we perform as if it were true that gods, heroes, or ancestors had thus performed. Perhaps archaeology itself is the sanction or text for reconstruction. If so, what is it that provides the ritual? Is it not the alleged exact nature of the proceeding? Even if the exact same tools are not used, much play is made with the notion that they are. A training function can be invoked for present-day artisans. The whole stress of the overall exhibit is certainly on the "real" use of "real" tools. Furthermore, contemporary comfort additions (new materials, heating, ventilation, security, etc.) are either unobtrusive or are not noticed by the public because they are taken for granted in the world they are living in.

What about the public? It can walk through the exhibition and give its children an alternative to school or television—i.e., it can be voyeur. Is there more? Tentative supposition: we have some sort of a need to experience our history as directly and concretely as possible; books are, for many now, far too abstract. Although it has come very close to its breaking point, the "American Dream" is still with us, and walking through a reconstruction could be a reenactment of that dream. The exact reconstruction, created with our ancestors' tools, inhabited by "actors" who stand in for those forebears, reestablishes for a short moment our participation in their lives. We can pretend that we stand in those early days full of mountain lions and murderous aborigines or pioneers—English, French, Spanish—whoever they may have been. And, on leaving, we load ourselves with "souvenirs" of a souvenir.

An aside from a collector: consumerdom America acquires a huge number of antiques and a larger number of reproductions of antiques. I am often surprised at how much this public will pay for a "fake" antique (often declared as such without any shame), for such a fake will frequently cost more than the real thing that, with some work admittedly, can still sometimes be found in reputable premises. Of course, the public may not know it can find the real thing, may imagine the real thing is more expensive than it is, or may succumb to convenience and buy the fake at the gift shop because this is part of the visit. (Some museum shops sell some real things; some even specialize in the real, albeit divorced from context. More and more "decorator"-type stores at home and in tourist destinations mix the real, the fake, the copy, the reproduction, often without much knowledge of which is which.) Another, somewhat frightening, possibility: that the fake is somehow more real than the original in the way the reconstruction is.

The market has sponsored the public's gullibility by various practices. One is to slap the words "collector's item" onto every object in sight. How many collectors of American stamps know that contemporary new issues are not worth collecting simply because such vast quantities have to be printed for this immense country that the stamp can never or rarely become rare? Today, the repro of a repro of a repro may well be "collectible," even though issued in thousands of copies, and there is also the "multi edition," affording a real object, albeit cheaper because multiplied. As the man said, we live in an age of simulacra. And there was Benjamin before him.

The gullibility converges with a belief, held in much of consumerized bourgeois culture, concerning the "amount of work" that has gone into a repro. My father used to argue that a great fake (such as, great or not, those of the Vermeer faker of his time he could grow lyrical about) was, "as near as dammit," as great an artist as the original painter himself and this because of the amazing amount of work involved in the copying. Here is the crux: forgetting the original labor of creation (and how easy this is when the whole covert intent of consumer culture is to demean, denigrate, occult, and silence the independent, absolute, godlike value of the original artist), the bourgeois mind lulls itself into believing that the fake could be more valuable than the real in that it takes more work to make than the real. To pay for such labor is a bourgeois obligation: noblesse oblige, as they say!

17.5 Return to the need to experience one's past. Few nations on Earth are such avid consumers and displayers of their own banners and flags, avid expostulators of their own myths at the drop of a politico-cultural hat as the U.S. of A. Among totalitarians and empire holders, the public, pro or con, loving or not, must constantly have in mind the "glorious goals" of the nation. The American empire is no exception. Yet because ours is a "democracy" in some internal respects (neglecting the fact that there has *never* been full democracy, even in Athens), there may be something else. And it may have to do with insecurity.

A moment's visit to another kind of nation. Studying the worldview of a Guatemalan *municipio* in the early fifties, I soon came to realize that the highland Maya then had very little, or no, knowledge of their own history. It is uncomfortably felt that some great disaster occurred in the past, but this is not necessarily associated with the real trauma: the Spanish conquest with its obliteration and transformation of so many native leaders and so much native culture. It may, rather, be associated with some version of an original cataclysm inherent in the Maya cyclical view of history—either pure, or possibly compounded with, whatever the Maya had apprehended of the Judeo-Christian Fall, Flood, and other disasters. The arrival of Christianity, for instance, is projected back into the beginning of time. The church, manifestly a sixteenth- or seventeenth-century building, is said to have been erected by the first father-mothers. The typical Maya blend known to some anthropologists as "Christo-Paganism" is seen as having been the real religion *ab initio*, the views of any present-day Catholic priest notwithstanding. Indeed, such a priest is often called a "protestant."

By focusing on those elements of the Maya and medieval Catholic worldviews that may have merged as well as on those that may have found it hard to merge, I proposed a model that showed up a crucial lack of agreement between a cyclical and a linear view of time. It so happened that in "my" village, I was able to postulate a link between three ritual figures (three *santos*) and three views of time: a purely cyclical, a purely linear, and an uneasily mixed view. I ventured the hypothesis that the crisis constantly boiling around the third figure between Catholic and native priests might have been symptomatic of a crisis native to the worldview as a whole from the moment the Spaniards first set foot in that part of the continent.

But what needs stressing here is the considerable unease that those Maya always manifested in regard to history. The constant, unending refrain ran as follows: "We do not know how the world was created; we do not know what the first men did; we suppose that they did this and that—and it is therefore incumbent on us to do this and that exactly as we think they did it." *La hantise de l'histoire perdue*: this haunting notion that real history had been irrevocably lost has in effect become a functioning part of Maya history to this day. It makes for conservatism in belief and ritual: the ritualist is always doing his best to approximate to the unknown original actions and intentions of the father-mothers, and he or she fears departure from them like the plague. It makes for an insecurity that becomes philosophically constitutive: the habit of thought becomes a good in itself, enters into the deference shown to native priests—those one-eyed men in the kingdom of the blind—and in the overall modesty of the Maya vis-à-vis the workings of the universe. You could even see that the old people did not want to be told the real story by venturing across the plaza to maps and charts available in the schoolhouse. They preferred to ask interminable questions, for in the questions themselves lay their sense of security born of repetition: the security of irremediable ignorance. Any answer that might get through the barrage of questions would be treated as one more uncertain speculation. Only among a few young people did I, in the early fifties, have the extraordinary experience of actually teaching Maya history such as anthropology and archaeology knew it. What this did to the contemporary data record I prefer not to think!

When one of us troops through a reconstruction, is s/he not enacting a ritual and confirming to him- or herself some kind of origin that may or may not correspond to a once-lived reality? Does his/her sense of security get involved in the action? Go further and assert that there never is or can be security? That insecurity is part and parcel of all "history," that the "original truth" can never be known, and that, therefore, any ritual, religious or not (here we get very close to the obvious!), is an antidote to insecurity?

We lack no evidence to show that any version of the American Dream— and this begins early, in Crèvecoeur, for instance, in de Tocqueville—is simplistic about the original democracy prevailing among us. Perhaps the people who came here were the poor, the hungry, the yearners after freedom. They set up sane governments that did away with European inequalities. All this entailed some slight disturbances among non-Europeans like "Indians" and "Negroes": Native Americans and African Americans. It also allowed, through the free play of free enterprise, of some people becoming more rich and equal than others, but, by and large, none of this interfered with the vision of the pristine origins of the United States.

Reformist historians apart, the refusal by the general public to face the facts of wholesale genocide, ethnocide, slavery, and class exploitation within, and outside of, the imperial nation amounts to clinging to a prelapsarian myth about the "greatest country in the world." We are constitutively, though ignorantly, insecure about the past. We do not, by and large, ever wish to know its truth.

It appears that any ritual affirms an as-if situation. As certain philosophers are heard to be saying today, there may never have been an origin that we can know for certain, and they, in turn, might meet certain cosmologists who would speak of everything having always/already existed.

Throw Eighteen

18.1 I have not done with the past. The problem of what to do with the past becomes more acute when considering natural and cultural islands—as I began to do in writing about heraldry. In some senses, the contemporary museum now unfreezes and constantly reinterprets the past for the present's and the future's purposes. It is still, though, a kind of "sole-surviving refuge" that, like certain lands placed in the public domain inalienably forever, can be added to and expanded but cannot truly disappear. (Except, that is, for destruction by war: writing in 2003 now, Iraq has just proved this again.) I suppose it should be added that, in many respects, an Indian reservation, whether in the United States or in, say, the Amazon, shares in the nature of the museum. Many tribal peoples face this dilemma. Public lands also: our whole national park policy oscillates constantly between serving God and serving Mammon.

The case is different with certain kinds of artificial islands. The ever-shrinking number of inhabitable "beauty spots," drawing the well-to-do like magnets, end by dispossessing the less rich, banishing and banning them. The moneyed then band together to protect these residential areas and transform them into museums. Nantucket, I gather, is such an island, and development there continues to be savagely contested all down the line. This kind of preservation often takes on the coloring of conservation *pro bono publico*: the less well-off can walk through . . . but not settle. Other locations are polluted instead. Nothing is perfect, though: a very beautiful old ferry was rotting in Nantucket in the seventies. It could have been saved then at a fraction of the cost of an inevitable reconstruction later.

No situation is ever "pure," hence innumerable compromises growing up in land use designed to keep the places functioning socially. Various "open spaces" projects have recently arisen in farming areas. The aim is to secure tax structures that allow farming to continue, even though economics would favor selling the land to developers. Such projects keep the land green but only for some people. I recently heard an open space leader tell of how pernicious it was for certain minorities and low-income folk to leave the cities and move, without the right etiquette, into the suburbs. Urban areas had only to be renewed to keep such colored waves from washing over the green open spaces. Here, conservation is socially regressive.

Another example is the glee with which corporations develop localities that should have been left untouched in the first place while putting up show programs of environmental concern: untouched acres for riding paths, bird sanctuaries, wilderness areas, marshes, and the like.

18.2 An unconscionable number of sins are committed in the name of tourism: a mechanism whereby both rich and not-so-rich are allowed the right to tramp through. Although rules still govern tramping through a museum or a national park, few govern tramping through a "living fossil" where tramping turns into trampling. In this sense, the poor can get vicarious pleasure from watching the rich live. I inhabit a "living fossil": New Hope, Pennsylvania, a charming Keystone State village on the Delaware River with historical antecedents, once serving as a staging point along the time-hallowed New York–Philadelphia route. On some days, usually weekdays until noon, the place belongs to itself and is delightful to live in. Then, in the afternoons, right through the summer and certainly on weekends, it becomes a place where you are not free to walk in your own garden, indeed cannot for the press of cars and bodies. And this not so much because of history as because the whole village is occupied by a multitude of gift shops mostly selling trash.

Most important: in America, all too often, the gates are raised against the hoi polloi. There are as many, if not more, "gated communities" as there are affordable-housing projects. On the other, or same, hand, America hates planning: it interferes with the "God-given right" of doing what you damn well please with whatever you think you "own." As a result, region after region, area after area, place after place are totally wrecked without a thought.

Tourism is almost entirely trampling. Even ecotourism has been shown to have drawbacks. I am aware of having belonged in youth to a privileged class: the independent travelers. A simple fact. When I first saw the Taj Mahal in India, in 1959, I saw it with, at most, another dozen people. Some twenty years later, I must have shared it with several hundreds. The days when one could wander around at will and whim are gone. Because of mass tourism, everything—flights, hotels, etc. etc. etc.—has to be booked well in advance, if it is not already full. One now has to book to see the Della Francescas in Italy, the Louvre in Paris, or the Zen Gardens in Japan. The national parks in this country should have examinations for prospective visitors to show bona fides unless they are to be trampled into oblivion. A similar phenomenon is the major art shows at major museums: the (fund-raising) "blockbusters." They are supposed to afford opportunities for study of an artist or a period. They are in fact almost impossible to see over the heads of everyone else in the world, while other marvelous rooms in the host museum are, of course, deserted. Do the trampling hordes genuinely want to see what they visit, or do they visit it because of pressure from the tourist industry or the museum moneymakers and their peers? Done this, done that, bought the catalog, the T-shirt, been here, been there. Hard to say. I do not know the solution. "Democracy" is involved: the right of anyone and everyone to do anything and everything they please. But anthropologists have come up with much study of tourism: this makes interesting reading.

18.3 I write in the wake of momentous news. A few days ago, I met a man who goes to Guatemala "for relaxation" as often as he can. Talking of Panajachel, he said, "Oh, we don't go there anymore: it is spoiled." To my horror, I heard that Panajachel had acquired two high-rise hotels. In 1969 I had noticed many changes on the Lake: hundreds of new houses among the trees at the water's edge between Panajachel and San Antonio Palopó. There were skiers on the sacred waters. But the main hotels had still been the low-lying Tsanjuyu and the rambling Monterrey. Now the Monterrey was a high-rise, it seemed, and another high-rise, nearer the lake, was putting the Tsanjuyu out of business.

Curiously enough, the current issue of the *National Geographic* arrived, containing a superficial account of flourishing Guatemala complete with portraits of smiling army colonels. It also contained full-color photos of the ritual *santo* I have mentioned, whose study was my main object in 1952–53. This too felt like desecration. I was suddenly as naked as the man in a dream whose clothes suddenly drop off him in a crowded place.

Holding on to my wits, I would suppose that the local Maya see little harm in the high-rises. I had never discovered the shade of an inkling among these people that they lived on the most beautiful lake in the world: I may well have been wrong, but landscape as such did not seem to be a value. The hotels would bring more jobs in an area condemned to tourism. In 1952–53, a certain quarter of Santiago lying close to the pier, which received the mail-and-tourists boat once a day, had begun to pervert the local costume with the tourist in view. I collected whole sets of clothes showing how the delicate, small embroideries on pants or *huipil* had grown in size and elaboration from some initial—this is always relative—geometrical patterns. The designs for tourists were vulgar "blow-ups" of the most figurative designs: they could probably be made most rapidly. Another feature of this part of town, decried by the rest of the village, was the habit of small children begging for pencils and coins.

You must differentiate, of course, between commerce (often baptized "airport art") and changes in the internal development of fashion. In 1969 the whole place sported clothes that, by the standards of twenty years before, were riotous. The very complex embroidery and the ever-widening stripes of indigo and white tie-dye (as well by now as every possible combination of colors) simply blotted out the original elegant patterns. In the rest of Guatemala, fashions had also changed at a delirious pace. This badly needed study, but only a handful of Peace Corps youngsters seemed to be interested in collection and research.

A central issue of my third poetry book, *The Beautiful Contradictions*, revolved around the poet/anthropologist's certainty that, however much he might want it to do so, the clock could never be turned back. This issue tears contemporary anthropology apart at the same time as it is being threatened by the desire of exotic peoples not to be "anthropologized." There are cases of Navajos, Inuit, and others asking the relevant authorities to establish a permit system for investigators: you interview an "informant" nowadays with the precautions and permits required to shoot a bear. Culture, it is understood, can be murdered as easily as people: ethnocide/genocide. The two forms of murder often occur simultaneously: Australian Aborigines, Tasmanians, North and South Amerindians. As Amazonia or Indonesia or Malaysia or Cambodia is being torn apart by logging and "development" at the hands of local and foreign capitalists, the only solution seems to be, yet again, national parks, reservations, preserves in which, for a time, the Indigenous can take their own time to "adapt." Living museums of yet another sort!

To what extent can menaced human groups be fully aware of the danger to their lives? Where genocide and ethnocide have come in, and may still come in, at one swoop, there is no argument. Exploiters and developers are past masters of interested tergiversation. If an Atiteco Maya tells me he sees no harm in the high-rises, can I put it to him that they may do good in the short run by providing service jobs—but do his people want to be servants all their lives, and are there not other solutions to labor problems less destructive to the most beautiful lake in the world? How to explain that *the* Lake is as fragile as Egyptian temples or Venetian palaces? Of which they known little or nothing . . .

Unlike Northern Native Americans, the Maya rarely confront directly but defend themselves through avoidance and separate development: in some senses their villages since the conquest have always been ghettoes. What help can the Anglo "liberal" give the Indigenous? Impressed by their occasional self-defense and creative initiatives, he or she can only bow out. They do not want help. I am not sure to what extent the word "help" still contains meaning despite all the NGOs in the world, when rich mankind will not interfere decisively in poor mankind's problems because they are too busy exploiting.

18.4 Do we save the planet or not? Does self-interest rule or the interest of the human race as a whole? Do we save the wildernesses? The animals? The "Indigenous"? Is this not in fact the history of the human race? My own belief, alas, is that our institutions are not powerful enough. The examples of people living cheek by jowl for ages without solving their problems is argument enough: the Northern Irish Catholics and Protestants, Palestinians and Israelis, Indians and Pakistanis. The planet will survive by the skin of its teeth. The human race will not. No need to listen to a poet. Read the number of science books which argue that the human race has approximately fifty years in which to decide whether it will survive or not. Right now: tundra melting, ice melting, vast fires, more and more violent storms.

There are too many institutions, and division does not make for power. Additionally, among institutions, too few understand that the conservation of nature and that of culture are indissolubly linked: you cannot save one without the other.

It seems to be a fact that each generation of students is less and less historically minded. Perhaps what we are dealing with is an ever-accelerating process of the destruction of time consciousness in our society. As global culture becomes more and more relentlessly similar to itself with its residence on the web, ancient tribes, buildings, and landscapes drown under one sea of neglect and pollution—conservation efforts never being strong enough to counter the tidal wave. A sense of continuity is essential to human health: only a firm grip on the past makes a future possible. We cannot survive by accepting the past as an object for museums, trampling over it on public holidays and making do with it in its prettified reconstructed forms.

For my own part, I project a heraldry in time where I have found it most at work in space. When working on Guatemala, I used to feel that New World history was an ideal historian's playground in that (archaeologists apart, of course) one had to deal with only a four-hundred-year span from the Spanish conquest to now. How different from the case of Old World cultures! Today, as I map once more the outlines of the North American continent (there is not a state or province I have not set foot in) because I cannot believe in maps without pacing them out again for myself, I face the same four-hundred-year gap—from pioneers to now.

Neshaminy Mall, near King of Prussia, Pennsylvania, sometime in 1973: standing in one of the largest shopping centers I have ever seen. Everything you can possibly want under one roof. An aircraft carrier! This too is a world model: the model for an ideal member of consumer society. Here are all his/her clothes, hats, shoes, toys, pots and pans, housing goods . . . even some cultural requirements—bookstores of sorts . . . and there is even an artist offering to do portraits out of a small metal shack in the middle of the monster. On the side wall of a central rest area, among artificial fountains, a half dozen dioramas of the foundational history of Penn's Sylvania. First ships on the horizon, the founder with Indians, the Liberty Bell. A taped commentary endlessly repeats the tale of the tribe. It is told in a very low voice, a voice almost drowned out by the Muzak playing everywhere in the building. Not many people around this morning. I stand by a male human being, an American citizen, seated on one of the benches around the fountain. Lonely old people come to the mall to watch . . . for a kind of company. He seems to be listening. He seems to be straining his hearing for the sound of the old story.

2019: the same tale continues. More and more places—the chief one being Venice disgusted at the arrival of obscenely giant cruise ships into its lagoon—are perpetually on the brink of deciding that tourism has to be limited. A visit to Paris this June reveals the huge space between Notre Dame and the Louvre as totally given over to tourist groups, mainly Asian it seems, following after their guides' little banners and flags. Information overload on a gigantic scale now precipitates both the traveler and the homebody in so many simultaneous directions that sitting alone at home may seem to be the only remedy. Remember Pascal! Meantime, a sixth extinction dangerously deprives our planet of necessary helpers such as bees and other pollinators. Murderous destructions continue in the name of providing certain cultures with foreign-animal body parts (elephant tusks, rhinoceros horns) proved by modern science to be useless. Criminal governments sold out to corporations and industry generally continue to limit citizens' liberties and to destroy the remaining great natural sites in their nations. Environmental help is negated and destroyed. I believe that the planet may survive—although wounded—while the human race may well not. I am a "terminalist." I deplore the making of babies at this time.

Throw Nineteen

19.1 At Princeton, Tarn taught in the Romance Languages Department, a pleasant enough group of people with one outstanding member: the poet Kenneth Irby's brother, James Irby, translator of Lezama Lima, among others. There were civilized departmental luncheons at Lahiere's once a week. Friendship with the great Dostoevsky biographer, Joseph Franck, brought an invitation to attend the Gauss seminars. Another with Theodore Weiss, editor of the *Quarterly Review of Literature*, occasioned one or two readings. Tarn's greatest enjoyment perhaps came from the riches of the Firestone Library, where the Western Americana curator, Alfred Bush, became a good friend, and from a close companionship with a young poet in the English Department, John Peck, who later, while remaining a poet, became a Jungian analyst. Stanley Corngold, professor of German—the man met on the final lap of the Rangoon–London journey in 1959—became a close friend for the whole length of Tarn's fourteen-year stay on the East Coast.

This was the time of the Cambodian crisis, and some people were trying to "share." The poem "The Great Odor of Summer" was written at this time. Tarn suggested that his own principal reading be shared with as many Princeton poets as possible in a group effort. Somehow this did not occur, and he remained with the feeling that his offer had been frowned on. The visiting professorship had been initiated by an aspiring poet/professor, Robert Fagles, who later made a name with translations from Homer. There was talk at the time of the possibility of being kept at Princeton, possibly as chairman of a European studies program. Before the end of the semester, it became clear, very indirectly of course, that a permanent position would not be offered. Was this a result of the visitor's political stance? Possibly to his theoretical orientation? Promotion regulations? No way of telling.

The search for a job began: at S.U.N.Y. Stony Brook, where Louis Simpson's wife seemed mainly interested in securing a London residence for a sabbatical, continuing at S.U.N.Y. Purchase, a new and promising campus. This last negotiation went on for a considerable time and became a classic "zeppelin" (Tarn's name for the academic technique of making a balloon larger and larger until a pinprick ends it). In the latter case the pinprick occurred during a long lunch with a dean at a Madison Avenue seafood restaurant called "Moby Dick." After two hours, it became clear that the dean already had someone in his pocket. End of story and out on the street.

There then came urgent courting by one Dean Ernest Linton of Livingston College, Rutgers, the State University of New Jersey, in New Brunswick—a kind of local alternative to Princeton: it was said that Rutgers professors were paid enough to live at Princeton while Princeton professors were ill-paid enough to live in New Brunswick. On his first trip from New York to see Fagles in the late sixties, Tarn had sat in a bus passing through New Brunswick and fervently hoped he would never have to deal with the place. (It has been spruced up since.) Linton, saddled with a small, extremely conflicted Comparative Literature Department that had been lured across the river to Livingston from the main campus (to the disgust of old-fashioned literary historian John McCormick, its *éminence* not so *grise*), had gotten it into his head that an anthropologist would be just the person to sort out the conflicts. McCormick made the best of a bad job by attempting to make Tarn promise that he would hew strictly to literary history—an impossible task for a structuralist. Two young poets, Miguel Algarín, later famous for his Newyorican Poetry Café, and Marilyn Kallett, later at the University of Tennessee, were very instrumental in the acquisition of Tarn.

It was sometimes said later that the Livingston campus had been built across the river on an old Army base in order to isolate the minorities and radicals who were, indeed, numerous on the architecturally dismal site. Life there was exciting in that the sixties did not really end until the mid-seventies and the "counterculture" in all its gaudy enthusiasm flourished at Livingston.

Much activity centered around opposition to the Vietnam War, and marchers were duly sent out to Washington, D.C. Tarn went to Washington. Some of all this entered the spirit of departmental affairs, encouraged mostly by an energetic young teacher, Elton Anglada, scion of an important Spanish exile family in Puerto Rico. Noticing that most of his students came to him as writers, Tarn, supported by Anglada, suggested that the department offer a Ph.D., or at least an M.A., for "creative writers." These would not be slouches in that they would do all the work for a straight Comp Lit degree plus their own work in writing. A horrified McCormick fought the project tooth and nail, swearing that "creative writing" belonged to English departments and would never, never sully a department of comparative literature. Eventually he defeated the project by vote. Tarn's contempt for the ever-growing "creative writing" industry came later.

This was probably the launching pad for an exceedingly wearisome fourteen years of infighting. During the summer before his first term, the department, unhappy at the idea of being led by a Ph.D. in anthropology, had made sure that Tarn would not, in fact, be chairman—a decision that Tarn used to ensure that he would never be saddled or saddle himself with such a post. It turned out over the years that it may be harder work avoiding administrative duties than taking them on—but the lines were drawn. No credit or recognition of any sort was given to Tarn's literary achievements, such as they were, with one exception: three years into the job, one colleague stated he was mildly surprised and gratified to notice that Tarn had translated Neruda. Not one absence, on sabbatical mainly, occurred without some attempt at demoting Tarn from some committee or title or other prerogative. This in spite of the fact that Tarn was at the top of the ladder as the Rutgers equivalent of a "distinguished" professor and therefore could not be demoted. Toward the end, matters became so bad that Tarn called on the Rutgers president. He took no action as far as one could tell. Ironically, the situation was helped by an outside examiner who turned out to be Yale's Paul de Man. This was before his youthful right-wing activities in Belgium had been denounced. Tarn asked to see him alone and outlined the literary historians' war against "theory." (Ironically, the moment Tarn left, "theorists" began to be hired.) De Man must have written some kind of defense into his report: after this, calm reigned until early retirement, in 1984–85, put an end to this period.

In some respects, life had become a little more endurable in that the department had finally managed to move back to the main campus, where one splendid Victorian building, its old furnishings, and its collections, the Theological Library, became a refuge. Although some departments were said and proven to be excellent, Rutgers as experienced by Tarn was a small place, far too busy worrying about its status in the hierarchies of academe ever to achieve anything substantial. A huge amount of time was devoted at one point to changing administrative systems, involving wasteful and adamantly repetitive paperwork, interminable committee meetings, etc. etc. In effect, Tarn drove in from Pennsylvania, did his work, and came away, participating only minimally and never seeking to do more.

Literary life at Rutgers was virtually nonexistent perhaps because of the proximity to New York. There were very few readings, and given his academic fate, Tarn, perhaps misguidedly, was not motivated to build any kind of "base" in that sphere. Reading programs were a power base for a number of poets in the United States, and little presses and magazines were and are also.

Undergraduates were uninspiring. Once, one of them, elated, rushed into the office with the news that Allen Ginsberg had been invited to give a reading. Tarn, somewhat sardonically, remarked that this would be that poet's nth visit and asked whether they could not have invited someone else for a change? The youth said he knew of no other poets! On another occasion, Algarín, going on leave, sent his infants to Tarn, who was giving a course on modern poetry from Baudelaire on down. A few minutes into the hour, many started to leave. To one girl: "Go, no problem, but may I ask you a question? Have you ever read Baudelaire?" Answer: "No, but why should I before I get my own shit together?" Graduates, by and large, were too far gone in specialization to be of any overwhelming interest.

Cultural life was limited for the most part to dinners and visits with Anglada and his wife. Elton was addicted to taping conversations and, at one time, ran a recorder in his house twenty-four hours a day. Topped up with certain substances favorable to conversation, his visitors were made to talk for hours with very doubtful results. Outside of the Angladas, there were few relations. One was with Cleo McNelly, an extremely bright young scholar in the English Department who eventually specialized in T. S. Eliot's Oriental research and in religious studies, teaching that discipline at the Princeton Seminary. She later married the Pound specialist George Kearns, and although both had the means to further knowledge of Tarn's work in the States and did not, they remained friends. A major painter, Leon Golub, with whom Tarn shared some activist doings, could have become a friend perhaps if Tarn had worked at it.

19.2 The breakaway to Guatemala in 1969 had come about in part because of Tarn's difficulties in dealing with the kind of breadwinning he had had to accept as head of a family. This is a very long, and to all concerned, a tragic story that, as argued in the preface, will not be told in this book. Unwilling for some seven or more years to consider separation or divorce, these were in fact eventually brought about by Tarn's move to America. It appeared that it would have been difficult for Patricia, and even more for the children, to leave England for good. They were very unhappy at Princeton because of culture shock, problems at school for the children, and the marital situation. At the end of the semester, they returned to London. Tarn has seen his family at least once a year every year, usually by going across to London but also, later, to Cape Town and elsewhere.

For the next three years: rentals in Princeton. The first, near the university, was a dismal, ill-lit place. Its worst memory: a small yard behind the house in which two unruly kids drove their father's car back and forth a few feet, gunning the engine and making an intolerable amount of noise. After days of the renter going nearly berserk, the police were finally called. The kids had a reputation. The second rental was a Princeton math professor's glass house set in a tight little wood—a most delightful, isolated place. On a platform back of the house, to Tarn's delight, a raccoon and her young would come to feed every night.

The place was also rich in birds: Tarn was a member of Audubon and has still never forgotten his first day going for warblers in the Institute woods with the heartwarming number of more than ten "American firsts" reached in one day. Many a trip was also taken to Cape May at migration time, where an added pleasure was the Lobster House and rich seafood. Cape May, reached by a long drive on the southern Garden State Parkway, was a magical destination, hemmed in by nearby "snowbird" motels in their hundreds and neighbor to a fascinatingly historical southern New Jersey coast reaching toward Philadelphia. The place appears mainly in the poetry within the "Seen as a Bird" poem of *Lyrics for the Bride of God* and in the sequence *Birdscapes with Seaside*.

This rental ended badly when the owners' cleaning lady—to whom Tarn had behaved, to the best of his knowledge, faultlessly and even generously—reported to the owners that he had held "orgies" in the house! These orgies turned out to be a few Rutgers classes where students were offered the chance of enjoying a lovely setting. For good measure, the owners decided to describe fictitious damages to the premises and furniture, all of which led to tedious exchanges with a lawyer. An inane little settlement "out of court" went mainly into the lawyer's pocket. This was one of Tarn's brushes with officialdom. Another occurred in his very first year, when he was hauled in for audit by the I.R.S. The accountant that Random House had found for him had gone to Florida, and Tarn, knowing nothing of such proceedings, went into the lion's den alone. An ancient curmudgeon found all sorts of faults with his receipts. For example, the pencil mark had not gone right through to the last page of an airline ticket. An immortal remark by this gentleman ran "Mr. Tarn—in this country when someone does not succeed, he tries something else. Why don't you give up writing?" Tarn had to resort to another accountant. The Feds ended up by owing the auditee fifty dollars, and a lot more than that went to the new accountant. A massive, continued, incurable detestation of all forms of burrokrassy as well as all forms of commerce and "business," dating admittedly from well before his arrival, was added to as the end product of this type of adventure. There were other problems for new arrivals: for instance, the obtention of a first credit card without a credit record in the United States. This was solved by insisting on and obtaining serial personal introductions to every single officer in the bank from the president on downward.

In 1972, after a failed attempt at buying a house near Princeton and a great deal of suspense and toing-and-froing including a period lived in a holding apartment in Trenton, Tarn became a proud Pennsylvanian by acquiring a small eighteenth-century stone cottage at 96 New Street, on the canal in New Hope, Pennsylvania. He had wanted to live outside the little town in the marvelous farming lands of Bucks County surrounding it, but there was nothing available at the time. One house, right on the Delaware River, somewhat north of New Hope, had been very desirable but in the kind of condition that made one suspect it would very soon slide into the water. Tarn maneuvered himself into a position of denial about the facts that New Hope was a tourist madhouse at weekends, that the canal in summer would be full of tourists on boats with loudspeakers, and much else. Principally, although he knew that the distance from Rutgers would make for tedious commutes, he persuaded himself, before purchase, by driving at top speed many times between New Brunswick and New Hope that this would not be too much the case. The location was even more problematic in the sense that so little time was actually spent there: between Rutgers, New York, Princeton, and Philadelphia there were enough places to keep one busy all week. Eventually, walls and fences had to be built around the property to keep out wanderers. On one trespass occasion among many, a mentally retarded man was found urinating into the canal from the back of Tarn's garden.

At 08.00 hours one morning, months after moving in, a totally unknown voice on the phone: "Mr. Tarn, I assume you like trees, and trees are very fine creatures. Well, you know those trees on the border of your property adjoining my parking lot? If you do not stop parking your car in the little box on that border, I am going to cut down all those trees." Although the realtor had assured Tarn that he had an easement there, some degree of panic arose. Consultations in the town. The man, a somewhat lunatic hotel owner, continued his harassments for several months in the street, by letter, and through other individuals, and then gave up as suddenly as he had begun.

Despite all the drawbacks, the place, its surroundings, and nearby Lambertville across the bridge were a joy. The botanical park in the Trenton direction (many a dawn birding surrounded by sleeping deer) with Washington's Crossing, the Revolutionary Tower, the Delaware itself, and its geese appear in the period's poetry, especially in the *Lyrics* volume, the book called *The House of Leaves*, and all the way over into the first "Rectangle" poems of *Seeing America First*. There were many trips farther afield—one in the Pennsylvanian German lands (and oh how German they had remained!). A favorite expedition was to Hawk Mountain to watch the raptor migrations.

There were good people there: the owner of the local hardware store, bearing a concentration-camp tattoo on his arm; the boys at the post office; the stationer and the garage owner in Lambertville; a number of antique dealers, one especially in Carversville who sold him a fine captain's chest, a rocking horse with an iron head (perhaps a shop sign), a Victorian rocking chair, and other goodies. Some of these objects now live in New Mexico. Not much society, except for the science writer John Pfeiffer and his lady, who lived in a house on the river. Pfeiffer was lively and enthusiastic company and very supportive through many difficulties.

19.3 Tarn's friend had visited a few times between 1970 and 1972, but during the glass-house period in Princeton she had finally decided against a permanent relationship and remained in London. Alone during the years between 1972 and 1974, Tarn felt he was living some of the "youth" he had never managed to experience properly before the rise of the "counterculture": whether it was satisfying or not is another matter. Savory or not—and Livingston was no exception—many teachers are known to have experienced the fact that, when and if they fall free, graduate students often seem very interested in filling the gap. In one way or another, a number of fleeting relationships followed one another, more than one occasioned by meetings within the course of the literary life. Among them, one inspired the "Between Delaware and Hudson" poems, another the *Artemision* section of *Lyrics*, and yet another some of the short pieces in *The Microcosm*. Many a story of craziness could be told but would bring matters too much into the realm of barroom talk. Whether they "approved" or not, and Tarn saw it as the most important social movement of the century, it appeared as if most men at the time were experiencing the difficulty of adapting to a tidal wave of feminism. Both sexes were extremely nervous of each other, afraid of commitment, uncertain of how to behave in almost any circumstance. Whatever the myth of the "sexual revolution" advertised (and it probably benefited only the very young), relationships were in virtually every case painful and insecure, perpetually generating mixed and confusing signals, and *tedium vitae* was rapidly developing. Tarn had always considered himself too committed to work to invest in any "singles" scene to the hilt, and there was also the difficulty of not having a central place from which to sally regularly into that life. At one point, the offer of a poet's rental in Westbeth and thus a period of time spent in New York City was very tempting, but, irresistibly, the spring leaves came out, and the city lost a potential resident.

19.4 One day when sitting in his Livingston College office looking at graduate student applications, Tarn came across one such from a slightly older student who described herself as a friend of Alastair Reid and Anthony Kerrigan—poets who had worked on Neruda with Tarn. Whipping round and composing a note saying "Oh, if you decide to come, stop by as a friend of friends and say hello" took but a moment. Janet Rodney, long living in Spain, wished, as a poet, to return to the United States, where she had been born in 1941. This, together with another letter from one professor, being the two "human responses" received, J., who had been accepted at Berkeley and other prestigious places, made the mistake of coming to Livingston.

With a high honors B.A. in history from the University of Maryland, Rodney had arrived to pursue an M.A. in comparative literature. In Spain she had considerable experience in publishing as a literary scout with Farrar Straus, McGraw-Hill, Seix Barreal, and Carmen Barcells. In 1987 she founded the Weaselsleeves Press at home in Santa Fe, creating ravishing books by the likes no less of Susan Howe and Lyn Hejinian. These, as well as broadsides, prints, and one-of-a-kinds, have been widely exhibited and archived in many major libraries. Her own poetry and her work in translation, reviewing, digital imaging, and CD recording have long been available and appreciated, but her modesty has prevented her achievements from being especially widely known. Among her main works: *Orphydice, The Book of Craving, Moon on an Oarblade Running, Alashka* (jointly with Tarn), and

Terminal Colors have gathered a faithful audience and will feature in the poetic history of our time.

J.R. was one of the creative people interested in the idea of a writing Ph.D. The UK law was no messing with students. When she had ceased being Tarn's student at the end of a year, the two began seeing each other, and after an initial trip together to Alaska resulting in the project of a jointly written book, she moved into the New Hope stone cottage. Years later, before the move to New Mexico, the couple came to Santa Fe as a symbolic gesture and got married there in the municipal building baptized "The House of Matrimonial Bliss."

19.5 A much valued link between the literary life in England and that of the United States was Nan Talese, Tarn's editor at Random House. She had originally published the first book, *Old Savage/Young City*, and had continually tried to forward her author's career, even getting him a short stint at the *New York Times Book Review*, where he successfully accounted for a book by William Gass and followed with other pieces—but, for whatever reason (again no explanations), this gig did not last long. Nan took *The Beautiful Contradictions* from Cape Goliard and in 1971 was the initial publisher of *A Nowhere for Vallejo*, which, in an interesting inversion, she then sold back to Cape. The *Nowhere*, written under great stress in Guatemala in the 1969 Panajachel stay, was witness to the very highest esteem felt by its author for any Latin American poet: above all possible others in effect. Were it not for the fact that Clayton Eshleman, another American poet and a man of immensely productive persistence, had invested a huge amount of energy in making that work known in English, Tarn would doubtless have tried to translate Vallejo himself beyond the tribute of the *Nowhere* volume. The friendship with Nan included the occasional publisher's lunch at a New York restaurant, a good chat and gossip, return to the office, and the generous gift of a number of books. This was valued far more than Nan ever knew because of her charm but also as a last token of a vanishing civilized rapport between author and publisher.

Nan's departure for Simon and Schuster was a typical author's tragedy: the editor leaves; the editor may or may not want to take his/her author to the new place; this works or not. The offer *was* made by Nan, but Tarn felt that S. and S. was even less interested in a serious poetry list than Random had been. In the meantime, Kenneth Rexroth, a generous patron since the 1964 Berlin conference, had very kindly recommended his protégé to New

Directions along with Jerome Rothenberg and David Antin. Jay Laughlin had been a publishing contact for Cape-New Directions business and had been visited on visits from London on this basis alone. On one occasion, Tarn arrived in New York to be told "Oh, what a pity—had you been here last night, you could have dined with Pound" and felt forever afterward that Laughlin could have avoided making that remark. On the other hand, when staying at Yellowstone, a bearded Tarn had hitchhiked, with difficulty, to the Laughlin ranch near Jasper and had enjoyed a heartwarming family weekend there. After a huge amount of palaver about Laughlin's uncertainty, his financial constraints, and similar obstacles, Tarn was permitted to produce the typescript of *Lyrics for the Bride of God* himself, given a cover design he disliked intensely, and became an N.D. author, experiencing this as a singular triumph and a sign of a successful transfer to American shores.

Laughlin's number two at the time gave the impression that this would be a permanent arrangement by asking for all previously owned rights to be made over to N.D. However, whereas Rothenberg remained, Tarn did not.

No satisfactory explanation was ever ventured. While under his favorable impression, Tarn, truly believing he would be taking pressure off N.D. by not following *Lyrics* up too closely, had offered a new work, *The House of Leaves*, to John Martin at the Black Sparrow Press. Martin had been asking repeatedly for a book for some years, and *House* came out in 1976. The following work was the *Alashka*. Parts of it were offered to Laughlin's annual anthology before Tarn and Janet Rodney had decided to make it a joint work, and the former subsequently asked N.D. to amend the signature accordingly. Rodney, joining Tarn in Nome, Alaska, before embarkation on the *Lindblad Explorer* in 1977 during their third Alaska trip, brought Laughlin's letter advising his author to stay with Black Sparrow. Tarn had foolishly not paid attention to his contractual obligations (these were never a problem at Cape or Random), and there was also a lady working at N.D. who did not like his work. Tarn discovered much later that Laughlin was extremely sensitive about authors abandoning him, doubtless or perhaps breaking contract, and had misunderstood Tarn's intentions. Had Tarn been more savvy, less sensitive himself, and less discouraged, he should have gone to New York and tried to talk to Laughlin. But thus began some thirty full years in the wilderness.

The Black Sparrow relationship did not work out more favorably. There had been one occasion on which the Martins and the Tarns had enjoyed a pleasant spree in San Francisco. On returning from the Alaska trips, Tarn, who had written to Martin outlining hopes for future cooperation, called the publisher on the phone, and they spoke about the *Alashka*, which was then approaching completion. Martin, claiming absolute disbelief in the possibility of successful jointly written works, refused to look at it as a matter of principle and declared that he would do the next "*echt* Tarn" work but nothing else. He then delivered himself of the unforgettable opinion that "a poet of standing wasting three years working with an unknown other—and a woman at that" was incomprehensible. The *Alashka* was eventually published very unsatisfactorily at Boulder, yoked with a Tarn *Selected*, while the couple lived in Atitlán in 1979. As a result, the book never received the attention it deserved, especially in Alaska, and Janet Rodney felt that the joint project had been harmful to her. This was a sad reflection on something that had begun in the excitement of men and women working together under countercultural and feminist impulses. Martin did not do "the next book." A final visit to him in 1986, when he had moved to Santa Rosa, resulted only in further insults. One of the greatest American printers, Walter Hamady, did publish some extracts beautifully. The "wandering life" had set in now, and over the following years no satisfactory publishing relationship, except for an extremely important one late in the day with Wesleyan University Press for a *Selected Poems*, was ever established.

19.6 Both *Lyrics for the Bride of God* and *The House of Leaves* covered the painful years of divorce, experiment, and search for a new life in new patterns—years that coincided with the sociopolitical ferment of the late sixties and early seventies. Tarn has always believed that, partly because of the lack of his continuity at New Directions, the *Lyrics* volume never received the attention it deserved—something possibly also brought about by a killer ad hominem review by one Helen Vendler, an academic totally ignorant—as such academics often are—of the realities of contemporary poetry. She had reviewed it in the *New York Times* with a full dozen of other books on religion and, when asking whether Tarn, if related to the bride, had seen himself as "God," she showed total ignorance of the meaning in Hebrew mysticism of the *Shekhina.* It is possible that Laughlin was also influenced by the Vendler murder, although Tarn was later told that he eventually abandoned any view of Vendler's relevance. David Lenfest, a friend from Loyola University who made a short film on "The Great Odor of Summer," felt that the book, in those difficult times, was too close to the bone for many readers on the subject of sexual relations, marriage, and separation. Perhaps he was right. If critical attention ever focuses, it may be possible to tell.

Throw Twenty

20.1 1978–79: an idea to take a sabbatical down in Atitlán and use the three fieldwork stays involved (1952–53, 1969, 1979) to provide the core for a travel book. What Atitlán had meant to me over the years could lead into other travels past, present, perhaps future. The book could be a sort of *voyage philosophique*, a layer cake, a French *millefeuille*, embedding as many life strata as I wished to discuss.

Came the sabbatical year, and I decided not to go down, at least not yet. The thought of renting 96 New Street inspired horror. Worries about the book: size, for instance—such a book could go on forever, and I had enough unfinished monsters in my drawer. Travel per se—or the peculiar travel in situ that anthropologists do—might no longer be my true focus.

The thought that my objects of study, in both my anthropological ventures (Guatemala and Burma), might somehow be included under the heading of the "heraldic vision," that the scholarly life might be brought into the literary life, was appealing. Specifically, I studied in Guatemala the worldview of one *municipio* (a village with its dependencies) among others, all characterized by a jealous and time-hallowed self-sufficiency—so that one could take the various *municipios* as shields and study variations in content. In Burma

I had become concerned with the way in which the Buddhist *Sangha* had discovered that by creating small, self-contained sub-*Sanghas* or, in fact, sects with their own leaders and own disciplinary requirements unattached to a pan-*Sangha* authority that any government might set up, they could best defend themselves against a host of troubles. The sub-*Sanghas* could also be envisioned as shields with varied content.

20.2 Friend and poet John Peck, who had helped me greatly in my Princeton days, put forward the simple but attractive notion that a lake is an inverted image of an island. Not a body of land surrounded by water but a body of water surrounded by land. In both cases, populated sites tend to be situated on the margin between water and land. Tourist books frequently talk of *the* Lake as surrounded by twelve *municipios* named after twelve apostles. Not so: not exactly twelve, not exactly all named after apostles. However, the idea is a nice one, responding to the situation of sites on the Lake, each nestling among its ravines and cut off by accidented lands or the massive body of water itself. There is a network of precipitous paths, but frequently there is no other recourse but to trust one's life to an inland sea—that can be savage—and a frail and capricious canoe.

The lake waters are often driven into turmoil by mysterious winds and chthonic underwater currents that drown a good many Indians and some tourists each year. "The Lake needs food" is sacred knowledge, occasionally whispered. The drowned are a special category of the dead. They must be buried face down to prevent them from "walking" at night: they do this backward. Once, on a Santiago–Panajachel mail boat, such a storm blew up. Atitecos threw themselves on their knees, begging the pilot to turn back, and when he refused, they prayed more vociferously than I had ever heard people pray before.

The Lake is a kind of home in the midst of the rippling highlands surrounding it on all sides. Guarded by its three towering volcanoes, its ravines, and sharp escarpments, it is like a sunken world as you come upon it from any direction. If the "meaning of height" was once made clear to me at Macchu Picchu, the meaning of depth revealed itself when looking down from the hills at Atitlán. I discovered in 1969 that the Lake had been plumbed but prefer to continue seeing it as depthless just like myths and guidebooks do. I also, when dreaming, prefer to forget pollution and fisheries concerns—the introduction of one species to solve one problem having merely created others. The Lake is one of the great tantalizers in the world. It has a thousand moods and ways of reflecting the light. I know of no great painter who has tackled it. Photographers, of course, by the dozen. I have a great many photos and postcards: in each one of these there is a new vision.

Leaving the Lake and returning to it always involved the kind of ritual, mental and physical, that the Atitecos practice as they salute the crosses placed in several layers at the entrances and exits of villages. (Even now, in a Maya mood and as a Maya-Catholic, I have at times crossed myself whenever arriving at or leaving a home place.) It is difficult not to think of the Lake as a temple or, at any rate, as a holy place in which one is privileged to live. The Tzutujil-speaking Atitecos call it the "corral," and for them it is "navel of earth, navel of sky," the center of the world.

Thus the fate of a Wordsworthian youth, replete with a baggage of Rilkean prose and poetics and the plangency of Rimbaud's "*O saisons O châteaux*," determined to associate himself with whatever mythology he intuited at the heart of this place, even going to the extent of sewing a yellow sun on a belt loop of his pants (a "conversation piece")—and how right he turned out to be! A fate linked to the cyclical theme of a "home" and "away" polarity. A fate tied to an immediate recognition of the Lake as a kind of spiritual home with overtones of the original, lost Eden. The story of one who is to be a fundamentally elegiac poet.

Any field trip always began with the hope that poetry and fieldwork could continue in parallel. Diaries were set up for this but almost immediately lapsed into single-channel quotidian records of ethnographic field events. However, the Lake continued to astonish for that whole first year. Once, I went high up into the mountain cornfields, the *milpas* behind the village, to interview a farmer about witchcraft. I climbed higher than I had ever been. The day was extremely sunny; the whole world seemed bathed in liquid gold. Solitude ruled absolute among those light-drenched acres. It seemed to me that I could go on walking up the flank of the volcano forever without thought of achievement. Far below lay Santiago, the patterns of its streets becoming clear as on an aerial map, and to the east the dependency of Cerro de Oro, where treasure was thought to have been buried in ancient times, and the village of San Lucas Tolimán. Further yet, where the waters began to curve toward Panajachel, the houses of San Antonio Palopó. Very high above, a plane was struggling to link one center of human business with another and seemed absolutely irrelevant.

Another occasion, setting out before dawn for the Pacific Coast with an Atiteco friend. Walking a long walk out of Santiago westward to the gap in the hills leading down into the tropical coffee farms and banana plantations.

THROW TWENTY

Soon I would be among lianas and orchids but, in the meantime, could view the volcanoes San Pedro and Atitlán, their tops circled by very thin clouds that seemed to dance and to caress the tips as if they were nipples.

I have already written of the extraordinarily unexpected last view, on leaving the area, of the waters from the window of a Chiapas-bound plane.

Leaving the Lake while living there: always carrying its image in mind and no rest until return. For one thing, I immediately became a blue-eyed tourist again and could not behave as naturally among people of other *municipios* as I behaved at home. "Give me a better price because of my blue eyes!" "It is exactly because of your blue eyes that I will not." On many occasions, I returned from some far-flung expedition across the mountains to catch the early-morning mail boat, sleeping fitfully on the wooden bench in the hold or on the cabin roof, the sun still relatively cool up there but beginning to burn.

For some seventeen years, I carried the image of the Lake inside me. I would dream of it once or twice a year. It was always the same dream: setting out, reaching the neighborhood very close by, though hardly ever catching a glimpse of its expanse and then being somehow prevented from arriving.

20.3 Summer 1969: time of personal crisis. Arrive Guatemala City. The awful night sick in a poor pension. Next few days buying equipment. Strange reluctance to move toward the object of my love. Then go. The city has grown; it takes longer to leave it; the road to the Lake is much better; the buses are newer; the ride is shorter and more comfortable.

I did not wish to settle in Santiago for fear of being drawn back into anthropology. With great difficulty I secured the house some twenty minutes' walk out of Panajachel toward the Palopó villages. The house large, totally comfortless: in bed, at night, I would read with my head ringed with a halo of scorpions. Moving the rainwater off the portal every night lest it flood into the house.

Six strange months: psychological turmoil on the one hand, quiet contemplation on the other. Work from 5 a.m. until 9 or 10, then the rest of the day to potter. Many mornings, nude, on George Holton's terrace directly over the Lake, swathed in bougainvilleas and hummingbirds. Walk to Pana for provisions and mail: a different one each day in that rains were heavy and the river kept on changing its course. On some days dangerous. Interest in birds that had been dormant during the anthropological years, now awoke again. One morning, fit for legend, the terrace bushes covered with black-and-white warblers creeping around. Some twenty or thirty of them.

Came the day, after staring across the water many times, I decided to go for Santiago. Wore the old white *cofrade* shirt with a cross pattern over the navel, the old *zut* head cloth with original colors of red, orange, purple, and brown round my waist—originally awarded back in the fifties. A sweater over this since it was chilly. In the mail boat a few Atitecos, paying no attention—just another tourist. Off with the sweater, a gasp of astonishment: these clothes were museum pieces. Only a very few old people still wore such things.

At the village, the walk up to the plaza now lined with shops, a candle lit on the floor in church after the Maya fashion, a few messages sent out and then a siesta flop in a small new hotel. On waking, the eyes of my old teacher Nicolas Chiviliu looking down at me. In his seventies now, probably, but still hale and hearty. Back to his compound: all his sons and his daughter come out with more than twenty grandchildren, everyone dancing and jumping up and down. I send out for beer and wine, and we have a great party. The last time I had visited to say good-bye, he had gotten very drunk, and I had left him shouting and wailing at his altar that his friend Don M. was leaving and he was now childless and apprenticeless.

On another day, we made *costumbre*, and he pushed my face into the great Mam bundle stinking of the alcohol he had poured over it. After this he shocked me somewhat by asking for money but relented roguishly when I reminded him I was apprentice, not client. We eventually took it out on a couple of Peace Corps youths who had the privilege of coming with me at my invitation.

I have kept diaries uninterruptedly since 1939 and am still saddened at the loss of the 1969 book, either picked from, or dropped out of, my pocket during a visit to Chichicastenango around this time. I did keep a few notes. Some were on the San Martin bundle in the chapel (*cofradia*) of San Juan. I was anxious to know if a certain ritual seen in the fifties, so secret that none of the Ladino (people who do not think of themselves as Maya) lifelong residents had ever heard of it, was still practiced.

A note: "Proceed November 10, 1969, I and L., a young Peace Corps man, to try to find *Cofradia* San Juan by ourselves in pitch darkness. Carrying one liter of alcohol from me; a half from L. and a large 20 cent candle. Through narrow volcanic lava and rock-strewn streets, guided by the sound of two marimba xylophones floating over the houses. Barking, snarling dogs, unafraid of our flashlights. Into the room, tiny as usual: bellows of welcome as I hand over the liter. 'We hope you are not just passing by.' Given seats on the wooden bench of the officials. Exchange of hand kisses. I am made to admire the familiar layout: full regalia of cypress and juniper twigs, plants and fruit in the eaves mixed with stuffed raccoons and other wild animals; a huge creamy *corozo* palm flower at the center; fiery red *pico de gallo* flowers and spikenards at the altar; huge yellow candles on the floor: the warm, comfortable light of home. On the altar, the cloth of the *Maria Yashper* bundle, the 'tripes of the Ancient Mother' (*Yashper* is female to the Martín, Lord of the Mountains and Wild Animals), in whose box sick children are rocked as they are returned for a while to the original womb of all things. And, of course, the Martín bundle, covered in rain-green velvet, some ancient silver crosses over it. There should be some small cakes of stone-hard corn there too.

"Delight when I ask who is *Alcalde*, who is *Juez*, *Primero*, and so forth, down the list of officials. Each pointed out to me, also the old *Nabeysil*, 'First Throne man,' charged with the heavy 'burden' of the ritual, wearing the oldest-style clothes. Five foot tall, white stubbly beard, gaunt face, large popping eyes: a very old Maya Bogart. They will be changing him soon, '*el pobre*,' the poor guy, with the usual stress on the tremendous spiritual burden of this *carga*, this holy duty.

"Usual 'reassurance' talk about keeping up the *costumbre*, letting nothing be lost since it is the way of the father-mothers. Chins on each other's shoulders in the old attitudes of ritual sympathy. It would not matter if I talked classical Greek: communication of affection and empathy is all. The friendly First *Cofrade*, the hoarse-voiced *Alcalde*, the rollicking *Juez*, all arm in arm, listening now to one, now to the other. From under the table the delicious smile of a thirteen-year-old girl, a friend of L's: I remember the haunting faces of those adolescents, hard to tell them apart from adults because the costumes are exactly the same; there had been one in the old days, in *cofradia* Santa Cruz I was very fond of. . . . Drinks start going round and cigarettes—a holy duty you do not refuse—with the old greetings at each gulp and puff '*Maltiosh* (Thanks) *Téeta* (Co-Elder) *Alcalde*, *Maltiosh Téeta Juez*, etc.' Not forgetting to pull a nasty face as if in disgust at the gut-wrenching liquor. Reminiscences, the passage of years, the sweet warm light, the smell of copal incense. The passage of years, deep contentment.

"My old watch-keeping role: *Primero* is for holding to the old strict rule of midnight; *Nabeysil* is impatient. Finally, two young men put on 'jaguar' costumes and two 'deer' costumes (animal skins and horns) and perform a perfunctory dance in the chapel before setting out for the hills. None of the old patterns, with the jaguar pawing at the back of the deer: the thing is quick and done by very young men. Some of the self-crossing at the cardinal directions but without much sense of order. Is some of this getting lost?

"About 23.40, *Nabeysil* goes up to the bundle and is immediately helped into one of the shirts it contains by the censer swinger. Starts dancing immediately, coming toward the *cofrades'* table, a quick, nondescript hop, hands swinging loosely at his sides, palms up. Not much of the graceful choreography of the 1950s official. No cardinal directions pattern: wherever he has room, kneels, crosses himself, picks up a little earth, kisses it. After a very little while, to my delight, takes up the 'crucified' position (I had only seen it once: not all dancers do it) with his back to the table fronting our bench, leaning far back on it, shoulders on the rim, left foot over right, arms spread out, turning his head from side to side and ogling.

"The room is very still, the doors and windows shut since the Bundle contains all the world's winds and could wreck the village if they were let out. Someone lifts the *Nabeysil's* joined hands: the impression as before that this is some sort of incarnation. [Dear reader, are you still there? The explanations have all been published in *Scandals in the House of Birds*!] The lead officials kneel in front of the dancer, cross themselves, kiss his belly, each arm at the wrist and the crossed feet. Women officials (the *tisheles*) follow, then the laymen. The dancer guzzles a soda. After the kissing, to the bundle again; takes out a second shirt. Dance repeated, ending at 24.15. After the dancer seated, a long drink is fed to the wooden Lamb icon (part of the San Juan regalia) sitting just above the bundle. Satisfaction expressed by all.

"Had always refused to dance in the old days, partly out of a lifelong embarrassment and shyness, partly in order not to miss any ritual. Now, could not resist *Juez's* invitation. Floor cleared for us and a slow stately melody called a *son* requested. *Juez* dances with grace; I get into his rhythm and perform well, despite the encumberment of the low rafters. Take another spin with a very drunk official: trouble in holding him up. 'Great fathers, I am among you, but if I speak not a word, forgive me,' a line from a poem in *The Beautiful Contradictions* going round and round in my head.

"*Cofradía* sweet smelling tonight, none of that smell of vomit, urine, stale alcoholic breath, and sweat that sets in toward morning or during the many-day rituals I used to sit through. Feeling of return so strong that I had not noticed the number of full *copitas* downed: some seven or eight maybe. [My record in the old days: thirty with pure chile juice on the day of departure in 1953.] Made the silly mistake of taking out a small smoke, thinking this would be a great place to have it. My companion L., after one puff, could not share it because of lung trouble. Smoked it all. Almost immediately began to feel wretchedly dizzy and sicker than ever before in all my life. Incapable of moving. Another round of drinks finishes me off:

you cannot refuse. Clutched at L.'s shoulder: he is anxious. Try to hold for a while, sinking like a ship at the slightest movement. After a few seconds feel slightly sick and keel over to the left, hoping to be sick behind the bench. *Alcalde* must have gotten up: I sense my head hitting the bench and my legs raised onto it. Pass out to the sound of amused comments and laughter, advancing and receding. Laughter with, not against: they are more than used to it. Strong desire to pass into sleep as in my own bed. Lovely feeling of being home intensified: home is where you can misbehave without being criticized.

"But passed into something else rather than 'out.' Stillness, knowing I must not move. Face deep into the very hard bench begins to ache. Bones wracked by hard wood. Very conscious: bits of talk floating in and out. Feel my mouth wet, cover my face with the *zut*: the men had taken it from my waist and put it round my neck in the correct position. Whenever eyes open, I see fragments of the bodies of women and girls sitting under the table near the great two-tongued drum—an instrument known from pre-Hispanic times. No one paying any attention to me: the most wonderful feeling of all. Believe L. has gone and believe I must stay till dawn. Don't care.

"After a while, who knows how long, begin to feel I can rise. Quite clear-headed. *Aguardiente* is more suave than most people make out. Purgation used to be total and a clear head in the morning. Come up ever so slowly to find L. beaming down. *Cofrades* laugh, say I've had a good sleep, invite me to dance again. Decline with as much grace as possible. L. gets me up and out with muttered thanks and promises of return. Walk quite steadily in the night air; converse as if nothing had happened. But my whole left side is soaking, and I am not exactly sweet smelling. Stink the whole of the next day until I can get back to Pana and wash off."

20.4 Back in time. Field diary entry for January 2, 1953:

"The other day, an Atiteco came in here to my office and talked with me. Suddenly he said 'You know, the people here love and respect you very much. There are many who are saying that you are a god who has come to visit the village.'"

I am surprised at the conciseness of this entry, considering its importance. The man had not been a regular "informant"; he had sat very casually on the table I used as a desk, swinging his legs and talking for some time about the price of corn. The question of my "divinity" came up very suddenly, and there was really no way that the conversation could continue from there. The man left very soon after.

Two things. Atitecos were undoubtedly curious about an outsider who spent a good deal of time making *costumbre* with a leading Atiteco shaman. Chiviliu clearly believed I fully knew Tz'utujil Maya although for mysterious reasons of my own I chose to only mutter it silently. My participation had intensified to the point that during the long, secret vigils, I would be helping the *cofrades* and officials by swinging censers, carrying torches to light the way, and keeping the time. One night, during the vigil following the ritual washing of the Mam-Maximón's clothes in the lake, I found that all the native priests were drunk. Somewhat under the influence myself, I took my mentor Chiviliu's Latin prayer book—a volume he believed to contain all the secrets of the universe—and, kneeling at the altar, began a long ritual in Latin with many local gestures and complex Maya ritual crossings. After this, I discovered that the little house we were in had belonged to a powerful native priest who had died some years before: Francisco Sojuel. He had led village resistance to powerful landlords. After this episode, I was often asked if I had known Sojuel or had been related to him. An old man told me that I had undoubtedly been born in Atitlán but had been taken away very early and could wear the shirts now but not the short pants, which would leave my legs cold. It was also true that I was instrumental in helping a party of traditionalists to regain certain rights in regard to the Mam (the Maximón), rights lost years before when a party of French Catholic priests had raided the Mam *cofradia* and taken away the sacred masks to be burned. (I also tracked down one of these priests and obtained a very old mask from him but could only do so on condition that it was not returned to the Atitecos. I deposited it at a museum in France and thirty years later returned it to Atitlán. That story is told in *Scandals*.)

I had also noticed that the names of certain dead Atitecos used to be appended to the names of gods, saints, and angels in the litanies of the native priests. It became clear after a while that, in keeping with ancient Maya practice, major impressive native priests—mostly rainmakers and makers of good weather after the rainy season—were thought to have ascended, on dying, into the ranks of the rain gods they served or the Christian "angels," which were transposed versions of the rain gods. It seemed that reincarnation could happen in some cases and that some of these "human" gods came back to help the village in times of trouble. Thus your humble as a relative of Sojuel, or even Sojuel himself, returned home.

G2.01 Author. Paris, 1970s. PHOTO: HENRI CARTIER BRESSON.

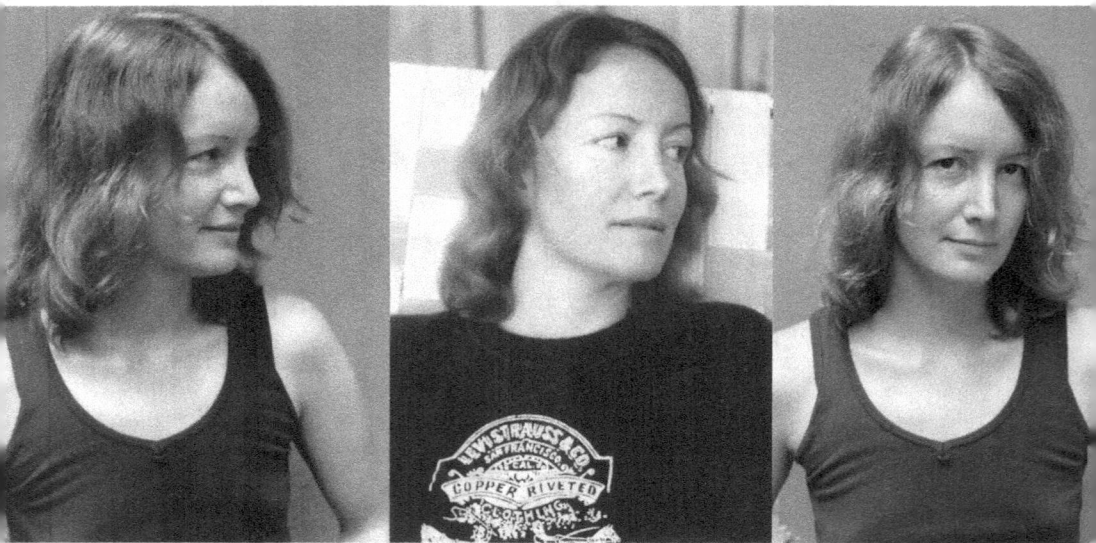

G2.02 (*top*) Janet. New Hope, Pennsylvania, circa 1974. PHOTOS: NATHANIEL
TARN.   G2.03 (*bottom*) Janet and author. New Hope, Pennsylvania, circa 1980.

G2.04 Marc, medical elective. Solomon Islands, 1988.

G2.05 (*top*) Author, Poets in Stanzas. New Hope, Pennsylvania, circa 1980s.
G2.06 (*bottom left*) Janet. St. Lawrence Island, Alaska, 1970s. PHOTO: NATHANIEL
TARN.   G2.07 (*bottom right*) Author and Yaxwan. St. Lawrence River, Canada,
1980s. PHOTO: JANET RODNEY.

G2.08 (*top*) Andrea and
Axel wedding. London, 1998.
G2.09 (*bottom*) Author and
granddaughter Ina Rain. London,
1990S. PHOTO: JANET RODNEY.

Throw Twenty-One

21.1 The Maya folk religion, which is a blend of medieval Catholicism (itself, as taught by Spanish priests of that time, very close to folk models) and of the ancient Maya religious heritage, has retained the notion that there is no absolute dividing line between humanity and divinity. A human being, under special circumstances, as helper or as especially gifted, can enter, alive or dead, into the ranks of the superhuman. Or to keep value judgments out (supra/infra) of the ranks of the parahuman.

This is the faith of most of mankind, and only our Judeo-Christian heritage in its exoteric form has prevented us for two thousand years from seeing it. There are of course hierarchies in all theophanies: in some, man can attain to the highest ranks of all, in some only to inferior ones. In Buddhism there is literally nothing else than man that can attain to the highest spiritual rank: that of a Buddha, superior even to gods, who, like humans, are impermanent. Although medieval Christianity had saints and mystics in the parahuman—the great white rose of Dante's Paradiso is the supreme demonstration of the notion of ecclesia—and although the three religions of "the Book" have branches in which it is held that more than this can be achieved (esoteric Christianity, Kabbalah, Sufism), our prevailing view is that there is an absolute break in continuity between God and man that cannot be bridged by anything human.

Nineteenth-century anthropology reflected this view by positing two domains—the sacred and the profane—and by postulating that much of religious ritual centered around the passage from one into and out of the other. I believe we are nearer the mark in suggesting that everything is sacred to the religious mind and that the passage to be mediated, if any, lies between a macrocosm, or great world/universe, and a microcosm, or small world, envisaged either as the society of men in general or the individual human soul. Very frequently, such a view involves the notion that in order to know itself or to experience itself completely, the macrocosm (envisaged as the godhead, the absolute unity or totality) has to fragment itself in a *sparagmos*—a part or parts of it to fall or to descend into plurality—and this, in itself, is the process that brings into being the microcosm or microcosms.

This detotalization is then followed, after a long period of involution (the notion of cosmic cycles is important here), by an evolutionary retotalization in which the fragments are reintegrated into the totality. We might think of this as a world breath in an endless series of such that constitutes the very essence and being of the universe. The drama of the "Fall of Albion" in William Blake's prophetic poems is of this order and recounts no other story. In some esoteric versions of Judeo-Christianity, the account of the Fall in Genesis is held to be but a truncated version of some such process: the whole Christian scenario then fleshes out the means whereby the microcosm in its fallen state is "saved" and reintegrated into the macrocosm. And ecclesia, or "church" more profoundly understood, then becomes the locus wherein the microcosmic pieces, fallen into existence through detotalization, are reintegrated into the body of Christ, which is his church.

21.2 What becomes of the priest in such worldviews? In the exoteric sacred/profane model, the priest has to stand as a mediator between two unbridgeable worlds. The more basic function of the priest in the esoteric view is more likely to involve him or her constantly keeping in the microcosm's sight the macrocosm to which it actually belongs the whole time if only it were able to see it. His/her function is to re-memorate continually the shape of the holy world, to hold before the practitioner the very shape and texture of the universe as it really is in order that the practitioner may have perpetually in view his or her actual status and inhabitation.

We know enough, in our day, about archetypes and their relationship to the psyche to accept that the world picture that such a priest keeps alive is not necessarily to be related, point for point, to the world picture held up by contemporary science. Its constant evolution apart, science often comes surprisingly close to the visions of religious psychologists and mystics, and although it may eventually be the fates of science and religion to be reunited in a common discourse, it is not necessary, at present, for the two views to coincide. The function of the religious picture is to reassert, time and again, a set of apparently permanent human needs. The scientific picture's function is to keep the record open, the doubt constantly at work. Both may still be necessary and may remain so.

World maps. We now have a good idea of these, whether Egyptian, Mesopotamian, Indian, Chinese, Australian Aborigine, Dogon/Bambara, Maya, or Navajo. There are pictorial representations often used in ritual: Tibetan mandalas, for instance, or Native American (Pueblo and Navajo) sand pictures. It is one thing to read about these and quite another to experience a picture coming alive before oneself—as I did in the case of the Atiteco picture, a fragmented variant of the great pre-Hispanic Maya picture still to be found in the Mesoamerican archaeological records.

21.3 To become a native priest in Atitlán, then, is to learn the disposition of the Holy World, the *Santo Mundo*, or *Remshus Kaj, Remsush Ulewu*—navel of sky, navel of earth—as it is embodied in the features of Atiteco geography. The Lake area is a holy land. The priest learns to recognize its features and to embody them in litanical prayers that constitute *costumbre*. *Costumbre* in effect is a promenade through the sites of the Holy World (villages, landscape features, crosses, hills, caves), a re-memoration of its features and a set of offerings to its powers so that these behave propitiously to the client. In early work, I used "native priest" to distinguish such an Indian person from Catholic priests, ordained members of the Catholic Church. I should have used "shaman" earlier because these native priests operate as shamans and do not recognize a gap between sacred and profane. By the time of the *Scandals* book, I was using that term.

I need a word other than "priest" to define the kind of religious leader I am talking about because not all these are shamans. "Guru" would do but has acquired too much pejorative weight in our culture. Let me try "guide."

Costumbre deals principally with the world body; other techniques, such as divination and dream analysis, deal with the man body in the form of *suerte*, a person's destiny or fate, and feed into the *costumbre* the information needed to "personalize" each particular ritual event. In cultures where psychology is more highly developed, it may be that the guide works more with the man body. The most extreme example of man-body guiding activity is perhaps the *Bardo Thodol* (Tibetan Book of the Dead), in which the guide, as psychopomp, addresses a dead person and shows his or her disincarnated imagination if not its salvation in enlightenment, at least the way to its best possible rebirth. There are some doubts as to the *Bardo*'s authenticity as presented, but the picture is still influential.

In certain cultures the world body and the macrocosm/microcosm correspondence are graphically illustrated in buildings. Paul Mus, in one of the greatest little-read classics of our time, his study of the Indonesian temple/mountain Borobudur, has shown this for the Buddhist *stupa* (often called "pagoda"), and Stella Kramrisch has shown the same for the Hindu temple. To some extent a medieval cathedral shares in this nature. The Burmese *stupa*, with the world of spirits at its outer rim and the world of totality at the very top of the golden bell itself, illustrates this as well as the role of such a building in orienting daily behavior throughout a life. Most *stupas* do this. Co-essential with the body of the Buddha—because it is a reliquary—and towering over the landscape, the *stupa* serves as a perpetual reminder of the primordial guide.

The guide is an initiator; he shows the mysteries like the Zen Buddhist master pointing at the moon. There is a moment beyond all ratiocination where the mind has to be stilled and has, as its only duty, to contemplate the mysteries shown, recognizing in them its own essence, its own nature. It is at this moment that the mind achieves illumination or "enlightenment" and the power of informaction. Merging into the mainstream of existence, becoming part of the Way, the mind cannot do other than act correctly: the being that supports it cannot do "wrong."

21.4 Who is or are the guide(s) in our cultures? On statistical evidence, the psychotherapist and psychoanalyst. In the hands of the right person, working within these arts can be an initiation. Yet, at best, and with the possible exception of the Jungians, the analyst can guide only the man body. Science is too powerful, and the task of exhibiting the world body is usually left implicitly to it. However, our physicists and our mathematicians are mostly encapsulated in a sphere so separate from the possibilities of our own understanding that very few of us literary folks have access to it. It is as if scientists were already out in space, out in the future, some fifty, some hundred, years ahead of ourselves.

Contra the desacralizing trend of our times, I long believed, perhaps had to believe, that the poet has to be our guide insofar as he or she is, in an age of ever-increasing specialization, the most generally available of humans. Writing at the threshold of the Industrial Revolution, which was to give us our present world, the Romantic poets were perhaps the first to grasp this. I turn back to ask Wordsworth, the poet of my youth, in words that should be far more familiar to us than they are, to describe this availability. We should intuit and insert an important change: To "Man" should be added "Woman." So in his "Preface to the Lyrical Ballads" you find this:

> "What is a Poet? To whom does he address himself? And what language is to be expected from him? He is a man speaking to men"

> . . .

> "He considers man and nature as essentially adapted to each other, and the mind of man as naturally the mirror of the fairest and most interesting qualities of nature."

> . . .

> "Poetry is the breath and finer spirit of all knowledge; it is the impassioned expression which is the countenance of all science. Emphatically may it be said of the Poet, as Shakespeare hath said of man, "that he looks before and after." He is the rock and defense of human nature; an upholder and preserver, carrying everywhere with him relationship and love. In spite of difference of soil and climate, of language and manners, of laws and customs, in spite of things gone silently out of mind and things violently destroyed, the Poet binds together by passion and knowledge the vast empire of human society as it is spread over the whole earth, and over all time."

> . . .

> "Poetry is the first and last of all knowledge—it is as immortal as the heart of man."

Wordsworth goes on to conjure up a time when the poet will cooperate with the scientist and, in effect, transfigure scientific language for the common understanding. We no longer believe in such a time, seeing science as being constitutively always ahead of us. For the rest, Wordsworth, however lovable he is in his intent to cleave as he best can to a fairly standard norm of the human spirit, shackles himself by his notion that poetry must necessarily cooperate with science. No such consideration, when he was stormed by his spirits from the outer world beyond normal consciousness, could have kept a far more radical mind like William Blake's from expressing the fullness of that human spirit, both in its beauty and its terror, its gold and its dross. Where Wordsworth limited himself to seeing the beauty in science's scholarship, contenting himself with following its worldview wherever it would lead a man of his time, Blake opposed himself, by a radical critique of Newtonian science, to the possibility that objective knowledge alone would save humanity.

In his myth of the fall and redemption of the cosmic man, Blake was the equal of the greatest initiators of all time, a mind so far ahead of his own period and even of our own that few, even today, can encompass it. His equation of the human imagination with the divine "Jesus" in each human person and in the cosmos was his true showing of the mystery. Far from merely commenting on science, he made the effort, through his radical critique, of building that science into the very procedure, the very texture of his work. That it has taken some two hundred years before certain scholars—Northrop Frye (who tried to get me to the U. at Santa Cruz), David Erdman, and Kathleen Raine perhaps principally—have begun to comprehend that texture; that we still wrestle with it today when Blake's spirit has descended, as Milton's once descended into his, into a community of poets in these American states is a sign of the high seriousness of Blake's original purpose. The intent of poetry now is no longer to merely "give pleasure" but to serve as a guide on the way to wisdom. No subject that can conceivably excite the human spirit is alien to it, no effort of the conscious or unconscious mind can be too great to challenge it, no form of expression can be too difficult to excite it into the possibility of voice.

Left behind by mainstream science, the average "reader" has been misled into creating, or following those who have created, alternative systems of cosmic explanation that offer complete, easy-to-grasp cosmic models. The phenomenal rise of "new age" literature demonstrates this. Philosophy and theology, enslaved to a Western worldview that is bursting apart at the seams, have retreated for the most part into heavily jargon-ridden academic specialization. There is no longer any one overarching body of knowledge that can serve as a reference keystone. In this situation, the poetic Word alone remains, naked and vulnerable as it is, almost overwhelmed by fakery as it is, the only fully available forum for the kind of discussion envisaged here whose aim is to perpetually re-create the exhibition of the mysteries of unified knowledge. Or would remain, I should add, if it went on fulfilling its function instead of abdicating it to the manufacturers of the pandemic known as "creative writing." But this is another subject.

21.5 Are the world models of archaic cosmographies and theophanies—with their cardinal directions, zeniths and nadirs, their navels of earth and sky, their heavens and hells, their mountains and valleys, lands and oceans (mirrors of those places our spirits are impelled to explore)—are these not the ultimate heraldic shields against the absurdity that menaces us from all sides at all times, against the Satan of doubt in all its terrifying forms?

My fascination as an anthropologist was always with these highly complex systems, their piercing together, their explanation, their eventual understanding. The very first system that drew me to the discipline at the end of the forties was perhaps one of the most complex ever uncovered, that of the Dogon, Bambara, and adjacent tribes in what was once the French Sudan, opened up so brilliantly by the sage Ogotemmêli for Marcel Griaule. Later I wrestled with systems found by my own work in Guatemala and in Burma: Maya Christianity and Theravāda Buddhism. The exhaustion entailed by the study of these systems may have something to do with the passive objectivity expected of the anthropologist. There comes a point, in Gary Snyder's words, when the anthropologist gets tired of asking questions and wants to become an informant. It is here, no doubt, that the anthropologist becomes the poet.

What I say now will be read by many as old-fashioned and hopelessly romantic in a culture that is itself in accelerated transformation and in a state of critical shrinkage, and where all power has been subtracted from poetry, not least by people who believe they are writing it but have actually retreated from the role of "poet" to the position, usually academic, of "writer."

But it is as poet/guide that such a poet has to make the passage, for little satisfaction can be expected from the role of one whose business is thought of as giving pleasure or (in more current terminology) providing entertainment. This too involves too much passivity, too much enslavement to the world as it appears to be rather than to the world as it is. The pleasure should remain: the poet retains full control of ludic and musical powers, but it is not enough. Only in that place where the poem can partake in the very making of the world body and man body in harmony together, assume their full conjoined weight, become part of the very spin of the world in motion, only there where it becomes what it beholds and what it shows will the poet find that rest which never rests, that stillness perpetually in motion, and that extreme puzzlement which will keep him or her occupied till the final day. Here is where the glove is taken up and worn, the shield fitted and adjusted to the arm. There is no need of sword or lance. The Word, as has been said at times, is mightier than both.

21.6 That by 2011, I have moved very far away from this view of poetry and the poet is the result of many factors I'll review later in this book—including society's impotence in the face of an environment being assassinated day by day—but, above all, vocationally speaking, to the fact that in a careerist, *pobiz*-dominated world devoted first and foremost to replication (the creation of more and more poets similar to one another blotting out any kind of sunlight from the landscape), the view has become, as they say today, "unsustainable." Culture, in the throes of the digital revolution, is going through nothing short of a cataclysmic change, and models of poetic creation, old as the world, no longer seem to hold any validity. I have no idea whether I shall live long enough to form any kind of conception as to any kind of outcome of this change. I doubt it. Meantime, in a great many senses, life has lost much of its color, interest, and value. However, a mystery yet unto me remains: how can I not consciously know those zillion human lives around me that I can never know?

Throw Twenty-Two

22.1 Acquaintance and friendship with American poets grew apace, favored by readings, conferences, short teaching assignments, and trips to the most far-flung outposts of the empire. While still at Princeton in 1970, Patricia and Tarn had gone to the Notre Dame Literary Festival, meeting Gary Snyder, John Matthias, and Michael Anania for the first time. The conference was beautifully run by young people who prided themselves on their first-class hosting abilities but apparently cared nothing about literature. Things went downhill until the last class, in which Tarn was fed to a group of very tough footballers whose sovereign detachment from the matter in hand led them to being dismissed after only half an hour.

Gary Snyder visited at Princeton after this, and Tarn suggested the interview that became "From Anthropologist to Informant" in an early issue of Jerome Rothenberg's ethnopoetics magazine *Alcheringa*. There were also visits to New Hope when Snyder was being pursued as an adviser by Jerry Brown, governor of California. The phone rang incessantly. Gary was especially pleased with a trip to the extraordinary Mercer tool museum in Doylestown: one of the earliest concrete buildings in America, with an inside very reminiscent of Piranesi's *I Carceri* engravings. A momentous visit to Gary's California home, Kitkitdizzie, followed at the end of one of a set of Alaska trips, with Tarn and Rodney being put out tentless to enjoy sleeping in a field under a giant firmament. The relation soured somewhat after a letter from Gary critical, as Tarn saw it, of Tarn's "failure" to manage ordinary, everyday American life. Sadly, it ended when Tarn disapproved of a student of Gary's editing the *Alcheringa* interview for a New Directions volume. Without any consultation, this young man cut out Tarn's modest contribution altogether and altered history by amending some remarks of Gary's on Olson and others. N.D. offered to restore all cuts, but, weary by this time, Tarn abstained.

22.2 New Mexico was first seen toward the end of the long entry-into-publishing trip in 1967. After drives all over Colorado and Wyoming, becoming acquainted with the splendor of the mountain West, Acoma was eventually reached while it could still be climbed on foot without the constraint of a tourist shuttle van. Acoma was the farthest point of the journey. Santa Fe was attained only during the 1970 summer vacation. Tarn stayed in a variety of places, retreated to the broiling old Vargas Hotel when he was forced to, fervently wished he had the money to buy a place on Canyon Road (fortunately, in view of tourism's future, he did not), and eventually shared an apartment for a while with Dennis and Barbara Tedlock. Although they and Jerome Rothenberg, also in town, were planning *Alcheringa* magazine together, Tarn had many an earful of dissentions and dissatisfactions felt by the Tedlocks—emotions that reached a breaking point sometime later when Dennis threw Jerry's typewriter out of the window, followed by poet and wife out the door, on one of the latter's visits to their home.

Dennis's father was a professor at the University of New Mexico and owned a house in Cerrillos from which he had, for years, run a small press for western writers. The first issue of *Alcheringa* was issued here and sewn together by the editors and their associates. A very-well-attended reading was also given at St. John's College, together with the Santo Domingo Littlebird brothers: poets, storytellers, ceramicists, artists. On subsequent visits a friendship developed with Larry Littlebird, also known as Larry Byrd. Larry offered a beautiful small painting of a red eagle in exchange for a poem. The only other artist who has ever made such an offer of trading art for poetry was also a Native American, the Inuit sculptor Ron Senungetuk in Fairbanks, Alaska.

For June 1971, Tarn had an offer to teach a summer writing school at the University of Colorado, Boulder, living in dorms and far too closely huddled together with the students. Other teachers were Senator Eugene McCarthy and Harlan Ellison, a well-known science fiction writer. The major interest of the students seemed to be concentrated on a bet as to "which teacher would get laid first." The only relief from all this came in a friendship and one or two bird-watching trips with the poet Jack Collom, who much later taught at Naropa. One tragedy occurred: a young African American girl, daughter of a U.S.A.F. colonel, who was going to get the prize for poetry was killed in a car crash just before the announcement: Tarn corresponded with her mother for some time afterward. Exhausted, Tarn was fortunate in obtaining from another local poet a two-week loan of his cabin in the mountains behind Boulder. The solitude was only broken at night when three diminutive big-eared deer mice came out on their tricycles and performed some delightful round dances. But Tarn was cured for life and never taught "creative writing" again.

A raid on Santa Fe from Boulder included a stay with Barry Hall, who was running the last Cape Goliard enterprise out of a ranch he and his lady friend—reputedly a recent close acquaintance of Georges Pompidou—had acquired by somewhat undefinable means. Various night raids—once to a writer's conference miles away, once to another dubious ranch replete with sexual high jinks—were very nervous occasions as if they had arisen out of the movie *Easy Rider*. A wonderful initiation into LSD took place among the Nambe cliffs, where ordinary desert stones were transformed into rivers of diamonds. There were also some comic episodes. On one occasion, a member of this "commune" failed to keep his powder dry. Frantically, he tried, by well-known means, to insert it into the noses of various friends before it melted altogether. Tarn avoided that occasion. On starting for the drive back to Boulder, however, a pill was administered, and the old Dodge Dart seemed to drive itself to the rollicking strains of the Hispanic radio station *Que Dice* until it came to a dead stop in sight of the Air Force Academy at Colorado Springs. A police car drew up behind immediately as if by magic; its driver bellowed through his loudspeaker at two inoffensive hippie hitchhikers standing by the road but was unaccountably kind to the traveler. Helped to a can of gas at a station nearby and sent on his way with many an injunction to visit the extraordinary Academy chapel, Tarn reached Boulder without further trouble and then went on back to the East Coast on a *periplum*, one of many long trans-America journeys.

22.3 During the seventies, a number of visits were made to California with stops, usually, at San Francisco and San Diego. A favorite place among the bookstores in the Berkeley area was Serendipity Books, then still run by Jack Shoemaker and his wife: early on in Tarn's American life, Jack had arranged a flatteringly well-attended reading for the visitor in his own house. Another memorable reading was arranged by Kenneth Rexroth at U.C. Santa Barbara, including a stay at Kenneth's home with its extensive gardens and superb library and liberal doses of his version of the Great American Monologue. Some satisfaction for Tarn arose at the reading when John Martin's daughter—he was still living nearby—told her father that he had been foolish to let go of this particular poet. Among large gatherings, a major event was the 1983 Second Ethnopoetics Conference held at U.S.C. in Los Angeles, where a great many poets gathered, headed up by Robert Duncan. Tarn felt that whereas he had prepared his paper, everyone else had come along to speak extempore, with the meeting suffering as a result. A much tighter meeting had been the April 1975 First Conference at the Center for XXth Century Studies of the University of Wisconsin, Milwaukee.

Robert Duncan was met with on a number of occasions. At first, Tarn had merely been for him a Cape representative. The turn came with a beautiful letter about *The Beautiful Contradictions* in which the younger poet was accepted as such and certain common interests and understandings between the two men were pointed out by the senior writer. Duncan visited on the East Coast, usually bringing sumptuous gifts of inscribed books: on one occasion, when departing, he entered a closet to fetch a huge overcoat and was photographed by Tarn as he turned around with the raised collar framing his face—one of his best portraits, still unpublished—though visible in this book. On visits to his house in San Francisco, you were rarely alone, and conversation was massive. One time, however, an interesting discovery was made. Face to face with R.D. alone for once, it turned out that intimate conversation was possible in such a duet, while the moment that three or more persons were involved, the event turned to theater and was completely dominated by R.D. On this occasion (Duncan may already have been on dialysis), the much-admired maestro confessed that he had not been very active lately because "there were so many young poets around that he no longer felt needed." One mystery—that of an apparent loss of interest on R.D.'s part in Tarn's work—never came clear. However, someone once told N.T. that he had heard Robert express a thought concerning an over-obvious interest in recording sexual feelings and occasions on both Robert Kelly's and Tarn's part, something which, for him, weakened the poetry.

During the Pound Conference in San Jose, Weinberger was in town and was having dinner with Michael Palmer and Cathy Simon in San Francisco. Tarn joined them hungrily. Palmer has remained one of N.T.'s major admirations in our time.

Among visits, Dennis Phillips, his wife, Courtney Gregg, and their daughter Sofia, the supreme printer Carolee Campbell (Ninja Press), and her actor husband, Héctor Elizondo, were family. Other fine poets met with on the coast were Michael Davidson, Leslie Scalapino, Kathleen Fraser, Lyn Hejinian, Duncan MacNaughton, Norma Cole, Andrew Joron, Steve Dickison, Susan Gevirtz, Sarah Menefee, Joe Lamb, and Martha Ronk. Brenda Hillman gave Tarn one of his finest ever reviews in the Australian *Jacket*. Anthropologists were not neglected: Burton and Marion Benedict at Berkeley, James Clifford and Judith Aissen at Santa Cruz. There was no way that our number-one store, Moe's Books, was going to be spared.

22.4 In the middle of the country, friendship with a beloved poet, Ken Irby, led to a powerfully inspiring correspondence. Poets George Economou and Rochelle Owens hosted Tarn at the University of Oklahoma when a substantial international prize went to Octavio Paz. Gerrit Lansing gave the Tarns a wonderful lunch before N.'s reading at Harvard and Susan Howe an equally fine dinner at S.U.N.Y. Buffalo. Forrest Gander offered a reading at Brown, and Tarn spent a beautiful verdant day with C. D. Wright at their home. There have been correspondences between poets such as Susan Stewart: once a Tarn student at Penn, now a power at Princeton. All these poets have remained strong presences in our lives. Also, other relations between Peggy Fox, once president of New Directions, and her husband, novelist and biographer Ian MacNiven. In the Far East, Professor Zhang Ziqing King of Nanjing University brought out his vast, three-volume *History of American Poetry* with some help from Tarn.

On the East Coast, companionship was provided by Eliot Weinberger and his wife, Nina Subin. Eliot, when still an eighteen-year-old college dropout and budding poet, had first visited Tarn at Kidderpore Gardens in a London writer's company, and contact with him had been renewed on arrival in New York, strengthening into a lifelong friendship when Eliot was running his magazine *Montemora*, a brilliant publication that, in many people's opinion, Eliot gave up running much too early. It was in this venue that Tarn first voiced his concerns about a society overproducing poets and underproducing readers, the major implication of the present state of "pobiz," a term that Eliot credits Tarn with creating. After marrying Subin, a highly talented photographer who ran part of the travel section of the *New York Times*, the couple, with their libraries and studios, settled in a most attractive and hospitable brownstone on West Tenth Street, traveling a good deal, especially in India, developing impressive careers, and becoming the proud parents of genial Anna Della Subin and Stefan Weinberger. While never losing his interest in poetry, Eliot gradually decided to leave that craft aside to become, as a series of volumes from New Directions amply testified, this country's leading literary essayist and most astringent commentator on the politics of culture. His anthology *American Poetry since 1940: Outsiders and Innovators* has remained the most effective compilation of its kind over three decades. Very sadly, however, it later fell prey to the inept handling of the Marsilio-New York publishing venture by its director, Luigi Ballerini. Discouraged by violent attacks from some quarters, Eliot unfortunately gave up any desire to keep the anthology project alive.

Another friend, George Quasha, was first encountered teaching at S.U.N.Y. Stony Brook when Tarn was interviewed for a job on that campus before joining Rutgers. George most hospitably welcomed the visitor into the group, which revolved around the magazine *Sumac* (among other poets involved were Jim Harrison, Dan Gerber, and Robert Vas Dias) and his own compendious two-issue *Open Poetry*. This was eventually followed by two anthologies and his cooperation with Jerry Rothenberg on that most vital of avant-garde anthologies, *America: A Prophecy*. Soon George and Susan were living in a diminutive two-room New York apartment high in a building at the river end of Christopher Street overlooking the most Chiricoesque piece of architecture Tarn ever found on any continent. The apartment was a constant refuge, especially during the troubled years of 1972–74, when the couple most kindly acted virtually *in loco parentis*, supervising Tarn's affairs and relationships with considerable care and affectionate concern, albeit with a touch of control. There was a considerable amount of smoking. Tarn often stayed nights—usually devoured by far-ranging conversations on poetry, poetics, and George's latest enthusiasms in the fields of esoteric and Oriental studies, healing, and the counterculture generally. His views were not always shared, but no one more systemically and infectiously enthusiastic than Quasha at this time had ever been encountered.

Early in Tarn's new American life, readings were mostly provided at Dr. Generosity's Poetry Bar in Manhattan. Groups would often form after a reading there, including Quasha, Armand Schwerner, Michael Heller, Jane Augustine, Jackson McLow, Toby Olson, Geoffrey O'Brien, Pierre Joris, Peter Cole, Paul West, Diane Ackerman, Jackson Mac Low, Ed Foster, Ammiel Alcalay, John Yau, Mark Nowak—before his move to Philadelphia—and many others. Tarn got hungrier and hungrier while endless palavers continued on the pavement regarding which restaurant should be patronized that night. All of this provided perhaps the most sociable period in this author's life, indeed perhaps the only one of its kind, an equivalent of a sort to that most civilized of sociabilities (the Parisian café scene) and has been sorely missed ever since. Such an assembly did not occur again until the 2015s.

One splendid occasion was a gathering of poets in a house that the Quashas had been lent during a Labor Day weekend. This was memorialized in the poem "At Gloucester, Mass., after Foreign Travel" in the *Lyrics* volume. Various Maximus sites were visited at this time, as well as the house itself, where Olson had written in pencil on the walls and around the windows and which was now lived in by Linda Parker, a delightful woman and a fine poet and herbalist. Luminist paintings at the museum were another highlight, as was the finding in an antique store of the flag of a US World War II battleship (white stars on navy-blue sky only), which Tarn promptly bought as *his* flag. A masterly painter, Thorpe Veidt, was one of the many people encountered here. Failure to acquire a painting of Thorpe's was a mistake Tarn has always regretted. A number of weird events took place during this weekend. One was George's insistence on Tarn's seeing the "Great Mother" in Suzan while under some chemical influence, another was a heroic run by George to fetch Harvey Bialy in trouble somewhere on the road, and yet another was a very pleasant evening beach flirtation with Harvey's then wife, Harvey coming along to watch and, in effect, closing down the event.

With the Quashas' rising interest in running a publishing house and the advent of certain funds—a possibility that had been abundantly discussed on Christopher Street—they rather suddenly removed to the neighborhood of Annandale on Hudson and Bard College, Robert Kelly presiding, and finally settled in with the establishment of a cultural center at Barrytown. Eventually, hearing of invitations going out to every member of the New York conclave to visit up there for readings and functions and not receiving any himself (for reasons that—as in so many cases in the "poetry life"—never became clear), Tarn felt bluntly abandoned, and relations with the Quashas became very spaced out. Later, George and Suzan became members of Namkhai Norbu's Tibetan Buddhist group, and Tarn once attended a retreat in the area with the Quashas' close friend and excellent poet Charles Stein.

22.5 Other New York–area encounters included Barry Alpert and his very fine critical publication *Vort*. Tarn was slated to be featured in that, but the money ran out just before this could happen. Being the last one in the door or, more frequently, the first to be kept out has been another marked feature of this "poetry life." The N.Y.U. professor and famous translator from French and German Richard Sieburth kindly introduced Tarn at a Poets' House reading. A reading for Nancy Kuhl of the Yale Beinecke was a treasure. Before this, her husband, poet Richard Deming, had come down for a reading of N.T.'s in the Village and has been a longtime friend. A lunch with Bei Dao organized by Eliot W. was another pleasure.

A later acquaintance was the distinguished Marxist anthropologist Stanley Diamond, a professor at the New School. Stanley fervently wished to be a poet and labored very hard to include himself in the circles just described. It appeared at the time, perhaps mistakenly, that he went as far as to project his present poetic activities into the past and was defining himself, with a great deal of rather embarrassing intrigue, as someone who had always been a poet, even perhaps before being an anthropologist. He edited a very meaty ethnopoetics issue of the professional magazine *Dialectical Anthropology* and ran a series of panels and readings at the New School. Unfortunately, he died far too young.

22.6 The Philadelphia connection was not as strong as the New York link but was significant nonetheless. Tarn kicked off a magazine, *The Painted Bride* (eventually morphing into an arts center in the city), when invited to read to and critique the poems of a small founding group whose first meeting this was alleged to be. Principal friends in the city were Toby and Miriam Olson, who had moved from New York to work at Temple University. A number of good readings were organized by Toby and his friend at a bar in a street behind the Philharmonic Hall. Toby, a major novelist and a very fine poet, experienced a year of fame (evanescent eventually as such things are) when he won the PEN/Faulkner Award for Fiction in 1983 and was able to offer week-long visitorships at Temple, one of which benefited his New Hope friend. Gill Ott, the editor of another successful magazine, was weathering fearsome medical difficulties at the time but survived to become a leading light on the local scene. Still in Pennsylvania, but farther out to the west, John Taggart visited New Hope and was visited at Shippensburg College. His area contained the Amish country and Lancaster with its great market—a favorite destination when traveling the state out of New Hope. Taggart very kindly arranged for a Pennsylvania State Award, the only such ever received.

22.7 Early in the seventies, Tarn, through an interest in the author's anthropological work in the Cranberry Islands, had made the acquaintance of Richard Grossinger and his wife, the poet Lindy Hough, both working at Goddard College. On a visit to Maine, he drove across country to Vermont for a brief stay with the couple. Something of his had been accepted by Richard's *Io* magazine: the essay titled "Toward Any Geography, Toward Any America Whatsoever." Grossinger was very unhappy with his situation in publishing—perhaps it was at this time that Black Sparrow appeared to be abandoning him?—and Tarn argued that he should add a book division to *Io* because the ideal of self-help was combining at this time with the success of little-press publishing and might well see him through. This was in fact the beginning of North Atlantic Books, a project that has been flourishing for many years and continues to do so. N.A.B. eventually published Janet Rodney's first commercial book, *Crystals*.

Throw Twenty-Three

23.1 A very different and more far-flung adventure concerned Alaska, which was experienced, three years running, as the skull of the American West at the top of the Rockies' spine, overshadowing in magnificence everything that had been seen of the whole continent before. Curiously, though always thinking of himself as a son of the tropics, Tarn discovered that his lasting nostalgia would be for the very far norths of the planet.

Not long after getting together with Janet Rodney, Tarn set off alone on May 15, 1975, for the great land (J.R. still had academic duties to deal with) in Rodney's new bottle-green Dodge 200 van, rudimentarily equipped with a box arrangement in the back whose top extended out to form a very hard bed. Battling the winds for whole days across the northwestern states (after a visit with David Lenfest "by the sea" at Chicago; readings at Beloit College, Wisconsin, and Carleton College, Minnesota; and visiting a string of Coloradan national parks and collapsing at night in some camp along the way) required endurance, but solace came from thousands of tiny ponds, each one occupied by a pintail or other wild duck with family. Moving into Canada toward Calgary, a group of Blood Indian passengers was acquired for a while before reaching St. George (via Banff and Lake Louise, whose famous sunrise failed to materialize), where Janet arrived by plane. A memorable evening before she came was endured at the great hall of the Sons of Norway: never had Tarn witnessed quite such a level of drinking, stomping, and miscellaneous ruckus raising before.

The pair then set out for the Alaska Highway. This was still an epic drive at the time, with many a fine rest stop: swimming in the shallow waters at British Columbia's Liard Hot Springs and spending a night at Lake Kluane, fortified by 100-proof Stolichnaya vodka and hearing, on waking, the xylophone-like music of shivering ice crystals on the lake edge. After the Yukon motel at Teslin, the last few miles into the state were difficult: unable to sleep or to stay awake, Tarn grew very cranky, and to make matters worse, there was no food in van or in camp.

The van, Rodney-baptized as "The Yukon Ritz," reached Anchorage on June 8, where very agreeable quarters awaited at Alaska Methodist University, thanks to Richard Dauenhauer and his Tlingit wife, Nora. These experts were joined by Andy Hope, another Tlingit writer, and many friends. An interest in the great changes taking place in Native affairs at the time, with Inuit and Indian groups attaining rule over their own lands, as well as in Native arts and in archaeology, prompted many visits and interviews that it would not have been incorrect to call "survey fieldwork." As usual when interest rose and peaked, substantial purchases began to be made for the home library.

A week's camping followed at Mt. McKinley National Park, with the classic awaiting of Denali's appearance: an epiphany amply recorded in the longest poem of the book *Alashka*, which, though not only a "travel poem," contains records of most of what could be claimed as "visionary" in the Alaskan travels. A pleasant river trip followed at Fairbanks. Immediately after: the flight to the Inuit village of Point Hope, distinguished by its extraordinary cemetery surrounded by a rack-of-lamb design of huge whalebones curving up and out in a complete circle around the ground. After this, the Tarns were lent a house by Willie, another Inuit friend in Nome, that had been almost wrecked by a rumpus between the owner and his girlfriend the night before, the ruins of their interrupted meal covering the only table in the house.

In late June, another house was borrowed for a week at Shismaref—Morris, the owner, running off to hunt at the very moment the pair arrived and throwing them the keys as he ran. This house's pride and joy was a mattress-less bed whose springs rose unequally into the air, ensuring expert circus acrobatics at night. Paths to outhouses were invariably protected by ferocious dogs, roped but just so their muzzles would line the very edges of the right-of-way.

Avoiding these, the problem was that one had to walk out a very long way on the flat land so as not to be visible from the village. On one occasion, the house had to be defended on the owner's behalf against Fish and Wildlife people who insisted on a search, inappropriate while Morris was away, and had to be thrown out. There were visits with a Shishmaref sculptor, Melvin Olana, whose work had been greatly admired on the mainland, and with an ex-Army man, Albert, mad on coffee and who, for many months afterward, would phone New Hope at ungodly hours of the night in search of conversation. As so often in Alaska, weather delayed departure—eventually a small plane, supposed to seat six at most, took off with more than nine. Tarn lay in the copilot seat, flattened by his huge backpack sitting on his face. The plane bravely rolled right up to the door of the jet for Anchorage.

A further flight took N.T. and J.R. to the Pribilof Islands—St. George and St. Paul—with heroic views of the volcanic Aleutian chain from the back windows of the plane. These islands were found to be rather depressing, not only because of the fur trade's seal clubbing but also because of the understandable but tedious behavior of the male seals sempiternally squabbling to keep control of their harems. In mid-July, some time was spent camping on the spit at Homer after long drives through coastal landscapes roaring pink with fields of fireweed. Whales, encountered so often out at sea on the ferries and other ships, could be seen in the morning promenading to and fro very close by. Camping one night on the drive back to Anchorage and short of food, an offer of half a salmon caught minutes before by another camper filled the bill exactly.

After this it was Valdez and on down through Whitehorse; the Tlingit village of Klukwan surrounded by bald eagles; Haines; Skagway (with a strangely inconsequential sign in a window of a side-street house saying "Go back to Boston"); a flight to, and cruise inside, Glacier Bay; the rich fir-lined totem-pole park and Russian cathedral of Sitka; Wrangell; Ketchikan; and Prince Rupert. In a Ketchikan store, rummaging among inexpensive bits of ivory described as sled parts, Tarn came across what he recognized as one of the fabulous prehistoric "winged objects" of St. Lawrence Island: it had indeed been damaged and possibly used as a sled part, but it was as beautiful as the Winged Victory of Samothrace in the Louvre and acquired for a song.

Out of Rupert lay the paradisal Skeena River, much beloved by Lévi-Strauss, and the totem-pole sites along it. Hauntingly quiet forest glades: some of the very few places in Northwest Pacific Coast culture where standing totem poles are still in situ. Kispiox, Kitwanga, and Kitwancool were visited as well as the craft-resurgence center of K'saan before turning south toward Vancouver, Portland (with a favorite oyster bar), and a first visit to the holy redwoods.

From August 8 to 12, a most generous host was Gary Snyder at his very spacious home, Kitkitdizzie, in the Sierra Nevada. Not unlike Ginsberg taking his guests out to milk a cow, Snyder took a couple of blankets out into a field and enjoined the Tarns to sleep in the open under the stars "with none of the usual protections." A splendid night.

Nevada, Utah, the extraordinary wall of dinosaur skeletons at Dinosaur National Park (never have these creatures been experienced so directly), and on to Boulder with more hospitality from the Naropa crowd and the invigorating sharing of an apartment with Jackson Mac Low and Sharon Matlin. Tarn had met Jackson at a party in New York in 1970 and attempted to voice his admiration for the *Light Poems*. But he had found the poet uninterested and ferocious. In Boulder it was discovered that one glass of beer or wine would transform this major figure into a pussycat.

With driving alone, a total of 14,669 miles had been traveled.

23.2 There were three seasons of summer travel altogether, with an interim winter visit to a Native arts conference at Sitka by Tarn alone. He flew out of Sitka in a blizzard with a sick woman in a stretcher strapped down just behind him.

In mid-June of 1976, the "Yukon Ritz" sailed out of New Hope on a similar route through Minnesota and Montana but then made for Spokane and Seattle (noting the great contrast between Oregon's hinterlands and its coasts), only to find that the Alaska ferry was delayed for two or three days. This opened the possibility of a quick raid on the Olympic Peninsula and the enjoyment of its impressive mountain ranges. The ferry went to Ketchikan and Haines, where driving resumed and a favorite camping ground at Mosquito Lake was revisited, continuing on to Tok Junction and Anchorage. On July 1 a bush-plane flight out to Gambell on St. Lawrence Island opened up the immense sun-drenched icescape of the Bering Sea. Three days of fine walks up and down the island, watching birds and admiring tundra flowers; talks with local Inuit folk in the small village, one's nose filled with the pungent smells of drying seal and whale meat; whale bones—ribs, jaws, vertebrae, etc.—all over the place mixed in with the skidoos (also used in snowless times) and hunting canoes upside down on their poles awaiting use. The two-hundredth anniversary of the United States on July 4 was spent watching Gambell folk lining up for a municipal gift of oranges.

In mid-July, while Rodney went off to McKinley Park, Patricia, Andrea, and Marc arrived and were taken in the Ritz on a fortnight's tour of bays, glaciers, and other sights. Andrea complained of one thing or another the whole way. Understandably, she was utterly miserable about the family situation (taking the children alone to Nova Scotia earlier had not been as trying), but to all intents and purposes, she came close to wrecking the trip.

On return an amusing episode occurred at the Anchorage Art Museum. A reading had been offered, and, the museum being very attractive, was accepted with pleasure. The poets were told that hundreds of invitations had gone out. Not a soul showed up, and a convenient bar was visited instead. It was then learned that the museum's invitations had all gone out of state! Another amusement was the El Matador bar, where Texan oil-pipeline workers danced with the utmost solemnity wearing their ten-gallon hats, pointed boots, and full Texan regalia.

In mid-August, a flight to Barrow on the Arctic Coast, visits with Bob and Rosita Worl (Rosita a Tlingit anthropologist working on Inuit issues), and very long walks along the coast and back of the town into the tundra. Tarn loved Arctic flights because, disbelieving in geography unless he could see it with his own eyes, the map was always dramatically visible from a plane window and our pilot flew very close to the ground. Like spirit visions, the longed-for great ivory snowy owls were seen ghost-gliding over the flats: there is nothing more silently majestic to be witnessed in the whole avian world.

On return, the reason for this particular trip came about in the shape of a conference organized by Andy Hope and Larry and Peggy Avakana to discuss matters of Native art and literature. Guests from the outside world were Edward Dorn, Richard Grossinger, and Robert Callahan. Among others present: Richard and Nora Dauenhauer, the Inuit sculptors Ron Senungetuk and Melvin Olana, members of the Frankson and Anderson families with their Inuit dancers, and a noble Tlingit elder, Jim McKinley, together with his entourage. Other friends in the whole area are identified in the *Alashka*.

There were performances, readings, and discussions. The latter were disappointing to all, especially to the outsiders. The Rodney-Tarns misinterpreted the situation in suggesting that nothing substantial would happen until Alaskan Natives took the means of production into their own hands. But the basic interest of the locals turned out to be obtaining a larger share of state funds for the arts. There were difficulties between locals and their guests. Andy Hope seemed to have serious problems with women and found it very difficult to deal with Rodney's presence. Later, on reviewing the *Alashka*, he refused to take her coauthorship into consideration at all! Regarding that book, only Richard Dauhenhauer and Andy reviewed it. A probable contender for being the most important long poem ever written on the place to date received no welcome whatsoever in the state. Tarn eventually wrote to Jim Haines, a kind of state poet laureate, asking if he could help: his reply was to the effect that the book was "too garrulous" to be worth standing up for. This situation has never changed.

The Tarns had stumbled on a dance for someone's deceased father at Gambell and had fallen in love with Inuit dancing, its intensely rhythmic music and steps, its rapid flowering toward a shatteringly sudden stop, the closest thing of all perhaps to André Breton's *explosion fixe*. One of the Point Hope Franklin family was especially moving and became the title dancer, "Willow," of a later prose piece, inscribed to Dorn, in which the essence of various Alaskan ethnographies was distilled.

A young guest at the conference, Mike Caron, a geographer and geologist, became a Yukon Ritz stowaway when the van's crew, in revenge for being most insensitively treated at ungodly hours of arrival by ferry crew members (virtually kicked off the boat), procured for him a substantial dollop of free travel. Through Hoonah, Sitka, Petersburg (with its giant halibut), Ketchikan, and Wrangell all the way to Rupert, Mike followed the routine of camping in one of the emerald forests of the South East, then lying down in a space between the bed support and a bunch of boxes in the back of the van. Tarn went up on deck; then Rodney and Caron followed. Caron and his hosts lounged on deck. There was never any interception.

This time, from Rupert, the whole Skeena route was followed, looking at the totem poles again and on into Jasper and Calgary. A fabulous birding day was provided by large flocks of cranes and pelicans at Last Mountain Lake in Saskatchewan. At Ottawa the riches of Canadian museums were enjoyed—especially those of the new Museum of Anthropology. Unfortunately, the new Museum of Aviation had not yet been built. Two and a half months after setting out, "reality" reasserted itself as a return to New Hope and Rutgers.

23.3 The third season, in 1977, was very different. Tarn had met George Holton, an excellent travel photographer, in Guatemala during his 1950s fieldwork and lived in his house there in 1969. George, now based in New York, was working for Sven Lindblad, the Swedish tourism entrepreneur, rushing all over the world at a moment's notice to photograph destinations of the *Lindblad Explorer*, the Swede's flagship. (It eventually killed him: he died, still young, of a heart attack in China.) Somehow or other, George persuaded his employers that his friend should lecture on Arctic anthropology on board the ship. A great deal of boning up became necessary, fitting in well with the readings done in 1975 and 1976, but did not entirely disguise the fact that the new lecturer was hardly an expert. Eventually, two trips materialized, and part of the deal was that Rodney would join the second and longest trip.

On June 21 the ship left Nome, reached Nunivak for the musk oxen glimpsed in thick mist, went on to Round Island for walrus, the Pribilofs for seals, Unalaska in the Aleutians for World War II memories, and on into various parts of the Aleutians: Unimak; Unga of the Shumagin Islands; Uyak Bay at Kodiak; Kukak Bay at Katmai; the Barren Islands and the Augustin volcano; the Nellie Juan and Columbia glaciers; Middleton Island, with its multitudinous bird colonies, the birds strung out on the cliffs like innumerable pearl necklaces; Dundas and Glacier bays; finally returning to Rupert via Ketchikan.

This and the following trip were haunted by a number of the most awe-inspiring landscapes on the planet—the word "awesome" in its original sense, not in today's infantile corruption—as well as abundances of wildlife only dreamed of before: birds, sea mammals (whale, seal, walrus, sea lion), land mammals (bear, gray fox, mountain sheep). Huge islands and volcanos would rise out of the sea at incalculable distances, the movement of the ship affording views from so many different angles; clouds of birds, golden in the light, would materialize out of nowhere assuring you that they were—at the very least—circling the world back and forth. It was possible, again and again, especially when standing on the bridge at dawn or dusk or even during the night, to be alone with motionless eternity thus housed in nature while only the ship moved against the stillness. As much of this as possible entered into the composition of the *Alashka* but also into the *North Rim* and *Jonah's Saddle* sections of a little book called *At the Western Gates*—published by poet John Brandi in Santa Fe and reprinted eventually by Shearsman Books.

The ship and its passengers were another matter. The Swedish crew was excellent, the quarters fine, the food delicious and abundant. Among the other lecturers, heartwarming encounters materialized with Ted Walker, an oceanographer from Scripps; Keith Shackleton, a descendant of the great explorer and a wonderful painter of birds (his gift of an eider watercolor is a family treasure); Des and Jen Bartlett, renowned documentary filmmakers. Among the stewardesses, Catherine Risdale from Britain provided much shelter and entertainment in her cabin below deck, where refuge could also be found among the Fijian and Samoan sailors, civilized beings living Melvillianly below the barbarian moneybag tourists.

Social duties for the lecturers were somewhat more broadly defined than expected and took Tarn by surprise, especially when it was suggested, during the first trip, that he should lavish some attentions on the single ladies. The most onerous chore was dining with different passengers every night. Some were very pleasant people. A surprise was meeting with Donald Anderson of Roswell, New Mexico, traveling with his first wife before her death from cancer. They turned out to have a house in Yorkshire that was looked after for them by the poets Jonathan Williams and Ron Johnson! Their extremely concise luggage inspired in the Tarns a passion for the Holubar brand of backpacks, used ever afterward until they disintegrated. (Eventually, Holubar, alas, went out of business.) Some people unwittingly provided entertainment. A Mexican gentleman initiated a talk meeting with a photo of an undistinguished-looking dog sitting isolated on a silk cushion and introduced as "*mi perro*." His hobby, though, was revealed by a picture of a circular room populated by a dozen vintage cars of inestimable value. Another gentleman at a fancy-dress evening got caught wearing a hula dress and gyrating round and round while the orchestra refused to stop. At one point, from a face contorted with anger and despair, his audience heard an agonized croak along the lines of "Hey, enough already!," which brought the house down.

Most passengers, however, were indifferent, uninteresting, or unpleasant. One dinner was suffered through with an Atlanta couple who seemed to belong to the KKK and began to defend the policies of a certain Mr. Hitler. More broadly, there was never enough one could do for them on board, on walks, or in the Zodiac rubber boats. Tarn, definitely not a hail-fellow-well-met, performed ever more unsatisfactorily as the days wore on. He was having his own acute trouble because of the letter from James Laughlin, brought to him by Rodney at Rupert, advising him to stay with John Martin's Black Sparrow Press.

A climax came during the second trip in the high Arctic. The ship had retraced the first trip's path, touching land at Nome on July 25 for logistical reasons. After a performance by the King Island Inuit dancers, the *Explorer* left for the Diomedes, arriving at the smaller US island (the larger one is Siberian) on the next day. Not exactly used to frequent visits from ships, the people had arranged a very substantial party on shore. Of course, some Inuit, wanting to sell little ivory animals as well as rides in their canoes, came on board and found their way to the bar. At some exact time on the trip's schedule, the ship was due to move up to the Arctic Circle for a champagne session. The visitors on board were unceremoniously and insensitively bundled off.

Many Fish and Wildlife officials were on board, and the whole emphasis on the trips had been on the conservation of nature rather than on that of culture. One little old lady was even heard to say that "the 'Eskimo' would not be civilized until they had learned to place lace curtains in the windows of their igloos" (no igloos in Alaska). As the sole representative of culture on board, Tarn had been getting more and more depressed and became downright angry at the treatment meted out to the Diomedans. Now, it was the custom before every dinner for the lecturers to wrap up the day with lighthearted little summaries. On the 27th, at Gambell, Tarn chose to be last, then, in four blistering minutes, gave the ship his views on how, at the end of a murderous century (some details adduced), this ship had not even seen fit to honor their hosts at Diomede but had gone off for a footling and totally meaningless drink at the mythical circle. A thunderous silence ensued. Keith Shackleton sidled up to the speaker, saying, "My God, Nathaniel, that was brave of you!" Nothing was said at dinner.

The next day, the ambassador of culture was hauled into the cabin of a pompous young ass—an Argentinian photographer who was the boss of the lecturers—none of whom had ever had a good word to say about him. He had all too often given untoward orders to his staff, ordered them around, issued critical directives, and made a "bloody nuisance" of himself. He had also angered some by diverting trip occasions in favor of his own photographer's requirements. On this occasion, Tarn was told that he would never work for the company again (hardly a major concern by this time) and that he had insulted the ship's crew: a tour was always obliged to fulfill a printed schedule, and the captain was only doing his duty. At the next preprandial occasion, the guilty party apologized to the captain and crew, leaving the rest as said, but wondered for a while whether he might not be dropped off to rot on some Arctic island.

23.4 The voyage continued on to Unalaska, where Father Veniaminov's eighteenth-century Cyrillic-Aleutian Gospel of Mathew could be admired, and then to Bogoslov Island—a couple of gigantic rock pincers rising hundreds of feet into the air. The drawbacks of ecotourism were illustrated here: despite all efforts, tourists disturbed birds on their nests, leaving other bird scavengers to pounce on them immediately and gobble the eggs. Rodney and Tarn enjoyed a little leisure together on the verdant hilltops of Atka Island. Then came the Gareloi volcano, the somber World War II archaeology of a Japanese Navy base at Kitka, Tarn's discovery of a downed Lockheed P-38 in good shape at Temnac (reported to the Alaskan Aviation Society and later "saved for the nation"), and a visit to the farthermost US west with the "Horny Bird" air crews of Attu. There was a monument here to a Captain Erik Nelson of the Douglass aircraft *World Flight*, who had landed at Chichagof Bay and left again for Japan on May 9, 1924.

And it was on to Hokkaidō, northern Japan, arriving at 10.30 hours on August 8, surrounded by fishing boats at Kushiro. Here, some passengers started a brief tour of the island: Tsuru Park for the dancing cranes, Akan with its ghastly "Ainu" souvenirs (mainland Japan had corrupted tribal Ainu crafts just as Mexico City had ruined the crafts of Michoacan), Kussharo, Bihoro Pass and the huge lakes of that region, the Shiretoko Peninsula, Utoro, a resort town built among rocks. Mindful of the role of a North Carolina Black Mountain in US literary history, Rodney-Tarn enjoyed a steep climb up another Black Mountain—Kurodake (1,984 meters)—as well as a visit to a reconstruction: a model old-style Ainu village. Here, dancers in gorgeous indigo costumes performed very credibly, and a remarkably beautiful old lady struck up a rapport dancing with Rodney, which lasted long in memory. Teuri Island, a pleasant tourist resort, provided fine birding.

The ensuing bus ride to the capital, Sapporo, was very long, and many felt that, while pleasant, Hokkaidō was nothing special and hardly merited a trip. An antique store rewarded a visit with rather bedraggled old Ainu materials. In a raid on Tokyo, the interminable discussions and calculations on board ship regarding photo equipment bore fruit in the purchase of much Nikon equipment (later stolen on the way down to Guatemala in 1979), some binoculars, and a radio/cassette player. In this, the admirable Japanese nature photographer Mitsuaki Iwago, a fine ship companion whose books are still treasured, provided much help.

23.5 Back in the Bay Area, part of a day was spent with John Martin, his wife, the Cooneys, and the Shoemakers. *Star Wars* no. 1 was showing—the Tarns duly lined up for tickets only to freeze until Rodney bought some newspapers, which were wrapped around the travelers' torsos. On August 22 Bob Callahan held a memorable dinner at his home with Ed and Jennifer Dorn. In the middle of this, Harvey Bialy showed up with his new Nigerian wife and launched into animated and rather monological conversation with his colleagues, paying not one jot of attention to his lady. She was left to wander around the house and round the table by herself. This displeased Dorn, but instead of showing his ire, the senior poet began to pull Bialy's leg remorse-lessly and at very great length, pretending all the while to be fascinated by the biologist/poet's contentions and arguments. Finally, the Bialys left, and with sighs of relief the Dorns and Tarns got away for a meal in Chinatown.

On the next day, New Hope brought new hope, or old hope, or no hope at all—it is now hard to remember.

Throw Twenty-Four

24.1 Until late in life, I experienced a marked inability to come to terms with the passage of time. Principally, it was with the passage from one time to another—that is, with the interval between one quantity of time and another, the division depending, of course, on the arbitrary systems we humans have devised to measure such a concept as "time." Whether there is, or not, behind such man-made cuts in the continuous flow a discontinuous pattern introduced into the continuous for the purpose of pandering to the human's unquenchable need to measure—deeper intervals or, at any rate, changes in the measure of time—whether, that is, something in the nature of bio-rhythms can be postulated for the Earth itself as well as for us, current science must be left to determine. I am in search of the subjective. Is this not, as an academic friend was pointing out the other day, the cardinal discovery of legions of academic ne'er-do-wells in our time? Is this not the golden gift of phenomenology?

You sit down one morning in front of your typewriter (written in pre-computer time). The blank page stares at you with its one unwearying eye— or its thousand eyes if you are in the mood for Argus this morning—the receiver in your brain refuses to answer, there is no answer within it, you could not answer if they paid you a million on the nail, etc. etc. etc. Despair.

Flight to Hades or to Hawaii. Gritting of teeth. Suddenly with the force of a hard-boiled egg propelled all the way from a star at your gray matter, the idea explodes in your head. The subject matter is the very difficulty you have in writing. The blank page itself. Suddenly reams and reams of paper are covered in writing: "returning to the terror of writing..." (etc.). The age-old discovery has its charms for every writer at the moment of truth. Basta! It has been done before.

If I am not mistaken, it was morning that was always the most difficult period to deal with. When I was still living with my parents, far too late into my twenties, the process of rising to the day always and inevitably took place on the wrong side of my bed. As a result of this incorrect determination of the primal orientation, I found myself unable to utter a single word until eleven o'clock. Because breakfast took place in the neighborhood of eight-thirty or nine and because it never became any easier for my parents to stomach and deal with this silence, the first meal of the day was usually consumed in a state of tension that would determine the logistics of indigestion for the rest of the day. Everyone's indigestion I would guess. I was diagnosed as "being in a mood."

I was, of course, perfectly well aware of the fact that my mood would very often come to dominate me and that I would then be as hard put to exit from it as I had found it difficult to ward off the mood in the first place. At such times, a certain amount of patient understanding and handling ability was tacitly requested of one or more of one's cohabitants. However, very few people are blessed with the gift of helping others out of such dark corridors: the gift of a magic smile, a very light joke, or a very discreet question that would ease you out. More often than not, then, I was left with the mood upon me far longer than I wanted until it became a royal pain in the ass to myself, and I was then obliged to exercise considerable ingenuity in order to figure out ways of exiting the mood without loss of face. Such moods were artificial, and note: only the exit might be deliberate, never the entry.

It is to be supposed that such moods gradually came to an end as I left the parental domicile and began to cohabit with women who, quite obviously, were not going to be as charitable to such tantrums as parents might be, for all their louring looks. It is also possible that my life took a turn for the happier or that I became more comfortable, more at home in my own skin (a very difficult place to inhabit as it has always been): rather hard to say. Perhaps the driving need to work, to cram as much activity into one day as possible, gradually took over from the mood demons. Enough to record that these early-morning blues gradually disappeared from my life. Without being bipolar (I have that as a question), there was always a manic side to my temperament so that moods were very much part of my climate. But they did not reappear in this form ever afterward. Depression is another story.

24.2 Nonetheless, it has always been difficult for me to pass from one state of mind to another without loss in the interval. An example.

Because I am given to arriving at appointments early, I invent a variety of means to keep me busy until it is really time for me to leave or, when older, I contrive to remain interested enough in my work to continue at my desk until it is almost too late. The time comes, and I go out. The mood is one of pleasant anticipation.

The sad truth is that by the time I have arrived at destination, my mood has changed, usually for the worse and often disastrously. Try as I will, it is hard for me to understand the process. Frequently, it has to do with the fact that the mind, when left unattended, has a tendency to dwell on the unpleasant and negative sides of life rather than on the opposites. Almost all my serious losses have been the result of "negativity." Paradigmatically, negative thoughts evoke others. Soon a host of them come out and parade around the mental arena. The arena turns into swill. I begin to swim in this sea of distress and arrive crestfallen at destination.

There is also the problem of negative anticipation. Life has a habit of turning out unpleasantly, of not being as rewarding as one believes it is going to be: it would be best not to expect too much. Nor to let hopes soar too high nor, in short, to be in so good a mood that a touch of cold will turn you into an ice storm. You make a small corner of your mind available to the possibility of disappointment. Such availabilities are contagious; they spread like a plague through the mind—pretty soon you become persuaded that "no" will prevail over "yes," and you arrive at your friend's door already defeated, foolish, and altogether ill at ease, even though the lady, if it is a lady, might, for all you know, be so desperate for your company that she has even entertained thoughts of rushing you. In such ways we often go through life defeating ourselves by negative thinking, negative suggestion, or the ignorance of how to make friends and influence people. In some strange way, one cancels oneself out. Experienced over most of a lifetime, this is quite simply satanic.

People cohabiting or married have often found that the ability to transfer one's mood to another person is sometimes a condition of one's own liberation from the mood. Could this provide an explanation for the business of making yourself late for an appointment? Let us suppose that you suspect the person you are to visit—being a "normal" person, well balanced, kind in disposition, and therefore not liable to be affected by such dark clouds as you inhabit—that such a person is going to be in a state of pleasant anticipation at the thought of entertaining you. There is nothing more difficult, if you are somewhat darkened yourself, than walking into a realm full of light. Come to think of it, who knows if the fear of encountering too much light might not lie at the base of the mind's action in turning to darker thoughts on the way to a meeting? Or making yourself late: would the purpose not be to introduce just enough darkness in the host's mind to ensure that you are not met with too much joy or enthusiasm? May you then not be in a position to console and cajole the host back into a state of equilibrium and be the seducer, displaying prowess in the dance and showing yourself off to best advantage? That all of this, in turn, is connected with yet more difficult sides of this nature strikes me as a distinct possibility.

I do not like, on most occasions I can think of, to be the subject of too much enthusiasm. Though not undesirous, in my deepest self, of being seduced, I am aware that the seduction must be of the very subtlest if it is going to work at all. Being pounced on in any way, I will turn as cold as the proverbial cucumber—frozen at that. It is probably worth recording that all the men on my paternal side have always had trouble with being physically touched. In short, I tend to experience all admiration, love, and affection as aggression unless it is very precisely and expertly offered. I have never been able to trust any kind of compliment from a family member or close friend: stupidly, compliments have to come from total strangers if they are to signify at all. Is this connected to a fear that praise is not going to be total and had therefore better be refused at the start? But the problem here, surely, is that such praise would be overwhelming. The upshot of this apparently vicious circle is that I seem to be sempiternally ready to face darkness as well as light at the same time. A Janus, I look two ways: toward ecstasy and toward disaster.

I have been dealing with situations in which the strongest emotions are brought into play. It is also true that the same mood changes may occur if feelings about the appointment to be kept are neutral. A business meeting perhaps, or one of those dinners where conversation flags and has to be kept aloft like a child's balloon: "And who, dear Madam, are you going to keep from his rest tonight?" It could be that most dreaded of all social events: the cocktail party, where people often turn into baying hounds. How then will Narcissus shine at a gathering unless there is just the right number of people present; the lighting, the wine, the food perfect; the host or hostess's opening words of just the right caliber; your own predisposition—O Lordy!—of just the right weight and color? We are dealing here with a very fundamental difficulty: that of passing from the street to the party, from one facet of time to another, from something akin to a Maya ritual *viaje* to another *viaje*. Why have *viajes* always been so difficult for me?

24.3 A connection occurs to me while writing with the ritual figure I have several times mentioned as being one of great potency in Atitlán. The legends tell us that just after being made and first manifesting its powers, this Maximón was subjected to a curious manipulation by its creators. The first father-mothers were looking for a tree out of which they could carve a figure who would keep order in a disordered village. As they walked through the forest, a certain tree spoke to them and informed them that it alone was the candidate. The tree was unimpressive, and they had difficulty believing it. However, they created the figure from the tree's heart. As soon as created, the figure began to walk, becoming a "great walker through the universe," marching day and night to its appointments. The "walking" (here signifying "working") and the exercise of its powers eventually led to a good deal of magic designed to counter disorder but eventually creating disorders of its own. Much of this had to do with seducing young women wrongdoers when in the male mode and young male wrongdoers when in the female mode. Fearing excess, the father-mothers became frightened. They twisted the figure's head to make it look backward in the hope that it would no longer walk too much or, at least, not walk out of their control. To my knowledge, and to the Atitecos', this did not prevent the figure from continuing its walks. Note also that the figure is patron of diviners: an art connected with knowledge of both past and future.

Atitlán, circa late 1969. I am living on the Lake again, after a long interval, and I am purchasing a few unimportant small items of Maya antiquity with a very small purse. One day a very curious figure is offered by the little tradesman from Panajachel who often appears with his bag of temptations at my solitary hermitage door. It appears to be made of stone, or a clay so hard it has turned to stone. A human figure, some six inches high. Cut off just below the sagging belly and at the shoulders. Small breasts. Wears a necklace from which depends a circle, followed by what seems to be a pair of inverted horns. Also wears a girdle just above its buttocks (cut away) and just under its belly (also cut away). From the lower back rise two heavy excrescences in the form of a *V*, broken off at the shoulders: impossible to know what they did above this level. Back of head very flat and pockmarked. Front of head divided into two faces, both bearded, sharing a central eye. It cannot be said that the two visages face two ways: they both look at you rather frontally, just the shade of a divergence having been forced on the sculptor by the nature of his or her problem.

I show the figure around. A well-known dealer in Antigua swears it is a fake. In his wonderful house, also in the colonial city, Dr. Edwin Shook, a friend from long ago and the greatest living expert on the Maya highlands, tells me it is a very rare piece: Archaic Horizon, probably from the Pacific Coast—one of only three such double-headed figures known to Maya archaeology. Due to live in a museum.

24.4 Where does all this lead?

A notebook entry (circa 1961?): "The poet is the original Janus. Faces forward and backward at the same moment, advancing and retreating simultaneously." The fascination of that bald statement from Descartes, encountered years ago in Paris: "*Larvatus prodeo*": I advance masked. Is that not the same as advancing and retreating simultaneously—for is not a mask the cover over a past you are leaving behind?

I retreat momentarily to dream. God of beginnings, give me strength to dream! "Jane, Jupiter, Mars pater, Quirine, Bellona, Lares, diui Nounesiles, dii Indigetes, diui quorum est potestas nostrum hostiumque, diique Manes. . . ." Let me dedicate my armies and yours to the spirits of the land and to Earth in general, for by this devotion will I enter more deeply into dream. I thank you, Lord of the "Prima!" This is where we plunge:

24.5 Once upon a time I was born among the gods. This birth must have come about in recompense for many good deeds performed in anterior lives, deeds of which I have, unfortunately, not the slightest recollection (that is the way it goes Orientally with reincarnation before enlightenment is reached!). I may have it someday but do not have it now. I then must have committed even better deeds than now in that I have been, this time round, reborn as a man—and everyone knows that, in the system-beloved-of-systems, there is no possible higher rebirth.

But to return to my onetime divinity. It was not my fate to be a major god: that, by Jove, was settled by the Big Guy in his own favor. I was part of the constellation of Latin deities important in our world some two thousand years ago though fallen into something like disrepute today and not even much remembered since a major decline in our educational system. In those days, however, we were of some note, the people who harbored and worshipped us being of the opinion that they owned a good part of the known world. In effect, many of these people's deities were constructed on the model of the Greek constellations: like another brash people, the Japanese, they had to get their gods from a prefabricated system.

In my case, however, something peculiar must have happened since no one was ever able to trace my origin to a Greek model. It is ironic, come to think of it, that my position had no origins because I was myself held to be the patron of beginnings and was invoked at the start of most enterprises and at the outset of various periods of time. In fact, the first month of the year came to be named after me in the Latin tongue, and this has survived in our languages to this day: "Januarius-January." It is even possible that one of my favorite people, the Maya, received this notion into their concept of the "year bearers," although this thought is strictly apocryphal and should be entertained by no one save an ex-divinity like myself. In addition to this matter of time, I was obscurely held—mainly perhaps by women (or again, it may be, by male priests, anxious to preserve the notion of patriarchy)—that I played a role in the conception of the human embryo, opening the way in the womb for the reception of the male seed. If my subsequent propensities are taken into consideration, touching the lovely entrances to the female body, there is nothing to my mind unlikely in this theory.

24.6 The writer Varro, as reported by St. Augustine, best defined my status in regard to beginnings by naming me as lord of the *Prima* in contradistinction to the Big Man, Jove, whom he called lord of the *Summa*: because the beginnings are in my power (*Prima*) and the summits (*Summa*) in that of Jove. So Jove is rightly regarded as king of all. For "beginnings are inferior to summits, since, though they precede in time, they are surpassed in dignity by the summits." Hard to deny!

In each month, the initial Calends were ascribed to me, *dues omnium initiorum*, while the Ides, the articulation of waxing and waning fortnights, were ascribed to the Boss. In very much the same way, I was assigned billets on a small hill marking the entrance to the Great City, whereas the Boss resided on the Capitol itself—which I occasionally protected (in the matter of the Tarpeian Rock, for instance, when I cooked the geese of the Sabines with the aid of hot sulfurous springs). In this matter of the Calends, however, I enjoyed an interesting relationship with the Boss's wife: Juno, goddess of childbirth. Juno was the goddess of only one kind of beginning—the human child's entrance into the world—I, on the other hand, was master of all beginnings and all transitions from one period of time to another. No one has ever gotten to the bottom of this relationship. For that matter, no one ever dared to question the matter too closely, and I am not about to reveal any secrets about those who are above my own station. I must say that the Maya again, in their concept of "the tripes of woman," the "original womb," and so forth . . . but there I go again: gods are relentless comparatists.

24.7 Known as *Cerus manus*—from the same root as Ceres, the name of the corn goddess, known also as *Creator bonus*, using creator in the sense of "initiator," I must have had something to do with the pushing up of crops from below the ground, although this has been denied by an expert in our own time: "having no connection with Ceres, who bears in herself the motive of growth." Shucks! I will admit at this point that I am disgruntled with this scholar. Gods, like other creatures, are social pushers wherever they can be: I would not have been averse by any means to add links with Ceres, Proserpine, and Hades to the other connection with my employer's spouse. That hellish lot up my street. So because no one helps he who does not help himself, I hereby roundly contradict the scholar—eminent as he is—and state that I did, most definitely, yes I remember it quite clearly now as we speak, give the smallest little push at the crops from below the ground whenever I could get down there, which, in the spring, when the ground becomes soft, you know, is not really all that impossible—even if the matter does not fit exactly into my month. And besides, I forget to tell you that at the Calends, they had special little cakes made for me, known as *ianual*—which is how people came to know of my Calends association if the truth need be told now. Vesta was *Ultima* to my *Prima* and the Boss's *Summa*, but whether I ever had any relations with Vesta or not, I truly cannot remember. And hey! The Maya were corn people par excellence!

Throw Twenty-Five

25.1 The poet Ovid, who had a good deal to say about me in his *Fasti*, relegated me to the beginnings of time, when gods and men lived in peace and, if I may borrow from another scenario, the lion and the lamb had drinks together. I suspect that this is because the Latins, landed with a god they had themselves invented, had to think very hard about the enigma and would not rest until they had positioned me as far back among the origins as they possibly could. By heaven, you do not have a god of your own every day of the month! "First of the ancient gods whom the Latins called *Penates*," sang Procopius; "Oldest god indigenous to Latium," sang Herodian; "*Creator bonus*," sang the Salii (as aforesaid but it will bear repeating); "*Cui primo supplicabant ueluti parenti et a quo rerum omnium factum putabant initium*," added C. Pompeius Festus, together with Septimus Serenus's "*O cate rerum sator, o principium deorum*," and Augustine flattered me with "*Omnium initiorum potestatem* and *potestatem primordiorum*." The Arvales Bros. even went as far as *pater*, which is to say daddy or lord of the lot of them. A beautiful language, was it not? The "Roman" Church lost everything when it decided to go colloquial! As for Macrobius, he even related a theory regarding my ability to rustle up the sun *quidam solem demonstrari uolunt*—although soreheads have it that this can only have sprung from my patronage of the morning.

As a result of all this, I was thought by some to be one of the original kings of Latium, perhaps the first, residing on that small hill I have mentioned, the Ianiculum, threshold to Rome itself. As such, I had a wife by the name of Camise and a son by the name of Tiberinus, who gave his name to the principal river of the city by obligingly drowning in it. In the matter of wives, I have always been a little forgetful only because, on another level, I remember all too well! Of this there is more to come. Let me say now that I am reputed to have married the nymph of the fountains Iuturna and to have born us a son by the name of Fons: this made me into the father of springs and waterworks, the beginning if you please of all waters. And in the matter of waters, I should also impart to you that I was a master of trade and commerce by sea, being also married (where are we? quadrigamously by now?) to the goddess Venilia— no doubt a lower lady of the Neptunian harem.

As king of Latium, moreover, I was able to be of service to old Saturnus when Jove did him wrong on Crete. He sailed for Rome and settled near the Ianiculum in a place not unnaturally baptized Saturnia. Early Latin coins had a ship on one side with my portrait on the other: which is why you toss for heads or ships down to this very day.

25.2 It was, however, in the matter of thresholds, doors, door pillars, and arches that I held most sway. After the *vestibulum* in any house, the *ianuae* consisted of two heavy folding doors which opened inward toward the *atrium*: I was their keeper and their i(j)anitor. My physiognomy was depicted on the *iani*, or arches, which spanned the city streets, as well as certain freestanding arches of the same designation that must have been used, initially, for ceremonial purposes. The location of my temple in the Forum has not been determined, Livy stating that it lay at the foot of the Argiletum, Macrobius countering that it stood at the base of the Viminal. Obscure as most of the above may seem to you, friend reader, you probably recall the fact from your schooldays that there was a prodigious amount of marching around their dominions by the Roman armies. They had to march all over the known world in order to impress the inhabitants and keep them in order—not like today, when we do this with missiles from the safety of some distant country. Think a little then, and determine in your most intimate mind whether the marching around was not bound to feature two most important aspects, aspects we might name *terminus a quo* and *terminus ad quem* or, to put it more simply, a setting out and a coming home. Now "there is a right way and a wrong way to march through a gate," according to Livy: the Fabii, for instance, go out to war *infelicia uia, dextro iano portae Carmentalis*, but I can assure you that the Romans always and on every other occasion knew how to go out and to come back in both.

There has been much disagreement too among the scholars, I gather, regarding the expression *Ianus Geminus* although, to my modest mind, it would seem to have to do with twins. The true function of the doors, according to the latest authorities, is undetermined, as well as their number (two or one?) and their exact nature and meaning. The account I favor runs as follows, but you must not take it on my trust—consult the scholars, always; they are the ones to know. However, the account:

25.3 On the road from the Forum Iulium to the Great Forum lay the temple of Ianus Bifrons, the two-headed one, or the Geminus (twin). The building was a temple and a passageway (*ianus*) composed principally of two gates, one facing east, one facing west, with the road passing between and under the gates. My image was engraved or sculpted somewhere on a wall between the gates, which is the reason for the appellation *bifrons*: that is, two-fronted, two-foreheaded, or what have you. At the time of the opening of the gates, I was known as Patulcius (from *pateo*: to be open); at their closing, I became Clusivius (from *claudo*: to be shut). As Ianus Quirinus (derived from the Sabine *curis* [spear]), according to an antiquarian from Rome herself, I presided over war. The army left by the open doors, returned through the same, after which return the doors were shut. I was a complex god, I'm proud to admit.

Knowing the scholars as you do, you will not be surprised to discover that a further disagreement of a very curious kind touches upon the opening and shutting of the doors. The question: were the doors shut so that peace might remain inside or so that war might not be let out? Did I keep the peace imprisoned, or was it war? I am not about to let out the secret, abetted all the more by a kind of senility, a sort of pre-Alzheimer's, you might say, if you could but recall the Latin word for it. The reason why I do not let out the secret: is it not obvious? Are these not religio-mystical times, and can a god ever swear that he won't be brought out of retirement? After Japanese Zen, Tibetan Vajrayāna, or Islamic Sufism, can the mysteries of Latium be far behind? Disinformation has been at work. We are far enough from Latium studies to bask in their unfamiliarity. The time for a retro season may have set in.

25.4 Besides all of which, it must be clear to you by now that there is something, to coin a phrase (and was I not the inventor of coinage?), duplicitous about my nature. All this coming and going . . . there is never smoke without fire. Being original, entirely, I issued forth out of no parents and was brought up by none, having to thread my own way through the thorns and dangers of this world. The key being my only weapon—I bear no sword—is it not the most natural thing in the universe that I should have acquired at times certain, let us say, questionable habits? That I should have learned, like a Peer Gynt in later times, to go round about or, like Homer's Odysseus, to have become a master in the art of deceit? Above all, study me well in the works of my bookbinding grandfather: for trickster was my name among the populations of this America we now inhabit, and over large expanses of plains and mountains, I royally screwed up the works of the creator. There is, always, at any time, in any circumstance, something . . . let us say . . . peculiarly unpleasant about my disposition in that, whether I am looking backward or forward or both, I can sit on a little swing, aloft between two pretty clouds, and survey my behavior from above, watching carefully as it tinkers with the behavior of others and, heaven help us, even modifies their emotions! Ovid tells of a delicious episode concerning the nymph Carna, who lived in caves. She belonged evidently to that order of persons who can never make up their minds, for she used to lure men into caves with promises that they might enjoy her there while, once they became lost in the cave's miasmata, she left them to their solitary devices and ran away. When she tried this on me, I saw her go with my backward-looking face, caught her promptly, and executed her. Before this, taking her in the normal manner, I bore upon her my son Proca, who later became king of Alba Longa—the endless dawn—and was saved from a wretched fate by the power I bestowed on Carna, to wit that she could chase away nocturnal vampires. Taking her in the forbidden manner, what she bore thereby I know not, save that her cave was known as an ill-smelling place from that time forward.

And do I not go, to this very day, among the gods, sighing backward at my old loves, sighing forward toward new passions, in a manner most unsatisfactory to the "gentle" sex? Change, change, is my refrain; I turn with the spinning world. One of my oldest recollections, self-envisionings I should perhaps say, is of myself on a stairway, about to spring upward but first looking back. Why? Wherefore? Hard to say.

Pater matutinus. My time is almost up for today (the amount that can be written, can be recorded at one sitting); the afternoon comes on. Let me recount one more event, which has taken place just this morning in the midday mail.

Above my bed, in *patris polis*, still lours the great engraving I purchased in Rome many years after the onset of my majesty, the work of that master of *I Carceri*, animator of our deepest fears, the lord Giambattista Piranesi. Many years I stared at that engraving on going to bed and on getting up in the morning. I must have stared at the cartouche many times, but I do not remember for certain what the inscription contains. Yet do you know that at this instant of writing, I am absolutely certain that it named the building depicted as the Tempio di Giano—that is, Janus? Now comes the moment of truth. In this very mailing, a package from the same beloved city contains a small engraving from the work *De la sphère* by one Mallet, Frenchman, 1683. The scene is a most delicate one. Rocks in the foreground, a gently rolling stream, trees, beyond that some fields and equally gently rolling hills. A ruin in the middle distance, two figures walking away from it, one carrying a cane. Above the tallest hill, a roll of gray clouds and a sky full of stars. Above it, in my very own mother language, its name, IUPITER. Gentle readers, ladies and gentlemen, it is time for a star change. I go to greatness like iron to magnet. The time of supremacy has come.

25.5 Now those same foolish scholars I have spoken of before have put it around that the god Ianus had no priest (*flamen*), probably because he was difficult to locate in any one time or place: he recurred at all beginnings. Among others who had no priests, they count the ancestral spirits, the Lares and Penates who could not be substantially differentiated enough to own a priesthood, as well as gods who were, by their very nature, multiplied to infinity. Of these the most typical is Genius, for as every person has a genius, mind you; it is clear that genius is as long and wide as humanity, and that is long and wide enough.

But is it not just as likely, I ask you, that I had no *flamen* because I was my own? In all we have said of priesthood, have we not claimed that it should be initiatory or at the very least initiatic? And if the key is my only weapon, am I not, like that later impostor Petrus, the holder of the key to Heaven, that is the opener of doors? *Belli portae*, the great guide of Dante Alighieri may have called me; nevertheless, I say to you that I was more than the opener of wars. In truth I opened every gate, including the gate of wisdom.

You will remember from your education no doubt that famous story of the three Horatii fighting the three Curatii in the Roman-Alban war. Until death did them part. One of the Horatii did live, though, and went back to tell the tale. On reaching home he found his sister in tears, for she had become engaged to one of the Curatii and was now grieving for her lover. "Ha! Ha!" said the Horace, in a turmoil of the passions, "this cannot be; it is an insult to Rome and to its gods!" Whereupon he dispatched his sister. Whether he hung up her guts at the place called Tigillum Sororium or performed some other kind of sacrifice—a melon let us say or a sick ox—the fact is that this tigillum was composed of two altars to Ianus and Juno, linked at the top by a beam. The common or garden translation for many years made this "tigillum" beam and "sororium" sisters, ergo beam-of-the-sisters. We have it on excellent authority, however, that *sororium* derives from *sororiare*: to mature (originally of the female breasts). Is it not clear that young men passed from adolescence to maturity at this temple and that I, Ianus, was their initiator?

25.6 But to return to the matter of the priesthood. In the time of this office, the gods' duplicity was regarded as a divine power. The divinity I worshipped and served as a priest was interpreted by my lay friend Pico della Mirandola, an alchemist, as "Lord of the Mysteries and Father of the Celestial Souls," those who animate the firmament. "In ancient poetry," wrote Pico, "these souls were signified by the double-headed *Ianus* because, being supplied like him with eyes in front and behind, they can at the same time see the spiritual things and provide for the material." (Not sure how before and behind transform into spiritual and material, but let it be.) Pico added, "Before they fall into this earthly body, our souls have two faces . . . but when they descend into the body, it is for them as if they were cut in half, and of the two faces, there remains only one, whence every time that they turn the one face that is left to them toward sensible beauty, they remain deprived of the vision of the other." Shades of Plato, shades of Philo, shades of the Logos Tomeus, the word as cutter that "produces creation by dichotomy" but is "the joiner of the universe as well!" I forbear to follow this into the mystery of the creation of father Adam ("*et erunt ambo in carne una*") and his original androgyny: the wind will take you there if you but care to follow it.

And yet, and yet, let me quote you but one other word from the admirable Pico. Picking up from the Song of Songs poet, Origen, Plato, Philo, and other worthies who had detected in the making of this Adam an attempt to depict the completeness of God, Pico wrote that "it is not without mystery that God created the celestial Adam male and female. For it is the prerogative of celestial souls that they fulfill simultaneously the two functions of mental contemplation and physical care without either of them obstructing or impeding the other. And the ancients in particular, as we may observe in the Orphic Hymns, adopted the custom of designating these two forces inherent in the same substance . . . by the names 'male' and 'female.'"

What, in short, was the task of my priesthood, and what the subject of all my care? A man came to me and told me of his troubles. "Look, priest," he would say, the language of those times being none too tender, "I have it in my heart to love a woman but am already married to another wife." "By the Lord," answered I, "and who be these women pray?" Whereupon followed names and measurements, detailing the ladies' qualities in bed, kitchen, and church, usually in that order. Some consideration of their potential as mothers might also enter into the equation. "No, no," said I, "dear friend, look into thyself!" and handed him a mirror. In this mirror he looked long and hard and, if the powers of Father Ianus were exercised correctly by his humble servant, the client would start, then sigh, then say in a joyous voice, "I see a single beautiful woman, a very young woman. I talked to her long ago in Ramoth Gilead of the Hebrews when she was bathing in the stream of beginnings. Is she not my very dear sister, my daughter, and my bride?" And the client would leave happy, wise, and satisfied. I need hardly add that my lady visitors were treated in like fashion and that they left with the image of the groom in their hearts as happy as with a newborn child. Dear reader, a warning in time: I have totally forgotten all Latin. Do your own research.

But stay with your own Janus: he will lead you well.

25.7 With my divine vision, I can look forward—to what? To the matter of merely a hundred years and quote you a poem by my friend George Wither, in his *Emblems* of 1635:

> In true divinity 'tis God alone
> To whom all hidden things are truly known.
> He only is that ever present being
> Who, by the virtue of his pow'r all seeing
> Beholds at one aspect all things that are,
> That ever shall be and that ever were.
> But in a moral sense we may apply
> This double face to man to signify
> Who, whatso'ere he undertakes to do
> Looks both before him and behind him too.

My father is lord of ships and celestial navigation. On a stone at Nimes, he is depicted in the same scene as Noah, father of the ark, who brought us all to the good life out of the flood. Is he not, looking before and behind him, at this very moment, sailing that sweet river up to Jupiter? Is he not going out, beyond all human oceans, to that multitudinous sea of stars, wherein our kind shall live in days to come? I give you the face of perfection, which looks into the abyss and sees the visible as one, into the corners of the Earth and sees the invisible as many, into its own profile and sees the many and the one as a single race. Passage! Passage! All is passage! We go from an Earth on fire into a celestial realm of flowers and bannerets; we are the sole survivors of disaster, of the great conflagration; our ship bears our brains up to heaven that they might become the fertilizing soil of the new world, soil of the Moon, canals of Mars, heavenly wedding bands of Jupiter! What matter, honest souls, if these transits are tribulations, if we suffer too much for our vision, if life becomes a hell for us because our eyes encompass too many beings and situations, if we cannot, in the end, handle the might of the ten thousand things? In passage is the secret, in perpetual movement the secret, in not resting anywhere the secret, in bearing the Grail to the heavens the secret, in seeing the one face in the mirror the secret!

"*Gate, gate, paragate, parasamgate, bodhi svaha!*"

"Oh Father of Dawn, or Ianus, if you prefer to be so called, from whom men take the beginnings of life's toil, such is the will of the gods—be the prelude to my song!" Thus father Horace. To all my songs. But have I not told you that there are no initiators on this Earth if it be not the poets?

25.8 At roughly the time when the above was written, I was composing essays in poetics that eventually became a volume called *Views from the Weaving Mountain* (University of New Mexico Press) and then became with some changes *The Embattled Lyric* (Stanford University Press). Out of one of my concerns came the suggestion that we needed, in criticism, three aesthetics rather than one. First: the aesthetic of the individual art object. Second: the aesthetic of the "opus": all the objects that a single poet would create in one lifetime. Third: the aesthetic of the "text" or "page": all the possibilities of poetry at all times. I argued that a poet, when a poem came upon him or her, would be bearing in mind, in one way or another, consciously or not—most likely not—these three aesthetics and acting according to that vision. More specifically, he or she would, when starting out on a new poem, be bearing in mind consciously or unconsciously all the poems he or she had written before and looking *back* at them (the "opus" to date) while also looking *forward* to the poem in hand (a future member of the "opus")—the background to this activity being the consciousness of all the possibilities of poetry insofar as he or she could encompass that.

For the backward-looking function in the making of poetry, I used the term "elegy/elegiac"; for the forward-looking function, I used the term "lyric/lyrical." I identified the moment in which the "lyrical" thrust would tip over into a second move as "rhapsody": that strange moment in which the poet feels that he or she will go on speaking/writing forever (the illusion of perpetual *process*)—which is precisely the moment when the activity ruled by the first aesthetic has terminated and the poem, now "elegiac," begins to slide back into *structure* toward completion. Note that, all of the time, there is simultaneous looking back and forward: the first "lyrical" stage, up to "rhapsody," is looking back at previous poems but mainly thrusting up inside the present poem in order to write it. The second stage, down from "rhapsody," is looking forward to the entry of the poem into "opus" but also mourning the fact that the poem is ending and "rhapsody" is over. This curious Janus-like status of the poet I have associated with prophetic power, which, quite literally, enables the poet, at creative times, to sense the abeyance of time as well as the boon that the poet owns of being secure in the poet's knowledge of the past and powerful in the poet's knowledge of the future.

In other pieces, this central moment of "rhapsody," where the poet is in reciprocity with self, is associated with a state defined as "the silence," whereas concentric circles of attention have to do with two functions in apparent contradiction with each other: the "vocal"—the self-other reciprocity of all competing poets—and the "choral"—the nonreciprocity of the community of poets in which competition is finally done away with completely. A new development of this would be to associate "the silence" with timelessness, the "vocal" with something like a Derridean "the same" (i.e., mostly past), and the "choral" with something like a Derridean "the other" (i.e., mostly future).

Throw Twenty-Six

26.1 After the last Alaska trip, there were still some seven lean years to endure before academia could be left behind. Like a painter who keeps a dozen easels in his studio and goes back to each in turn, Tarn often let go of a subject completely to return to it after some years. It chanced that a very bright, energetic, and ambitious young archaeologist, a Brit by the name of Norman Hammond, came to the Rutgers Department of Archaeology and reawakened a dormant interest in Mayan studies. In 1977 Tarn attended Hammond's class as a student, then co-taught with him. By 1978, the Tarns were down at Cuello, Belize, as dig assistants "to see what the archaeologist's life was like," cleaning potshards with a toothbrush and occasionally lending a hand on the pyramid. Life in thatched huts was enlivened by the occasional tarantula in a shoe and by other troublesome critters (one of the team's favorite memories is of this senior professor streaking almost nude through the camp at maximum speed, covered in fire ants and heading for the one and only shower). The senior's position was resented a little by the juniors, including Janet Rodney, as it was felt that he enjoyed some privileges like sitting to read the London *Times* in the morning (Hammond insisted on the *Times*) while the juniors slaved. But privilege did not stretch to the maximum. Expeditions by the main staff to various places for beer and entertainment did not include the senior professor. One night, while this staff was away, Tarn opted for dividing a large cheese among the juniors. The cheese belonged to the staff: Hammond had procured it with great difficulty.

There were interesting visits by archaeologists working in Belize. and Hammond once brought in a British Army helicopter, "protecting Belize—previously British Honduras" at the time, to do some surveying photography. Everyone, including the delighted Mayan cooks and other assistants, was taken up for a ride. After the dig, the Tarns visited various sites in Belize—Altun Ha, a favorite—with a stay in Belize City, whose open sewers, Victorian buildings, and deluxe seaside hotel provided some tropical interest: unfortunately, the renowned keys were not visited. At one point Rodney was called away to attend to her father in the Naval Hospital at Bethesda. Her husband visited the two major sites of Xunantunich—from which one could see Guatemala—and Kohunlich with its giant stucco masks. Then there was Chiapas with headquarters at San Cristobal las Casas, initially in the wonderful colonial building of the Posada Domingo de Mazariegos hotel. At this point, Tarn fell extremely sick with dizziness, fainting, and vomiting. This dragged on until a very long time later, when salmonella poisoning was diagnosed in Mexico City. Work continued, however, including the trip by small plane to Yaxchilan and Bonampak, a flight described in some detail in the poem "Palenque." Frustratingly, contact was lost with Rodney for what seemed an eternity. At one point, the traveler was taken in by the family of the poet Allen Tate's widow, Caroline. At another, when Rodney had returned, a house was secured that sported a very beautiful garden. The poet W. S. Merwin had lived here at one time and planted the garden with nothing but an abundance of white flowers. A small party was given in this house for Tarn's fiftieth birthday. There followed a trip to Atitlán in order to look into accommodation for the 1979 research sojourn.

26.2 Tarn had conceived of an experimental project aimed at an overabundance of jargon. It involved looking for a "new" language in which to write certain kinds of cultural anthropology, a language that would not depart from scientific exactitude and rigor but would not, either, abdicate one jot of its literary potential. A great deal of work and energy went into securing a sabbatical and grants from the Wenner-Gren Foundation and the Social Science Research Council, both in New York, also the American Philosophical Society in Philadelphia.

The old Dodge van was brought back into play, although it was not realized until the Mexican roads were encountered that it no longer had shocks and suspension worth a red cent. The drive down to Guatemala included visits to some fifteen sites—Veracruzan, Olmec, Mayan—all down the Mexican East Coast into Yucatan and Belize and through the Guatemalan Peten to Tikal and the Atlantic site of Quirigua. Despite serious security measures, a dreadful robbery was suffered with virtually all the Nikon equipment bought in Japan taken and a day endured with the local police chief, who delighted in crowing about his love for his Nikon collection! An Olympus OM1 was acquired at Cancun.

Followed a year at Santiago in a rented house on the Tzanchicham peninsula. Much of the story of that year is told in a text that eventually became *Scandals in the House of Birds: Shamans and Priests on Lake Atitlán.* In the course of extremely complex adventures regarding the return to Atitecos of a mask saved from fire some thirty years before and deposited at the *Musée de l'Homme* in Paris, the Tarns teamed up with a young New Mexican, Martin Prechtel: painter, musician, and healer, married to an Atiteca. He had risen to the high position of *primer mayor* (responsible for the major village Easter ceremonies) in the Indian hierarchy—partly because of his remarkable talents and partly no doubt because of gringo money. It is not being suggested that he was well-off.

A number of trips were undertaken—to the Pacific Coast sites, to Copan and elsewhere, jaunts to Guatemala City often based on ferrying Martin's sick child back and forth to hospitals. Significant adventures included a mushroom "trip" during which a shamanic consciousness was experienced; frequent *costumbre* with old Nicolas Chiviliu, Tarn's teacher and Martin's; daily, weekly, monthly harassments from the nascent political situation, which was to lead to the Civil War from 1980 onward; the chance acquisition of a dachshund (baptized with the Maya name of Yaxuan (Juana), which escaped repeatedly from a German family in the city and was finally kept and taken back to Atitlán and all the way to the United States; the modest continuation of textile-acquisition habits, although prices had risen by this time to astronomical heights.

The return drive home, up the West Coast this time, began dramatically. Matters concerning the Guatemalan burrokrassy, like car registrations and such, had been handed over to an agency in the city. One of their men had been supposed to deal with all outstanding matters. On arrival at the border between Guatemala and Mexico, with sites visited and planned, the Guatemalan border officials declared the van's papers invalid. A soldier was assigned to the couple, armed and drunk to boot. Rodney flatly refused to deal with him, and he was replaced by an equally armed but very amiable younger man. Seating arrangements in the van on the return trip to the city can be imagined. The young soldier advised emptying the van before it was impounded. A good Chinese dinner was brought to him because he had to spend the night in the van. Fortunately, a friend, Cherry Pancake of the Ixchel Textile Museum, awakened in the middle of the night, provided a floor in her house on which all belongings could be lined up. Several days of travail in the city and a couple of thousand dollars later, the van was able to leave again, and the program could be continued: another fifteen sites or so visited and photographed all the way up to Zacatecas and Casas Grandes in Chihuahua. The interest of a very rich trip—the astonishment of natives of Oaxaca City at the sight of Yaxuan trotting along (*"Ay! Mira la salsicha!"*— "Look at the sausage!") one memory among hundreds (Atitecos had refused to believe this was a dog)—was somewhat diminished by the fact that Rodney was burned out. She retained virtually no recollections of that return drive.

The first hamburger in Texas tasted like ambrosia, as did the food provided by the poet Keith Wilson and his wife, Heloise, in Las Cruces, New Mexico. Tarn had nourished the notion of showing Santa Fe to Janet with a view to a possible future there and had somehow imagined that he could evoke all of N.M. in the three available days! This plan could not but fail, but as it turned out, roots were planted. Rodney said that it looked just like her Spain.

Papers arising out of the 1979 research were given at various conferences during and after this research—one, on the *Popol Vuh,* the great sacred book of the Quiché Maya and one at a Sociedad Mexicana de Antropología Round Table in San Cristobal de las Casas. Also related were visits to Mexico City with time spent with Octavio and Marie-Jo Paz and other friends. A picnic visit to the extraordinary newly discovered site of the Cacaxtla frescoes was one such occasion.

26.3 Life continued at Rutgers with over-frequent and, in the long run, arduous commutes between New Hope, campus, and major centers: New York, Philadelphia, Princeton. On average, only two days a week seemed to have been spent at home! New York, with Eliot Weinberger, Nina Subin, and family the generous and ever-hospitable vortex, continued as the focus of the literary life. In Princeton, Stanley Corngold, professor of German, was the main friend, and in Philadelphia, Toby and Miriam Olson, who had moved there from New York to work at Temple. There were frequent visits to the coast—at Cape May and at the decoy fairs on the Chesapeake Bay (an area that rivaled New Mexico in attraction for a while as a possible eventual residence). Cobbleskill, New York, where John Ferguson, a Burma studies colleague, and his wife, Katherine, had a magnificent farm was another attraction.

Tarn had been interested in Buddhism since something very akin to a nervous breakdown at the Seigle house in Penne in 1954. He had Buddhologist friends in the United States: Robert Thurman, D. Seyford Ruegg presiding. The Tarns committed themselves at this time to serious Zen training at the New York Center of the *Dai Bosatsu* Zen organization, Tarn leaving off after a year, Rodney continuing for some time after the move to Santa Fe until 1986. After a while, Tarn's daughter, Andrea, had arrived in New York as an art and architecture student at Parsons, with an apartment on East 10th Street. This provided a welcome opportunity to catch up with her and to attempt to work on the traumas left over from divorce, and while Rodney went to the Zen Center, Tarn used all the spare time he had in the city to be in Andrea's company. She also came out west in 1982 and toured with the family as, somewhat later, did son Marc, now training to be a doctor at St. Mary's Hospital, London. On one long tour of major Western sites, Tarn took care of the travel and the archaeology while Marc, a somewhat sybaritic youth at the time, found the best rooms and the best food available. One lapse, however: considerable time and rhetoric was expended on one occasion in luring Tarn into a McDonald's. Annual or biannual visits to the family in London, with side trips to Paris, continued year after year.

Tarn and Rodney took a few days off in Santa Fe in 1982 in order to get married there as a token of interest and commitment to "the future." The "wedding" was mildly hilarious with a judge at the "House of Matrimonial Bliss" (Tarn's name for the municipal building) anxious to show off his jewelry shop in case a ring was needed, secretary witnesses who had to be tipped, a visit to the Chimayo church to salute the local spirits, and a dinner in solitary splendor at the Rancho de Chimayo, where a bottle of wine was graciously offered to the newlyweds. Rings had extravagantly been commissioned from the great Hopi jeweler Charles Loloma. The summer of that year was spent in the painter Paul Sarkisian's house in Cerillos, a splendid old-school edifice whose only drawback was exceedingly sulfurous water.

26.4 In that same year, profiting from a sister-university relationship, and following the usual interminable negotiations, came a two-month teaching stint at Jilin University in Changchun, Manchuria. After a time visiting as much of Beijing and surroundings as possible, including the Great Wall, the

Ming Tombs, and (a favorite place with the hills, temples, and villages around it) the Summer Palace, 150 books were lugged to Jilin as a gift: they were promptly impounded into the teachers' library and never seen by students.

This was supposed to be, after language training, the first year of teaching literary theory, and the students were apprentice teachers themselves, people of a certain maturity. It proved very difficult to cleave to theory, however, for matters were always driven back to language: How do you say this? How do you spell this? What is the meaning of this word? One class on Marxist literary theory was memorable: the students had no knowledge whatsoever outside of a few strictly Chinese sources. Anyone coming with spouses or relatives at that time would find those immediately enrolled de facto into the faculty, so Rodney soon found herself teaching English-language classes.

Foreseeing some of the place's realities, the Tarns had assembled a collection of slideshows before leaving, and these proved to be their most popular contribution: the whole university would turn out for them. American small towns or villages were tolerated, but no secret was made of the fact that slides revealing the sights of New York, Chicago, and San Francisco were by far the most popular. At a later date, Rutgers formed a relationship with Beijing University, and some regret was felt at not having had a crack at that—although it must be admitted that the travelers were far closer to the moment's "real China" in Changchun than they might have been anywhere else. Housing was in a jealously guarded building for foreigners, with student visits severely discouraged. A remarkable old tai chi teacher came every day, after the bellowing radio and waking bugles, to animate the guests in the courtyard. The university president's acupuncturist was dispatched to plant his immense and dreaded needles in Tarn's legs every morning. From time to time, impossibly formal banquets took place with attempts to drink the guests under the table. On one occasion, the wife of one teacher who had been entertained at Rutgers reciprocally commissioned an eleven-course meat lunch at a Muslim restaurant that nearly caused apoplexy in her two guests, left to crawl back, almost on hands and knees, to their compound when she had taken her leave.

There were many amusing episodes. Item: that of Professor Tarn's bed. The bed in situ was too small, so the pair moved to the floor—which was perfectly fine. Suddenly, carpenters arrived and proceeded against all imploring (there was danger of electrocution in the bathroom light fixtures that literally screamed for attention) to manufacture an extraordinarily cockeyed extension to the foot of the bed. Item: one night, a bright light shone inexplicably into the bedroom window. Happening to wear bright-red pajamas and thinking this might be a robber, Tarn stood up on the bed and roared at the window with every decibel at his command. A terrified shriek rose from the neighborhood of the light, and some unfortunate janitor had to be treated for shock: he was certain he had seen a red spirit in the professor's bedroom. Item: another adventure arose out of the fact that the guests' feeble earnings had to be spent in China. A couple of padded jackets—black silk on the outside, crimson on the inside—were commissioned in town as well as a Mao jacket for the professor. The fittings of what turned out to be a Party secretary's blue, silk-lined garment, taking place in the diminutive shop, drew a large part of the town to the door. A very few, very late antiques were available—especially jade archery rings—and a stamp collection was formed at the local post office, somewhat gingerly in that the local philatelists were prevented from entering and were kept outside exchanging stamps they had obtained in the past. On returning from that office one day Tarn ran into an execution procession with the condemned, wearing placards, standing in the front vehicle of a line of trucks, heavily occupied by police. The defiant face of the lead victim, jaw thrust forward, eyes popping out of his head, was unforgettably painful. Shots were heard soon afterward.

Changchun had been the capital of the Japanese puppet state of Manchukuo, and the occupiers had felt it desirable to erect a good many gray buildings in the classical Greek style. Compared to Harbin north of it and the old Manchu capital of Shenyang south of it, where colored clothes had come into fashion, Changchun was still very gray, and its male citizens wore the old regulation Mao suits. It was also subject to being drowned in coal dust most of the year. Despite all this, evening strolls in its streets were not unpleasant, especially when the "June snow" of the cottonwoods fell in thick drifts. There was a park in which traditional music and singing would occur at night while lovers, with nowhere else to go, lay in the bushes.

Harbin was a fascinating place. Remnants of Russian art deco architecture could still be seen. It would have been good to explore this junction of the great Siberian-Chinese railway system, but there was too little time. One moment brought home some of the realities of the Cultural Revolution. Tarn had been asking about a famous wooden Russian Orthodox church said to be the largest outside of Russia itself. A guide pointed down from the hotel window to a very extensive circular green lawn around which trams were circulating: no church. Another historical moment: a hotel elevator full of very cheerful and proud elderly Japanese men returned to visit the sites of some of their wartime exploits.

Shenyang was memorable for its huge complex of Manchu tombs set in a very fine park and also for some visits to popular restaurants where, surrounded by friendly workers enjoying their weekend in fiesta style, some extremely good food was devoured.

26.5 Teachers were paid in travel rather than salary, and extremely long and nerve-racking negotiations took place concerning the amount of travel allowed: the usual being Shanghai and an East Coast Canal town or two. Tarn was dead set on the Silk Road. Eventually, his seniority did allow a very substantial journey. Most of the travel was done by train: foreigners were almost always placed by the train conductor in a first-class compartment by themselves so that it was possible to work, rest, and sleep in great comfort for very long stretches. As companion, guide, and assistant, a favorite student was chosen—here called Y—who had been an "official friend," and a very good one, throughout the teaching stint. During the term, one of the day's more pleasant moments was to see Y arriving, invariably late on his cycle, to the tai chi classes, his hair in a mess and his eyes still full of sleep. He came along all the way to Urumchi and back to Xian, at which point the travelers were left to their own devices. It was possible to talk to Y during the trip, although tedious separations were imposed at all restaurants and feeding stations. (Y could not sit with his charges. Even foreigners, traveling on different circuits, were not allowed to sit together.) Much came forth concerning the Cultural Revolution. The most graphic revelation: how often trains in the area would be jolted on their rails while rolling over the bodies of suicides.

The long Silk Road journey took the Tarns to all the places that were "open" at the time. Going north through Inner Mongolia for a while on the way to the massive Buddhist Yungang grottoes near Datong, Shanxi Province, as well as the superb temples in Datong itself, then on down and across China to Langzhou—the museum, more rock temples at the end of a day's river trip through wondrous beige and brown sandstone landscapes—and across to the Dunhuang Buddhist caves, perhaps the most famous and history-laden site on the Silk Road in that the depredations of those known as "foreign devils" to the Chinese and as great scholars to Westerners (British Aurel Stein, German Albert von Lecoq, French Paul Pelliot, American Langdon Warner, et al.) had been amply recorded in many large scholarly volumes. The evening before visiting the caves, all travelers left the hotel to try to climb the huge sand dunes nearby. This was very hard work, and even members of the People's Liberation Army were finding it a strain. From the top down, the other side was pure pleasure: a long skiing glide on the sands.

At the bottom an old man pointed to a small lake and said that a great Han period monastery had stood there but had been razed to the ground during the Cultural Revolution. It felt very much as if this old man might have been one of the monks. The immense scope of the destruction that had taken place certainly made itself felt during that journey as well as the knowledge that China had not inflicted on others' arts (Tibet's, for example) anything that it had not inflicted on its own. There must still be very heavy books to be written about one of the greatest cultural disasters in history.

Difficulties at the caves. Permission papers emanated from Beijing's archaeological offices and not from Lanzhou's. Because of problems with visitors' breaths threatening the paintings in the caves (a known and universal phenomenon admittedly), the travelers would be restricted to five caves out of over three hundred. Invoking the wrath of the whole international community of scholars and the probability of a host of diplomatic incidents (a sterling technique), the professor, immediately constituting himself as an expert on the Wei Dynasty, demanded a great deal more help than he was getting. In the end, some thirty-five mostly Wei period caves were visited, but every day was a trial. One particular cave, ardently wished for, had been totally verboten. On the last day, this cave was passed by yet one more time, and some thirty "Hong Kongs" (students from that city) were found inside. More raising of scandalized voices: "What? Thirty students and not three scholars!" Finally, the Tarn party was allowed in for two or three minutes, but the psychological pressure was such that the miracle could hardly be enjoyed.

Another trial throughout the journey was the prohibition on photographing the inside of most monuments: it appeared that the Chinese had made arrangements with Japanese publishers to bring out imposing illustrated studies of just about all Chinese treasures. This had some curious results. For instance, on a later occasion in Tibet, it was found that cameras were not allowed but (as yet uncomprehended?) video equipment was. One sad result of this: a fellow traveler promised a copy of a very long film of temple interiors but had not learned anything of technique, and although the film was sent, it proved to be vacant. Y did try to persuade his charges into various subterfuges, but this was felt to be unworthy as well as tedious.

Nothing should be said here about the splendor of these monuments. The paintings and sculptures have to be seen in their sheer majesty, they have been amply published, and any reader can study them at leisure. A passionate love and admiration for Central Asian Buddhist art continued live here.

Sadly, a number of sites were not "open" yet, including the very imposing cave-riddled mountain of Maijishan in Gansu Province.

Many train rides later, with visits to ancient desert cities, other caves, and fiery mountains, the Islamic region of Turfan and surroundings were finally reached. Here one entered a charmed Uyghur world of irrigation ditches and stone canals running through each side of willow-lined streets, men in turbans squatting by the canals at great ease, women and children in colorful dresses doing their chores or playing, diminutive donkey carts running up and down laden with produce or with firewood, the whole scene evoking old memories of Persia and Turkey in previous travels and the charms of Islamic poetry.

Nothing could be done in Urumchi except wait. There had been some mistake in the train reservations from Turfan, and a car had had to be hired, whose cost Y was trying to recuperate for a whole day. A remarkable visit to the Kazakh horse riders in the flower-laden fields of the surrounding mountains made up to some extent for these frustrations. It was like being in a Chinese Switzerland, with many childhood memories of lovely and carefree green expanses, the meadows of heaven.

All the way back to the fabulous city of Xian with its museums, collections of ancient calligraphic stones, giant terracotta army burials (now universally famous through exhibitions sent abroad from China), old streets and houses, and, not least among its offerings, the beautiful Muslim temple in the Chinese style set among the most ravishing of gardens. In Xian, however, new problems. The plan had been to continue through Central China to visit the other major Buddhist caves of Longmen with the possibility of boating on the Yangtze River and finally running into the canal cities of Shuzhou and Hangzhou in the direction of Shanghai. A great Yangtze flood was a barrier to this. Y had left for Changchun. Alone and left with Rodney's rudimentary Chinese, plans were switched in some forty-five minutes toward the south.

Rodney had a strong desire to climb one of the great mountains of China: Mt. Omei. The climb would have been arduous at the best of times, but it fell out that this was the beginning of school vacations. At the first stopping point, after a long day's climbing march through bamboo forests, considerable competition for food and sleeping places was encountered and very little help from the other pilgrims. Rodney felt unwell during the night, and the pair went down again to rest in a hotel at the base of the mountain. Strangely, the gardens here were very reminiscent of Rangoon's.

Kunming was looked forward to as an opportunity to glimpse some of the most luxurious tribal costumes in the world, costumes of a kind that had been admired years before in the hills of Northern Burma on the "other" side. There were such opportunities, although the extreme shyness of the tribal people made portraits impossible: indeed, it was extremely difficult to get anywhere near the individuals involved. Birdwatching with the sought-for bird several hundred yards away, almost invisible among the branches! More: a visit to the Stone Forest (nearly lost in there) with its Sani tribal people sitting in long rows by a lake and selling very attractive textiles. A climb up a very narrow neighboring mountain path to visit a series of Taoist temples disposed along the surface of the rock.

The Guangzhou exit from China was painful: a small, inexpensive tape recorder that Tarn had given to a student was thus unaccounted for (complete lists of belongings always had to be made on entry), and the travelers were made to suffer disproportionate indignities. Further problems awaited in Hong Kong, where a very comfortable Chinese hotel afforded some respite from torrential rains. The wife of a fellow student from Tarn's Chicago days had turned out to be a travel agent and had managed the tickets for this trip but had forgotten, though with over two months in hand, to confirm the Korean Airlines return trip to the United States. After several soaking wet days and frustrated efforts at the airport to find a way out with *any* airline through *any* combination of world destinations, the Tarns finally had to buy two ruinous first-class tickets on Pan Am back to their home. Degree of exhaustion and shock: not a single word was exchanged between Hong Kong and San Francisco.

An unhappy and initially unsuspected outcome of the trip concerned Y. When it was discovered that Y's boss was relying on Tarn to get Y to Rutgers, Tarn was on the point of retiring. Everything possible was done to persuade the Chinese scholars in his Comp. Lit. Department that Y should be helped in his travels, but the outcome was negative for any one of a hundred infinitely tedious academic "reasons." This has lain heavily on Tarn's conscience to this day. Y's travel, residence, and tuition fees simply could not be afforded.

26.6 Nineteen eighty-three brought a sabbatical, which was spent in New Mexico with a view to seeing whether settling there would be a possibility. A house was rented from the daughter of Charles Bell, poet, novelist, and eminent tutor at St. John's College in town. The house was an old adobe with a large orchard garden in El Rancho, not far from San Ildefonso pueblo. In great secret, land was looked at in all areas of Santa Fe and the county. Two basic choices. Either: the old Hispanic model of living next to a river with a great deal of greenery, mainly from cottonwood trees, but few views. Or: the younger model of living on hills with extraordinary views but a very basic vegetation, mainly of piñon pines and juniper. Finally, a beautiful and very hilly place called Las Dos, behind the large settlement of La Tierra in the northwest of the county, was found to have a richer vegetation than any other site looked at. A house was put into the works, first with an architect who dropped his clients when offered a job of state architect, then with a building contractor. The architect had not solved the problem of books. The builder's opinion was that although basements were not frequently found in the area, a hole in the ground was the least expensive way to go. The concrete Bunker Libraries famous among poets were born.

It was then back to New Hope for a final year. After worrying a good deal about selling the house, it was finally disposed of to a next-door neighbor, who eventually changed the place a good deal by filling the garden area with a studio on one side and a pool on the other. The Tarns were given a dinner by the department after surprising and upsetting the faculty by announcing their departure only two weeks before the end of an academic term. An enormous amount of packing was done over a number of weeks. Some boxes had had to be stored in order to make the house visible for sale, and these had already been taken off: it was found much later that they had been stored in a wet place, and many books were damaged. The rest were to go to Santa Fe with movers. There came a day when the sales contract said that the house should be empty. Not feeling well that night, Tarn lay down on the floor in a fetal position, declared that this was still *his* house . . . and, to Rodney's great amusement, refused to budge until the next morning.

26.7 Thus, in the middle of February 1985, a convoy left New Hope in the old Dodge and a newly acquired blue Cherokee jeep. On arrival at the New Mexico border, the drivers got out and performed a joyous little dance within sight of no one in particular. There was also a ceremonial meal of New Mexican food at some roadside restaurant: since that occasion, every week to ten days, a hit of the local food has been a permanent habit—until kidney problems arose. After a night at La Posada Inn, the Tarns drove out to the new house on March 1. It had never been seen, except as a hole in the ground when an invitation to a conference organized by the Center for Contemporary Arts of Santa Fe brought the pair to town in 1984. The house seemed miraculous: the classic adobe brown outside (although made of inexpensive adobe); the brilliant white walls and the totally empty spaces inside; the dizzying 360-degree view from the top of the property over the massive landscape stretching out west to the Rio Grande and the Jemez Mountains, south to the Sandias near Albuquerque, north to the Colorado border, and east to the Sangre de Cristo Mountains.

26.8 Soon the house began to be filled. For the second time in Tarn's life (the first had been in London), he was able to see all his books together—now those from France, England, and New Hope—all over the house and in the largest Bunker. Desks were put down and studios organized. Rodney eventually had her own building in which to open her Weaselsleeves Printing Press: she had trained in New York with Leslie Miller of the renowned Grenfell Press. Leslie had been met through Brad Morrow, the editor of *Conjunctions* magazine in New York. Owing to Rexroth's continuing kindness, Morrow had picked Tarn as his first contributing editor at a loquacious first breakfast meeting on Cornelia Street that ended twelve hours after it had begun! Tarn's extensive work on the magazine for a long while can be seen in the first part of its archive, lodged at Ohio State University.

Throw Twenty-Seven

27.1 And we live at Las Dos still at this date, December 2021, a mile or so south of the native American pueblo of Tesuque with a P.O. box at the Hispanic village of Tesuque (most people think we live there: we do not) and one at the main P.O. in Santa Fe. Our relationship, while greatly loving and affectionate, is, in some senses, more like that of two coworkers than a "marriage" in the old-fashioned sense: in fact, we have imagined an ad we joke at every now and then about "two writers seeking 'husband' or 'wife.'" *Pero no puedo vivir sin ti.* The place is often referred to as a monastery for two. Despite some difficulties at times, we have had new things to say to each other every day for some twenty-five years, and that, by all accounts, must be rare.

I believe that the minute you put down a desk in a place, it ceases to be paradise. Banalizing begins. However, I continue to find the landscape enchanted, and the view out of my study window is a permanent miracle. The infuriating ads endlessly vaunt "New Mexico *True*," and you wonder what "New Mexico *False*" would look like. Granted that I came here to work and be alone—finally to do my own work and not everyone else's—I do miss whatever sense of community I once had on the East Coast. For some reason, this is an almost impossible place in which to sustain social relationships with fellow workers, who are also probably here to be alone. One keeps discovering that a large range of interesting individuals live and work here, although we are not at all likely to meet them. Which is not to say that we have had and have no colleagues: the Bells of St. John's College; Woody and Steina Vasulka in video; Linda Klosky in film; Eleanor Caponegro in book design; Frank Ettenberg and Christopher Benson in painting; Morton Subotnik and Peter Garland in music; Clifford Burke in printing; Joan Myers, Edward Ranney, Meridel Rubenstein, and Eddie Dayan in photography; Gene Youngblood and Brent Klewer in film; the playwright John Mencken and the poets John Brandi, Renée Gregorio, Philip Foss, Arthur Sze, Carol Moldaw, Anne Valley-Fox, Mei Mei Berssenbrugge, Gene Frumkin (in Albuquerque), and Larry Goodell (in Placitas); in books, poet Leo Romero and Nick Potter. Further out: Charles Alexander and Peter Warshall (Tucson). As I update this in 2019, some of the above have died or disappeared from view.

Like so many other attractive places all over the world, the town of Santa Fe has been ruthlessly boutiquized and except for the architecture has in many ways ceased to exist as the rough but charming small burg it was for so long. Apart from some of the long-standing Native American art galleries, there are perhaps only two or three small businesses that can be called local left in the center: the Plaza restaurant, where you would expect it to be, a bar nearby in West Francisco Street.

On the other hand, we are very rich in music, with the Santa Fe Opera, the Chamber Music Festival, the Santa Fe Symphony, the Desert Chorale, and other musical groups and festivals; and also in film, with at least three "art" movie houses (the Center for Contemporary Arts, the Screen at the College of Santa Fe, and the Jean Cocteau); but 90 percent of the visual arts is kitsch, and there is such a glut of "new age" practices that they seem to have shut out traditional intellectual activities altogether—although the School of American Research, the Santa Fe Institute, and the Museum of New Mexico are fine assets. From the time, long ago, when Santa Fe is said to have chosen the state penitentiary rather than the state university (which is in Albuquerque), the scholarly library problem (beyond anthropology and Native Americana at the S.A.R., the Laboratory of Anthropology and literary classics at the College of St. John's, and a few other very minor specialized libraries) has been acute. You would have thought that the state university would have established a strong branch in this town, but it never seems to have done so. I learned to fly for my *Avia* book.

For many years, one friend in Albuquerque made the literary life here stimulating for me: the brilliant young poet and critic Lee Bartlett of the university's English Department. We have worked on many N.T. projects together, including a *Bibliography* (1987), which now needs refreshing, and *Views from the Weaving Mountain: Selected Essays in Poetics & Anthropology* (1991), and have shared a great many enthusiasms. He has succumbed to misfortune and illness in the last few years and moved away from the center: this has been a major loss. In 2019 he is living in Las Cruces with his very dear and brilliant musician wife, Anne Foltz. We are also in touch with daughter poet Jennifer. Henry Roth, the octogenarian author of the magisterial novel *Call It Sleep*, and his composer wife, Muriel Parker, were two other Duke City inhabitants whom we saw with pleasure in their mobile home before their deaths, as was the very fine poet Gene Frumkin, also a teacher at U.N.M., and Larry and Lenore Goodell. Further down, in Las Cruces, the man who should be poet laureate of New Mexico (if "poet laureate" means anything anymore), Keith Wilson, with his wife, Heloise, had been treasured friends—although Keith had died by 2019. Janet and I have sometimes taught at the Naropa Institute in Boulder. Its poetics school is particularly lively in the summer and most welcoming to artists of every stripe. Allen Ginsberg, Anne Waldman, Anselm Hollo, Jane Dalrymple, Bobbie Louise Hawkins, Jack Collom, and Andrew Schelling are among the people who brightened that place (many gone by 2019). The visits from the extraordinary Clark Coolidge, Stan Brakhage, Clayton Eshelman, Michael Ondaatje, and David Hockney were special treats. Meanwhile, Edward and Jennifer Dorn contributed their lapidary talents while Ed's incandescent wit set fire to many a mediocrity out of his or her hearing. Dorn was one of the major poets of his time and the author of *Slinger*—perhaps in my view (I am not alone) the very first totally, one hundred percent American long poem ever written. A cancer victim, he is violently missed.

27.2 Many hold that Santa Fe is best when combined with frequent travel out of town. We get to both coasts as often as possible, similarly Chicago. Poet Peter O'Leary with wife, Rebecca, and boys—musician Gabriel, also musician but a copilot of mine, Lucian—are family. Close also are poet Ed Roberson and scholar Harris and architect Emily Feinsod.

In Ohio, one good reading trip through the state included meeting poets Norman Finkelstein and Tyrone Williams at Cincinnati.

A fellowship to the Rockefeller Center's estate at Bellagio on Lake Como in November 1988 was preceded by an intensive-study trip to the small towns of the river Po out of Milan below the river, all the way to the East Coast at Ravenna, and all the way home above the river. Tarn was back to his passion for Renaissance painting, a passion yet to be fully fed.

In the summer of 1990, Tarn fulfilled a lifelong ambition by going to Tibet with a small group led by the Buddhist scholars Elizabeth Napper and Jeffrey Hopkins. We entered from the North via Lanzhou, the Labrang and Kumbum monasteries, and the central plateau along the very long road to Lhasa, spending one night perforce in a military encampment along the way. Despite the atrocious fate suffered by the vast majority of Buddhist establishments in the country, the few centers and buildings left—the Potala itself, the Jokhang, the Gyantse monuments, Samye, and others—do give you a sense of the splendor and utter tragedy suffered by this culture. Of all the manifold impressions left on the mind, a leading one is perhaps the matter of proportion between the towering altars and Buddhas and Bodhisattvas in the monasteries and the smallness and narrowness of the spaces in front of them—not in the main halls but in the great many chapels around them. This simple spatial device brings the great towering statues home to you like no other architectural feature Tarn can think of. There were sad occasions such as witnessing the departure of military wagons loaded with prisoners on coming out of the Dalai Lama's Summer Palace one morning and, of course, the manned posts on the roofs of buildings above the central Johkang temple. The group left the country via Chengdu, Giangzhou (onetime Canton), and our "old friend" Hong Kong.

27.3 Shortly after this, the Tarns toured Rajasthan by car with a very fine gentleman driver who never left his vehicle by day or by night, even when somewhat ill and offered a hotel room. He was British educated, a Protestant, and a musician. Tarn had some run-ins with him because he often decided that a place we wished to go to was nefarious and should not be visited. This was a time of curfews, however, and his management of that issue was impressive. The way in which he found roundabout ways of traveling, his upbraiding of policemen junior to him, and his canniness in finding gas despite great scarcity saw us through a journey that could easily have been disastrous. We were blocked a very little in Jodhpur—otherwise not.

Rajasthan is one of the most enchanting provinces in India and indeed on Earth. The trip began at Bikaner and continued on to the famous painted houses (*haveli*) of Shekhawati—abandoned to some extent, but there are efforts at renovation. Depictions of Rajput life on the walls constitute a great illustrated encyclopedia of that fascinating folk, from their beginnings to the age of flight. Then it was on to desert Jaisalmer, near the Pakistani border. Our reservation was lost, and we ended up with a beautiful pillared room (not unfrequented by rats) in a modest ministerial palace. A balcony directly overlooked one of the great Jain temples. The lady of the house made *lassis* fit for the gods. Walks in the city were taken hand in hand with Ali Baba—so age-old and hallowed seemed the streets and buildings. Likewise with walks on the dunes outside the city to visit various archaeological sites.

Udaipur followed. Because of mass tourism and mass bookings it was always a struggle to secure rooms where wanted, but it finally became possible to stay in the Taj Lake Palace. A large kingfisher lived outside our window. This was one of the great moments of the trip, recorded in the poem "Bartok in Udaipur." There was an Edenic feeling about living on what seemed to be a floating garden in the middle of a very large lake.

Jaipur, staying in a princely palace with art deco rooms, enchanting gardens, and an excellent bookstore, followed with its astronomical monuments, its principal city palace, and a palace outside the town, where Tarn was severely mortified by an elephant ride Rodney insisted on taking because her mother had once taken it. The swaying of the beast brought out his best vertigo, and he did not enjoy the stops she made to complete her thunderous excretions. (2019: activists said to be relieving elephants from this chore.)

In Jodhpur, Kota, and Bundi stood other palaces, all equally delightful. At Kota the prince's guests were entertained in his dining and sitting rooms replete with photographs of royalty and relics of bygone eras. At Bundi some of the finest murals in the province were found on the palace walls. Before reaching the camel fair at Pushkar, we insisted—against the advice of the driver—on visiting the tomb of an extremely famous Sufi saint in Ahmedabad and were fleeced at every corner of the monument for our pains. Having our noses thrust quite sharply into the perfumed cloths with which the tomb and other relics were wrapped became distinctly unpleasant.

The Pushkar tent city, though comfortable, was crazily overgrown, but once in the fair itself among the camels and tribal people, the adventure became worthwhile, and somehow there were very few tourists. The town also was enjoyable: there were small cafés on rooftops from which you could watch people moving about in the streets far below in their clamorously beautiful clothes. This was the place to buy Rajasthani textiles with their genial main combination of red and orange. At Kota I had fallen in love with Kota saris. They sport very delicate colors and exquisite repeated small woodblock prints, of flowers mostly, quite different from the standard Indian garment.

In a place whose name I cannot recuperate, one of the more difficult to find, on the sand-track way about which even our driver became anxious, we discovered that we were not expected. This had happened at Jaisalmer and was to happen once or twice more. Famous for the decibel pitch to which my voice can reach, I was insistent. The prince came out and gave us his room, adding that this would be the first time he would sleep in his wife's room since their marriage. This gentleman, now a member of the Indian Parliament, was expert at sending us out on all sorts of enjoyable but costly little trips, one of which was to see the rare black buck of the region.

Many other sites were visited, including the extensive deserted fort city of Chittorgarh, the jungle site of Ranakpur with its major Jain temples, and, at the end, a famous bird sanctuary at Bharatpur (now the Keoladeo National Park), where expert guides take you around on rickshaws pointing out various ornithological treasures. After this—because Janet had not seen northern India—we went to Delhi, Fatehpur Sikri, Agra, Benares, Ajanta-Ellora, and Bombay, staying at the old section of my favorite hotel, the Taj, and visiting Phillip's Antique Store, with which we have been exchanging New Year cards ever since. The difference from my first trip coming out of Burma in 1959 was marked: where I had been fortunate to see the Taj or Fahtipur with a handful of people, fellow tourists now numbered in their hundreds, and truly pestiferous sellers of the sempiternally identical postcards and other souvenirs were as abundant and troublesome as flies. I once tried to describe to one of these how "miserable" he and his like made tourists feel, however much they might sympathize with them for many a reason. His anguished "But why? Why miserable?" measured the whole extent of the separation.

At one point we had had to drive from Khajurao to Bhopal because all other possibilities had been booked by mass-tourism groups. A driver who had come through the night collected us and took us, without rest, for the whole day over a road so bad that it could truly be described as nonexistent. All he wanted was a cup of tea from time to time. His chest was scarred by acid from an episode in an unruly youth, and he had terrible tales of the effects of the well-known Bhopal Union Carbide gas leak disaster (1984) on his mother and family. On arrival at Bhopal to visit the Buddhist temple at Sanchi, our booking was not recorded—at which point the aforesaid decibels threatened "an international ambassadorial incident" and finally obtained a room in an annex for a night before moving in properly the next day. The Sanchi visit went off well, as did another to Bodhgaya. Both these illustrious Buddhist sites were mercifully uncrowded.

27.4 In May 1991 there were readings in Berlin, Prague, and Budapest. In Berlin (where Lee Bartlett joined me on a rare foreign venture), my host was the poet Joachim Sartorius at the German Academic Exchange; at the Prague University reading I saw Miroslav Holub for the last time, and in Budapest

I met Agnès Gergely, a dear friend with whom translations were exchanged over some years; Ferenc Juhász; János Kodolányi, married to the daughter of poet Gyula Illiés—whom I had met at Bled. I also saw the filmmaker Gyula Gazdag and his art historian wife, Eva Forgács, first encountered in Santa Fe at a festival of his films. Between Prague and Budapest came a reading at the University of Olomutz, a delightful Moravian town that reminded me of Cambridge and where I had a room in which Mozart is supposed to have slept. Because flights home started from Vienna, I obtained some three days there, reaching it by hydrofoil from the center of Budapest. For whatever reason, I found most of the people I happened to encounter here (in a bookshop, in a philately store) extremely difficult and unpleasant. There were, however, the marvelous monuments—the great Art Museum (whose Brueghels inspired the poem "Brueghel at Wien"), the Museum of the Austrian Imperial Army (an astounding historical feast), and the Technological Museum, as well as a night at the Opera with *La Clemenza di Tito*.

It would take a whole book to describe all the visits made in cities such as these—some of which were repeated: Berlin with my daughter, Andrea, where we studied the aftermath of the fall of the Wall; Prague and Moravia with a young American composer entering the latter through East Germany; and the medieval town of Görlitz.

The truth is that I have too many travel plans for the time I have left on Earth. Over the years I have discovered that my greatest joys come from a great museum or a great monument: nature is everywhere present in my work, but culture is a sine qua non of well-being. This seems to activate for me the fundamental age-old philosophical debate between the particular (the "ten thousand things" of the Chinese) and the general: one of the two or three koans of my existence and a great trigger for the poetry. I also find that moving around prompts writing more than staying still: travel, with notebook in pocket, is a vital part of method. A book such as *At the Western Gates* depends heavily on this activity: part one: Baja California; part two: Chiapas, Mexico; part three: Alaskan and North Japan waters. I would not necessarily call them "travel poems": the setting is one thing; the matter is another.

27.5 Other substantial travels included a month in Bali with a side trip to the vast Borobudur in Java and surrounding temples, Ladakh, Bhutan, and several trips to Russia. For the Ladakh trip we joined a small Anglo-Welsh group, proceeding to Delhi, from which we were to fly to Leh. We were back in an old Delhi *querencia*, the Imperial Hotel. Because of some radar problem on the Air India plane, the flight to Leh was aborted at Amritsar: just before landing we flew over the famous Golden Temple of the Sikhs. Hopes that we might visit it were dashed, but perhaps that would have been forbidden anyway. Return to Delhi. We then boarded a bus for an extremely long trip to Srinagar in Kashmir, spending the night on one of the famous lake houseboats mostly made of fragrant sandalwood. I had never thought to see the lake or those houseboats in this life. We received, in the anteroom to the boat, visits from traders desperate because of a great shortage of tourists; canoes laden with flowers; other canoes slithering alongside our own when on the lake, carrying more traders with offers preposterously priced. A morning visit to the Mughal gardens along the lakeshore. Then the long bus climb through a paradisal countryside into the mountains, with constant interruptions by long Indian Army convoys going to, and coming from, Ladakh. A world of its own: Muslim Kargil—site of recent battles between India and Pakistan. The bus again into Zangskar, the wildest part of Ladakh, and after a kind of no-man's-land, the beginnings of Buddhist country.

We had walked but never trekked, and this was a ten-day camping trek at 13,000 feet, walking some eight hours a day or more with stops in fields or monasteries. The going was extremely hard and not all that well organized: told, for instance, of a lunch rest coming in ten minutes—two hours later no rest yet. Again, it is necessary to look at photographs to appreciate the splendor of the landscapes. The story of the trek with its water obsessions, its gleeful sightings of the Blue Himalayan Poppy dreamt of since adolescence, is told, as always, in diaries and in the poem "First and Last Trek, Zangskar." Memorable, the monuments aside, were the overwhelming desire to cast yourself into the river rushing in a direction opposite to ours along the deep gorge below and the way in which we would throw ourselves into every one of the springs we passed. On one occasion I took it on myself to make trouble for some Christian fundamentalist missionaries who came into a monastery peddling their faith through medical know-how and supplies.

More bus through the great sites of Lamayuru and Alchi to Leh in Ladakh proper. Alchi with its painted walls had been looked forward to as the apex of the voyage, but work here was exasperating: a single monk opened the door of one building while closing all the others—thus preventing comparative study—and the lighting was virtually nonexistent. In Leh a delightful small hotel with a very colorful garden afforded some respite. I had wanted to stay on in Leh after the others' return to attend a conference and see more sights, but for the first time in my life, I felt too exhausted and returned with the

THROW TWENTY-SEVEN

rest on a bus descent to Srinagar that seemed to last forever. On approach, we were caught in a crossfire between insurgents and the Indian Army: I forgot to lie on the floor. No one has turned a bus round so fast and fled so many miles as our driver did. At the airport, security involved some dozen idiotic body searches in the two hundred yards separating the bus stop and the plane door: "What is this?"—"It is a pencil." "And this?"—"This is my handkerchief." "And this?"—"These are Indian coins." Hard to believe but true.

At Delhi, we took refuge in the twenty-four-hour café at our dear Imperial Hotel. I then went with the others to the airport only to find out that I did not have a seat. Janet went off not knowing what had happened to me, and I went back to the Imperial, having to force the cyclo driver virtually at gunpoint to take me there and not elsewhere at his convenience. An Indian Airlines strike did not help matters. I finally managed at considerable cost to leave for London on the next night, sharing a Lufthansa jet with a crowd of Italian hairdressers. A rest by myself on Herm Island, where I managed to be extremely sick, then the return home.

27.6 I flew to Bhutan with Lindsay Hill, a poet and dear friend who had invited me more than once to Memphis, Tennessee, on poetic projects and was now considering leaving his prestigious job in business for the literary life. Going and coming from Bangkok, we flew over Burma—I should have expected this but had not focused yet. The event was very moving, although nothing was recognized.

Bhutan, with traditions jealously maintained by its royalty, is one of the most beautiful countries on earth: its landscapes, especially its wooded hills and valleys, define the essence of green better than emeralds. We journeyed west to east by minibus, visiting many monasteries and many of the great administrative castles (*dzongs*) and witnessing two major ritual events involving giant *tangkas* hung from towering walls, monastic masked dances of gurus and demons, large crowds of Bhutanese dressed in their finest. On one occasion, we had walked at some length up to a monastery in the hills where our guide, a scholar from Berkeley, indulged in some research. Night came on fast, and we went down the mountain in total darkness at considerable risk to knees and ankles. I upbraided this scholar for putting us at such risk, but he was happy with his research. Day by day through the trip, Lindsay Hill became thinner, more quiet, and more transparent: I was moving around with a ghost. At the very end, my vertigo could not contemplate the trip up to the famous Tiger's Lair monastery. This caused much anguish, but I ended up spending a pleasant day and finding a magnificent gray textile in the hotel store. Day by day, Lindsay looked more and more ghostly. Two days after our return, he resigned from his business job and went on to becoming an extremely successful writer with his very first novel: the extraordinary *Sea of Hooks*.

Throw Twenty-Eight

28.1 The penultimate Asian trip, accomplished fortunately before the up-heavals in Afghanistan and Iraq, was to Northwest Pakistan, Xingiang, and Uzbekistan. After Dubai, with its extraordinary shopping center of an airport, Emirates Airlines took us to Peshawar, where we were treated to lectures and museum visits centering on Gandharan Hellenistic-Buddhist art. Taxila, a major Buddhist site, was not on the itinerary, but at my insistence we were able to go to it. We were also taken to the Khyber Pass under armed escort—all the way to where one could see the Afghan border in the distance, with cyclists indulging in the immemorial Khyber smuggling trade back and forth under our very noses. The pass, with its many historical monuments to the British and Indian armies on its hillsides and its giant fortifications, was far more interesting than expected. Another feature of the stay at Peshawar was an acquaintance formed with a retired Pakistani Army colonel who took us for tea to the Peshawar Club (with its musty old library full of incredible treasures) and organized a tea party and concert for us at the Great Fort after viewing the changing of the guard in dazzling uniforms. He then turned out to own a very large shop selling most souvenirs—but mainly carpets. Never having found carpets to be of the slightest interest, I very suddenly fell for a pigeon-blood-red Afghan item, waited until the very end, then negotiated for it. Months after our return it turned up at Albuquerque airport wrapped in a very soiled white canvas. It now lies at the foot of my bed, and I love it deeply although, mysteriously, it insists on travel and has to be repositioned every three days.

We then moved north, visiting more such sites, along the Karakoram Highway following the river Indus (another part of which we had known in Ladakh) up through Swat, Gilgit, and Hunza toward the Chinese border. More extraordinary landscapes. A favorite aspect: imagine a huge drop from the top of a mountain down to a fairly narrow ledge on which a village stands with adobe huts and fine tall trees, the drop then continuing on down again to the valley below. The Aga Khan is the lord of these parts, and signs of praise to him, his foundations and establishments, are everywhere. Many very pleasant inns run by an Indian chain. At the Swat District museum, I discovered a magnificent large textile: an old embroidered cloth for carrying bread. Where to find such a thing? In a textile shop nearby, skyscraper piles of rough and uninteresting textiles disappointed, until the proprietor brought out such a cloth—probably the most astonishing of all the textiles I have ever dealt with—saying, "Perhaps you are looking for something of this quality?" He claimed to be keeping it for some embassy lady but was fairly easily persuaded to part with it. It is now framed above my bed, hovering over the Afghan carpet.

The landscape gets starker and starker; we go through a desert no-man's-land to a single point of rest where travelers of various nationalities eat . . . and we lose our leader—a British writer with a residence in Turkey—at the border with China because of some transgression in China of his journalist son's for which he was being made to suffer. We do not get him back until Tashkent. Meantime, Kashgar brings a visit to more Muslim monuments, including a mosque with several football fields' worth of adobe tombs and the bewildering market, advertised as the largest in Central Asia. At a hat section one merchant completely squelches my desire for a hat by ramming one example of his wares on my head after another until I am completely dizzy. There is a touching visit to the old British and Russian consulates—now hotels—which figure so largely in accounts of the Silk Road by the "foreign devils" who haunted it.

A night in Almaty, Khazakstan, but no tourism because of rain. Finally a luxury hotel at Tashkent and the trip out to the fabled cities of Uzbekistan, guided by a hauntingly beautiful woman, wife to an engineer in Bokhara, Fatima by name. Again, Samarkand, Bukhara, and Khiva: you cannot elaborate on them here except to say that—Soviet reconstruction notwithstanding—these three were immensely impressive: for me the first sight of the dazzling deep blues and turquoises of tiles against the adobe of the building walls since my visit to Iranian Isfahan in 1959. Not a single room in any monument was devoid of people selling arts, crafts, and souvenirs: despite the excitement of temptations, this, in the long run, became tedious. One saddening sight along the way: the giant Oxus shrunk to a rivulet in the desert on its crawl to the disaster of the dried-out Aral Sea. The Soviet regime had demanded a total devotion to the raising of cotton, and this had injured the whole area. But there were also many pleasant visits to potteries along the way and tables heaped with fruits and vegetables under vine canopies for our meals. At various places, it was possible to buy the wondrous *ikat* tie-dye textiles of the country, but any older piece was subject to Russian-style denials at Customs, and I was in no mood to risk those. Strangely enough, an old and very famous Uzbek Jewish wedding singer, now living in Denver, performed in Santa Fe within a few days of our return.

28.2 The Russian journeys are another matter altogether. The 1968 trip with the *Société Européenne de Culture* was interesting but produced no special affect toward the country—even though I had often declared that "my soul was Russian." In 1995, however, this land reached my feelings for good, and I became passionately involved. There had been a number of meetings organized at the technical college in Hoboken, New Jersey, by the poet Edward Foster and his Russian colleague, Vadim Mesyats, between American and Russian poets. These were disastrously lacking in structure, so the Russians went off to drink among themselves without much contact with their hosts. However, it turned out that Vadim was the son of a very important official in the Russian Academy of Sciences. I ended up by receiving an invitation to visit Petersburg and Moscow in the care of the Academy and was lodged at the Academy house on Millionnaya Street next door to the Hermitage in Petersburg. Some scientists were put in charge of me in both towns.

I complicated the matter almost beyond belief by simultaneously being on a tour with a British group whose main objective was the biannual Aviation Fair at Moscow, staying at the old Stalin-built skyscraper of the Ukraina Hotel to which I had transferred. In the end, I would devote alternate days to the Academy and to the aviation group while keeping some time to myself for some own choice: the huge Ismailovsky flea market, the antique stores on the Arbat, or the wonderful architectural outdoor museum of Kolómenskoye. The aviation group was full of "spotters," whose main enjoyment seemed to consist in collecting names of aircraft types and their registration numbers—something

I could in no way get into. This took us to the great Aviation Fair (we had the roof of one of the aircraft designing firms' headquarters to ourselves), to many airports, to the outdoor Russian Air Force Museum at Monino, and to a number of bases. At one of these, the group was split up and taken for rides in two different aircraft. One of the aircraft, piloted by the base's colonel, crashed, killing all on board. My old Antonov made it back to base.

While under Academy care, I visited Space City, where Gagarin's widow still lived, and ran into American astronauts training there; the Zhukovsky Aviation Academy, with its superb collection of historical models; and the MIG factory (this had been subject to much negotiation), where we were taken around by one of the sons of Anastas Mikoyan. He in turn put me in touch with his brother, Stepan Anastasovich Mikoyan, the reigning test pilot, whose translated memoirs I eventually housed at the British publisher Airlife.

The Ukraina was still run on old-fashioned lines with extremely surly waiters. On one occasion I was very rudely upbraided for taking a bottle of water from a vacant table because no one had brought me one. My window, high up on an umpteenth floor, did give out onto the White House and the river: a fine view. The lobbies were haunted by a great many good-looking women. There were uninterrupted phone calls to your room offering company until two a.m. In the end, my only recourse was to take the phone off the hook and muffle it in a blanket after ten p.m. (By 2019, the hotel had been renovated as a Radisson.)

28.3 Back at home, after a very basic course at the community college, I worked on Russian by myself for a year and a half but found that my aging memory did not allow enough storage to ensure a real takeoff. For months, I read nothing but Russian materials: all the classics I had read as a youth, then modern literature, the arts, history, political science, and contemporary affairs. The Russian section of the library grew apace.

In 1998 there were two trips. One in winter. A run-down but still presentable apartment next door to the Lesnaya subway station was loaned for a very small fee by a young actor who spent most of his time in Moscow. The apartment sported a very decrepit cat rejoicing in the name of Saddam Hussein and one room entirely given over to an enormous collection of rubber uniforms and other sadomasochistic gear—evidently the secret passion of its owner. A number of parties with poets and young intellectuals of various stripes, Arkadii Dragomoschenko in the lead, held here in suffocating cigarette smoke and vodka fumes.

I explored the city, mostly in fear for my bones because every inch of the streets was covered with ice. New discoveries included the Arctic Exploration Museum, which I had entirely to myself; the extensive Naval History Museum, at the point of Vasilyevsky Island facing the Hermitage; the even larger Artillery Museum, behind the Peter and Paul Fortress; the fortress itself, with its mint and its Imperial period tombs; the *Aurora* cruiser (on which a sailor became furious when I would not be lured into visiting the captain's cabin for a substantial fee); the Siege of Leningrad Museum; and much else. Perhaps the only things I failed to see were the great cemeteries of the World War II siege and the legendary naval establishment on the island of Kronstadt.

One very dear friendship was formed with Y, a retired engineer, his wife, and daughter: an extremely bright young teenager. His own collecting passion was for contemporary coins of the world, but he was introduced to me as someone who could take me to some small flea markets in distant parks where militaria and old badges could be found. Apart from toy soldiers, I had become addicted to the study of Imperial period badges, both civilian and military, drawn to their elaborate heraldry and jewel-like qualities of workmanship, some even by Fabergé. Unfortunately, I came into this very late, when Russian collectors had renewed desire and where the market was already quite bedeviled by fakes. One well-known banker had published two sumptuous volumes on the subject and was buying up virtually anything that was for sale anywhere in the world. One could tell from events at the great auction houses in London—and who could honestly complain of this?—that one no longer stood a chance against Russian repatriation.

28.4 In the summer of 1998, after more extremely elaborate planning, Janet and I went to Russia together on a two-month home-stay venture. A professor in Petersburg had set up a system whereby you stayed with families in their own homes, and he had established quite a collection of families and of places. Conditions were mostly extremely arduous in that almost all the homes were very small, some of them primitive and—like so much of Russia's infrastructure—broken down to a disastrous degree. After an initial difficult experience in Moscow with an academic couple obsessed with their pension problems, most of the people we stayed with were extremely thoughtful and anxious to give us the best time possible. Our Moscow hostess did make possible our participation in a group excursion to Tolstoy's home, Yasnaya Polyana. This was the fulfillment of a long-held ambition, but the bus trip down was not: an old lady guide, left over from Soviet times, felt obliged to talk and explain on and on all along the way. Tolstoy's grave in the forest, a mound covered with a few flowers; the overall smallness of the place; and the presence of the author's grandson were among our recollections.

From Moscow, we went to the old towns of Rostov Veliki, Suzdal, and Vladimir, where all my architectural desires were thoroughly fulfilled: the whole setting and townscape of Suzdal and its gardens, the two cathedrals of Vladimir, and the heavenly little church of the Intercession on the Nerl, reached like a grail after a long walk through marshy fields. Then it was back to Moscow for a day and on to Novgorod, where I saw a great deal more than I had seen in the sixties, with a particular interest in the oldest Novgorodian frescoes, their destruction by German troops in World War II, and the truly heroic efforts made toward their restoration. A visit to Dostoyevsky's dark-green house in Staraya Russa on a street corner by a lovely river—we were graciously permitted to visit in spite of an academic conference going on there—allowed a strong sense of the author's presence: some house museums exude this; some do not. A later attempt to visit Pushkin's place at Mikhai-lovskoe was frustrated: we were told that the place was in danger of being transformed into a tourist center. Pskov and environs followed, including a superb monastery near the Estonian border. Then it was Petersburg, which Janet had never seen, but seven days were not enough to remedy that. This was the one place where we managed to have an apartment. A visit to Pavlovsk was especially delightful.

In the Ukraine we went to Kiev, my "maternal hometown" of Odessa, and Lviv. The stay at Odessa was curious, involving the home of an army officer and his family dominated by an elderly dame who had obviously been a high-ranking Soviet official and was still able to pull any number of strings when the occasion demanded. Problematically, they lived forty-five minutes out of town by the seaside, which made acquaintance with the city rather difficult. Driving daily to and fro through extensive but barren fields, one could enjoy the sight of nouveau-riche faux-Disneyesque houses, their architecture of the most hallucinating grotesqueness, surrounded by high walls (against whom?) and hundreds of acres of absolutely nothing. This was a far cry from City Center with its opera (under restoration), its stately houses, and its exquisite and unbelievably elaborate Art Nouveau Passage, still standing among rather derelict buildings. Also the Black Sea Fleet's museum. A separate book could be made out of the stories of the people who hosted us in all these places. Eventually we ended up in Lviv, Western Ukraine.

28.5 The trip was to end in Lithuania, but we had no desire to go through visa problems in Belarus and so ended up unexpectedly on a very long train ride to Warsaw through ravishing countryside. In Poland came a sudden change in our circumstances at one of the major American-style hotels: the, by now, completely novel availability of *luxury*. In the city, the strange experience of a totally resurrected medieval center; the National Art Gallery, with a whole unknown-to-me dimension of medieval and Renaissance painting; a Chopin tour; and several bookstores and print shops. The whole Warsaw Ghetto experience, however, was an abyss, this "nowhere" being represented at this time by very little more than a couple of souvenir stands and a statue.

In Lithuania we saw as much as possible of Vilnius, a fine city with a host of fascinating monuments, and I noted again that everything seemed to be done to cover over the whereabouts of a ghetto that had once been the "Northern Jerusalem." On one occasion, near the university, we were approached by a young lady with a questionnaire for tourists: "What improvements would you make?" I answered that a more substantial Jewish presence would do no harm. We visited the extremely helpful Lithuanian State Records Office (it is kept alive at the moment by Americans, Gentile or Jewish, looking for roots), where I did my best to commission a set of family records, but nothing was found on my grandfather or his father. We celebrated my seventieth birthday in the city by attending a performance of Beethoven's Ninth offered in the imposing Great Court of the University. Our seats were near the edge. A couple of little boys, undisciplined by their mother, played noisily throughout the performance and wrecked it for me. We went back to the hotel and watched World Cup football on television.

A day was spent visiting the castle at Trakai and another in Kaunas, where a complete exhibit of the pilots Steponas Darius and Stasys Girénas's New York–Lithuania flight of the *Lituanica* aircraft on July 15, 1933, occupied a whole vast glass case in a special room of the Army Museum. The plane, after a highly praised flight, had crashed near Soldin in Germany, not far from a later Nazi concentration camp. We also visited the main synagogue and were amicably received there by the caretaker and a friend of his. While having lunch some way away, I was most amused to have this friend suddenly pop up out of nowhere with a request for a small personal donation. The situation felt like one out of an old tale of Martin Buber's. Further on, at the old town square, were some bookstores and antique shops, one of which was selling prewar Jewish bills of sale and receipts franked with Lithuanian revenue stamps.

It had taken me some time at home to trace the real location of my father's "Neustadt Schirwindt," a German name, the name he remembered as being the place-name of his father's origin. One book I had read on our cousins the Shuberts placed this origin in a wholly different place near Danzig.

However, "ours" turned out to be Nayshtot Shaki in Yiddish, Wladislawów in Polish, and Kudirkos Naumiestis in Lithuanian, this last being the name of the composer of the national anthem, and it was right at the other end of the country over by Kaliningrad, aka Königsberg. We went there with a young woman, Regina, who specialized in helping people looking for roots. We began in a field outside the little town where a goodly number of old burial stones were drowning in brambles and weeds. Regina toiled for some hours of very difficult reading, but nothing with our name on it was found. Behind the field, there was a mass grave for hundreds of Jews murdered during World War II. However, the only monument was one to a handful of Lithuanian partisans who had been buried in that place.

The town was most attractive and most verdant, with a pleasant square organized around the statue of the composer, a bridge over water with a border post at each end leading toward Russian Kaliningrad but obviously unused, and a variety of remnants of Jewish housing and other buildings. There happened to be a fiesta of sorts going on in the center that provided us with beer and sausages and a heavily Gentile atmosphere. On the way back, we visited one of the wrecked wooden synagogues, which had been used for years as a barn. Only the skeleton remained. An old lady, given a pension by some American Jews, did her best to look after the place.

Thus the travel records of this life end, for the time being, at the place where anything that can be remembered of the past began, the only location missing being, I suppose, at my mother's Iasi/Jassy/Iassy/Yash in Moldavia, Rumania. On finishing this sentence I called my old Parisian college friend Chiva, originally from Iasi, on the phone. He is in his late seventies by now, has had very severe health problems for many years, and finds it very difficult to write even once a year. For an hour, we ran through the whole of the French situation in the social sciences, to which he is still emotionally attached. We talked of archives and how France had virtually stopped caring about the preservation of papers of civic concern (that is: other than literary) since the end of the eighteenth century. I asked him about Lévi-Strauss's papers. He had asked the maestro—who answered that he did not wish to think about the matter and that his children would deal with it . . . Chiva, much missed, died not long afterward. 2020: I learned more about Chiva's friendship with Paul Celan in the huge Celan-de Lestrange correspondence. The closeness made me even sorrier that I had turned down a meeting with Celan in my student days.

THROW TWENTY-EIGHT

Throw Twenty-Nine

29.1 August 2019: I am forgetting a number of important occasions and travels. During the teen years of 2000, Tarn enjoyed readings several times in San Francisco, at the Rain Taxi Festival in Minneapolis, in Ann Arbor and Detroit, and at a whole Tarn weekend to himself organized by Duke University in November 2011 as guest of poet Joseph Donahue and his wife, the brilliant sociologist Priscilla Ward. On two occasions there were readings in Great Britain thanks to Tony Frazer, a friend and publisher of the Shearsman Press, who had brought out a number of N.T. titles and, in 2019, reprinted four of his out-of-print books: a very rare boon in the field of books.

In 2005 the anthropological Tarn, very desirous of seeing Borneo and its "legendarily" handsome Dayak peoples, volunteered to work for a group in Berkeley that provides aid to Borneo people in safeguarding forests and lands. He traveled the area, after a spell in Kuala Lumpur, for about two months seeing a great deal of Sarawak and Sabha. A major event was to be a fifteen-day tour of mainly nomad (Penan) settlements together with a local leader affiliated with the Berkeley group. On arrival at the first long house, Tarn dutifully took notes on the place's gardens and agriculture, and after a session of discussion and advice, he and his colleague were put to sleep on the floor in the headman's house. Tarn had been sleeping badly and swallowed a pill.

In the morning his colleague was found dead. The process of settling matters with the village, the colleague's village, and getting the body back to hospital and to base, followed by a funeral and talks with the colleague's daughters, took much time and much discomfort. After which Tarn had to decide on a whole new program.

The tragic side of the trip was to see how much of Borneo had been taken over by the oil-palm industry, with its devastating effects on Indigenous rights and the rights of nonhuman fauna, mainly the orangutan. All this is covered in the book *Ins and Outs of the Forest Rivers* (2008).

29.2 In 2006 Tarn had joined a group birding in New Guinea, specifically to look for birds of paradise. The miracles were seen: some close, some not so close. This was followed by a trip to Melbourne, where he gave a talk at the Melbourne Festival, and Sydney, where there were readings of and seminars on his work. He became very fond of Sydney, visiting all the museums as well as the zoo out in the bay and befriending Australian poets such as Robert Adamson and John Tranter, who had given him space in his publication *Jacket* not long before this was turned over to Penn Sound at the University of Pennsylvania, where it became *Jacket 2*.

Tarn's eightieth birthday was celebrated in June 2008 at Sils Maria, Switzerland, to which he and Rodney had been invited by Patricia, Andrea, and Marc. Reuniting with alpine botany in those magnificent fields and visiting Nietzsche's house were the highlights of that vacation. That year also brought a voyage to Antarctica on a small research boat that had once been Russian, the *Professor Multanovskyi*, with a very sympatico Russian crew. A few days were spent in Ushuaia and its surroundings. Regret at not seeing more of Patagonia. The best memories here are of the immense landing on South Georgia with its thousands of penguins and a last day with a rare amount of sunshine cruising past seal-invested rocks within the peninsula proper.

In 2010 Tarn joined a birding group to Ecuador (Tarn and Rodney had previously seen the Galapagos and the Ecuadorian Amazon), enjoying not only the birds but also the flowers on the sides of roads and paths throughout the Andean center of the country, his favorite part of Ecuador. November 2011 was celebrated with a visit to the family in Cape Town, continuing on to the splendors of Namibia on the West African coast—chosen over the east and thus visiting the Etosha National Park instead of the Kruger. The southern Namibian dunes are a national treasure. In 2014, with an offer from Eliot Weinberger's daughter Anna Della Subin to join her in Morocco, Tarn flew

THROW TWENTY-NINE

via Lisbon (only the airport alas) to the Marrakesh airport, meeting A.D. there, followed by a long night's train ride to Fez. Taken to the gates of Fez by car and entering the old city was like entering into the Old Testament. Days were spent walking up and down the two main arteries visiting craft and antique dealers, eating in delightful little restaurants, and, above all, seeing the magnificent sculptured walls of old Islamic madrassas, chapels, schools, and colleges. Much later, in 2018, A.D., who had been working on a book about "accidental deities," brought a chapter titled "The Apotheosis of Nathaniel Tarn" about N.T.'s "deification" in Guatemala to Tesuque so that N.T. could look forward to some anthropological recognition—in the ever-delayed expectation of gaining some of that benefit in the poetry field. In 2014 also, Rodney and Tarn followed the Piero della Francesca trail in Italy, seeing every one of his available paintings with a single exception: the astonishing *Resurrection* was in *restauro*, and all pleas and attempts at having a peep were firmly repulsed. How to account for the marvels of Siena (the Piccolomini Library and its Donatello!), Arezzo, Urbino, and Assisi?

29.3 In February 2018, Tarn's work was made the subject of a panel at the Louisville Conference on Literature and Culture—the largest and perhaps the most significant of its kind—a panel organized by his literary executor, Peter O'Leary, and his Duke University friend Joseph Donahue—both distinguished poets. In January of 2018, in very unpleasant weather, came a visit to the Maya Meetings, renamed that year as the Mesoamerican Meetings, at the University of Texas. Tarn took two classes in glyph recognition and enjoyed the symposium papers. However, meetings with other Mayanists did not go well, with one exception: a lady who happened to have moved recently to Santa Fe. In particular, a much-admired archaeologist from California turned out, on being approached, to be an ill-natured boor.

Later, 2018: the Tarns flew all night to Tahiti, then again for three hours up to the Marquesas—the islands of Melville and Gauguin—also part of French Polynesia with Tahiti but with quite a different culture. At Nuku Hiva they embarked on the *Aranui 5*, a Tahitian-Chinese–owned ship divided into two parts and calling at all the main islands in the course of roughly a week. The low front part carried and picked up cargo while tourists occupying the high back part went on trips to the archaeological sites. During the week a friendship was cemented with Didier Benatar, a tourist organizer on board whose French youth had matched with N.T.'s so that they knew a great many names of writers, philosophers, anthropologists, and other such in common. Didier, after a visit to Paris to see his mother, came to spend two days at

Fort Tarn. Rather than sailing back to Tahiti via Bora Bora—which Tarn had taken Rodney to for her fiftieth birthday and which was now said to have become hugely touristified—they elected to spend two weeks in a little *pension de famille* on Hiva Oa: Tarn spent much time resting and gazing at the green of the trees' leaves—so much lighter than the verdure of junipers and piñons back home. The owners, delighted to have someone stay for more than a couple of nights, brought the The Tarns into their family. It is very sad that Hiva Oa is so far from home!

2019: a visit to Paris, long unvisited, for the Franco-American conference on Robert Duncan's hundredth anniversary at the Sorbonne. Many poet friends there from all over the place, including Rachel Blau Du Plessis, the Aussie Robert Adamson, and some British who claimed to have read me in ancient times. Florence Trocmé, editor of *Poeziebao, the* French poetry website, and Olivier Brossard, American poetry scholar, also in attendance. At the senior reading of seven poets on night one, Tarn read alphabetically last and brought down the house by reading first a poem from *The House of Leaves* inscribed to Duncan and then an early translation of a Duncan piece into French. This was followed by an invitation to a reading Tour de France much desired for years but coming, alas, too late. A dinner with very old friend Michel Deguy was lost as a result of schedule misunderstandings. Four very pleasant days were spent on the Atlantic Coast at Rochefort with N.T.'s translator, poet Jean Paul Auxeméry, and his wife, Katie, who had visited them in Santa Fe. Tarn brought out a *Selected* of Aux's in 2020.

Paris was no longer the Paris that Tarn knew. Huge crowds, huge traffic, people obsessed and quite different in their behavior, massive groups of tourists all over the space between Notre Dame and the Louvre. Everything was now done by internet: it took two days and much luck to get into the great Hittite exhibition at the Louvre. A first sight of the Quai Branly Museum, Chirac's replacement of Tarn's *Musée de l'Homme* with its Oceania show coming from the Royal Academy London, went well, and the unicorn tapestries at the Cluny also. Chartres was reached by train, again with digital tickets: it had been more substantially enjoyed back in youthful times. The tourist madhouse must be avoided in future and travel probably sent to the winter months.

There was another Louisville Poetry Conference in 2020. Tarn was to read extracts from his *Atlantis*, the book that you are now holding. Many poet friends there: Nathaniel Mackey, Peter O'Leary, Joseph Donahue, Norman Finkelstein, Ken Taylor, Jed Rasula, Jeanne Heuving, Forrest Gander, John Yau, Mark Scroggins, Geoffrey O'Brien, Elizabeth Gray, Albert Mobilio,

Michael Heller, Jane Augustine, George Quasha, and many more. Robert Kelly and John Peck avoided it. Coral Bracho was invited from Mexico, and renewals ensued. We were given a room with some twenty seats. A hundred persons showed up, and we had to move into the main auditorium. The star moved up a millimeter.

A book, *The Hölderliniae*, began its journey at New Directions helped by my editor, a fine and friendly poet, Jeffrey Yang, while this book was waiting in the realm of the uncertain.

Then came the COVID-19 pandemic.

Throw Thirty

30.1 I think it was Stendhal who instructed us never to discuss our triggers—those emotions or events in the writer's life which bring writing about. I have believed all my life that what remains for me a central mystery—the poet's marriage not mainly to content but to language (as matter, stuff, form) and the ways in which this marriage plays itself out through time—should not and need not be discussed by the poet. And, further, that although poets eventually depend for diffusion on reviewers, critics, and biographers, the mystery is as often weakened as strengthened by that socially apparent necessity and, if any survival is to take place, unavoidable intervention. Introductions, afterwords, notes: equally harmful. Why not allow the poems to speak for themselves and, if mystery remains, why not? How much mystery is there left in the world anyway? If asked, I far prefer to talk about the matters and disciplines that concern and engage me at any given time and leave it to readers to find out how, if at all, they enter into or influence the "content" facet of poetry. It is mainly for such reasons that I have always been wary in regard to academic procedures. For students, I would often write on the blackboard the name of a writer to be studied and then draw underneath the picture of a house, a garden, a lawn, a garage, a scholar, his or her spouse, children, and pets. The fervor with which critics build their careers around the activity of one kind of "canon formation" or another (the decision as to whose reputation shall live and whose shall die) has always led to the ugly feeling that poets are slaves in the basements of the critics' houses. The more literature finds its one and only home in the academy—universities and professional institutions—the more this feeling grows and overshadows any concern, often passionate, about the role of the poet in society.

30.2 I hope it is clear from this book that a lifelong interest in religions and symbolic systems—primarily, but not exclusively, classical, Mayan, Buddhist, and, to some extent, the monotheistic three of "the Book"—has been a very powerful motivating force. A strong sense of the interrelationships of man and *polis* and an ever increasingly somber view of man's inhumanity to man have also provided the "matter" of much poetry. In childhood and youth, a passionate involvement with nature, especially ornithological and botanical, occasioned many poems. Over the years, this has to some extent given way to an inextinguishable romance with culture in the form of great human works in any medium (the arts, architecture, technology) and a theoretical interest in the interplay between civil ecology and conservation: that many can even discuss human habitation and the environment apart from each other seems to me an impossible and intolerable aberration. The urge to totalization is still strong; the problem of how parts and whole can be integrated and understood is still all-devouring. I constantly suffer the utopian dream of uninterruptible art/writing/poetry (Paul Eluard's "*Poésie ininterrompue*" perhaps), against which the discontinuities of creative energy always loom. *Ars longa, vita brevis* as they say: in fact, the qualifiers are interchangeable. Life is both far too long and far too short simultaneously. Everything comes up every single moment against the intuition that, to be exhaustively true and just, one should live and write *for ever*. Death is simply a scandal.

Perhaps the only change noted in these patterns over the last two or three years is what most would call a "loss of faith." Rather suddenly, on a morning walk, after attending a very long multiday session of "teachings" by the Dalai Lama no less, a *Kālachakra* cycle in fact, I was overwhelmed by the sense that all these beliefs and rituals, all these attempts at meaning, were illusory and had only one aim: to cover and mask (*Bardo Thödol* et al. notwithstanding) the brutal, insulting scandal of death. Perhaps an exceedingly long-lasting, virtually permanent, state of clinical, that is chemical, depression engendered a sense of the meaninglessness of all phenomena. In any event I entered a phase of absolute agnosis: I do not know and I do not believe it possible for anyone to know any "ultimate truth" in any sense of the word "know" whatsoever. There is a ceiling above the human head that cannot be pierced. This came with a strong sense that "life," as well as "death," is a scandal: something that you are dragged into without your permission being asked and something that you are dragged out of without your permission being asked. Further, the fact that there is no explanation for emerging in birth and disappearing in death remains everlastingly infuriating, meaning that no explanation for the pure facts of life and death can ever be forthcoming. This evidently and almost certainly leads to a state of anhedonia. That the agnosis leans heavily toward "atheism" should be obvious. It does not go there entirely because the word implies a judgment about what is or is not in the whole cosmos, and agnosis cannot judge. But for Tarn the three major monotheistic religions have, one after the other, brought more harm than good to the world: a sense of things that he does not visit upon his religious friends. Plus the fact that monotheistic rituals, while, yes, having a consolatory function, are almost totally repetitive, thus blocking all possibility of change.

A last thought on a single value of depression. That malady looks down on all peoples and not just on the poetry itself. Depression then can be seen as a path which leads to the poet's involvement with the world and not just his or her little self.

More recently, it has seemed to me that there can never be any meaning in the absolute but only in the relative meanings which humans ascribe to things, persons, and events: in fact, that any idea of an "absolute" is non-sense. The sociological puzzle of why so many people share such meanings remains to some extent, but structuralist interpretations of our mental processes probably solve it for me to a large extent. You can also argue that if life is so difficult, or even terrible, some kind of comfort has to be imagined. The fact is then that "meaning" is a marker, a signal of human survival: without this it is difficult to continue living. Is it impossible? I do not know yet. That, in the end, we almost always manage to secrete meaning is without a doubt part of the answer. The human animal hopes to be ceaselessly curious and out of curiosity ceaselessly makes meaning. It is what keeps that animal going. The same, I suppose, applies to "hope," and the only excuse I can find for the persistence of religion is that it keeps some kind of "hope" alive in many people as well, very importantly, as giving the human animal a sense that it is being cared for and looked after. The fact that it is possible to *know* with absolute certainty that you will die while, at the very same time, finding it inordinately hard to *believe* that you will: this strikes me as a sign that hope is strictly unavoidable and is doubtless necessary from an evolutionary

THROW THIRTY

viewpoint. That this "hope" manifests, through the fundamentalisms which are obsessing so many of us today, in the most infantile as well as politically murderous guises does not detract from that point.

A question in my mind has to remain: I have always felt that poetry was impossible without "hope." What is the relation between hope and meaning? Do we secrete hope as well as meaning by the mere fact of being poets? Undoubtedly that forward-looking aspect of poetic creation for which I have used the term "lyric" seems to contain a constitutive element of hope, even if it is only the hope that the poem may be successfully completed in order to take its place in the "opus." In a life reduced to the constative function of being attentive to existence, to what I have become used to calling "the isness of is," this may, in the end, be all that can be expected. Living that function turns out to be "not so bad." Immanentism, "living in the moment," as it is widely known today in this (ha!) "new age," seems to be the "answer" given by most wisdom systems when the trappings of orthodox "religion" have foundered. Perhaps it would have been better if this had been the motto of all cultures from the beginning and if religions had never arisen. Attention to the planet and our relation to it might have benefited from a lack of attachment to fictions of the invisible. If a divinity is necessary, Gaia, this Earth, is the sole possible candidate. I feel very strongly that if all the work and the expense of energy and of goods could be transferred out of religion—mainly the monotheistic ones—into work and devotion on behalf of Gaia alone, the human race might have the possibility of surviving.

30.3 The sense of the ending of an era, perhaps even of a whole concept of "civilization," has been strong throughout and has nourished my interest in the notion of "elegy" not as a species of poem but as a formal function of poetry concerned with the act of looking back at previous poems, and by implication previous culture (fully realizing, fully attentive to, and possessing that backward look). In an essay that has been very important for me, "Archaeology, Elegy, Architecture: A Poet's Program for Lyric," I have manifested these processes through polymorphous interpretations of the Orphic myth—the various possibilities of Orpheus's interaction with his female manifestation, Eurydice-Persephone. This myth I take to be the essential charter of, in Hugh MacDiarmid's words, "the kind of poetry I want."

"On the third hand," as I like to put it, we have all been warned, through the use of such terms as "future shock," that the world my generation thought we knew has all but vanished and that the world we are about to know, in many ways are already knowing, is and will be "changed, changed utterly."

In a life I lead that has become, in many ways, very closed, isolated, and re-
stricted, I see as threatening an enormous proliferation of machines over
which the average person, not technologically "savvy," has very little genuine
control. The whole growth governed by communication theory and its prac-
tical results in the digital revolution—so that we are forever more and more
dependent on legions of expensive "experts" continually upping the ante to
force us everlastingly into consuming the latest "upgrade." So often, this has
no more significance than the "forward" of the polspeak expression "moving
forward." ("We have to put this behind us . . . so that we can move forward.")
What has happened to the telephone is a good simple example: in my opin-
ion, the system began to become intolerable when the answering machine
was introduced. Before that, if you were there, you were there; if not, you
were not, period. Right now, the octopus-like tentacles of everything that
goes under the heading of automation makes the thought of a simple phone
call something that might come to be dreaded through a whole sleepless
night. The insane stress on "security" in every department of life responds
to the growing variety of technological crimes against the individual. In the
name of our new god "security," born from a misreading of the facts of "9/11,"
this stress ends up by complicating every single one of the formerly simplest
possible chores and errands, and infesting these with the menace of one
loss of civil liberties after another. In the process, we become a package of
numbers: passport numbers plus Social Security, driving license, credit card,
debit card, membership, rapid reward, cell phone, remote, registration num-
bers . . . as well as a morass of PINs, passwords, and other codes that every
organization requiring them knows in advance we will forget. Technology,
security, police methods—all in the absurd and failed pursuit of making us
feel "safer"—are reducing daily life to an infernal charade, which makes me
very happy to be my age with the thought that I do not have to bear it very
much longer. These complications lead to an overuse of a single word that
has by now become meaningless: "busy." Is there anyone today, faced with
these complications, who can be said *not* to be "busy"? Not to have his or her
time devoured by meaningless burrokrasstic procedures? The word is used,
however, and used abundantly to cover the fastest-growing phenomenon of
all: either no response or an irritatingly multiplication of response (ads and
appointments mainly). In the overall criminality of late consumer capital-
ism and corporate domination, as well as the polities which are subjected
to them, the small, quotidian criminality we sempiternally resort to because
we are "busy" lies in the fact that the postmodern form of response is very
simply: no response. The brutal truth is that this has killed correspondence

stone dead and has dragged friendship down in its wake. There is no longer such a thing as a "friend." There is only enough time for an "acquaintance." And a Facebooking, texting, twittering one at that.

30.4 All of this, corresponding to an earthy approach in my makeup, the legacy of a social-science training no doubt, has led me to much concern with what I finally have to see and accept as the declining role of poetry and the poet in our increasingly illiterate culture. At a very banal level, almost all of us poets of my age sense some kind of great difference between the life we used to lead and the one we lead now. I daresay I was more fortunate than many in my beginnings, but I treasured the sense of having a publishing home, an editor who would stay put, the occasional lunch, a few free books on going back to the office after lunch, the pretense that the next book was actually awaited with some degree of "excitement" (that miserable cliché for anything to happen in the future) and that your vocation was in some senses "real" and of some "use" to the world, the semblance of moderate attention paid in reviews and notices, the gradual buildup of a very modest reputation—all of which I was blessed with at the start, although it hardly continued. There was also the coincidence with the sixties (lasting into the mid-seventies): a time of extraordinary interest in poetry; the possibility of substantial and extremely well-attended readings; the experience of a kind of "siblinghood" with other poets visited all over the land in their far-flung hangouts, their *querencias*; the sense of a potential (probably illusory) for significant political action; the signs that the "redskins" or Americaphiles in American poetry might finally burst through the containing walls erected for generations by the "palefaces" or Anglophiles of the establishment.

G3.01 (*top*) Author and Pablo Neruda. London, 1970s.   G3.02 (*bottom*) Author and
Octavio Paz. Harvard, Massachusetts, 1970s. PHOTO: ALBERTO DE LACERDA.

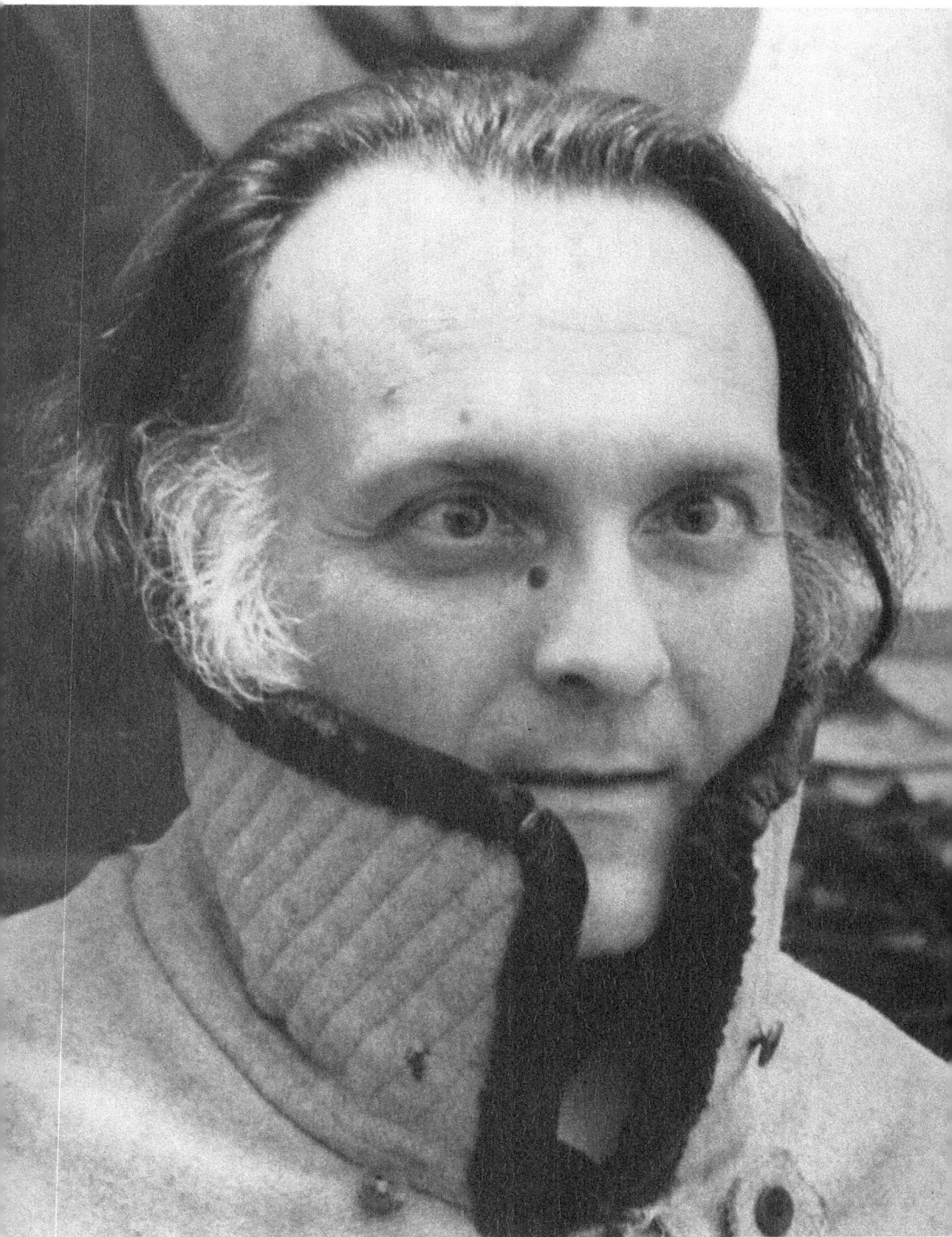

G3.03 Robert Duncan. New Hope, Pennsylvania, 1970s. PHOTO: NATHANIEL TARN.

CHARLES OLSON

for Nathaniel —

Nicolas Dean 1963

G3.04 Charles Olson. 1963. Gift to author from photographer Nicolas Dean.

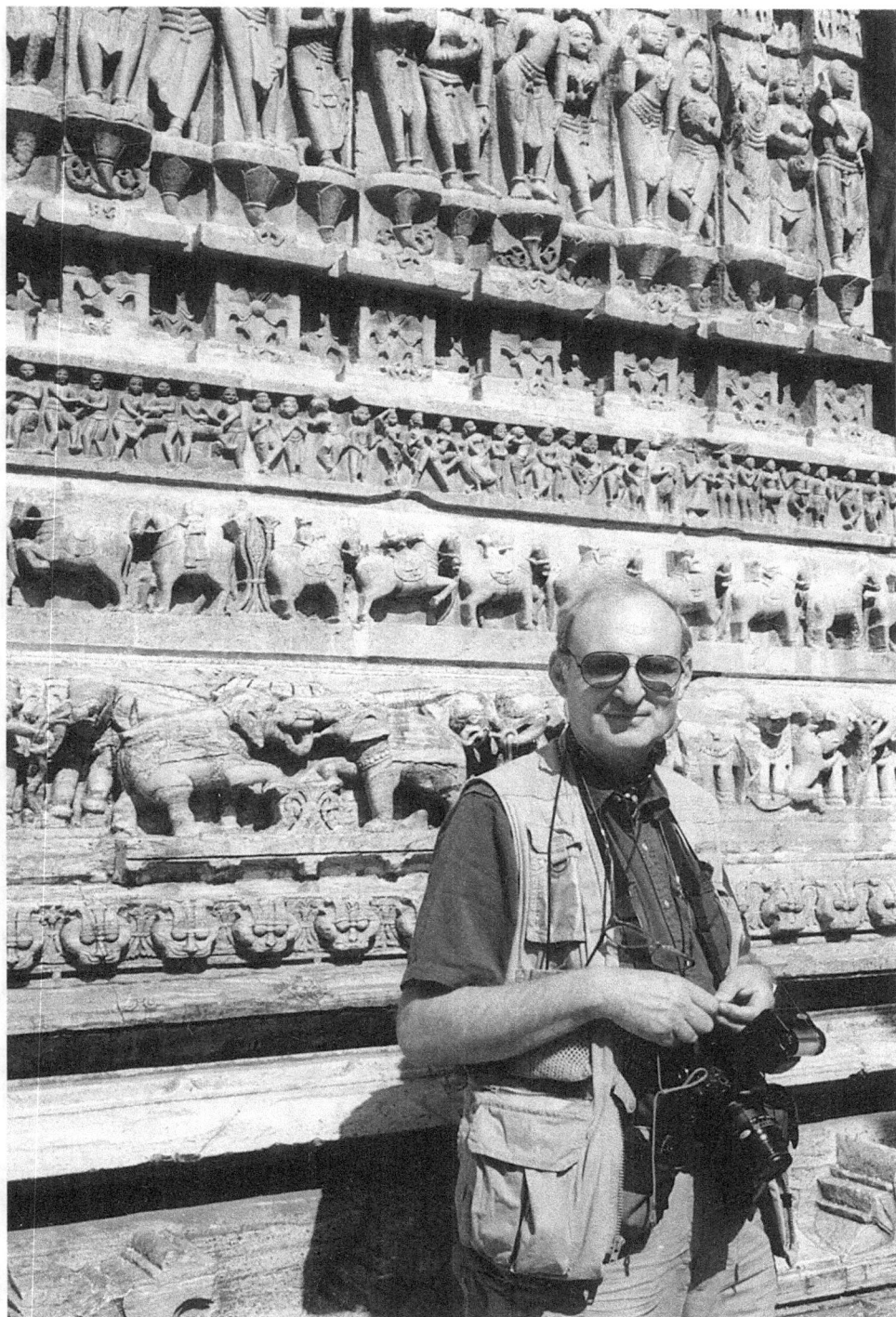

G3.05 Author. Khajurao, India, 1980s. PHOTO: JANET RODNEY.

G3.06 (*top left*) Marc, M.D., Cape Town, 1980s. G3.07 (*top right*) Fiona, R.N., Cape Town, 1980s. G3.08 (*bottom*) Author. Dartmoor, UK, 1980s. PHOTO: TONY FRAZER.

G3.09 Author. Samye, Tibet, 1990s.

G3.10 (*top*) Janet and Yalor Ratzan.
Santiago Atitlán, 1979. PHOTO:
NATHANIEL TARN.
G3.11 (*bottom*) Playwright grand-
daughter Katya. Cape Town, 2019.
PHOTO: MARC.

G3.12 Fort Tarn, New Mexico. Bunker One, Library One, 2013. PHOTO: CHRISTO-
PHER BENSON.

Throw Thirty-One

31.1 All that began to give way *on the very day* the Vietnam War ended, when the public's attention span at readings fell somewhat miraculously from something like three hours to approximately twenty minutes. Only the very smallest number of "known," "famed," "noted," "recognized," "admired," "respected," "prized," "awarded" bards now enjoy such luxuries. Note that the word "poet" has disappeared: no one—either the truly famous or the unknown—can be described as what s/he is except by a combination of the above words with the word "poet." The other arts follow suit. In "bio notes," "introductions," and all forms of "citations," the poet becomes nothing more than a list of his or her "awards," "prizes," "grants," or "fellowships." Rarely does anyone bother anymore outside of academia to say anything about the nature of the poetry produced—although nine times out of ten, if it does occur, it occurs as blather. And it should be added that every "prize," every "award," has its source in one form of pobiz corruption (I kiss you/you kiss me) or another from the Nobel on downward. They give the public the illusion that there are "judges" out there who know what they are doing and who can be trusted. Again: nine times out of ten, pure illusion.

These efforts at distinguishing an individual from the mass, smacking more of Madison Avenue than of culture, arise, of course, out of the fact that we now deal with a mass. The entrance of "creative writing" into the university, roughly since the end of World War II, means that the culture overproduces "poets" while at the same time underproducing readers—the old-fashioned *general readers* that is, not the specialized readers of today who are . . . the "poets" other than oneself. These "poets" have nowhere to go except back into the academy, where their job is to produce more "poets"—usually cloned in their own image—with the understanding that every student has a "poet's" baton in their backpack and (this is the most awful hypocrisy) that there can be no such thing as failure and no such thing as not getting a job. The academic *nomenklatura,* unavoidably subsisting in committees, dictates what is to happen and what is not to happen in the poetry world: in that virtually every "poet" is now an academic, the conditions for the existence of a meaningful "avant-garde" have vanished.

On its side, the world of mainline publishing, sold out to corporatism, is deliquescing beyond all recognition. There is now not even the pretense that poetry can be published by sacrificing a few of the profits made on best-sellers. It is true that a few bastions exist in the shape of university presses—I can think of one single "commercial" press that still works—but the academic presses are all more and more subject to commercial pressures and are not, for the most part, equipped for building coherent literary lists. Gradually, under economic pressure, they are relinquishing their mission and following the rest. For the first time in history, perhaps, the material, sociological conditions exist for the drowning out of quality by quantity—cultural stereotypes like "there cannot be any mute, inglorious Miltons: sooner or later talent will out" notwithstanding.

Virtually everyone, except other "poets," has given up the pretense of producing, reading, or enjoying poetry, so incestuous schools and movements flourish—existing, because of their sheer complexity, way outside any general readership and doomed, one would think, to extinction by the resulting overspecialization. Ever-increasing emphasis on the inside progress of the craft (*pour épater les autres poètes*) has led to ever-increasing "obscurity" (manifested above all today in the craze for "disjunctive" writing, with a huge stress on form rather than content) and the abandoning of the craft's outward reaches toward making some kind of contribution to society and culture as a whole. The academic requirement that, in order to be worth considering, a body of work should be available for interminable exegesis favors increasing complexity: it is necessary for the Ph.D. mills to keep on grinding. An unavoidable stress on the intellect in these conditions leads to what seems increasingly to be called "writing" as opposed to what has been called "poetry." For myself, I take, broadly speaking, the former to be the product of the head alone, the latter to be the product of head and heart, intellect and emotion, conjoined. One of the great victims has been music: Pound's *melopoeia*. Needless to say, the matter is confused by the fact that much "writing" continues to be called "poetry" by its producers in an attempt to go on enjoying the ancient privileges, as they perceive them, of being a "poet." Tarn often wishes that universities could be totally destroyed and rebuilt on very different bases.

In these conditions, competition for infinitesimally minute pieces of turf, in smaller and smaller "little-press" publications and venues, has virtually lost all meaning in that the turf itself is becoming meaningless. Continually injured and insulted by the kind of reception s/he for the most part suffers out there, the poet comes to see that the "poet's" life, far from being a god's, or even a dog's, is now worth less than that of a liver fluke progressing through the guts of a sheep.

And very few risk saying so for the blindingly simple reason that the job-market applecart cannot be upset: one of the only forms of employment a poet can aspire to is as a "creative writing" teacher.

31.2 The relatively most recent "big event" in the poetry world, the donation of a hundred million dollars to a single (dinosaurial) magazine and a supporting staff with hugely fat salaries, begs the question of what could have been done with that sum if properly distributed. The demonstration that the foundation born of the magazine had, at the start, not the faintest idea of how to deal with the gift illustrates the nature of the Poworld's present situation. All the *New York Times* can do on the consecration of a mediocracy in Chicago on October 6, 2004, is to announce that "Poetry Starts to Wear $100 Million Crown."

31.3 One interesting scandal appears to remain in perpetuity. I referred to a conflict as old as American history between Americanophiles and Anglophiles. Whatever powers may have been obtained by participating in the academy, the various groups able to have a crack at claiming to be an avant-garde—from the "New Americans" to the "Language Poets," all of whom eventually belong to Americanophile lineages—have not been able to break completely the stranglehold exercised by the Anglophiles. These rule by means of their hold on the Ivy League universities, their majority in most "creative writing" departments or programs as well as grant- and prize-giving bodies throughout the land, opinion-forming publications, and corresponding fellow travelers in the UK and elsewhere. The education in poetry that most Americans receive allows these folk to rule by one single pretense. They rule by pretending that they produce the only poetry there is: it is not even a question of nothing else being worthwhile; it is a question of nothing else *existing*. One only has to look at the anthologies, the canons, and the lists produced by the leading conservative critics to recognize the extent of the crimes they are committing against American culture. Many of these critics may be fine when writing about previous centuries but reveal the most devastating ignorance when commenting on or anthologizing our own times. As of the latest writing (2019), the major difference lies in the conquest of writing departments by the Language Poet movement so that one version of Americanophile writing is maintained, but not the one I would follow.

I need here to say something about "creative writing." My sense of it is that when soldiers came home from World War II, some academics, sensing that the one thing they had suffered in the military had been the diminishment of, or even the loss of, *ego*, invented or stressed a degree called Master of Fine Arts (M.F.A.) easier to obtain than an M.A. or a Ph.D. and that would involve activities favorable to a rediscovery of ego. This led eventually, beyond a returning military, to the development of M.F.A. programs in the US and then in the whole world.

Now, from a "democratic" point of view, and here discussing only poetry, not all the arts, there is no reason whatsoever why young people should not be educated into being anything they would like to be. The problem is that whereas there are *born* poets—individuals who know from childhood that this is their fate—the poets *fabricated* by M.F.A. programs rarely ever get beyond a certain facility. For the system to survive the teacher needs to assure the student that s/he has a poet's baton in his or her backpack: a lie in that there can never be as many jobs in "creative writing" as are needed, the same being true anywhere else in the academic world. In short, as in any other aspect of life now, we have the problem of overpopulation. Because poetry has never been a money earner, this leads to a far too large number of manuscripts lying unlooked at and uncared for among editors, among publishers, among prize and award givers. The situation leads to every kind of abuse that one "fabricated poet" can inflict on another in the rush toward success and the pobiz type of behavior—further masking any rise in achievement among "*born* poets." This is saying that quantity is drowning out quality all down the line as overpopulation will always do, making it difficult for poetry as an art to survive at all.

31.4 Under these conditions, I have always greatly wondered why so many young people continue to ache as much as they do toward gaining their poetic wings. It must have to do with valuing status above wealth, even though I find battles for status to be far more cruel than battles for wealth. So that, of course, it is in those young people one is forced to believe if avoiding suicide ("Eighteen of the ranking U.S. poets of the Twentieth Century committed suicide," wrote Kenneth Rexroth to James Laughlin on October 26, 1950), and from that point of view, poetry is the only "principle of hope" I can still enjoy. My own belief is that we have reached a point when only a major sociocultural revolution on a *universal* scale would be capable of changing the conditions I have described, and it is not at all certain that they would lead back to the world of "poetry." If, in the opinion of a major astronomer—Professor Martin Reese, astronomer royal and master of Trinity College, Cambridge (Anglophiles please note)—who is very far from being alone, the human race has only around fifty years in which to make the decisions that will cause it to live or become extinct. If the serious daily news assures us that we are destroying the planet for the sake of profit, endlessly favoring the rich over the poor and conducting criminal operations against each other, if it is not too late to realize this and to take action, will any of this lead back to "poetry"? It is after all possible, as Claude Lévi-Strauss once pointed out, to imagine a world without culture, without art, without poetry.

What revolution can we be thinking of, in any case, when the triumph of consumerism seems as complete as possible and when only more and more consumerism seems to be the lot we can look forward to and the lot we can offer occasionally to "technologically underdeveloped" populations? The one total, all-encompassing, absolute merchandising store is here to stay. This, incidentally, being to me, with the addition of the collapse of communism, the true moment of "postmodernism"—if such a thing can be meaningfully categorized.

We have to conjugate the words "young" and "technologically underdeveloped" or "evolving" (such terms as terms always, of course, from our ethnocentric viewpoint and no other) and put our future hopes perhaps not so much in ourselves as in the poets of other areas of the world. The voices of the future, ancient in their own homes, may come onto our stages out of Africa, Asia, Latin America: many, and great ones, already have. The major conflicts looming on the internal empire's front in these United States, in the form of the question of "multiculturalism," prefigure this in the same way as "ethnopoetics" prefigured "multiculturalism." At this time, the entrance of "liberation poetries" onto the scene complicates the American White-Anglo statistical picture drawn here almost beyond measure. I am talking of any of the hitherto underappreciated poetries of African, Asian, and Native Americans, and the poetries of women across the board and the poetries of the L.G.B.T.Q. communities across the board. Even at the cost of the self-scuttling or destruction or radical reformulation of the White-Anglo literary world, these "liberation poetries" are becoming the poetries of the future and are reorganizing the landscape. I do not believe that this is a "liberal" kowtow to the burrokrassies that are imposing "diversity" on this nation in a mostly crass and unimaginative way. I believe it to be the simple truth about the changes that have to occur in society as a whole if "poetry" is to survive as "marital" rather than "incestuous"—that is, as meaningful to a truly substantial and general audience and readership. Much, perhaps all, will depend on the extent to which the liberation poets can cleave to their own values rather than joining the Anglo consensus for the sake of some imagined "prestige." Also in contention remains the attitude to the liberation movements and to the social groups they represent. A large variety of snobberies have to be strangled.

I will then hope that the new "poetries" will be more generous to us than we have been to them and that, after the initial alienations, we will once more be allowed onto the scene as part of a universal culture. For while we dispute among ourselves, the Earth itself is in the process of becoming as endangered as those cold masses out there in space might at one time have been. And we all need a home, to whatever species we may belong. Given the time frame in question—there is not enough time to get away into space—this home may be all we have.

The tragic fact any lover, any admirer of this nation comes to sooner or later is that, in one way or another, it has been based from the very roots on matter, on consumption, on gain. It seems to me significant that, to this day, the country has never had a Ministry or Secretariat of Culture. There is a powerless National Endowment of the Arts (with an infantile motto: "A great nation deserves great art") that does not even begin to be active in the art world in ways that such a ministry anywhere else would encompass. This institution can even be the regular prey of conservative politicians intent on destroying it. There are no honors for people of other nations who serve our culture in their arts such as are found in virtually every other country. Example: in the realm of national wealth acquired by taxation, the personnel are perpetually in search of artistic activities defined as "hobbies," which end by implying that art is a "hobby" until it is commercial enough to make a financial mark. This apes the eternal bourgeois attitude that an artist, a poet, should have a steady job in something "sensible" while exercising his or her art as a spare-time pursuit.

Adding to this, we live (October 2020) in an execrable social world led by illiterate criminals and are moving toward an election. The insulting hysterics arriving every day on the web with one and only message—we beg you for money—make one wonder how we could not have a simple system: let government give an equal sum to all candidates and then no further gabbling. France allows little or no gabbling during elections.

Throw Thirty-Two

32.1 I here liberate the word poetry from all inverted commas and return it to the sense that I know.

I referred in an interview recently to a state of mind in which two contradictory impulses coexist at the same moment. On the one hand, the passionate desire to put an end to one's life at that very moment; on the other, and at the very same time, the passionate desire to experience and express in poetry the joy of being alive in the only world there is, beautiful or not. It occurred to me only a few days later that this state of mind was a good description of the central station in a tripartite model that I have long written about to try to describe what happens in the creation of a poem. This is the model of three stations: the "Vocal", the "Silence" and the "Choral."

The "Vocal" refers to everything that is made by reference to a self, to an individual's talents and ideals in competition with those of other individuals. Using the anthropological sense of reciprocity, the reciprocal situation at this level would be described as self-other reciprocity. The "Choral" refers to everything that is made by reference to the Community and its culture, its world of *cooperation* as opposed to competition, where reciprocity would disappear in that where there is self there is automatically other, and where there is no self there is no other. In the model, the "Vocal" and the "Choral" are described as reciprocal illusions of each other—a way of indicating that the only "real" station is that of the "Silence" because it is here that the praxis of making a poem is ultimately situated.

Most critics have discussed poetry as emerging out of silence and returning into silence. This is a binary model. In the trinary model I propose, the "Silence" is, as it were, sandwiched in the middle between the "Vocal" and the "Choral" and is found to be a state of self-self reciprocity in which the poet is completely alone with him/her self at the most crucial moment of composition. This: the site in which the backward-looking elegiac function (What have I done in the past?) implicitly compares and balances what is to be with what already exists in the "opus" is where the "Silence" resides. This same moment (What am I doing now for the future?), the site in which the hope of progress inherent in a new poem, thrusting forward *lyrically*, will add itself to the opus and alter its whole nature is also where the "Silence" resides. Obviously, this is a crucial moment: there can be none more crucial. And it is precisely here that the decision implied when facing the two possibilities—that is, to be or not to be—becomes merged with, becomes expressed by, the two possibilities: to work or not to work. In the fascinated and absolutely wrapped, silent, and intense *attention* (nothing imaginable being capable of more intensity) paid to the conjoined and co-inspiring vision of the state of the self, that of the community and that of the world, lies the secret of poetic composition.

If the "Vocal" is the station of self and the "Choral" is the station of community, then the task of the "Silence," looking around every aspect and the whole of the scene, is to establish the station of world. For the poet, poetry and the world become commensurate: there literally is no world outside of poetry. I often noticed, before the days in which disillusionment threatened, that I would constantly wonder how people who were not poets could consider being or remaining alive at all! This, of course, stretched to all the other arts, and it is in this genuine wonderment (to the poet, while to anyone else it is simply laughable) that the arrogance of the artistic fiat, totally at odds with a "reality" situation of complete powerlessness, maintains itself. The fiat: this art object comes into being because I is, because all You are, because World is: the isness of is. This book is also known to its author as *Atlantis: An Autoanthropoem.*

I questioned, while writing this at some point, why so many young people wanted to be poets: the answer is here, in the illusion as well as in reality, because it is the only place in which you can create world. This is why the making of art—while considered such a small thing by nonartists—seems to be such an immense one to artists. And to the extent that any human being is an artist, in however infinitesimal a degree, the possibility of World can continue in existence.

Poetic liberation is the oldest liberation movement there is. Anyone can join. Anyone should.

But then the last thing to say and to repeat. Poetry is dying because, almost, there are in the nature of things so few *born* poets: those who hear an internal voice the moment they are born. There are innumerable *fabricated* poets: little machines whose one function and one pleasure and one reason for existence is *to eat, to devour, and to delight in admiration.* The immense effort required, in an insanely overpopulated world with so little space in which to live, to build a self—as opposed for a moment to an ego—cannot be put out by more than a handful. The *ego*: an admiration devourer that can brook nothing other than admiration. The *self:* a devourer of experience capable of learning from criticism, both positive and, especially, negative, in order to grow. I can no longer count the number of times in which an ego has proffered its compliments in order to purchase admiration—only to disappear into the great silence if that purchaser is other than *totally* satisfied. The few who retain any meaning live in a world not of poets but of cowards. It is immensely lonely, immensely without borders.

32.2 I sometimes try, as an exercise, to give credence to the ancients who held that most things, if not all, are probably parts of a whole greater than themselves. Although we sometimes enjoy the possibility of verifying that certain things are parts of a whole and that this whole incorporates no other things than those, we live most of our lives uncertain as to whether we know, recognize, possess, or have some sort of control over all of the parts composing any given whole. The age of angst, following another poet's age of anxiety, is also the age of over-information and is one in which that uncertainty has grown to such a pitch that there is too much suicide of one kind or another on this planet. It is imperative that this ignorance be diminished.

Uncertainty/unknown: the two are very close. One way in which I have played at attenuating the uncertainty—or tolerating the unknown (it comes to that)—is to play the game of supposing that time and space, especially time, are illusory. It follows that more or less everything, oh let us say everything, must be happening at the same moment in the same spot or, to put it another way, in a simultaneity far more vast than we know. This ensures that some of the parts may remain *acceptably* unknown while not losing their place and also that the sum total of phenomena is bound to amount to

Justice. Among one's readings, there are frequent encounters with views of this sort emanating from poets whose ability to prophesy (to speak from a no or all time and a no or all place) permits them to give no more credit to time and space than is strictly necessary. I think of André Breton with his point at which all contradictions can be said to end and be resolved—can, in short, cease to be contradictory—or William Carlos Williams, whose vital moment, the "it" of his ardent chase and purchase, closes in so much upon itself as to exclude the most frightening dimensions.

I have always been fascinated, to take one instance, by the debate between one life and many lives: do we have just this existence, or do we, in one manner or another (every level of sophistication is permitted here), "reincarnate"? In the first possibility there appears to be so much injustice that the weight of the known component(s) in the solution becomes intolerable. The only acceptable possibility would be that the total existence of that being over the eons, and even more so its species, would end up by making sense. However, this calls for a massiveness in the unknown that strains most credibilities.

Take the alternative. Because only a being that might be hypothesized as "completely enlightened" can, in most philosophies of this understanding, know its past lives (and, probably, its future ones), it is such a being that has to end up defining the whole. We unenlightened beings must lead, in a state of ignorance, whichever life *this* present one happens to be—merely trusting, however, that there is *some* meaningful relation between (should it be the case) all lives in the series. The belief helps keep in place a sense of Justice, for it would be unthinkable that a number of lives (the parts) lived one after the other would not eventually tally into one great, good, and meaningful life (the whole). To think of a long series of existences that would *still* end in meaninglessness moves from the intolerable into the chaotic and absurd or, translating, into the insane. Thus, if every life series ends up as one great, good, and meaningful life, there need be no strain in thinking of the compatibility of *all* lives—and we can go back to merely wondering what is the point of such an orchestration of perfection—if point there is to anything at all.

Poetry could be supposed to be the privileged place in which the suggestibility of the unknown parts of any whole becomes so potent that we speak/write as if the unknown were equal in opportunities to the known: that is, as if the unknown, in the last resort, were part of the known and could rise to the surface of consciousness as such. Perhaps this is what we could mean when speaking of poetic prophecy.

But what happens when, as is the case now, you fail to make sense of existence within a set structure of belief? This leaves you with the question, which I have always entertained, of what the reason can be for the immensity of the known (and unknown) universe, an immensity to which it is necessary for man to be blind (you cannot look at the night sky most of your time) on pain of losing sanity. Added to which the persistent feeling that a reason there must be if the word "meaning" can still respect itself. And one is not necessarily aided by failing to be a physicist or a student of evolution.

If then all belief systems put forth to date are infantile—if not evidence of mental incapacity or even mental illness—can one survive in a mode of "as if," continuing to live *as if* life had meaning without being able to tell whether it has or not?

One thing does occur. What I would call "the *isness* of *is*" appears more and more strongly "to be the case." The modern poem, as initiated by the lineage to which I claim to belong, is a flowering of that "case." In addition to uncountable weeds, there is a considerable field of flowers to be enjoyed. It is for this animal the last manifestation of "hope" in this fallen world. I have always sensed that poetry without "hope" was simply impossible. Which one assumes is what Adorno meant. I write *as if* I were hopeful. This, at the very least, continues to compel my interest and speaks to a universe's trillions of presences way out there.

Throw Thirty-Three

33.1 All this debate about hope and the lack of it, about a fundamental pessimism and a perpetual attempt to approximate to some form of optimism, is said without any detriment to an overwhelming sense of how rich I have been in my ability, without major hindrances, to be a poet without suffering many of the material deprivations that this low-caste position often carries with it. Nevertheless, under the guidance of a baleful star more often than not, I am grateful that I have reached the age of potential departure—the true "death band"—in that I do not wish to live very much longer in the world that is emerging.

By choosing to live in "the country" rather than in "the city," I have worsened my chances of finding companionship and avoiding loneliness. I say loneliness, not solitude: they are different. Solitude is an essential requirement; loneliness is painful. This "country," in effect the edges of a southwestern "cultural capital," is one in which I have not been able, beyond my spouse, to find in all these years more than one or two persons who had some inkling of who and what I was. Nothing major implied in the "who" and the "what"—merely a recognition of a situation, in French a *constatation*. Added to the decline of friendship, this makes for loneliness indeed.

A related uneasiness is the distance between self, with Janet, and family. My first wife, Patricia, lives in London, fervent in re concerts and opera, and has become to all intents and purposes an unofficial Cordon Bleu chef. Son Marc is a major M.D. in the field of infectious diseases, especially antibiotics, and a university professor at Cape Town. His spouse, Fiona: a highest-degree R.N. and M.A. who works with African refugees. Three grandchildren: one is Katya, highly literate and already a playwright with whom Tarn has a very full correspondence. Ben is a lawyer and Joshua a student in history and politics at St. Andrews in Scotland. Daughter Andrea, also in Cape Town, is a psychotherapist, the mother of an adopted Lakota daughter, Ina Rain, and the spouse of Icelandic Axel, an expert in dyslexia. So there is also this loneliness.

33.2 While recognizing the fact that I usually get tired eventually of places I live in (Paris the only exception perhaps—although time was cut short), I should insert here my growing disenchantment with Santa Fe. When I first saw it on immigrating into the United States, it seemed to be extraordinarily lively in all the dimensions I was interested in. There were poetry events and readings that included members of the three cultures: Native American, Hispanic, Anglo (though far too little of African American). This describes the early seventies—to my mind the end of the rebellious sixties. There were at least two bookstores whose owners were writers or interested in writing. There was the possibility of assisting at Native American rituals and dances: I saw a whole week of such at Hopi and a whole night at Zuni plus dances all over the area. A major draw had, after all, been the work that Lévi-Strauss did on the Pueblos. The richness of musical life and film was huge compared to that of other small provincial cities. Even without the state university (and although there is a classical education at St. John's College), I found myself believing that Santa Fe would grow into a serious intellectual and artistic capital. I failed to look at all the distances involved. When Rodney and I came back up from our year in Guatemala in 1979, I wanted to show her Santa Fe as a possible place to move to. It reminded her of her eighteen years in Spain. In our first years, the illusion continued. However, one gradually discovered that there was no such thing as sharing in the three-culture situation unless one devoted one's whole life to that end. For instance: one could use Spanish with Mexican immigrants, but New Mexican Latinos were very often unwilling. Also that most of the "good stuff" was imported from the outside. There were and are major artists here and there, but they show their work elsewhere and evidently keep to themselves. The local arts virtually never change. Apart from which, it is not easy to meet people in Santa Fe: so many come to hide away and to retire. As far as poetry is concerned, the emphasis has been more and more on the "local," with neglect and little or no knowledge of the national and international. The "locals" read to one another 365 evenings a year in bookstores with virtually no poetry shelves. All benefits (grants, awards, etc.) go to "locals." The one foundation that could be of assistance does not deal with residents of this city. I do not know where to find city life. Repeating: the city, such as it is, has been boutiquized to such an extent that we hardly ever go there; therefore, the tourist season makes life difficult for citizens, and this will doubtless increase. The day I wrote this, a new seven-story hotel in the middle of town was being planned. Very large contingents of people from California and such are arriving daily, planning to stay.

33.3 I always say that "I am here for the land." But is it even possible, apart from the occasional excursion, to enjoy "the country" any longer? The city has in fact invaded the country with all its ills: the southern part has been growing furiously, and I imagine that if it were not for the Pueblos, Santa Fe and Albuquerque might become one city. A whole study would be worth making of the verbal and behavioral codes whereby we are forced to pretend, even in "the country," that "slow food" and "friendship" and other country virtues still exist. The privacy that is a facet of friendship and a sine qua non of a "comfortable lifestyle" and a tolerable "quality of life" is fast disappearing: phone interruptions of routine at any hour, invasions of every sort in the mail and in everyday life, and the mania for "security" already mentioned are putting an end to it. Time for reading, for reflection, for meditation is gobbled up by the ever-proliferating and ever-more-redundant demands of the burrokrassies: the mandated communications; the calls, postings, tweets; the forms to be filled in to keep those infernal machines running. It is dazzlingly clear that every move that is made by the rulers or the corporations (they are the same) to "make life easier"—their everlasting claim—is *guaranteed* to end by making it more difficult. We are more and more, even in "the country," at the mercy of machines provided with more and more "bells and whistles," in new versions engineered every year, ensuring both our inability to cope with them and our consequent slavery to hordes of specialists who, sometimes, are able to. The sheer complexity of the commercial world's operations makes it certain that more and more things can go wrong: quite apart from the environmental dangers already mentioned, we live on the rim of catastrophe day by day given the horrendous number of disaster scenarios that the material substratum (take nuclear proliferation and weapons of mass destruction on the loose, for example) engenders. This "rim" makes it more and more doubtful that we can live very much longer as human beings, and I am appalled by the ignorance of the populations who continue to bring children into this kind of world.

I recently tried to speak at a conference about the results in this poet's life of a loss of "hope." The question: how could a poet continue his/her activity when s/he had become persuaded that the view from here raised the most serious doubts as to whether the human race would survive? Delight in the moment, of course, unalloyed with any other sentiment, would have to be the answer. But the interesting thing was that no one in the audience had any comment. I was not approached afterward, not communicated with. It seemed to me that the audience was unanimously annoyed, cross, even angry. Perhaps what was there was *fear*.

I cannot agree with Robert Duncan's famous statement in his H.D. book that humanity has now "come into one fate." In the sense that the fate is extinction if news from ecologists is not heeded: yes. In the sense that a member of our elites is not "fated" in the same way as a Central American person trying to cross our southern border into this country, for example: no. (In any event, I also remain more of an Olsonian than a Duncanian.)

Two additions in September 2020. For some thirty-five years—that is, since the East Coast period—I have had virtually no poet companions. Recently, I was asked to join the editorial board of a brilliant and combative web magazine: *Dispatches from the Poetry Wars*, edited by poets Michael Boughn and Kent Johnson. They published me and gave me a niche full of writings and photographs.

A major change occurred from the Louisville conferences onward, where I began to feel that a number of poets whose work I was interested in were interested in mine. The powerful Nathaniel Mackey at one point created, jokingly of course, a Society of the Lamb Chop based on our menu selections in a delicious Louisville restaurant. I have no other future.

33.4 A book should probably end with a bang. As one distinguished poet once warned us, it can hardly avoid ending today in a whimper. In spite of this, I conjure up a bang. There is nothing else to do. There is nowhere else to go. Arrange the wagons in a circle for a while. However: expect nothing. On the other hand, every thing and every one should *secede*. So then Move! So then Forward! So then Go! Write "The Last Poems."

www.ingramcontent.com/pod-product-compliance
Lightning Source LLC
Chambersburg PA
CBHW071730270326
41928CB00013B/2625